CAN TECHNOLOGY BRING HUMAN DEVELOPMENT

JOHN LOK

Contents

Foreword

Introduction

Our business society had developed long time from farming period to manufacturing period, then to service industry period, till to nowadays technology service and manufacturing period. It brings this question: Can technology or human behavior may influence economic development? Human ourselves foolish or enjoyment behavior whether which can bring economic recession? If human can forgive to do enjoyment behavior, we can help economic growth? I shall apply behavioral economic theory to indicate cases to attempt to explain these questions. Whether technology influences ecommerce development or customer online shopping behavior influence ecommerce? Whether labors or robots may help organiations to improve performance? All these questions, I shall attempt to indicate answers to let readers undestand.

Prologue

Contents

- How artificial intelligence influence e-business
workers market?
- How robotic becomes one kind of factor of production to the owning robotic task participation organizations?
- Why can robotic avoid productivity challenge and the firm does not need to employ extra worker ?
   How robotic brings positive and negative social change
- Why does robotic seem to McDonaldization franchise sale method
   - Why robotic seems to McDonaldization's operation?
   - Why does robotic seems to be common social commodity?
   - How can robotic bring global social stratification positive and negative change?
   Robotic how influences global economic change
- Encouraging new economic development
competitive factor
- How much robotic productivity can raise competition to cause effects of limited competition disadvantage to our
society.
- How and why robotic brings long time intellectual development to global factories ?
- How can robotic help manufacturers to raise productivities or improve efficiency?
- Why does production possibilities curve may explain why robotic participation may assist few workers to raise
productivities in factories ?

Must Developed And Developing Countries
Need Artificial Intelligent To Replace Human Job
- How AI help developing countries to communication and agriculture and learning and medical delivery
development
   - Emergency Response to developing countries' earthquake natural damage sudden occurrence predicting
- Smart AI Agriculture
- Medicine Delivery to developing countries' patients urgent need
- Assistance to reduce teaching work workload or psychological pressure to teachers in developing countries'
schools
- Why does smart phone help developing countries communication ?
- The Positive Impact of Mass Media in Developing Countries
- Why do developed countries need to develop AI
- AI may bring what benefits to developed countries
- How can AI be dangerous when developed countries continue to develop AI to become weapon to replace
soldiers?
- Why the recent interest in AI safety ?
- Why do developed countries people need AI ?
   Reference

Artificial intelligence bank service working environment
- The Future of Artificial Intelligence In
The Workplace
- A positive future with artificial intelligence to
bring remote online office working environment chance
- Artificial Intelligence (AI) in Banking working environment
AI technology can bring better Customer Support in bank service environment
- What does artificial intelligence mean for the bank service office worker?
   How AI influences our daily working culture in any office working environment
- The Future of Artificial Intelligence In The

Human Behavioral network job brings social
economic benefits p.216-230
What does human network job mean
Why human network job behavior may influence economy

Robots take our jobs behavioral and economy influences
Robot job behavior brings economy influences

Intellectual human economic behaviors
What does intellectual human economic behaviors
mean ?
The relationship between social change and human
behavior
How human productive behavior may influence economic development
● New Zealand farmer individual wine productive behavior
● America high technological productive behavior
● China share market investing behavior
Why has any individual country have many people invest share behavior which can influence the country's macro
consumption desire?
Can technology influence human shopping behavioral change?
Why and how human behavior may influence the country's economic growth or recession?
Technology how impacts human behavior changing?
How and why employees behaviors may influence economy development?
Robots invention whether they can help organizations to raise efficiencies or inefficiencies?
Why social behavior may influence organizational strategy needs to be changed ?
How and why human behavior may influence economic growth or recession?

CHAPTER ONE

Technology or human behavior whether may influence economic growth or recession

Human Behavioral network job brings social economic benefits

What does human network job mean ? Why may human network job be popular? Why human network job behavior may influence economy ?

Nowadays internet is popular to use. We can apply internet to find data , search any new things, even earn money. Why does internet

may become huma network job source. For example, e-publish may be one kind of new human network job. Any authors may apply internet

channel to help them to sell electronic or paper books from e-publisher web store. They may apply facebook, you tub etc. any online

channel to promote themselves new books to let new readers to know whether when they may buy themselves favourable new topic books to read

from electronic publisher web store.

Thus, future electronic publisher industry may help any authors to build internet network platform to help them to sell and promote

ot advertise their any one new electronic or paper book topic to let global any one reader to choose to buy their any new topic books from electronic publisher web store easily and conveniently. However, it implies that electronic network platform author may be one kind of future new human network job in our societies.

How electronic network platform author job may bring economy benefit in macro economy view? A person can have few friends, contacts and still be very influential if these few

friends and contacts are themselves highly influental, e.g. one author must not need to know any one reader in global society. When they like to choose any electronic books from electronic internet network platform. They may become the author's any one topic book buyer, when they feel the author's any one topic book is fun and attract they make decision to buth the strange author whose the topic book from electronic book publisher's platform web store conveniently in short time. Although, they are strangers, they do not know themselves , but the reader can understand what it way that made Google from writing platofrm to create new creative mind and typing network job method to replace traditional hand writing book method for global authors. It will be one kind of new human network writing job.

Hence, global any one reader can apply an innovative search engine , such as google.com to find whether whom author personal new topic books are value to read from internet.

Then, the electroniuc publisher's web store may be new book store platform sale network to help the author to sell many electronic or paper books from electronic network platform

in short time. So, internet may be future new network plaform to help global any one author to create network

writing job absolutely. Furthermore, internet may be popular social media
to help any one author to build goold relationship between his/her readers. It is one kind of new network, human network job. New authors do not need to buy many paper books to prepare to put in any one book shop warehouse. Their every book can print on demand to reduce out of book stock in any one book shop. They may choose to sell either electronic books or paper books both from any one book publisher web store. So, electronic network platform may be one kind of good writing channel to help human authors to create income and it can also help authors to bring new creative mind and new topic fun content books to let readers to know and buy to read from electronic publisher network platform.

Why does human behavior may be one kind of new human network job to bring global economic advantages. ALthough, it may be free income or without inocme, but the person does the network behavior, his/her behavior may be bring advantages to influence many other people's health. For this case, when a worker in a coffee shop in an airport gets a vaccination aganinst the flu, it does not only helps him or her stay healthy, but also helps the many travellers who might otherwise have been inflected if that workers caught the flu. So, the externality , the result implies the vaccination of even a part of a community conveys benefits to the whole community. For example, governments pay special attention to the vaccinations of school children, teachers, health mothers, and the elderly, categories of people particularly susceptible not only to catching, but also to transmitting a disease.

It is not accidential that governments are heavily involved with vaccination . When there are externalities, free market, fail to persuade individual incentives with society's
their the worker's decision of whether to get a vaccine ends up attracting whether other people get sick. The workers might not fully take all these other people's potential suffering into account when making her or his vaccination decision.

As Stanford University does many suggestions, understand this and tries to help them make the right decisions and so providers free flu vaccines for its staff and students.
Small pockets of unvaccinated individuals can allow a disease to gain a spread more widely well-being. For example, parent weighing the costs and benefits of a vaccine for their child is not always thinking of the consequences of that vaccination to other people. THese are markets in which subsidizing or regulating behavior can make everyone better off. Because the reason for requiring that a child be vaccinated before enrolling in school is not just to protect that child, because each child's vaccination affects others via potential contagions.

Robots take our jobs behavioral and economy influences

Robot job behavior brings economy influences

If one day robots can replace human to do simple, even complex jobs. They will bring what influences to our global societial economy.The popular economic refrain declares that the
global middle class is dying and robots will soon take our jobs, e.g. shopping center customer service jobs, library service jobs, cinema ticket sale jobs, restaurant kitchen cooker jobs,
even, bus drivers, taxi drivers etc. public transport driving jobs, accountant, doctors etc. professional jobs. Whether it is beautiful or petty matter if our future societies have many human jobs can be replaced to do from robots. Businessman must may reduce to employ employees and reduce to pay salary or wage, when robots can be replaced to do their employees tasks. But, societies must bring unemployement rate rises , due to societies will have many people loss jobs when their employers choose to buy robots to serve their clients or do any office tasks or customer service or cleaning etc. tasks.

In micro economy view, employers may save money in long term, but in macro economy view, it will cause unemployment ratio rises , even crime rate rises when there are many people lose
jobs in societies. These models of doom, though, fail to account for the hundreds of businesses riding the waves of change in their industries when robots may be invented to replace human to do many simple , even complex tasks in our future societies.

WE may image that one small factory needs to manufacture fishes canes to sell to supermarket, the small , cheaper stuff and higher margin parts of the fishes manufacture industry. Before, this factory needs to employe many human factory workers need to help every fresh customer makeing the perfect fishing gear, designed for performance, durability, and cost in order to achieve to manufacture every fish cane in whole fished processing manufacturing stages. Every worker needs to spend about 15 to twenty minutes to finish every fish cane , till to delivery to any supermarket to sell. If this fish canes manufacturing factory can apply manufacturing robots to help them to finish any one working tasks , every robot can only spend five minutes to finish whole fresh fish cane manufacturing process. Thus, every robot can

help this factory save 10 to 15 minutes time to finsh every fish cane manufacturing process. IN fact, time is money, because when every robot can help this factory to reduce 10 to 15 minutes time to compare human worker. Then, this factory can finish about 20 fish canes in one hour if it can use robot to help it to manufacture fish canes. Otherwise, if this factory still use human workers to help it to manufacture fish canes, then it can finsh about 3 to 4 fish canes in one hour. SO, the manufacturing efficiency ensures that robots must help this fish manufacturing factory to raise fish canes number more than human workers. So, in robotic behavioral economy view, manufacturing robots must help this fish canes manufacturing factory to raise fish canes manufacturing number and deliver increasing number to supermarkets to prepare to sell every day. Robots can help this fish canes manufacturing factory bring manufacturing time saving, rising manufacturing efficiency, improving performance and reducing wages expenditure long time advantages in micro economy view. However, manufacturing robots can also bring disadvanages to society, e.g. increasing unemployment ratio, increasing crime rate,

this factory workers will lose jobs and income, they need earn social welfare from government and increasing government finance pressure in short time, even long time in macro economic view.

Stanford University graduate program in economics, Scott lecturer explained that "in demand and supply economic theory for robots supply and demand case, robots supply number increasing may influence human workers demand number decrease. It sometimes calls " the efficient frontier".

No specific human beings were mentioned in any of economics classes. As robots supply and demand in market case, They (robots) may be purely theoretical " agents" who reached to the most reasonable sale prices in order to persuade any one businessman buyer to make manufacturing robot buying decision whether robots can help him / her to bring how much saving time , saving money, saving cost, improving performance, efficiency economic benefit before he/she plans to reduce workers number when he/she decides to apply robots to replace human workers in his/her factory or office or any service department, e.g. cinema ticket sale service, shopping center customer service, shopping center cleaning , supermarket customer service etc. service or sale tasks. When robots can replace human to do any one of these tasks in any organizations. So, robots may be human worker agents who reached to prices the way robots would react to a software

command. There was nothing that explained why some people thrived and others did n't or why truly brilliant, hardworking people could fail when much lazier folks succeeded." Having been admitted to the Stanford University graduate program in economics, Scott lecturer hoped to get his answers there.

How robots influence our future social changing? Using the right technology can be a boon to your business in this economy. For internet example, it is easier than ever to find well-matched customers all around the world, to stay in contact with them, and to more quickly design the products they want. If you focus solely on being cutting -edge, though you risk letting the technology

take over what should be very robust relationships with your customers , employees, and colleagues. IN nowaddays society, technoligical advances and cutomation, personal

relationships in business are more crucial than ever. I mean that robots can not replace human to serve clients to let them to feel more comfortable and passion more easily. For shoe shop case example, if the shoe shop apply one robot to serve its clients to replace human shoe salesperson to serve its shoe customers. Robots ensure that they can not persuade every shoe potential buyer to make shoe buying decision more easily when robots need to contact every shoe potential buyer. The reason is simple, because robots can not touch any one shoe buyer individual emotion very easier.

If the shoe buyer needs the robots to help him/her to choose any right shoe styles when he/she can not feel himself / herself can make the most right shoe style choice decision. The robots can not replace human shoe salesperson to make shoe style choice judgement more easily. They must need longer time to analyze whether which shoe style may be the most suitable to the shoe buyer. Otherwise, human shoe salesperson may attempt to make the most right shoe style choice decision to help any one shoe buyer to chooce the most right style shoe because he/she owns shoe style sale experience, shoe style knowledge, the most important reason is that they can feel every shoe customer individual emotion to touch whether he/she will feel comfortable or happy when they attempt to help every shoe customer to seek the most right shoe style in every shoe customer whole shoe searching processing. Othwerwise, serving robots are only one machine, they can not touch or feel every shoe customer individual emotion whether he/she feel comfortable or unhappy or happy when they need to contact them in whole shoe searching processing. Hence, I believe that some tasks robots can

not repalce human staff to do very easily. Otherwise, robots may bring disadvanatges to let any one businessman to loss his/her customers, due to robots can not touch every customer

emotion to compare human staff in service tasks more easily. Robots serving customer behaviors may cause money lose and customers number lose to the shop in micro economic view.

Intellectual human economic behaviors

What does intellectual human economic behaviors mean ? I believe that when we choose or decide to do intellectual behaviors, then our societies will be influenced to bring economic growth in consequence.I shall attempt to indicate pollution case to explain how and why eithet our intellectual or foolish behaviors may bring economic growth or recession in consequence as below:

On one hand, for air pollution social case aspect example, if we only consider to buy cars to drive for working aimr or holiday leisure aim. Then, our societies air will be polluted. Our health will be influenced to bad. Our car driving behaviors may cause global environment air pollution serously. In long tiem, global air pollution will bring our bodies health to be bad. Although, ourselves car driving behaviors may bring our driving travelling leisure enjoyment and comfortable feeling in short time, also we so not need to pay public transport fare often, but we need to compensate ourselves health economic intangible loss due to air pollution , when cars number increases, dirty air will cause ouselves health to become bad.

In the result, we will need to pay more medical expenditure when we are old age, due to ourselves bodies will become bad, due to we breathe global dirty air every day, due to ourselves cars pollute air in long time, e.g. 10 to 20 years, even 30 more without limited air pollution environment. So, driving cars behavior may be one kind of human foolish behavior and our foolish behavior may bring ourselves future long time medical expenditure absolutely.

One the other hand, water pollution social aspect, if we often keep much rubblish to pollute sea, oil exploration porcessing pollute ocean , ships gas pollute ocaen, then fishes will eat polluted food and drive dirty water, due to global ocean is polluted.

In fact, because human only to conside how to buy boats to carry on leisure enjoyment activities, or catch cruises to travel on the sea. Also, oil manufacturers only consider researching anywhere to find new oil exploration places to manufacture oil product, when their oil exploration processes pollute ocarn . Consequently, global fishes drink polluted warer or eat polluted food. They will have poison. SO, human will have high chance to eat poison polluted fishes, due to fishes are poison or are polluted.

So, human is doing foolish activities, we only hope to find oil exploration places to pollute ocean or we only spend money to buy ticket to catch ships to travel anywhere in global ocean. All of these human foolish behaviors will bring pollution to global ocean. On consequently, we will need to compensate to eat polluted or dirty or poision fishes, ourselves bodies health will be bad. In long time, we need have high chance to pay medical expenditure when we are old. So, pollution case may be one good example to explain how and why human foolish behavior may influence ourselves future need to compensate serious medical loss.

All of these human foolish behavior will bring pollution to global ocean. On consequently, we will need to compensate to eat polluted or dirty or poison fished , ourselves bodies health will be bad. In long time, we will have high chance to pay medical expenditure, when we are old. So, pollution case may be one good example to explain how and why human ourselves intellectual or foolish behaviors may influence future long time economic loss or economic growth or recession in micro and micro economic view.

On another water pollution aspect hand, if we often keep rubbish to sea, oil exploration processing pollutes ocean and ships' gas pollute ocean, then fishes will eat polluted food and drink dirty water, due to fishes will eat polluted food and drink dirty sea water because the global ocean is polluted seriously.

In fact, because human only consider how to buy boats to carry on any leisure water activities, or catches cruises to travel on the sea. Also, oil manufacturers only consider any where to find oil exploratin places to manufacture oil products from ocean, when their pol exploration processes can plooute ocean. Consequently, global fishes drink polluted water or eat direty food. They will have poison. So, human will have high chance to eat poison fishes.

Otherwise, such as pollutin case, it can infuence inflation or deflation. Consequently, the reason indicates supply and demand theory. If air pollution is serious, then we will consider health issue, global cars demand number may be influenced to reduce, when global cars number demand will reduce, global car prices and supply number will need to change to fall down in order to attract or persuade global car consumers choose to make car purchase decision.

Hence, global car manufacture number and car price will be influenced to reduce, due to global air pollution issue. Consequently, deflation will occur because when the country citizen usually does not spend much extra saving money to buy car expensive goods. Money value will be low. Otherwise, if global cair pollution is not serious, human considers to buy cars to enjoy driving leisure lives. So, global car demand is influenced to increase , also global car price will also influenced to increase.

Consequently, gobal human will choose to buy cars to drive. Due to we accept to spend extra saving to buy expensive car goods. Car sale price and supply may be influenced to rise up. Money value is influenced to reduce. Inflation may be influenced, due to global car consumers number increases, we would not have extra money to spend easily. Car expensive goods expenditure influences our spending habit to avoid to make car purchase decision more easily. So, human intellectual or foolish activities may bring inflation or deflation consequency in possible indirectly in macro economic view.

On conclusion, above pollution case explain that how and why human intellectual or foolish economic behaviors may bring inflation or deflation consequency as wll as economic growth or recession consequency as well as any goods demand and supply increasing or decreasing consequency. It implies that human behavior may have indirect relationship to influence any goods demand and supply number to either increase or decrease result as well as any goods price will be influenced to increase or decrease in micro and macro economic view.

The relationship between social change and human behavior

Why does economic changes may influence human individual behavioral change? I shall attempt to indicate shopping behavior and staying at home behavior to explain their case and effect relationsip as below:

Human behavior can be influenced by economic change or economic change can be influenced by human behavior? Why does recession may influence consumers reduce shopping desire? In social recession suitation, it is possible that many people lose jobs suddenly, due to businessmen lose many customers. They need to make decision to reduce employees number in order to continue to keep businesses. Consequently, many firms (organizations) their employees may lose jobs. When they have much time, due to lose jobs, they will feel to avoid to spend too much time and money to go to shopping often. Many losing jobs people, they will often stay at homes.

So, they will reduce time to go to shopping, then non essential products won't their preferable choice purchase products. Hence, recession will change many losing jobs people their shopping or consumption desires to avoid to buy non essential products often . Usually when economic boom, many people have jobs to do because consumers number must increase when many people have jobs to do. Then, many people can accept to spend money to buy non essential products often. Many people feel spend time to go to shopping can satisfy their purchase of any kinds of new products useful psychology or desire. So, recession is one good example to explain it can influence many people do not like often to leave homes to go to shopping easily. Many people like to stay at homes, becaue they feel worry about spending too much shopping time when they leave homes. Their staying home time is one good negative shopping behavior example. So, economic change may influence human individual behavior changes , they have direct cause and efect relationship in behavioral economic view.

May human behavior influence economic change? Is it possible that human behavior may bring the country social economic change in macro economic or micro behavioral economic view ? I shall indicate publishing industry example. Do you feel that if there are many students feel learning is very important when they read many books or many of students feel interesting to read or they have reading new books in habit, then it is possible that the country will have many students like to spend time to go to any book shops to choose the books, they feel that they can help they learn new knowledge. Then the country will increase students number, they often spend time to visit any one book shop every week. Their visiting book shops behavior which may become their habits. So, the country will increase students number, they often spend time to visit book shops. Also, it implies that visiting book shops behaviors may be their behavioral habits.

So, when the country has many students often spend time to visit book shops , their visiting book shops behaviors may help any one book shop to raise books sale chance. So, the country's student individual often visiting book shop behaviors, their habitual visiting book shops behaviors must may assist help any one book shop to increase books sale number absolutely.

Consequently, any one book shop , its books sale bumber must be influenced to increase to increase because the country will have many students like or feel need visit book shops habit in order to choose any suitable books to buy to read at home in order to raise themselves learning effort. When the country has many bok shops often have many students visit their book shops, then their books sale number may be influenced to increase. It explain why student individual visiting book shop behavior may help any one book shop sale number increases also.

How human productive behavior may influence economic development

May any country which citizen behavior assist themselves country development? It is one cause and effect economic question. I mean that if the country itself citicen can not concentrate mind or energy to choose to do one kind of industry in order to let themselves country can bring the most benefit, then whether the counry itself economy can bring the most serious economic benefit. I shall attempt to indicate these countries themselves indistry choice to explain whether these countries themselves citizen productive behavior may help themselves countries to achieve the largest economic benefits. I shall indicate as below:

New Zealand farmer individual wine productive behavior

For New Zealand country example, this country concerns itself effort is foucs on farming agricultural aspect. So, this country has many farmers concentrate on farming agricultural aspect. May New Zealanders choose to spend time to produce different kinds of wines, e.g. wine or red grape wine is for the people are eating meat, or they are eating dinner.

When these New Zealanders their behaviors choose to do farming or agriculture to grow and produce different kinds of taste of white or red grape wine drinking products job. Themselves grape agriculture behavior will influence these New Zealanders themselves, they can learn how to improve different kinds of grape wine drinking products in order to achieve every kinds of white or read grape wines taste improving aim during their white or red grape producing process.

Why can New Zealander every individual white or read grape wine producers improve their white or read grape wine taste more easily? In behavioral economic view, it can explain that why any one New Zealander white or read grape wine producer can be encouraged or excited or persuaded to concentrate nervous and energy and effort to learn how to improve their white or red grape wine products easily.

In fact, New Zealand is one agricultural food export country. It has good natural environment resource , e.g. land, seed to provide any one farmer to produce themselves any kinds of agricultrual food products, e.g. fruit, or wine food products. Because New Zealanders know themselves country has enough natural resource . So, in common, many New Zealanders choose to attempt to do farming agricultural jobs in order to export themselves any kinds of fruit or meat or wine products to overseas or sell to domestic in order to earn profit.

So, when these New Zealand farmers number has been increasing every year. This country farmers will feel themsleves competition between this New Zealand farmers themselves are serious due to they may feel New Zealanders choose to do agriculture businesses in order to export themselves different kinds of farming food to overseas or sell to local to earn profit.

Hence, when many New Zealand farmers feel that farmers number has been increasing every year. They will feel themselves competition is serious. They must need to spend much time and nervous and effort to research what method is the best how to produce the best taste of white or red grape wine products in order to let local or overseas wine buyers to choose to buy his/her producing white or read grpae products to drink.

Hence, in competition psychological view, may influence many New Zealand white or reaad wine producers had been beginning to change their learning behavior on researching what method is the best in order to produce the best quality of taste red or white wine products to sell in order to attract overseas or local white or read grape wine drinkers to choose to buy his/her wine products. Their behavior will focus on learning how to raising or improving white or read grape wine taste method more than only focus on producing a large number white or red grape wine products. They believe wine quality is more important to compare wine producing number. So, New Zealand wine producers themselves wine producers behaviors have been changing on concentrating on researching wine quality method aspect more then wine producing number aspect in behavioral economic view.

America high technological productive behavior

For America example, US is one high technological country, it owns many high technological knowledge talent inventors, e.g. computer science inventors. Hence, US must attract many diferent countries owning high technological computer inventors choose to go to US to develop their computer science profession career. Also, it seems that when many computer science inventors or professions choose to go to US to develop themselves computer science new career. In behavioral economic view, due to their leaving themselves countries choice, which may bring influence themselve country job behaviors need to be changed. They must need to adapt US new live. Because they will forgive their past computer science job. These computer science professionals need to spend time to adapt US new lives. They " past computer science job behaviors" will need to be changed to their new US any computer employer's new computer science job model.

Because their traditional computer science jobs needed to be forgot in their themselves countries. They will feel their old computer science job knowledge and behavior needed to change in order to let their US any one new of computer company employer feels satisfactory to accept their new working behavior in any one US computer organization.

So, on the other hand, many US computer company employer will feel that they must need time to accept any one new overseas computer science professions their working behaviors, their working attitude daily, because these foreign comouter science professional, their past computer working behaviors and working attitude must be different to US domestic computer science professions.

In behavioral economic view, these overseas computer science professions, their working behaviors and attitude must be needed to change in order to adapt any one US new computer company itself domestic or local computer science professional stafs themselves daily working behaviors and attitude because these overseas and local computer science professionals must need to team work together.

In behavioral economic view, it is only one way that foreign computer science professionals must need to change themselves past country traditiona daily working behaviors and attitude in order to cooperate with these US local computer science professionals in teams more easily.

Consequently, if these foreign compute science professionals can change their past working behaviors and attitude to let any one US local computer science professional feels to cooperate with them easily in short time. Then, the US computer company itself whole computer professional teams themselves efficiencies will be influenced to raised or improved by the changing past working attitude and working behaviors of these foreign computer science professionals. So, in behavioral economic view, only if US any one computer company hopes itself computer teams themselves efficiency can be raised or improved when it decides to employ foreign computer science professionals and US domestic computer science professionals. They need to work in teams together. They must need to let these foreign computer science professionals to know how to change their working behaviors and attitude to let their domestic computer science professionals feel easy to work together. Then, the US computer company itself whole team efficiency must be rasied or improved easily in short time.

● China share market investing behavior

For China share market example, economic development depends on financial market. Because if many Chinese have interest to invest to carry on shares buying and selling activities in orde to learn how to earn shares interest and share profit when the China shareholder can make decision to sell himself/herself shares in the the high price, then he/

she can earn money when he/she can sell the China company's shares in the high sale share price position.

If China has many Chinese like to spend time to carry on investing shares activities. Themselves shares buying and selling behaviors will influence China has many companies can increase fund from many Chinese shareholders in order to have enough money to expand or develop themselves businesses in China in long term.

Consequently, when China can have many Chinese like to attempt to carry on buying and selling shares investing behaviors in China share market. Themselves buying and selling shares behaviors can help many Chinese companies have effort to increase enough money or capital in order to continue to do their businesses in long term absolutely. So, it explains why when many Chinese become shareholders , they can assist China will have many companies continue to develop their businesses if many Chinese like to carry on shares buying and selling investing behaviors in long time in China financial investment market nowadays in behavioral economic view.

Why has any individual country have many people invest share behavior which can influence the country's macro consumption desire?

I shall apply shares market buying and selling investment behavior to explaiin why shares investment behavior which may impact the country's overal consumption desire as below:

In behavioral economic view, I assume that when the coutry has many people have interest to attempt to carry on shares buying and selling investment behavior, then their frequent shares buying and selling behaviors which may bring negative consumption desire or shopping desire of these shares investors their consumer behavior.

The reason is simple, when the country has many share buyers number suddenly been increasing rapidly. Consequently, these large group share investors must need to spend much time to research any kinds of company shares variations, whether when their share prices will rise up of fall down in order to achieve buying the company's shares in the lowest price and selling the company's shares in the highest price level in order to earn profit.

Basic on this reason, they must need to spend much extra time to research share prices changing behavior every day, e.g. one working person will wait to leave his/her job, after he/she can spend time to gather data to research the day's share price changing behavior after dinner. So, the working person's right time may be his/her share price market research behavior. Before he/she may spend his/her night time to go to shopping after dinner, but nowadays, he/she will fogive to do his/her shopping behavior before dinner or after dinner at hight sometime. He/she will make decision to spend much night time to turn on computer to click on share market website to research his/her share purchase choice to investigate whether his/her share price whether it rises up or falls down at the moment in order to make his/her share buying or selling decision at ever night time.

I mean the when the country has many people are share investors, their shares investment behavioral spenging time which will influence many shops lose customers at might often because the country will have many people feel need to spend night time to turn on computer or watch television to investigate share price variation. So, the country will have many people / share investors choose to stay at home in order to carry on share price variation investigation behavior, they need to listen share market update news from radios or watch the share market update news from computer or TV at home every night. Consequenly, they must reduce times to leave themselves homes at night. So, their shopping behavior also will be reduced. Because these share investors feel need to spend time to investigate share price variation news at homes which can bring economic benefits (high opportunity benefits) when they choose to forgive to leave homes to go to shopping times (opportunity cost) every night.

On conclusion, it seems that when the country has many people are share investors, then their share price investigating behavior may bring negative shopping emotion at night. Consequently, the country's any one shop may lose many customers from this share investor consumer group in behavioral economic view. Hence, when the country's share investors number had been increasing rapidly, it will influence any shops lose many customers from this share investing customer group at night frequenly in short time, even long time in behavioral economic view, because their shopping desires or shopping emotion will be brought negative feeling when they make decisions to spend much time to listen radios or watch TV or computers share price update nes at night. Hence, share market will bring negative impact to influence consumer shopping desire or negative shopping emotion in behavioral economic view.

Can technology influence human shopping behavioral change?

Nowadays, technological development has reached mature stage, whether technological mature stage may bring positive or negative shopping emotion influence to global consumers. I shall aplly internet inventin or ecommerce shopping channel tool to explain whether internet technology can bring postive or negative influence to global consumer behavior in behavioral economic view.

Internet is a good technological tool, it brings e-commerce business chance. In fact, commonly, global has have many businessmen choose to use internet channel to carry on their products transactions between global online-buyers and their electronic websites. So, global many shoppers had begun to feel online shopping is more convenient to compare visiting shops shopping. Their shopping behaviors have been changed from internet technological tool. Global has many shoppers choose to buy any products from any overseas or local businessmen their web stores. They only need to spend time to find any businessmen their webstores to choose the most suitable products to pay visa to buy from their webstores. at homes. So, in general, global had have may shoppers had changed their shopping behaviors from visiting shops to visiting webstores at homes often.

So, it seems that internet technological tool had influenced global many shops disappear, but internet webstores will be replaced their actual shops on streets. Some of businessmen either they choose webstores to replace shops or choose websotes and shops both or still keep shops only. Hence, internet tool influences global businessmen have three kinds of products sale channels to let globa local and overseas consumers to choose how to buy their products. However, in fact, many of global shoppers, youngers and olders had begun to accept to buy any products from webstores. They feel to spend time to leave homes to visit shops , their shopping behaviors will be wasted time to not essential part to their daily lives. Hence, since internet technological invention, it had changed many consumers their traditional visiting shops shopping habit to change to buying products from webstores channel.

However, on the one hand, internet creates webstores ecommerce shopping channel to let global many consumers do not need to leave homes to go to shopping. It brings negative visiting shops shopping emotion to global general consumers nowadays. But on the other hand, it also brings positive visiting internet webstores shopping emotion to global general consumer nowadays. So, it seems that global many consumers feel that they often do not need to spend much time to go out shopping. Many global consumers feel convenient and enjoy to choose any products to buy from different internet webstores, when the online buyer chooses the most suitable product, he she only needs to pay visa card to buy the product from the online seller's webstore conveniently at home.

Hence, online shopping can bring economic benefit to online buyers, e.g. avoiding walking time or spending transport fare to visit the shop to go to shopping, shortening or reducing shopping time to do another important matter.

On conclusion, global many consumers began feel online shopping can bring more economic benefits on shortening shopping time, avoiding transport fare spending aspect. So, online shopping will be popular shopping behavior for future long time. It may encourage global many shoppers can make rapid shopping decision in short time in order to carry on any products buying transaction to global any one online shopper in short time easily in behavioral economic view. So, global many businessmen had begun to build themselves one attraction webstore in order to persuade different countries consumers to choose to click themselves webstores from internet channel to buy any kinds of products in short time easily.

So, internet technology had changed consumers traditional shopping behaviors to build positive online shopping emotion as well as raise online sellers' any products sale chance easily in behavioral economic view.

Why and how human behavior may influence the country's economic growth or recession?

When one country has many people choose to do the same matter for one period, whether their behavior may influence the country's pvera; economic growth or recession . I shall attempt to indicate cases toexplain their relationship as below:

For flowing rubblish behavioral case example, do you feel that when the country has many people often flow rubblish on the streets, instead of their flowing rubblish behavior may bring streets dirty? But, their flowing rubblish behavior may explain that this country has people may have enough money to buy food to ear, or enough cloths to wear, enough bottles of water to drink, even they may have enough money to buy new television, radio, refrigeraters , washing machines, desktops or laptops electronic home products from old to new to use in order to satisfy their living needs. So, when they flow old electronic home products, their flowing old home electronic products behaviors may seem that they have enough money to buy other new home electronic products to replace old home electronic products to use at homes.

However, it seems thaat this country ought have many people have jobs to do. So, many of them, they can easy to make purchase decison to flow any old home electronic products and buy any new home electronic products to use . Because this country has many people have jobs to do. So, they can often not use old home electonic products to become rubblishs to flow on streets after they had bought any kinds of new home electronic homes.

In fact, it also implies that this country's economy grows rapidly. So, many businesses can glow up rapdly. When they expanded their businesses, they must need to increase employees number in order to let they help themselves to raise productivity or serve their clients absolutely. So, when the country has many businesses can grow up, it seems that its economy must be better or it is improved to compare past. Due to many different kinds of home electronic products had been often bought to use by this country people in this period. So, this country's any streets can be observed that expensive electronic home products were flowed on streets anywhere. then, this country will have many electronic home products sellers can sell their home electronic products very easily. When this country has many people can find any kinds of jobs to do easily. So, due to unemploymen rate had been decreasing.

In behavioral economic view, as this many electronic home products rubblish country case, we can observe this country may have many people have jobs to do. So, consumption number has been increased long time. So, cheap food, or expensive home electronic products may be rubblish on any streets. This country's people , their flowing rubblish behaviors may be explained that many of people have enough jobs to do, so they have ability to buy any good taste food to eat or buy any kinds of expensive electronic home products to use. So, this country's economy may be improved for this long period. So, in behavioral economic view, when this country can have many electronic home products rubblishs are flowed on anywherer in streets frequently. It seems that this country will have many people have jobs to do, so it causes they often change old home electronic products or replaced them easily, when they have enough income to spend to buy any kinds of new home electronic products to use at homes easily. Moreover, their flowing old electronic home products behaviors also indicate that this country has many people their salaries may be increased in possible from their emplyers. When this country can have many different kinds of home electornic products are sold. It means that this country's electronic home products needs or demand had been increasing, due to many people have jobs to do and income increases to excite their living of needs also improve. Consequently, this country may seem have better economic improvement. We can observe from this country's electronic home products rubblish increasing income in theis period.

On conclusion, this country ought experience economic growth at this period. So, " flowing expensive electronic home rubblish increasing number " may seem that this country's economic growth is rapidly in this period, due to many people have jobs to do as well as salaries increase in this period.

Technology how impacts human behavior changing?

Technology how influences human behavior to bring changing? For example, online share purchase and sale transaction from smart phone brings share investor can do share buying or selling transation in any where and any time conveniently, non manual driving auto vehicle, bring car owner feels comfortable and spends free time to do other matter, e.g. reading, listening mucis in himself or herself car freely. electrical energy vehicle can help car owner to reduce air polluton and it can brings the drivers do not feel drive long time in any journeys in order to avoid air pollution for environmental protection responsible car drivers in our societies. Thus, they will drive long time in any journeys when they can drive electronic energy cars to replace oil energy cars.

However, online technology can also bring consumers can choose to stay at homes to buy any things from seller individual online webstore conveniently. Such as online technology can bring shoppers do not need to spend much time to visit shops to buy any things. They can choose any kinds of products from any online sellers individual online webstores conveniently at homes. Online technology excite busy consumers can make purchase decision easily as well as it can help online sellers sell any kinds of products from internet easily.

In behavioral economic view, technology can change human behavior to be improved, it can let human feels comfortable, more free time ro use, rapid making any decisions, such as apply smart phones to make share purchase or sale transaction decision, online shopping decision, even travelling any where decision in short time, when the traveller finds the most cheap hotel accommodation room price and air ticket price frm any travel agent online tourism webstore, then the potential travel customer can follow the online hotel accommodation price and air ticket price data to make decision when to buy the air ticket from the airline travel agent or make decision when to prebook which hotel accommodation room to go to the country to travel from online travel agent tourism webstores. So, technology can encourage global any country travelers to make anywhere to trvel rapidly. If the traveler can find the country's general hotel rooms and airline tickets prices had been decreasing more sightly. The traveler may make travel decision to choose the country to travel in short time, then he/she can prebook the country;s any hotel room and airline ticket to pay by visa fraom the country's any hotel and airline travel agent webstores., before one week, even one month or more easily. Hence, online technology can also encourage traveler individual frequent travel times to be increased, due to global travelers can find any hotel rooms and airline tickets prices from internet conveniently at homes. They do not need to spend time to visit any airline travel agent to enquire travel choice country's hotel rooms prices and airline ticket prices. They can compare global travel of countries choices ' all hotels rooms and airline agents air tickets prices to make prebook airline seat and hotel room decision before one week, one month even six months early.

On conclusion, online technology can encourage global travelers can make travelling any where and when traveling time desicions easily. It can excite tourism industry develops in long time. Also, such as electricity cars invention can encourage environment protection car owners do car purchase decision easily, because they can choose to drive electronic energy cars to replace oil energy cars in order to avoid air pollution occurs easily. So, electronic cars can increase electronic car purchasrs number, due to many of environmental protection attitude of car owners can choose to drive electricity cars to bring air cleans, even non -manual driving cars can encourage lazy driving and free time driving car owners to choose to buy non-manual (artificial intelligent) cars to drive , because they can spend much free time to read, listen music or do any matters in themselves cars, they do not need to drive cars, robotic (AI) auto driving machine is such one non-manual driver to help them to drive themselves cars confidently. So, non-manual driving cars can attract lazy and enjoying free time driving car owners to choose to buy to replace traditional manual cars to drive easily. Moreover, online share transaction can help any share investors to make share buying and selling decision in short time easily. When they can apply smart phones technological tool to carry on share buying and selling activities easily. They can observe any share rising or falling price suitation from smart phones in any where any any time easily. So, smart phone technology can help global any shareholders to make share purchase and sale transaction easily. So, technology can encourage human makes decision in short time rapidly.

How and why employees behaviors may influence economy development?

In behavioral economy view,I believe the country's any organizational employees behavior may bring indirect relationship to influence the country's long term economic development. I shall indicate past manufacture industry social development period to explain their relationship. For many countries' past business activities had belonged to manufacturing industry, such as US, UK past before 1980 year, it focused on steel manufacturing and steel manufacturing related machine products. So, US, Uk developed countries manufacturing industries may be past main country's economic income sources. I assume US , UK past had one million number different kinds of industries. They ought had about seven houndred thousand number organizational businesses were belonged to manufactured industry. They may include:

Steel manufacturing and steel related machine manufacturing, e.g. vehicle manufacturing, home appliances, e.g. washing machine, television, radio, refrigerate cooler, heater, air condition etc. different kinds of different kinds of steel -related manufacturing machine, they were manufactured from US, UK steel machine manufacturers. So, US, Uk the other three hundred thousand number industry may be general service industry, e.g. hotel service, restaurent, cinema, public transport service, tourism lesiure , wine bar, supermarket etc. different kinds of non-manufacturing industries business organizations were operated in UK, US past before 1980 year.

So, in UK, US developed countries industry development history, they ought have high percentage of businesses belonged to steel related manufacturing machine and steel products. Also, in the past before 1980 year, US, Uk business employers , they employed many workers are manufacturing workers. They needed to spend long time to work in factories. They were skillful workers, and they are trained to manufacturing cars, washing machine, television, heater, etc. even steel itself different kinds of steel related products to prepare to deliver to their shops to sell to US, Uk local or overseas clients.

So, I believe that past UK, US ought employ many employees, they belonged to skillful manufacturing workers, manufacture increasing steel machine or steel related machine number of products rapidly daily. So, if UK, US had had many of these manufacturing factories owned high skillful workers, then their manufacturing steel-related machine or steel both kinds of products number must be influenced to raise rapidly. Consequently, their steel machine manufacturing products would been exported to overseas or would been sold to local both markets , they may be influenced to raise sale number. They (these manufacturing workers) needed to be trained to know how to manufactur these different kinds of machine products in the efficient teams and they ought to be trained to raise their efficiencies in order to shorten time to manufacturing many kinds of steel related manufacturing machine or steel itself products rapidly. So , if their efficiencies and manufacturing performance was improved, these US, UK any one manufacturing worker and their teams ought achieve raising productivities significantly.

Hence, when past UK, US manufacturing industry development period, if these two countries' any manufacturing factories could have many manufacturing workers could be trained to be skillful and proficient manufacturing workers. Then, in past every day to these factories workers, they ought help their steel or steel related manufacturing employers to raise any kinds of machine or steel products number in every team. So, when past in the manufacturing industry development, US, UK could have many factories' manufacturing workers themselves steel or steel related machine products manufacturing skill could be trained to to improve to any kinds of these machine or steel manufacuring products quality as well as their products number could be influenced to raise by themselves skillful improvement significantly every day.

Then, what would be influenced to occur to past UK, US manufacturing industry period? In behavioral economic view, when these two manufacturing industry developed countries, such as UK, US , if they had many factories workers can be trained to improve their skill in order to achieve any kinds of steel or steel-related machine products quality could be improved as well as products manufacturing number could be also increased absolutely.

In consequence, past UK and US both countries ought increase themselves any kinds of steel and steel related machine products number to be supplied to themselves local shops to let local clients to choose any one kind of machine manufacturing products to buy easily as well as they could also export to supply overseas any countries to buy their different kinds of steel or steel related machine products to let overseas steel or steel related manufacturing machine product buyers, they can have many of these different kinds of these steel or steel-related different kinds of manufacturing machine from UK and UK these both countries easily to compare other countries.

On conclusion, I believe that past US, and UK macro manufacturing industry income GDP would increase significantly. So, they would have good economic growth performance because when many of these manufacturing workers themselves manufacturing effort could be improved. So, it explained when employees manufacturing abilities can influence economic growth indirectly.

Robots invention whether they can help organizations to raise efficiencies or inefficiencies?

In behavioral economic view, in any organizations, when the organization hopes its worker teams can raise efficiencies , the organization may choose to increase more workers number and/or it can provide training to improve these workets themselves skills in order to raise their efficiencies. For one warehouse example, when the warehouse increases many goods , they are needed to delivered these goods from the shelves to the delivering destination locations. If this warehouse supervisors feel these workers themselves goods delivery speeds are slow, which is possible due to this warehouse's workers number is not enough. So, this warehouse supervisor ought increase workers number in order to increase their goods delivery speed in order to deliver goods from the shelves to every indicated goods delivery destination in order to let any one lorry driver can transport the right kinds of goods and ensure the accurate goods number to transport to any one client home rapidly.

However, if this warehouse supervisor planed to buy several warehouse goods delivery robots to assist these warehouse workers to find the right kinds of goods from shelves and then deliver to the right destination location in the warehouse. So, these warehouse orkers can concentrate on counting the accurate goods number and ensuring the right kinds of goods in order to prepare to let lorry drivers to transport these goods to these goods of buyers themselvers homes rapidly. Consequently, in the first step, robots can concentrate on finding th right goods from shelves and delivers them to the right goods transportation of location destination. Then, in the second step, these warehouse workers can concentrate on counting the accurate goods number and ensuring the right kinds of goods in order to prepare to put them to the lorry. Consequently, when warehouse robots and warehouse workers can cooperate to work together, the most important, robots, can deal on finding the right kinds of goods and deal on delivering the accurate number of goods of job duty as well as these warehouse workers can only concentrte on counting the right kinds of goods number in order to avoid it has none any mistake of wrong kinds of goods and inaccurate goods of delivery number to be transported to the lorry and to deliver to any one buyer's home.

So, it seems that warehouse robots ought help any one warehouse worker to raise himself efficiency and avoid goods delivery of mistake occurrence easily as well as their help to warehouse workers that can let any one goods buyer feels their goods can be delivered to their homes rapidly. Moreover, warehouse robots can also help these warehouse workers to raise efficiencies because warehouse robots can help them to shorten goods delivery time between any one shelf and any one goods delivery destination of location in the warehuse because robots may help them to find the right kinds of goods from the right shelf in the short time. So, any one worker does not need to spend long time to seek anywhere is the right shelf location for the kind of goods when the kind of goods are needed to deliver to the buyer's home from lorry. Warehouse robots can help them to do this aspect of " finding the goods from the right shelf in short time job duty". So, any one warehouse worker only needed tospend less time to do the counting of any right kind of goods number and ensuring the right kind of goods job duty. Consequently, this warehouse 's any one worker, his any one kind of goods delivery time may be reduced, because robots' assistance and they may have more confidence to avoid mistake to deliver the wrong number of goods and/or the wrong kind of goods to any one goods buyer's home.

On conclusion, it seems that warehouse robots ought may help any one warehouse worker to raise efficiency for any one team in the warehouse as well as the warehouse any one supervisor does not need to spend much time to observe any one worker individual performance for " goods delivery job duty aspect" because their goods delivery job duty that had been replaced to do by these several warehouse robots. Robots can achieve the more accurate of right kinds of goods and the right number of goods delviery job performance to compare any one of human warehouse worker themselves right kinds of goods of delivery and right number of goods of delivery job performance. So, when robots can participate to cooperate with this warehouse's any one worker to do their goods of delivery job duty in this warehouse every day. Then, robots can raies any one of supervisor individual confidence in order to let they do not need to spend time to observe any one of worker individual whose goods of delivery job performane. They can concentrate on supervising any one worker whose goods transport to lorry in the final step in order to avoid to deliver wrong goods number and / or wrong kind of goods to any one goods buyer's home every day. Consequently, this warehouse's overall teams of their delviery of goods performance many be improved by robotss' participatin to goods of delivery task as well as this warehouse's oveall teams themselves efficiencies may be influenced to raise by robots' goods of delivery task participation.

Why social behavior may influence organizational strategy needs to be changed ?

Why any organizations need to know whether nowadays social behaivor how has been changing in order to implement the kind of the most right strategy to achieve the profit aim pursue in possible. I shall indicate nowadays ecommerce or online, customer shopping behavior to explain above question concerns they ought have close relationship between social behavior and organizational strategic choice or organizational behavioral changing need. On nowadays ecommerce business, or online shopping model, this kind of shopping model in global many young and old age consumers like to apply internet tool to choose any country sellers website stores in order to stay at home to buy any kinds of products from themselves webstores in global societies.

In fact, online shopping model had been popular for long time above to twenty years. Most of global sellers will make decision to design themselves webstores in order to attract global many online buyers to choose to buy their products from themselves webstores. So, it seems that social consumers purchase behaviors had been changed to online shopping from internet invention.

Hence, social consumers purchase behavioral changes may influence any organizations' strategies need to be changed from visiting shops purchase strategy model to online purchase strategy model, if the seller still concentrate on concentrate on considerate how to design itelf , but neglects to considerate how to design itself webstore, e.g. how to design attract product photos to put on itself webstore, how to arrange sale price information location to be putted on webstore and visa card payment location on itself webstore in order to let any one online buyer can feel very easier to buy itself any kinds of products from itself webstore. Then, its potential online buyers will be influenced to increase number when they can find this online seller itself any kinds of products photes and every kinds of product sale price information and visa card payment channel locations easily from itself webstore.

So, it implies that nowadays any one seller ought need to design one webstore to let any one online overseas and domestic consumers can have chance to click itself webstore to choose any one kind of product to buy conveniently when he/she does not hope to leave him/her home to go to shop, because nowadays social shopping behaviors had been influenced to change when internet invention, them it gives another online purchase method to replace visiting shops purchase method to global any one buyer in nowadays societies.

So, if nowadays any one seller still concentrate on how to design itself shop display in order to put any kinds of product on shelf in order to let any one visiting shop customer to find the kind of product to buy, but it neglects to change to choose to pursue another new technological shopping method, such as webstore purchase method in order to implement effective strategy to design the most right webstore as well as in order to attract global overseas and local consumers to find itself webstore easily from website and find its any one kind of product phots and sale price and visa card payment button in order to choose to buy itself any kinds of products in the short time. Consequently I believe that the seller will lose many customers from overseas and local when its other same or similar product sellers choose to design themselves webstores in order to let global any one product buyer can buy themselves any one kind of product when they can pay visa card to buy their products from them webstores conveniently when they stay at home habitly. Then, the seller will lose many global potential customers in long time.

On conclusion, in behavioral economic view, any consumer behavioral social changing, which will influence any in order to avoid customers number loses significantly . In future time, organizations need to make rapid decision in order to implement the most reasonable and the most useful strategy in order to avoid global potential customers number reduces or lose them in long time. So, social behavioral changing environment ought influence any global organizations need to decide how to change themselves strategies in order to avoid customers loses significantly in future time.

How and why human behavior may influence economic growth or recession?

May ourselves daily behaviors influence our global societial continue economic growth or recession? Do they have cause and effect close relationship between human behaviors and global economic growth or recession? I shall apply behavioral economic theory to analyze and explain whether ourselves daily behaviors and our global societial economic growth or recession which have close cause and effect relationship as below:

Every country itself economic development must depend on any business activities, otherwise, any kinds of business activities must need ourselves business activities or behaviors in order to achieve any business activities as well as achieve the country's overall economic development in macro view.

However, any country's overall business activites or behaviors which must depend on any kinds of individual businessmen, themselves employees daily working behavior or activity or performance in order to help them to attract or increase many clients number to acieve " earning profit" aim. So, it seems that any individual business, itself overall every department individual working behavior is one main factor to influence the company's overall business performance.

For agricultural fruit and meat food farming industry example, such as New Zealand is a farming main target industry country. It had had many New Zealanders were daily themselves own farming businesses for many years. Their farming businesses include growing fruit, sheep, cow, pig pork, meat etc. food sale business. If the New Zealand farmer owned a large size farming land, then he will choose either growing fruit or feeding sheeps, pigs, cows to be meat to to transport to New Zealand supermarkets to help them to sell to their farmers meet to New Zealanders in order to earn profit. Thus, if the New Zealand farmer owned large size of farming lands, then he needs to employ many farming employees (farming workers) to help him to carry on farming business daily tasks, e.g. picking up friuts, feeding pigs, cows, sheeps to eat food daily. These daily farming jobs are very important to influence this New Zealand farmer's meats or fruits sale number whether they can be easy or diffcult to sell in New Zealand supermarkets , if these farming workers can own encough farming knowledge or skill to know how to pick up fruits method and make judgement to know whether it is right time to pick up the kind of fruits from the trees , as well as know how feed this pigs, sheeps, cows to eat food in order to let they are better health. Consequently, their farming behaviors which can let these animals can provide the best taste and enough meat from these animals to let New Zealander to buy to eat from New Zealand any one supermarket. Even these New Zealand farming workers can know whether the kinds of fruits, e.g. oranges, apples, gapes etc. fruits whether they ought be picked up from the trees at the right time. Consequently, they can make judgement to decide to pick up any kinds of the best taste fruits to let any one New Zealander to buy to eat from any one supermarket in New Zealand. Otherwise, if they do not make judegement to know whether the kind of fruit ought not be picked up because they still need longer time to continue grow up to increase fruit size and better taste from the trees in order to let any one fruit buyer can feel better taste when they eat this kind of fruit later. If they can buy this kind of fruit to eat later, then this New Zealand farmer's his fruit buyers can buy the best taste of this kind of fruit to eat from an yone supermarket in New Zealand. Consequently, many New Zealand supermarkets will choose to buy any kinds of fruits from this farmer fruit supplier when they feel this farmer's fruits can provide more better taste fruits to compare other farmers' fruits.

Thus, due to New Zealand is one farming main income source country. It's any kinds of fruits and meats need to be export to overseas to sell , instead of local sale. It's GDP percent is very high to whole country 's overall income source. So, any one New Zealand farmer individual and any one farming worker individual working behavior will influence its economy whether it is influenced to grow or recession possible. Moreover, it also seems that farming workers' farming knowledge and skill will influence themselves farming daily activities to achieve the aim of the number of increase or decrease to any kinds of fruits whether they are better taste or the number of increase of decrease to any kinds of meats whether they are better taste to supply to any one New Zealand fruit or meat buyers to eat from any one New Zealand supermarket. So, it implies that any one New Zealand farming worker individual farming behavior may influence any kinds of fruits or any kinds of meat taste because they are transported to any one supermarket to sell in New Zealand.

Consequently, if New Zealans had many farmers can teach god farming knowledge and skill to let their any one farming workers know how to decide judgement to decide when it is right time to pick up any kinds of fruits from trees , or how to grow them on soil in order to let they can grow rapidly. Then, many different kinds of fruits can be provided to let any one New Zealanders can eat the best taste of fruits when their fruits are supplied to any one New Zealand supermarkets. Even, if they knew how to feed foods to pigs, cows, sheeps to eat daily. Then they can be more health and they can provide the best taste of meats to let any one New Zealanders can buy their meats from any one New Zealand supermarkets. Moreover, their fruits and meats can be transported to overseas to let any one country fruits or meats buyers can choose any kinds of New Zealand meats and fruits to buy to eat from themselves countries supermarkets. Then, many overseas fruit and meat buyers will perfer to choose New Zealand any kinds of fruits or meats to buy to compare other countries fruits or meats to buy when they go to any one local supermarkets. On conclusion, it seems that New Zealand farming workers themselves farming behavior may influence their farming employers any kinds of fruits or meats sale number and income because their farming task behaviors must influence whether their fruits or meats taste are the better taste or worse taste to compare their other local farmers (the farmer competitors) whose fruits or meats taste. If tthe farmer's any one farming worker can be trained to learn how to know to feed animals skill and when is the most right time to pick up any kinds of fruits from trees or how to grow them on the soil methods. Due to these farming worker individual farming behavior may influence his different finds of fruits and meats sale number to be increase or decrease, so these any one New Zealand farmer must need to depend on any one farming worker whose farming working methods, if their farming working behaviors can be the best to influence any kinds of fruits to grow rapid or any kinds of pigs, cows, sheeps animals grow up rapidly , then their sale number may be increase significantly and their taste can be improved to let any New Zealand or overseas meat or fruit buyer to buy to eat to feel from any one New Zealand or overseas supermarkets, then New Zealand's agriculture industry must be influenced to increase. In the world, any one fruit or meat buyer must choose to buy New Zealand's fruit and meat to eat in prefer to compare other countries' fruits and meats. So, New Zealand's GDP may be influenced to raise from any one New Zealand farming worker individual farming working behaviors.

Reasons why human behavior may influence economic recession or growth?

Can ourselves daily behaviors or activies influence ourselves countries' economic growth or recession? I shall attempt to explain the reasons why they have direct or indirect relationship between human behavior and economy growth or recession as below:

I shall indicate environment pollition case to attempt to explain above question. Our societies had been experiencing servious environment pollution challenge. However, environment pollution , such as air pollution is caused by air planes and vehicles emission by air planes and vehicles emission as well as water pollution is caused by plastic rubblish, or dirty water or oil or gas chemical material, these both kinds of pollution ought may bring economic recession and this both kinds of pollution are caused by human ourselves daily foolish activities.

I believe human behavior and economy and pollution which have cause and effect relationship. I shall analyze this environment pollution case to explain why they have case and effect relationship between human foolish behavior and environment pollution and economic recession as below:

When global societies had many people like to buy cars to drive to bring emission to fresh air on the roads as well as many manufacturing factories will bring emission to pollute fresh air in their manufacturing processes. Factories and cars will bring air pollution , due to factories need to pollute fresh air in order to manufacture many products and car owners need to drive their cars to go to offices or leisure places. Their cars will also bring emisson to pollute fresh air. On consequence, car owners themselves frequent driving behaviors and factory workers themselves frequent manufacturing behaviors may bring environment pollution. Technology or human behavior whether may influence economic growth or recession. Moreover, air planes also brings emission to pollute air when they are flying in sky. Also, when ships bring oil pollution or sea plastic rubblishs bring pollution to global oceans.

In fact, manufactuers and cars owners, such as factories workers manufacturing behaviours ans car owners driving behaviors and pilots driving air planes flying behaviors and ships transport behaviors, which may cause plastic rubblish, oil or gas emission to sky or sea or on the road to cause ocean and air pollution is serious. However, human ourselves need to buy cars to drive to satisfy ourselves driving leisure or enjoyment, travelers need to catch air planes to travel to enjoy leisure needs, factories workers need help factories to manufacture many products to sell to customers to satisfy their using needs. oil exploration needs to find lands to explore new oil lands.

All of these business and leisure activites may bring serious air and water pollution. However, due to serious air and water pollution will bring earth warming challenge , such as some countries temperature will be influences to rise up to 40 degree or higher br earth warming. However, earth warming is caused by air and ocean pollution. Pollution must be caused by human ourselves, driving cars leisure and factories manufacturing business activities. Hence, if human decided to continue to do these foolish behaviors, we only pursue to manufacture different kinds of industrial products or drive cars to enjoy leisure aims, but we also neglect ourselves behaviors may bring environment pollution. Then, earth warming or earth temperature will be influenced to rise up absolutely in long term. Moreover, if our future earth will be influenced to bring serious high temperature effect by human ourselves these foolish behaviors.

On consequencey, warth warming will bring serious economic losses in possible because when ourselves earth temperature had been influenced to rise up to 40 degree or high. Ourselves health will be caused poor, due to we will feel difficult breath, we must need often tried and hard to work, due to our nervous and health will be influenced to poor by pollution and earth warming effect. Also, we need to pay more money to see doctors when we had long life. Then, our societies will lose may strong labors to help manufacturers to work, e.g. factories will reduce workers number to help manufacturers to produce more different kinds of products, due to workers health is general poor. Due to lacking enough workers to manufacture products, our societies will begin to reduce enough supply number of products to sell to global consumers to satisfy their use needs.

On conclusion, in behaviroal economic view, our societies will lose many labors due to their bodies are not health by air and water pollution. Global economic and business activities will be influenced to worse by global workers reducing number reason. So, economic recession will begin to occur in possible when pollution reaches the serious level.

CHAPTER TWO

Customer online shopping behavior or technology influences Amazon e-commerce development

Amazon Knowledge innovation strategy

There are both kinds of knowledge innovation influences to Amazon ecommerce organization develops in success, one is e-commerce technological knowlegde as well as another is social innovation knowledge. I shall explain the reasons why these both knowledge may cause Amazon e-commerce organization grows in success as below:

E-commerce technological knowledge innovation

What does knowledge innovation mean? Why and how does Amazon ecommerce organization need to continue to innovate its online shopping knowledge sale channel? Can knowledge innovation impact positive online shoppers number grow to Amazon? Why does Amazon ecommerce organization apply knowledge innovation strategy to grow itself organization to achieve global online buyers number in success? In fact, when we can prepare to innovate our knowledge to be perfect. Consequently, it can help our social development more success, e.g. non manual driving vehicle, e-commerce, construction houses on water skill, hospital new robocit surgeon equipment, manufacturing robotic technology , even space touriusm leisure development etc. different kinds of technology innovation, they are depended on how human can attempt to learn to innovate or improve ourselves traditional old knowledge to be changed to any kinds of new or not discovered unique knowledge. So, human ought need to continue to learn how to innovate our old traditional knowledger to be more perfect. The question concerns how human can continue to change our old knowledge to innovate in succeed. I shall attempt to indicate how Amazon ecommerce organization can apply knowledge management innovation strategy to improve itself online puchase and sale platform to attract global many online buyers number choose its any kinds of product online purchase channel in preference as below:

What does knowledge innovation mean? The role of knowledge innovation means that knowledge management assists in building competencies required in the innovation process. Though knowledge accessibility and knowledge flow to organization, staff memebers are able to increase their skills levels and knowledge both formally and informally. An increase in skills can improve the quality of innovation as well as in society. When the country have many people can attempt to learn how to change and knowledge old knowledge to new knowledge, then they my bring their societies to develop more rapidly. So, it seems that knowledge innovation may help society, organization and individual to bring new knowledge to attribute to our future societies easily. It wil be a very important factor influence human future development in success.

However, knowlege innovation concept is not just represented by introducing or implementing new ideas or methods. The definition of meaning of innovation can be defined as a process, but involves multiple activities to uncover new ways to do things. Innovating helps developing original concepts and is to driver of optimizing operations. The purpose of innovation is to come up with new ideas and technologies that increase productivity and generate greater output with the same input on organizational aspect.

So, knowledge innovation may be applied on organization aspect, such as Amazon ecommerce organization, even individual and social aspects. On Amazon ecommerce organizational knowledge innovation aspect, innovation secures tomorrow's revenue, lowers costs and differentiates companies from the market. However, a good business model that only provides a brief market advantage and disappears after a year is not the right approach. Hence, organizational knowledge innovation aims to help the organization to raise competitive effort in long term.

Does knowledge provide innovation in Amazon ecommerce organization? Knowledge managment creates a culture conductive to tacit knowledge creation, sharing ideas in the organization, which plays an important role in the innovation process. Is knowledge management ncecessary for innovation? Beside the financial basis knowledge is the most important resource for innovations, in order to lead a company successfully, systematic handling of " knowledge", becomes more important. Today, the increase in value develops from the productivity and the innovation in business society.

What is the role of knowledge for individual? Knowledge is important for personal growth and development, knowledge sharpens our skills like reasoning and problem solving. A strong base of knowledge helps brains function more smoothly and effectively. We become smarter with the power of knowledge and solve problems more easily. Hence, innovation is about knowledge creating new possibilities through combining different knowledge sets. These can be in the form of knowledge about what is technically possible or not particular configuration of this world meet an articulated or latent need.

For Amazon knowledge innovation can bring the positive effects of technology improvement example, there are just a few of the ways in which technology may positively affect our physical and mental health. Health apps to track chronic ilnesses and communicate vitual information to doctors , health apps that anyone tracks diet, any kinds of sport exercise and mental health information . Hence, technololgy innovation had been applied to health apps smart phone product to help we to track our health from ourselves smart phone apps equipment easily any time.

What impact did this innovation have on daily life? It increased the regional differences among various groups of people across the country, it become a major method of long distance commnication to many years. It allowed people to sign documents from across the country. So, innovation can be applied to administive tasks aspect. Also, it can increase productivity and brings citizens new and better goods and services that improves our overall standard of living.

The benefits of inovation are sometimes slow to materialize. They often fell broadly across the entire population. According to Krathwohl (2002), he indicated that knowledge can be categorized into four types: (1) factual knowledge (2) conceptual knowledge (3) procedural knowledge and (4) metacognitive knowledge. So, if human hopes to implement knowledge innovation in success, we need to know how to learn these 4 types of knowledge innovation elements. For organizational knowledge management components example, the best four components are people, process, content/ IT and strategy.

Regardless of the industry size or knowledge needs of Amazon ecommerce organizations, organizations always need people to lead, sponsor, and support knowledge sharing. Sharing knowledge innovation how influences social development. Social innovation includes social processes of innovation, such as open source methods and techniques and also the innovation which have a social purpose, like activism , virtual volunteering, or distance learning. Social innovation may include the social processes of innovation. However, social innovation is important because it can provide a unique opportunity to step back from a narrow way of thinking about social enterprise, business engagement and to recognize instead the interconnectedness of various factors and stakeholders. For science and technolgical social innovation example, science and technology can help a nation's process and development science and technology innovation are connected with development because they have hostorical record of bringing advances that have led to healthier, longer, weathler and more productive lives and they are key ingredients to solutions to the most serious poverty and economic development challenges.

Social knolwedge innovation

So, social innovation may bring human benefits, such as providing food and lifestyle products world wide with focus on environmental and social innovation , giveing every child in the world the chance to learn code and helping the visually impaired interact with their surroundings. Hence, social innovation means new solutions (products, services, models, markets, processes etc.) that stimultaneously meet a social need (more effectively than existing solutions) and lead to new or improved capabilities and relationships and better use of assets and resources. However, a social innovation process consists of a sequence of activities that seals to find solutions to a special challenge. The process itself brings a new approach that has social impact in its means (process) and ends (solution).

There are 6 keys characteristics of a social innovation, as told by Colombian social enterprises, they include: Adresses real needs of people in a community, requires a deep understanding of the problem, localizes and humanizes the problem, builds trust and collaborates with the community in need, is sustainable and scalable and adapts constantly. Hence, every one may attempt to learn in social innovation. You will learn what social innovations are and understand how they are help solve societal problems. You will get an overview of important literature and debates on social innovation. You will also learn and apply methods to develop , implement and scale social innovations.

How can social innovation be improved to apply to Amazon ecommerce organization case? Major cross business/ cross functional projects should also have social innovation objectives include: leadership programs that include volunteering activities may help employees develop their skills and lead to greater innovations during their daily work in any organizations. How does the idea of social innovation connect with social needs? We define social innovations as new approaches to addressing social needs. They are social in their means and in their ends. They engage and mobilize the beneficiaries and help the transform social relations by improving beneficiaries' access to power and resources.

For social innovation on education aspect, teaching technological literacy, critical thinking and problem, solving through science education gives students the skills and knowledge, they need to succeed in school and beyond. The essence of how science and technology contributes to society in the creation of new knowledge , and then utilization of that knowledge to boost the prosperity of human lives, and to solve the various issues facing society. Hence, when many consumers believe online shopping channel is one kind of convenient visa card payment and safe purchase , rapid goods transport to different countries, many different kinds of products choice channel. Consequently, global societies will be influenced to accept online shopping method / mode to replace traditional shops visting purchase mode. This kind of social online purchase knowledge innovation may influence Amazon ecommerce organization develops in success in long future days.

Amazon ecommerce organization warehouse products transport process and workplace innovation
How Amazon needs to consider warehouse goods delivery service tasks ?

Why does Amazon need to innovate its wareshoise products transport process to raise rapid products delivery service to different countries consumers as well as let buyers can view any products photos to feel their good quality, good design shape to attract customers consideration from its websites/ web stores in short time? What advantages will be bought to Amazon after Amazon warehouse delivery products had been innovated in success? Can products innovation help the product to improve its market image to Amazon? Can product innovation raise Amazon growth? I shall attempt to indicate reasons to explain above questions?

In our business societies, any products ought need to be concerned how to innovate them to be good quality. The key practical benefits of innovation may include: Improved productivity, reduced cots, increased competitivenesss, improveed brand recognition and value, building new business partners relationship, helping the business to increase turnover and improved profitability.

So, it seems that product innovation may bring positive impact more than negative impact to any businesses. In fact, after the buysiness innovates itself products, innovation ought may help the business to charge higher prices for new products before competitors products come on the market. Being innovative good for the firm's reputation, even people naturally interested in its future products, if they have been first in the past as well as innovations in processes can add value to existing products/ services.

So, the meant is by product innovation, it means that a product innovation is the introduction of a good or service that is new or significantly improved with respect to its characteristics of intended uses. Maninly, these reasons can explain why innovation is important: Innovation grows business, increasing profit, innovation helps any businesses stay ahead of the competitiion, innovation helps businesses take advantage of new technologies, such as Amazon ought need to innovate its warehouse products delivery service to let global buyers feel Amazon can provide rapid products delivery service to themselves homes after they paid visa card to buy any Amazon products from its web stores rapidly. On organizational benefit aspect to Amazon warehouse products delivery service innovation, innovation may help Amazon organization differentiates its 3 rd parties sellers themselves products when they decide to display their products photos on Amazon webstores, e.g. if your organization is using innovation on its processes, its because doing so will save your time, money, or other resources, and give your organization a competitive advantage over other companies stuck in their system.

In common, innovation may include four types. Incremental, disruptive , archihectural and radical, they help illustrate the various ways that companies can innovate. For technological innovative advantages, it increases productivity and brings citizens new and better goods and services that improve their goods and service that improve their overall standard of living.

The benefits of innovation are sometimes slow to materialize. They often broadly across the entire population. Hence, the advantage of product innovation may include: Growth, expansion and gaining a competitive advantage. A business that is capable of differentiating their product from other businesses in the same industry to large extent will be able to reap profit. Examples of product innovation in improved products involves introducing beter or more functionality to existing products, e.g. electric and gas lawn mower, GPs in car , battery car, non-manual driving auto car etc. So, product innovation is the creation, development and implementation, a new product, process and service, with the aim of improving efficiency, effectiveness or competitive advantages. Such as Amazon case, it needs to make products AI warehouse delivery service innovation, e.g. chaning to artificial intelligent products delivery service from workers delivery service in order to raise its goods can delivered to different countries buyers homes in the shortest time rapidly every day.

How does innovation help Amazon ecommerce organization grows its online buyers number? In fact, one of the major benefits of innovation is its contribution to economic growth. Simply put, innovation can lead to higher productivity, meaning that the same input generates a greater output. As productivity rises, more goods and services are producted. In other words, Amazon online buyers number grows.

Instead of innovation on product aspect, innovation is also important in the workplace, it can help staffs to raise efficiency. Innovation is vital in the workplace, because it gives companies an edge in penetrating markets faster and provides a better connection to developing markets, which can lead to bigger opportunities, especially in rich countries or developed countries.

However, when an organization decides to implement innovation before it implements , it needs to concern these possible risks of innovation. Operational risk, e.g. failing to meet your quality, cost or scheduling requirements, commercial risk, e.g. failing to attract enough customers, financial risk,, e.g. investing in unsuccessful innovation projects. But, when the organization decides to implement any innovation, it may hope innovation how contribute to success. Especially as customers become more demanding. Entrepreneurs need an innovation to survive to boost your business productivity, growth and profitability more easily.

IN simple, innovation may improve sales and customer relationship, reduce waste and costs boost your market position, improve employee relations. What does the right time to organizations make decisions to innovate ? When the firm discovers its customers use the product and they field praise and complaints. And they probably have ideas, however, that can be refined into a better product. Innovative companies make it clear they want ideas, that the door is open and there is always a friendly ear for changes, then they will start to come it. It may be right innovation time, when customers have any unique idea to concern the product after they use.

What is required to introduce innovation in an organization, such as Amazon ecommerce organization? To successfully implement innovation, you need to know exactly what makes an innovative organization as well as how it contributes to its growth. Our organizaitons also need to require an innovative culture where everyone is able to think independently . So, these reasons can explain why our organizations ought need to innovate, being bold in taking on the innovation challenge build people's readiness and receptivity to change, assisting people to resolve their unconscious biases and resistance to it, developing both customer intimacy and customer empathy. However, although innovation can bring positive impact in a business, but it is so difficult to implement because new ideas and initiative depend on the people who work for the organizations. It is a lot harder to achieve desired results.

Innovation is not about optimizing gross margins , but about attempt how finding new ways to create more value for yourselves profit image to attract more customers consideration.

Innovation is difficult to implement, because no system, process, or industry knows how to change, more innovations are worth exploring for many. Technology for example, can be re-purposed into new innovative solutions provide your customers with new value. The challenge is that when it comes to disruptive innovation, it almost always involves " higher risk" compared to incremental changes and thus can not be managed the same way as regular business projects are managed.

Hence, maintaining quality and product improvement and process development often involves standardization, whereas innovation can rarely be standardized . Also, new innovationds can not be measured using the same metrics and value drivers as the existing products and services . To overcome this major barrier to innovation, companies should approach disruptive innovation differently compared to how they are used to approaching regular projects. This, any organizations need to understand that they may fail to innovate. In the beginning, innovation and most specifically disruptive kind, is inferior to the existing products and services on the market. Because product improvement takes a lot of time and requires multiple iterations, the value for the customer at this point is minimal , when distuptive innovation initally caters only to a small and not so profitable customer base, established organizations are focused on serving more demanding, high and customers using their existing value channels. This is where it typically has higher profit margins, which is why established companies with rational decision-making processes usually choose not to invest in disruptive initiatives in the easrly stages. The problem ocurs when incumbents attempt to apply new technologies to trheir existing value networks or refuse moving into new markets because they are seen as too small to drive growth goals or are simply perceived to have too low margins. So, for organizations that prioritize reaching scale through operational efficiency, it makes more sense to focus on growing the business through incremental means, such as invest in risky and uncertain innovations.

On conclusion, in reality, however, Amazon ecommerce organization needs to do both simultaneously improve the core business and exploit new business opportunities . Hence, when Amazon organization decides to innovate its 3 rd party sellers their product, on warehouse goods AI delivery processing or AI workplace safe working environment . Amazon needs to find a balance between different types of innovations to choose which is the most effective goods delivery and warehouse workplace safe and efficient goods delivery innovation, which is a lot more sustainable may be stay in the Amazon e-business growth in the long term to in order to implement Amazon AI warehouse goods delivery service and warehouse working environment efficient and safe workplace innovation in order to let its all warehouse workers to feel comfortable and safe feeling and raise their goods delivery tasks efficiently.

AI creates Amazon efficient service growth

How does (AI) technological development will influence Amazon develops in success ?

(AI) robotic automation technology can bring Amazon warehouse goods delivery service task more efficient Future, (AI) robotic automation technology can be applied to Amazon warehouse goods delivery tasks in order to help it to shorten goods transport time to be delivered to overseas different countries buyers homes in the shortest time rapidly every day. For example, nowadays, UK computer and space explore technology had reached the mature stage. It means that UK government ought not need to continue spend much resource to research these two kind technologies. Otherwise, the (AI)robotic automatic manufacturing technology, e.g. human intelligence new product. It has need to develop because human intelligence machines will bring beneficial to satisfy human everyday life need, e.g. hospital patients' activities need, if the patent who can not walk easily, but the human intelligence machine can assist the patient walk to anywhere conveniently. So, he/she does not need to sit on wheel chair and apply the human intelligence machine man to help him/her to drive on the intelligence automatic driving vehicle to go to anywhere conveniently.

Otherwise, increased automation in low wage countries, e.g. China, Korea, Africa, Hong Kong etc. which have traditionally manufacturing firms, could use automatic technological manufacturing to bring lose cost advantage and potentially lose their ability of achieving rapid economy growth by shifting workers to factory jobs. So, UK government and businessmen needs to consider automation technology development, i.e. 3D printing manufacturing industry will encourage UK companies to move manufacturing process, closer to gain the biggest advantage from this 3D automation technology development.

A growing concern of premature de-industrialization in energy and developing countries could require new models and a need un-skillful the UK workforce. In the future, the best way toward for UK cities will reduce their exposure to automation is to boost their technological dynamic and attract more UK skilled workers. Automation technology progress can give UK manufacturers' employee benefits, such as long term healthy productivity improvement, raising productivity efficiency and product quality, macroeconomic and microeconomic effects of automation technological change, it's change will be beneficial to UK society, i.e. automation active labor market policies, which could help UK job seekers find jobs from training to incentive to support self-employment to create high technological job employment chance in UK society. So, raising science, technology, engineering and math subjects update skills level are needed to UK any universities, which can be increasingly important in UK society, these factors could complicate the ability of UK high automation technology education to adopt to the UK automation manufacturing technological change. A talent mismatch already exists in UK, with many well UK educated workers can find employment in lower-skilled jobs. To combat this, greater coordination will be needed between the education, training and employment sectors in UK society.

Why are high automatic technology product development models needed to improve to Amazon warehouse goods delivery improvement service ? UK government and manufacturers need to consider how to achieve high technology product development models. According to Hauser et al. (2006) indicated the high technology (high tech.) development process, is influenced by the innovative process, bringing products on exception value which stimulate product market demand. Innovation provides products the specific basis for which world economies compete with each other on the global market. Able to find new solutions, innovations generate significant changes in existing markets, destroy them, or create new marketing (Hauser et al. 2006). So, UK manufacturers need to concern on any manufacturing high technology product development process because which can influence any new products development to manufacture to sell to any overseas or domestic both markets successfully.

What does high tech. product warehouse goods delivery transport service improvement mean? Mohr et al. (2010) argues that there are two reasons why it is important to clarify and specific high technology : (1) due to the impact of technologies on the economy, attempts are made to classify economic production and incomes ; (2) due to the impact of high tech. on the environment. Standard marketing strategies are being modified and adopted , therefore, it is necessary to know the products to focus on. Why does Amazon need to consider warehouse high technological product delivery transportation process? Nowadays, high tech. products are complex, advanced, requiring specific technical knowledge, which is technologically not discontinued and being produced at the companies which have twice as many technical personnel and invest twice as many in scientific research and development than other companies. Moreover, these products are time-sensitive as scientists are continuously searching for new approaches for invention of more advanced technologies which make all preceding ones lower-ranking. The most important, nowadays global consumers will adopt the particular technology. It means that Amazon needs to improve high technological goods delivery service process to avoid the delay when global any online shoppers choose to buy any kinds of high technological products from Amazon web stores.

Anyway, nowadays customer individual needs in high tech. environments are characterized by sudden changes related to unpredictable fashion. Even, consumers concern about how to preserve new product' competitive technological standard is completely incompatible with technological uncertainty. The most important factor is the prevalence rate of any new products development process, which is influenced by slower than of traditional products. In many cases high-tech. automatic product market are being materialized slower than which are expected. The technological uncertainty challenges will exist in development process, such as uncertainty related to the timetable for development of the question whether the new product will be function as promised. In automatic high-tech. industries, the time requires for product development is difficult to predict as , commonly, it takes longer than expected , uncertainty related to unanticipated consequences and uncertainty about the product life cycle related to competition products. In conclusion, these factors will influence future Amazon any kinds of new automatic technological product warehouse delivery process to avoid to delay to deliver to different countries buyers themselves homes rapidly every day.

Future economists predict automatic technology how to influence future ecommerce goods efficient delivery service

Before, all over the world presented picture of demonstrate in London on the occasion of the meeting of the G20. Some economists indicated disastrous economy consequences will occur to any one of Western country , such as UK, so if any one of Western country did not consider automatic technology development to itself country. They indicated one example, such as material incentives to produce disappeared throughout Russia and, when Society leadership called off the experiment, the country faced industrial output reduced to 10% of what had been registered in 1914 and agricultural output reduced to such low levels as to cause widespread famine.

Why would UK encounter disastrous economy consequences if UK government did not encourage manufacturers spend money to invest to innovate automatic technology industry, such as Amazon online goods global delivery service case? According to a variety of anthropological studies, a collectivity is unable to operate efficiently with everybody giving talent workers have chance to devote whose best effort to manufacture any high technological products, e.g. human intelligence vehicle or airplane. Hence, economic incentives are needed to manufacturers to invest high technological automatic industry development. Because the economists predict future ecommerce organizations will have many talent worker numbers, their number will be more than a certain number of normal effort workers, due to technological education level is very excellent to provide to train many young technological manufacturing students to find this kind of high technological manufacturing job. So, the high technological manufacturing job seekers need to future ecommerce market in order to raise ecommerce any organizational development.

Assuming that future UK ecommerce market will have high technological automatic manufacturing workers who would desire only to introduce changes in the workings of the international e-commerce economic order and policies of countries participating in the present economic order rather than change the order itself, what will be UK manufacturers their specific economic preferences in the future? It implies tnat either concentrate on spending more investment to automatic high technological development, e.g. human intelligence automatic high technological products or still concentrate on spending more investment to common traditional technological products to future UK ecommerce market.

However, UK was a developed Western country which had had strong automatic high technological development effort very long time. Otherwise, it compared to some developing countries, such as Asian China, Hong Kong, Korea etc. Asian countries their future economic growth rate will show un- surprising , different patterns, so the Asian countries has weak effort to invest high automatic technological product development, such as human intelligence technological development. The catching-up process suggests low economic growth rate in the high automatic technological product development to the Asian developing countries in the future.

Hence, the future economists predict that it views as probable successors of the Western world economic leadership if any Western country , such as UK manufacturers who prefer to invest to any high automatic technological products development , e.g. developing on human intelligence automatic technological products more than traditional common technological products development. On the one side, but it seems important to stress that two very poor countries among the challengers-China and India-are examples of countries that changed their institutions and economic policies from no or little economic freedom to more economic freedom. Because there two countries whose governments prefer to lend loans to encourage their country manufacturers prefer to invest high automatic technological products manufacturing. On the other side, attitudes toward foreign direct investment (FDI) have undergone change since the 1960 s and a large majority of less developed countries, e.g. China and India are now competing strongly among themselves and with developed market economies for direct investment from multinational companies. So, UK will face China and India high automatic technological product competitors in the future. And in fact, all countries that joined Western developed economies did that without much (if any) external inflow of public resources. It is right time that UK government needs to lend loans to encourage domestic manufacturers to invest high automatic technological products to raise whose international high technological products sale effort to win its future competitors. So, machine resources will be increased demand to o UK manufacturers if who chose to spend machine resources to innovate to manufacture any new and high technological automatic products to raise human daily life needs in the future. It means that it is right time UK manufacturers need buy much machines to prepare to manufacture many future high technological automatic products when these machine prices are low. Because the future global machine prices will possible be raised if many China and India manufacturers will also buy many machines in the future. For example, USA government had provided much financial support to assist sugar cane producers to develop their businesses. And they are dependent to a much larger extent than sugar cane producers and sugar processors in the USA on government. Without very high subsidies to renewable energy generation, they would not have survived at all. So, USA government had been the first country which could lent much financial assistance to encourage domestic renewable energy generation manufacturers to develop high technological energy manufacturing business. So, UK government needs follow USA to lend financial assistance to encourage domestic high technological automatic industry development.

Future economists also predict China and India will be competitors for future leadership in the global e-commerce economy, special high technological products. China has been the media and analyst's favorite for quite some time. Quantitative projections have seemingly supported such expectation. Such as China and India had manufactured many high technological new space rockets products, ocean war large ships etc. Moreover, China has become one of the major world trade players in the early twenty-first century.

Many long-term forecasts, assuming similarly high economic growth rates in the decades ahead, predict that China will surpass the USA in terms of aggregate GDP somewhere between 2020 and 2030 or later, say between 2030 and 2050 year. The future economists conclude on the basis of these predictions that China will not only pass the USA in aggregate product (GDP), but its economy and economic policies will influence the rest of the world to a similar extent that the USA does at present.

I stressed a very important point to future global ecommerce organization growth, namely that the UK future high technological automatic product competitor China and India, namely that economies not only grow, but in the process change their structure. China and India have been industry very rapidly (the first transition) and building the physical infrastructure that accompanies industrialization changes to technology in the future. However, at a certain per capita GNP level the two countries, such as China and India will face another structural shift when which technological development will reach the mature stage in the future. China and India had been primarily historical pattern of economic development because the shift in the role of engine of growth from industry to services is to a much greater extent a qualitative shift. Both higher and different skills are required. And, even more importantly, interactions generating ideas driving the highly human-capital-intensive service economy require a much freer environment, not only in the economic area. Chinese exports have been heavily labor-intensive. This being the case, they contributed to the expansion of industrial employment, offering for the first time in the history of China a taste of (very modest) prosperity to more than 100 million new industrial workers and their families. This is the major component of the success accomplished by Chinese economic growth. Richer trade partners create room for more trade, so the Chinese should hope that intra-South trade, that is, trade between the emerging economies of Asia, the Middle East, Africa and Latin America, will open up new and growing opportunities. I presume that if Western economy , such as UK did not developed high technological automatic industry to stable their social welfare, so thoroughly slowed down their economic growth.

Will it allow China to accomplish the transition to a mature, innovation, service-sector-based ecommerce market economy? It has allowed the economy to industrialize much more successfully, even if the labor shift from agriculture to industry has not yet been completed. But it is a long way off the next major test: the second high technological industry transition of the economic structure to China. Bear in mind that Russia attempted it twice and failed at both attempts.

But even, assuming that China at some point in the future does succeed in accomplishing the second transition, will it be able to supersede the USA, for example, as the main global high automatic technological innovation center if it wants to become the No.1 global high technological industry ecommerce economy? Given the nature of the centralized state and its stability to collect financial resources , China's ability to increase research and development expenditure to high automatic technological products and to hire a mass of researchers, engineers, technicians and other specialists should not be doubted. This process in already taking place.

But , again, Soviet Russia already exceed the USA in the R&D/GDP ratio in the 1970s, long before the communist collapse, with no effects on its innovativeness. Inputs matter less than outputs, quantity in the innovation process mean much less than quality. The latter characteristics depends importantly on economic, civic and even political institutions. Otherwise, independent India had three options open to it in 1946s. It could pursue spontaneous economic development, with some state intervention to be sure, along the lines of basically free market capitalism; it could turn the clock back and try to recreate the rural-agricultural and handicraft based. The dominant way of thinking was Society -style priority to industrialization and , within industralization , priority to heavy industry. In other words, not textiles and clothing, which has been developing well in India since the mid- nine teen century, but production of sewing machines and , even better, production of machines the produce sewing machines.

The results were only to be expected. The heavy stress on the expansion of capital-intensive heavy industries in a very poor country quickly strained the ability of the Indian economy to generate adequate savings. Moreover, some of these industries were above the level of industrial competence of an underdeveloped economy. Thus, the amount of required resources (capital, skilled labor) was usually larger per unit of output than in the same industries in more mature, richer industries economies. In another view point, India will develop light industries, just as any other poor country with a great deal of unskilled labor, had a comparative advantage and no less importantly, an economy in which, due to their low capital/labor ratio, light industries could employ many more people, spreading prosperity more widely in a poor country. So, it explain that why China will have more effort to develop heavy high technological industry in the future. Thus, India got less economic efficiency, less employment than in a spontaneously developing economy, less ability to compete internationally in light industries suitable for an underdeveloped economy and finally got heavy industry unable to compete even on the domestic market and, therefore requiring no less heavy a dose of protection. Overall India got an underperforming economy, in particular in its relations with the rest of the world.

To conclude by comparing the performance of the traditional sectors of the Indian economy and the performance of its modern, human -capital-intensive subsector of manufacturing and skill intensive service sector. The latter both employ workers with high-and medium -high skillful level (in branches ranging from computer software and biotechnology and pharmaceutical high technological light industry). India is ahead of China in terms of the output and export of such products and services. Thus, it implies that Amazon ecommerce organization ought concentrate on developing high automatic heavy high technological warehouse goods delivery service industry, e.g. human intelligence technological warehouse delivery products because these industry is not better development to other many countries' strong effort , such China and India large population countries, they still have weakness to develop warehouse AI delivery service skills in themselves ecommerce organizations.

    Amazon succesful leadership management behavior

    How Amazon leader be one successful CEO?

If it is not, what are the unique personal characteristics between one general CEO and one successful CEO ? Instead of personal characteristics, which kinds of skills to any successful CEOs, they will need? Why do some CEOs encounter fail to manage themselves companies? Why do some CEOs feel difficulties to manage themselves companies? This book can indicate some evidences to explain what factors can influence the person can be successful CEO to let readers to understand. Readers can learn whether what personal factors can help general CEO to become excellent CEO in any organizations.

The different characteristics between common CEO and successful CEO

The characteristics of common CEO

What are the common characteristics to general CEO? IN general, CEO person specification includes: High level of self-motivation, creativeness high level of self confidence. So, In general, qualitiies and traits of a chief executive officer, he /she may have courage, passion , but an excellent CEO is draw to change and effective action. Also CEO needs have resilence and drive ability. It means theat the CEOs, leaders ought know that taking risks and making large-scale changes can lead to organizational growth or can fall dramatically.

A CEO must posses certain traits to be an effective leader, e.g. ability to learn from the past experience, strong communication skills, buildinh relationship, realistic optimism, easily understanding, listening people and adapting to necessary managment styles.

What makes a good CEO leader? At a leader, a common CEO needs to posses strong communication skills. From motivating your employees to meeting set deadlines. You should have the ability to communicate your needs, when you hope to become a common CEO. If you want to be a good CEO, you must be consistently clear in your communication. But, some succesful executives may have these 7 perdsonality traits, such as visioning, in-depth problem solving and analysis, attapting change, driving for results, influencing and persuading, managing others, organizational resources allocation.

Hence, it seems that it is not all people these 7 successful Ceo. In fact, many companies own common CEOs more than successful CEOs in human resource view. In general, an organizational leader (CEO) , he /she does not need special management train, he /she depends on his/her past working experiences training to climb up to become the company's leader. SO, taking risks and acceptance fail or acceptance attempt, they may be general CEO personal characteristics . All of these personal characteristics, it is not difficult to own to general CEOs in any organizations. But if the organization hopes to help the business owner to manage himslef/herself overall organizational different departmental operation more effectively and efficiently. The CEO must own unique personal characteristics and excellent managing ability in order to gelp his/her boss to manage whole organization excellently. Hence, one successful CEO must own unique personal skills or abilities and personal judgement characteristics to compare common or general CEOs in any organizations.

For example, when one organization has serios financial resource allocation to provide different departments challenges, it is the best chance to examine the CEO how to apply shortage financial resource to provide to different departments in order to still keep efficient operation aim. If the CEO can know how to arrange shortage financial resource to provide to salespeople salaries expenditure , shop or office rent, water , electricitiy , telephone fee etc operational expenditure, factory workers salaries and factory machines productive energy expenditure, product manufacturing processing material expenditure etc. resource managment expenditure allocation effectively. Consequently, the overall organizational performance can still keep positive growth, or profit can still raise. Then, I believe that this organization leader may be one successful CEO , he/she does not ne one common CEO or failure CEO role to this organization.

The characteristics of successful CEO

What factors cause the CEO can be one successful leader to his/her organization? What are this CEO personal unique characteristics own? I believe that any successful CEOs must oen unique personal characteristics that common CEOs must not own, I shall explain as below:

Usually , any successful CEO must need time from common CEO to become. Every successful CEO must communicate with their employees using concise, easy-to-understand language, open-mindedness, approachability, growth mindset, ethics, decisiveness. All these characteristics may need to any successful CEO. A chief executive officer (CEO) is the highest-ranking executive in a company , whose primary responsibilities include: making major corporate decisions, managing the overall operations and resources of a company, acting as the main point of communication between the board of directors (the board) and these corporate .

Hence, a successful CEO needs have these 5 key managerial skills: Technical skills, conceptional skills, interpersonal and communication skills, decision-making skills. The roles that a manager plays in the organization require having some skills. Hence, one successful CEO must need to know how to supervise and manage stsffs for his / her overall organization. A successful CEO also needs to understand every part and function of the business: accounting, finance, HR, marketing , legal , operation supply chain, sales and information technology. Also, one successful CEO also needs to consider organizational cultural fit, industry understanding , building good soft communication skills between staffs and him/her or between customers and its sale service staffs. Moreover, a successful leader with a CEO mindset has a clear direction for the future, and is not afraid to share it. Do not be scared to set yourself, when you are the organizational CEO and your team, ambitious and exciting goals, sure that you have smaller, achieveable steps in these as well. So you can maintain motivation.

For next example, if you are your firm's CEO, you can help your firm shareholders grew in power and their demand for booming stock prices led to booming pay. It means that you 's CEO salaries increase or decrease, it depends on share price driven salaries, when your organization's share price can often keep high price position to compare similar competitors ' share prices. Then, you 's CEO salary may keep increase, because your can manage firm's share price often keeps on high price position in share market. However, one successful CEO must need to own there managerial skills in order to help his/her organization can grow rapidly. The managerial skills may include as below: Technical skill, it means that the abilities, knowledge, or expertise required to perform specific, job-related tasks. Technical skills are related to jobs in science, engineering, technological, manufacturing or finance. They are learnt through on-the-job experience or structured learning, e.g. data analysis, project management, technical writing, software proficiency, programming languages, artificial intelligence, machine learning, data engineering, visualization, network and information security, cloud computing.

The next is conceptual skill, a successful CEO also needs have conceptual skill, it is the ability to analyze and evaluate whether a company is achieving its goals and its business plan. Conceptual skills are skills that enable individuals to identify , conceptualize and solve problems. It is important in the workplace because it allows professionals to think and woth though abstract ideas and come up with multiple solutions to complex issues. Hence, conceptual skills include the ability to view the organization as a whole, understand how the various parts are interdepetend, and assess how the organization relates to its external environment. These skills allow managers to evaluate situations and develop alternative courses of actions. Conceptual skills may include: abstract thinking, analytical skills, congnitive skills, communication, contextualizinf, creative thinking, critical thinking, decision making. Hence, one successful CEO may be a conceptual person, who is one conceptual thinker, he /she has an understanding of why something is being done. The conceptual thinker can think at an abstract level and easily applythe CEO himself/herself insights to the suitation. So, any comon CEO may attempt to improve conceptual thought processing and increase work performance by these methods:

Observe leadership. using challenges as case studies, seeking outside knowledge, staying up-to-date on the industry, applying new practices, disucssing concepts with colleagues, finding a mentor, learning about the organization. So, one successful CEO needs to own critical thingking skills: Analysis, interpretation, inference, explanation, self-regulation, open-mindedness and problem solving, strategic thinking includes careful and deliberate anticipation of threats to guard against and opportunities to pursue.

Ultimately strategic thinking and analysis can help CEO to lead to a cleear set of goals, plans, and new ideas have abstract thinking and feeling, it is the ability to understand concepts that are real, such as freedom. So, analytical skills refer to the ability to collect and analyze information , problem solve and make decisions. Successful CEO can know how to use analytical skils when detecting patterns, brainstorming, observing , interpreting data and making decisions based on the multiple tailors and options available to you, such as the organizational CEO, e.g. creative thinking visual art, communication skills and open-mindedness to any one successful CEO, he /she ought own.

Finally, successful CEO needs have excellent interpersonal communication and decision making skill. Why is decision making and communication an important skill? It can help any CEo to raise the ability to make a decision of good leadership skills. Decision making is an on-going process in every organization, large or small. Having critical thinking skills allow the CEO to ascertain the problem and come up with a solution that is benefical to the company and its employees. So, one successful CEO needs to own soft and hard skils both.

For making decision for the organization, the successful CEO must have decision making skill to find the best solution to the challenge in process. He /she can define the problem, challenge or opportunity clearly, generate of possible solutions or responses, evaluates the costs and benefits or pros and associated with each option, selects a solution or response and knows how to implement the option chosen clearly.

Any CEO can learn how to improve decision making in workplace, such as following these steps: starting with the desired outcome, or goals, rely on data and insights to spot patterns, use S.W.O.T analysis, simulate the outcomes, trust your instincts and identify your cognitive biases. Identifying critical factors which will affect the outcome of a decision, evaluate options accurately and establish priorities, anticipate outcomes and see logical consequences, navigate risk and uncertainty,, reason well in requiring quantitative analysis. On conclusion any one CEO must need time to improve his/her hard and soft skills in order to become one successful CEO to his /her organization.

What skills to one successful CEO owns
We can learn that it is difference between one common CEO and unique successful CEO personal characteristics. Then, it beings this question: What are the skills that one successful CEO ought own? I believe that one successful CEO ought own these skills that one common CEO he /she won't own.
Building excellent communication skill:
Top performing CEO, ough know that strong communication skills are the secret to influence final success. Successful CEOs understand that influence is required if they are to inspire people to willingly act upon what they have to say. Highly influential CEOs deliver on these communication skills daily as below:
Successful CEOs understand the importance of clear, concise communication. They recognize that in the absence of simplicity comes confusion. For example, one organizational CEO sent an email to his employees listing only three objectives he wished for the company to focus on : " customers, team and execution". Instead of providing a dozen areas of opportunity . This CEO also maintained a short list of objectives that were clear. He kept employee goals concise, guiding them to focus to perform excellent services to let customers feel satisfactory. Such as this case, it explains that where one CEO focuses on concise and clear communication, he makes it easier for others to follow. This level of influence ensures that others remember what was said and are inspired to act accordingly.
Top CEOs are known for their sharp minds, and business acumen. They know that frequent communication between employees and senior leadership to be very important in their ability to stay engaged. For conference discussion case, when a successful CEo discusses ongoing company objectives and action items. he begins each all by sharing status updates of previous discussions, including what the executive staff is doing to secure the company's future. Each call concludes with a 30 minute open question forum, where all empllyees have the chance to ask questions and on ideas the executives discussed. Allowing employees to collaborate and share ideas creates a sense of ownership . It permits insight into the company's goals and encourage employees to engage in its success with ideas of their own.
By creating an atmosphere, successful CEOs encourage employees to share ideas. As a result, CEOs build stronger relationships and deepen trust in leadership . For example, when one CEO maintains an open-door policy and is known for frequently visiting employees on the floor, no matter the department or position. As a result, the CEO builds personal relationships that foster trust and candidacy that only comes with real influence. So , the difference between the successful CEO's communication skill and common CEO's communiction skill is that a common CEO has influence based solely on his /her title may intimidate employees to act on direction, but successful CEO is a leader who influences others to act willingly has establish the trust and credibility necessary for lasting success. Unfortunately, too may ledaers fail to share this level of detail with their staffs leading employees to question their intention. They neglect communication weaknesses that need improvement . As a result, the entire organization will benefit from improved performance and communication . When leaders admit they are not perfect and are willing to improve, employees follow suit.
What makes a CEO successful? Findings from a database of 17,000 c-suite assessments reveal that successful CEOs demonstrate four specific behaviors that prove critical to their performance. They are decisive, they engage for impact, they adapt proactively, and they delive reliably. So, as a leader, you need to posses strong communication skills. From motivating your employees to meeting set deadlines, you should have the ability to communicate your needs and even show your employees how things are down. If you want to be a good CEO, you must be consistently clear in your communication.
What is the most important skill to a CEO? In short, the single important role of a CEO is to make absolutely certain that the right CEO is running the company and then do what is necessary to encourage that CEO's effectiveness, strategy, vision, culture shareholder value, all crucial and all within the scopr of the CEO's role. Hence, successful CEO needs to know whether what he/ she actually does. A chief executive officer (CEO) is the highest ranking executive in a company, whose primary responsibilities include making major corporate decisions, managing the overall operations and resources of a company, acting as the main point of communication between the board of

directors. Hence, CEO needs to report to the board of directors, with most CEOs being members and sometimes chair of the board, president, they report to the CEO and the board of directors and cometimes they are board members. Hence, a CEO needs to understand every part and function of the business: accounting, finance, HR, marketing, legal , operations, supply chain , sales , information technology . In business speak, the CEO's job is to define the mission (purpose), strategy (direction), and metric (pace and performance). These three elements provide the essential elements that a growing company needs to be able to perform. So, a successful CEO must need to find the effective strategy to help his/her company to solve any challenges in ay time. When the chairman technically has higher level power, the CEO is indeed the boss of a company. The CEO does by the law answer to their board of directors, which is ultimately headed by the chairman. In general., the CEO job starts when the organization reaches about 20 employees, prior to 20 employees, the job resembles more of a product management role. CEOs at this stage are trying to develop a visable product and generate some revenue.

In general, successful chief executives tend to demonstrate four specific behaviors that prove critical to their performance. For example, holding people accountable and the ability to motivate a team, high-performing (CEO) do not necessarily stand our for making great decisions all the time, rather they stand our for being more decisive. They make decisions earlier, faster, and with greater conviction. Also, they do so consistently, even with incomplete information, and in unfamiliar domains . Interestingly, the highest IQ executives , they are intellectual complexity, when the quality of their decisions is often good, because of their pursuit of the perfect answer, they can take tool ong to make choices or set clear priorities and their teams pay a high price. These smart but slow decision makers, their teams either grow frustrated , which can lead to the attrition of valuable talent ot become overcautious themselves.

Moreover, high-performing CEOs understand that a wrong decision is often better than no decision at all. It means that a bad decision was better than a lack of direction. Most decisions can be undone, but a successful CEO has learnt to move with the right amount of speed. To that end, successful CEOs also knows when not to decide, whether a decision should actually be more lower down in the organization and if delaying, it is a week or a month time, would allow important information without causing harm.

Hence, strong performers balance keen insight into their stakeholders' priorities with focus on delivering business results. They start by developing an understand of their stakeholders' needs and motivations and get many people on board by driving for performance. So, CEO needs to bring others along plan and execute disciplined communications and influencing strategies. Indeed, the skilled CEO gains the support of their colleagues by confidence that they will lead the team to sucess, even if that means taking uncomfortable or unpopular moves. These CEOs do not shy away from conflict in the pursuit of business goals. The ability to handle different viewpoints significantly faster than average.

Factors Influence CEO Success Or Fail

In fact, any CEOs will be influenced to succeed or how how to manage their organizations by personal psychology and personal skills or knowledge and external environment factors. However, CEO is such leader role to any organizations. Can owning high level leadership skillful CEOs manage their organizations more eaily to compare owning low level leadership skillful CEOs? May leadership skill be main factor to influence any one CEO's person success or fail? I shall attempt to explain as below?

In fact, I feel any CEo must need have these kinds of leadership skills. They ma y include: First, recognizing strengths, everybody with an organization has their strengths, and it is essential that you are able to identify the strengths of individuals, and recognizing weaknesses, second, reacting to employee needs, third, clarity and fourth, willingness to make tough decisions and conflict managment skill. Why does every CEO need have leadership skill? Effective leaders have the ability to communicate well, motivate their team, handle and delegate responsibilities, listen to feedback and have the flexibility to solve problems in an ever changing workplace. Hence , in CEO personal psychological view, an excellent CEO is drawn to change and effective action, courage , passion and resilence and drive attitude . A good leader knows that taking risks and making large-sacle changes can lead to organizational growth or can fall dramatically.

Why is CEO leadership important to the performance of a firm? Research evidence provides overall support for the positive relationship between leadership and firm performance (Lowe et al, 1996). CEOs with transactional leadership can successfully manage goal accomplishment and contribute to the enhancement of the firm performance. So, it seems that CEO's leadership has indirect or direct relationship to influence his / her whole organizational performance whether it can grow up rapidly or slowly, even fall fown rapidly or slowly, because if the firm's CEO can not manage different department teams cooperate efficiently. Then, the firm's leader personal leadership effort may influence whole organization different department teams to cooperate smoothly. Although, CEO must not need to contact all department staffs every day, but he /she needs to contact any department managers in order to know whether their departments have any challenges , when managers feel difficulties to solve. If the CEO had low level leadership ability, he /she won't discuss with any department managers to conclude the best opinions to solve the challenges more easily. For example, when financial budget department manager discovered that his organization had deficit challenge recently. If he can not solve lack of cash available problem. Then, his organization's deficit will be increased easily. Consequently, it will influence staffs salaries can not pay on time, it won' t have cash to buy enough manufacturing material to prepare to be supplied to manufacture to provide products to provide to market to sell, factory can not have enough money to buy new productive machines to replace old productive machines etc. different kinds of organizational operational needs.

However, if the CEO owning high level leadership skills, he may know hoe to lead this financial budget manager to solve " deficit" challenge. Although, deficit seems to be simple matter, but if this financial budget manager can not know how to manage cash available in order to allocate to different departments operations, e.g. allocating the limiting amount of cash to urgent departments to use in prior. Then, deficit challenge will increase cash shortage number more seriously. So, high leadership skill mist need to any one organizational CEO in order to help his/ her organization can solve any challenges more efficiently and easily. Otherwise, low leadership effort owning CEO only influences his/her organization can not grow up more rapidly, even it can fall down rapidly. Consequently, the organization will only liquidate or it will be sold out rapidly.

What does excellent leadership skill need to CEO? Many psychologists indicate excellent leadership may include these essential elements: Integrity, ability to delegate, communication, self - awareness, gratitude, learning agility, influence effort, empathy.In common, characteristics of a good leader, he / she can help staffs and makes the essential large-sacle decisions that keep the organization can operate efficiently and reduce challenges occur. Integrity is especially important for top-level executives who are charting the organization's actions and making countless other significant decisions. Ability to delegate , delegating is one of the core responsibilities of a leader, the goal enables the CEO's direct reports, facilitate teamwork, provide autonomy, lead to better decision making and help the CEO's direct reports grow. Effective leadership and effective communication are intertwined.

So, any CEOs need to be able to communicate in a variety of ways, from transmitting information to coaching your staffs (managers). Any CEO must be able to listen to , and communicate with, a wide range of staffs across roles, social identities and more. The quality and effectiveness of communication across the CEO's organization directly affect trhe success of the CEO's business strategy. So, better communication skill can actually improve the CEO's organizational culture. Self-awareness is focuses skills for leadership. The better leadership skill to the CEO , he / she can understand himself / herself managing ability, the more effective , he /she can do. Do you know how other people view you or how you show up at work?

Gratitude can lead to higher self-esteem, reduced depression and anxiety, learning agility is the ability to know what to do when you do not know what to do. So, great leaders are great learners, with strong learning agility to get started , when you are one organization's CEO in beginning, you must need to learn how to influence your whole organizational staffs behaviors to be the perfect.

" Influence" may be through locial , emotional or cooperative appeals, is a component of being an effective leader, influence is quite different from manipulation, and it needs to be done and it requires emotional intelligence and trust. Empathy is correlated with job performance and is a critical part of emotional intelligence and leadership effectiveness. A successful leadership CEO needs have empathetic behaviors towards his / her direct reports, empathy can be for improving workplace conditions. Courage is such that when the CEO wants to voice a new idea, provides feedback to a direct report or flag a concern for someone above him / her. That is part of the reason courage is a key skill for good leaders. Rather than avoiding problems or allowing conflicts to faster, courage enables leaders to step up and move things in the direct direction. A workplace with high levels of psychological safety and a strong coaching culture will further support truth and courage. Finally CEO needs to know how to treat people with respect on a daily basis is one of the most important things . A leader can do that it will ease tensions and conflict, create trust, and improve effectiveness.

On conclusion, when the CEO can know how to build these psychological and emotion feeling, then the CEO can be trained to improve leadership skill in order to know hoew to manage his / her organization efficiently and effectively.

Can training provision raise CEO leadership

Any organizational CEO is the top level managerial position. So, it is one job to anyone. Any organizational positions may have training provision in order to improve the staff personal job skills, e.g. organizations can provide internal accounting training to accounting clerk, even accounting manager training in order to let they can learn company's accounting policy in order to improve their accounting tasks more proficient, or a law firm can provide legal draft training to general law clerks in order to improve their legal draft writing skils, or one company's data processing department can provide data processing training to improve data processor typing speed to learn more proficient to type its documents, or property agent firm can provide property sale speaking training to its property sale agents to improve their property sales presentation skill or insurance agent firms can provide insurance sale speaking training to its insurance sale agents to improve their insurance sales skills.

Hence, it seems that any organizational positions may apply training methods to improve any staff individual performance in any organizations. So, it brings this question: Can organizations provide training to improve CEO performance to achieve more proficient? To answer this question, we need to suppose same kinds of business CEO positions , they ought be trained to improve their performance. If it is true, whether what kinds of businesses CEO positions, they may be applied training method to improve their managerial skills? How and why to these kinds of business CEO positions, they can be trained to improve their proficiency? I shall attempt to answer as below:

In fact, general CEO typically have a bachelor's or master's degree in business administration or a fiels related to their industry. Some CEO positions require that candidates have a master's or even depending on the industry , education, for instance. So, one university CEO or president, he /she needs have education psychology master or doctorate level to any kinds of degree. They need have high educational level to do university leader. Hence, CEO, training can focus on learning or educational aspect, e.g. certified CEO program is general education certification course designed for business leaders globally (CEO senior managers) and aspiring business leaders who are looking to build upon existing qualifications and business experience.

What does CEO coach training method mean?

However, every CEO needs a coach in organization , because a coach suports the CEO to manage conflict effectively often decisoin of the CEO please one group and displease another. The CEO needs a partner who the CEO can be open with, one who is going to be sensitive, and objective, honest and respectful. Hence in any organizations, a coash can teach the CEO these managing skills to manage their organizations more easily, e.g. flexibility, value driven decision making, delegating, leadership, clear vision implementation.

Hence, in general, coach training needs ususaly take 2 to 3 years to complete. The organizational CEO will does on the-job-training and spend time with a training provider. Employers will set their own entry requirements. So, in popular, many CEOs use a CEO coach over the course of their career. No athlete would be embarrassed they use a coach. Yet, CEOs believe they do not need a coach of their own. However, any organization is the final deicion making person, when the organization feels that the CEO's managerial effort is poor, it can attempt to provide a proficient managing experience coach to train this CEO's management skill in order to achieve this organization's CEO ability requirement within 2 to 3 years. For example, a CEO peer group training, interchangably called CEO peer groups or networks, these organizations generally arrange reqular meetings in confidential environments where CEOs can share ideas, best practices, experiences and advice together to attempt how to improve their managerial skills.

So, executives look for in a coach, a good executive coach does not need to have the exact background or experience as the CEO , but a familiarity will help him or her better understand the CEO thinking and needs. More importantly, the CEO coach needs skills, the CEO either does not have and wants to attain, or ones that can help strength the CEO opportunity areas.

In general, what leaders want from coaching. Coaching empowers leaders to do expectional work. Coaches establish and advantageous relationship that uncovers hidden strengths and weaknesses within the leader. Goals will be created to enable leaders to indicate their weaknesses and track their progress. What is better up coaching? Coaching training can address the CEO must pervasive organizational challenges with the organizational unique combination of coaching to achieve a growth approach to mental fitness and organizational health more effectively.

Have a CEO coach is similar to the executive or leadership coach , but with the added responsibility of working with the CEO who is working in the firm. So, coach can attempt to help the CEO potentially make the most significant difference in the company's success and lives and careers of those who work for the company. Hence, any organizations can provide executive or leadership coach to improve the CEO's leadership skills by these 5 caoching styles, such as below:

Democratic coaching, this method gives the term freedom and accountability, with the coach stepping in only when meeded to keep the process going, or authoritarian coaching, holistic coaching, authcratic coaching and vision coaching training methods, for example, entrepreneur coach can help new and existing business owners with any number of tacks to foster their entrepreneurship. In fact, entrepreneurship is not about having a business, but about having an entrepreneurship mind. So, CEOs can be trained from any style of coach in order to improve their management and leadership skills to more proficient in their organizations. So, it means that coaching training is one kind of effective training method to improve CEO's performance in any organizations.

On conclusion, I believe that it is only one kind of training method to train any organizational CEOs to become proficient CEO, it is coaching training method, instead of providing general educational level to the CEO for leadership knowledge, because coach training is one kind of organizational leadership practice training, it can satisfy any CEOs to raise leadership effort effectively to help the CEO to manage his/her organization easily.

Amazon leader / founder owns new business foundation strategies mind

Any new business founders, they ought hope their new businesses can run long time. The question concerns that how they can help their new businesses run long time, e.g. at least above 5 years . I shall attempt to apply behavioral economic theory to solve this common challenge as below.

Keeping a new business is in difficult economic time is challenging. Every new business is different and each carries its own risks and rewards in behavioral economy view. These sifferences cause some new business founders attempt to copy another similar new business founder strategy. Still, these are save general strategies business owners can follow to help themselves new businesses to copy another similar new business strategy succeeds in possible.

However, some of these copying another new business founder strategy's owner still feels their sopying another new business founder strategy may help them to succeed. So, they still have risk or they may encounter failure, if the another similar new business founder strategy can not be suitable to be adopted to themselves new business similiarly. So, it explains that why some new business founder can not keep their new businesses can run long time, because they feel the other similar new business founders their strategies can help to develop their new businesses succeed together. But in fact, there are may new business founders their copying strategy decisions are wrong. They feel their copying another new business founder's strategy can help them to develop in success. So, their new business strategies ought also help their new businesses to develop or grow long time. However, there are many new businesses can not run above 5 years, due to there new business founders choose the wrong copying strategies from another similar new business or old business competitors.

New business founder needs to look at the big picture, it means that long term customer behavior change picture. Because consumer behaviors must often change suddenly in any time. So, any new business founder ought attempt to discover whether what their product buyers behaviors will change after 5 years, even 10 years in predicting. People have a tendency to attack the most obvious immediate prodblems without hesitation. That's understandable and might make good business sense in some suitations. However, it is also advisable to step back and look at the big picture to see what is still working and what might need changing.

Its an opportunity to better comprehend the size and the scope of exciting problem and further understand your new firm's decision model, determining how its strengths and weaknesses come into play. What is a business model? The term business model refers to a firm's plan making a profit. It identified target market, e.g. which is age customer group, where is the geographical sale place, and anticipated expenses. However, business models are improtant for both new and established businesses. They help new developing companies attract investment, recruit talent, and motivate management and staff. Establishing businesses should reguarly update their business plans or they will fail to anticipate trends and channelgens. So, business models both levers are pricing and costs. It is a high -level plan for profitably , a business in a specific marketplace. A primary component of the business model is the value proposition. This is a description of the goods or services that a new business offers and why they are desirable to customers, ideally stated in a may that differentiates the products or services from its competitors.

A new business enterprise's business model should also cover projected startup costs and financing sources, the target customer base for the new business, marketing strat egy , a review of the competition, and projections of revenue ans expenses. It may also define opportunities in which the new business can partner with other established companies, e.g. the new business model for an advertising business may identify benefits from an arrangement for referrals to and from a printing company. So, successful new businesses need have good business models that allow them to fulfill client needs at a competitive price and a sustainable cost. Over time, many new businesses revise their business models from time to time to reflect changing business environments and market demands. However, the business model may not tell new business founder everything about a company's prospects, but the investor who underatands the business model can make better sense of the financial data.

New business founder also needs to consider organizational internal matter, e.g. suppose a new business founder discovers that two employees are making mistakes with inventory that cause certain supplies to be overstocked or understocked. When a initial reaction might be to fine those employees. It might be wiser to examine whether the manager who hires and supervises them properly trained time. If the manager is to blame, that person could be fired, but this might not be the best solution. If the manager's relationship with client have a history of bringing in repeat business and substantial revenue. They are likely someone, you would want to keep. However, retraining might be a better alternative than termination.

Infact, by thoroughly reviewing the strengths and weaknesses of the employees, the owner is looking at the issue from a top-down perspective, reducing or eliminating the chance that the problem will occur when avoiding a change that could adversely impact future sales. Hence, a similar kind on analysing how youe new products or services fit into the marketplace in your new business beginning stage, how the economic crisis has affected your customers and suppliers and all the other key aspects of your new business. You need to know how well your new business model fits the current environment and forecast what various alternative scenarios of the future mighr mean for it.

For one interesting new business behavioral economic view to recuriting new employees view example, any new business owners or large corporational founders tend to be either wise or follish when they hire the least expensive workers sometimes, the productivitiy of these workers may be suspect. Hiring one worker who costs 20% more than the average workers, but works 40% more effectively make of crisis. By seeking resumes and interviews from new applicants. New business founders can make change to new staff when needed to increase efficiency. So, how to choose any department new staff recruitment , it is very important to influence the new business furher develops for long time. Don't sacrifice quickly, keeping a handle on costs is crucial in tough times. Owners need to stay on the offensive and get employees on board with changes that are being made. However, any one new business founders need have good sense to predict when their new products or new services need to be changed in order to adopt customer behavioral changing environment.

ON conclusion, so any new business founders hipe to keep themselves new businesses can run long time, they must need to know " consumer behavioral psychology" how and why to cause their change in order to implement the most effective new business strategy to improve their sale methods to achieve the most satisfactory level to their potential clients' purchase needs or service needs in long time. Consequently , their new businesses ought keep long running time in this old and new product / service competitor market.

    Avoiding new business low value method

Internet marketing promotion strategy

Any new business founders do not hope their new business market worth falls rapidly or share price falls rapidly. What facors may cause new business share price or market value falls rapidly? What methods to help new businesses keep the same share price is stable long time or market value can be kept in the stable worth, even share price can be influenced the rise or market value can be influenced to rise? I shall attempt to explain some useful methods, they may influence new business market value to avoid falls down, or share price can rise more easily.

TO avoid new business low value, these ways may be used in developing new business. They may include: Knowing what your client individual actual need, e.g. rice cooker product, cooking rice function must need , but avoiding to spend long time or short time to cook rice rapidly, big rice cooker size to cook more rice, long time keeping rice warm function. All these factors may influence rice cook buyers individual choices. Some housewives also need the kind of rice cooker has above all these functions, before they make rice cooker purchase decision. So, knowing what your clients real needs, they are essential to product manufacturers, offering great customer service, e.g. repair sevice, after sale enquiry (following up equiry to the client, nurture existing customers and look for new sale need opportunities, use social media attending networking events, give back to your community, measure what works and refine your approach as you go. So, if the business founder can manage sale and customer, service both teams to achieve the best service performance to let clients feel , then they may persuade many clients continue choose to continue to buy their products more easily. So, salespeople and customer service staffs training method may be one main influential factor to help the organization to raise market share value. If the organization can design useful training course to raise its salespeople sale skills or customer service staff service performance.

Which businesses can be started with less investment? For India country example, these low investment business wil be helped the new business founder to earn the most profitable, e.g. dropshipping is one of the most successful business in India, because in India, even global there are many tall offices need dropshipping equipment to transport window cleaners to clean tall office windows. So, dropshipping cleaners'window ability may influence India deopshipping firm share price changes to rise up or fall down. Because India dropshiping companies window clean workers window cleaning performance can bring property management company clients to make dropshipping window cleaning service provider choice.

I mean that India dropshipping office window or global dropshipping office windoe clean service providers, their new business market value or high stable shar e price value, their value is depended on whether their dropshipping window cleaners clearning window skills or window clean priperty management clients' window clean needs. So, for dropshipping office cleaning service provider case example, how to improve dropshipping office window cleaning workers' windows clean ability, it is only one influential method to influence dropshipping office window cleaning firm service providers their shares prices whether they can keep stable market position, even share price can be risen easily. How to improve dropshipping office cleaning workers' office windows cleaning skill is very important to influence dropshipping office window service providers' shares prices are at the stable high price level. For courier company example, how to improve courier service performance, e.g. shorten the document / goods delivery time between the document or goods sender countey and the document or goods country receiver, when the document or goods can not bt delayed to send to the overseas receiver whose home from the another country sender, e.g. From US sends the document to China in common general couriers need 5 days , but the US courier company can send the documents to China, it only needs 2 days delivery time. Then, it may attract many China goods or documents receiving clients to choose the US courier service providers. So, how to keep the US new courier servier providers, or market value or share price value, it depends on whether it may help its overseas documents or goods receiving clients to reduce how long time to let they can receive the documents or goods from US. So, the avoiding delivery time delay is the import factor to influence courier goods / documents delivery service provider new business market value.

Moreover, any one new business founder may promote themselves new business in a low budger. These methods may include: posting amazing content on your new firm's blog, creating a google my new business account, building a free or cheap email list, contributing an article to an industry magazine, attending local networking events, co-sponsor a contest. So, internet channel may help any new business to build a rapid promotion network to let many people to know that this kind of new business exist, it aims to let potential clients number increases in short time in possible.

So, internet may be a kind of new promotion tool to help any new business market share value rises in short time, the internet strategies for effective promotion of new business, e.g. creating a website, geting listed on google, advertise on facebook, email customers, and potential customers use google Adwords, paid media advertising , social networks and viral marketing, internet marketing, email marketing, direct selling, point-of-purchase marketing, co-branding, cause marketing , conversational marketing .

All of these internet promotion methods may help new businesses to rise market growth value or share price in short time. Hence, internet promotion method is preferable to choose to compare general TV, advertising , newspaper, advertising, magazine advertising, radio adverting, sales promotion, general selling, publicity promotion methods because internet promotion marketing is one kind method, it may bring the new product or new service providing message to let many potential clients to know from the new firm's email ot website in short time rapidly. It is one kind of new global promotion method for any kinds of new busienss development in beginnning.

So, any new business founder may prefer to choose internet promotion method in orde to let many potential cients to know their new products ot services are existence. So, attracting new customers method may use social media optimizing the new business founder's social media account, improves website and engage with loyal customers, give branded gifts , referral discounts, social media contects, and giveways, sending email to survey customers, researching your competitors and finding out who their customers are, target email advertisement, smart social media, responding to every email, tweet , facebook comment, e-publish user reviews from internet media channel. All of these new internet promotion strategies may help any kinds of new businesses to promote their products or services to let clients to know in short time rapidly from internet media promotion channel. The internet promotion marketing strategy is one kind of low cost promotion strategy, low cost marketing stragtegy for startups, cheapest new businesses to start and focused low cost strategy company.

Why internet promoting strategy can help new business to avoid low market value? The reason is simple, because when the new firm sends one email message to let any one country's email user to know. This new product or new service email message can let global any one emaill user to know that this new product or new service business is existence in market. When the email user receives the new business' semail message, it may keep in itself email box. So, the email user won't lose the one email message and it can often remember this new product, or new service provider is existence in market. So, any one email user when he/she receives new product or service provider 's email, this email is such as the private advertisment between the new business founder and the email receiver. So, email advertising is different general product magazine, TV, newspaper , radio advertisment. It is public promotion advertisement.

Hence, the feeling of private advertisment, it is the most influential factor to persuade potential consumers to choose to buy the new product or use the new service from this provider, because when the potiential client receives the email promotion from the new product/ new service provider, he /she may feel surpise to raise interest to click the advertismeent email to see whether what benefits can be given ti him/her if he /she chooses to buy the new product or use the new service. If one say, the new product / new service provider can send about 1,000 promotion email to let global 1,000 different countries possible potential clients to know its new product/new service is existence in market. Consequently, this email network promotion method can help this new business founder to advertise his / her new product /new service to let global 1,000 email users to know in one day. When, its potential clients number increases, it implies that its new product or new service market existence value will be possible to influence to rise up. Hence, emial promotion method may influence any kinds of new businesses to rise market value in short time in possible, because when may email receivers become to the new business potential clients. Consequently, the new business's share price may be influenced to riase up then its market value may also be follow to influence to rise up. So, it seems that email promotion method may be nowadays a kind of the most effective promotion method to help any new businesses to raise up share price or raise market value in short time.

Becoming talent human how influences social changes

Nowadays we tend to think about social and digital technology more from a personal or consumer perspective than their business or professional applications, but as the Digital Era continues to progress, many of technology's most profound impacts are likely to be in the world of work. In addition to changes in product and business development, knowledge management, data analysis, and other operational processes, transforming talent management will be a key priority for organizations striving to be employers of choice.

● Digital technology encourages to create talent human

Why does digitial technology encourage to create talent human or excite human to learn new things ? The human capital implications of social and digital technologies impact virtually everyone, regardless of the type of organization they work for, their profession, their functional area, or their career stage. That means that the talent management functions in all organizations, as well as the professionals who staff and lead them, have a critical role to play in ensuring the efficient and effective transition and transformation from Industrial Era models and processes to their Digital Era upgrades.

It's no surprise that talent management has already become more "high tech." Many employment related activities have been digitized, and there has been a corresponding increase in employee self-service. It's important to remember, however, that digitization is not the same thing as digital engagement, and that the rise of "high tech" solutions doesn't necessitate the loss of a "high touch" approach to managing an organization's human assets. Transforming talent management requires digitization, to be sure, but it also involves leveraging social and digital technologies in ways that promote and enhance communication, collaboration, and engagement - not just between an employee and the organization, but between and among employees themselves.

Talent Acquisition

The logical place to start when talking about the impact of social and digital technologies on talent management is talent acquisition, where the greatest advances have been made. Anyone who has searched and applied for jobs in the past 10 years is very familiar with how technology has transformed the application process, which in most organizations (and virtually all large ones) is now almost completely digitized and automated. However, there are other ways in which social and digital technologies are impacting talent acquisition that may not be as well-known or commonly understood. Social media sites in particular (such as Facebook, YouTube, and Pinterest) are a great way to promote an employer's brand and offer realistic previews of work life, people and culture in organizations. Online games and simulations can also be used to get a sense of what working for an organization would be like, and give organizations themselves an opportunity to determine if a prospective candidate would be a good cultural fit and potentially successful.

On organizational working environment aspect, some employers are recognizing the value of digital alumni networks or communities to maintain strong relationships with former employees. One of the primary motivations for doing this is that the employees may return one day and/or make referrals to or from their personal and professional networks. Similarly, talent networks enable organizations to establish and maintain relationships with professionals in key areas like IT and engineering, even when there isn't a current opportunity to have those folks be a part of the organization. Moreover, social media can bring positive influence to impact organizations to encourge employees to attempt or feel needs to learning new things for their tasks needs. Due to social media has actually transformed every stage of the recruiting process in significant ways - so much so that the traditional recruiting funnel can be recast in "social" terms. At the top of the funnel are activities like social advertising (i.e., placing job ads on social networks like Facebook), social sourcing (i.e., searching for candidates who meet certain criteria on networks like LinkedIn), and social referrals (i.e., having current employees share position openings with their online personal and professional networks). And at the bottom of the funnel is social screening (i.e., reviewing a candidate's public activity in social networks to identify potential hiring risks).

● Learning management is needed to feel needs to any organizations

Learning management is probably the another most advanced area when it comes to adopting and adapting to new technologies. As with recruiting and other processes, the initial advances are in the area of digitization, with social software applications evolving next. One of the obvious digital impacts is the increased use of elearning and online learning platforms with self-paced study. There are also countless instructional videos on the web, both free and fee-based, that address a virtually unlimited range of topics. And we can't forget MOOCs - massive, open, online courses - which have proliferated in the past couple of years. Finally, many organizations have also started to leverage tablets and other mobile devices for learning, as well as using simulations and games to help employees develop specific skills. In addition to offering training through a variety of multimedia channels, organizations are increasingly using a range of digital tools for assessing employees' skills. They're also allowing employees to play an enhanced role in identifying their key skill sets and training needs, and can even have them create their own learning and development plans. Allowing employees to take a more active role in their own learning and skills management enables organizations to develop and maintain a more complete and accurate knowledge and skills database, which in turn enables them to maximize the value of the workforce in which they've already invested.

1. Formal learning management systems and platforms are also beginning to incorporate social technologies in a variety of ways. Promoting connections and interactions among participants, as well as with the instructor, can enhance the learning experience both during and after a course. Creating course-based cohorts that allow people to continue to interact with each other via a digital community - even when their shared learning experience is face-to-face - can promote both knowledge transfer and retention, in addition to increasing commitment and engagement through interpersonal connections.

2. Informal learning - which is now also referred to as social learning - is greatly enhanced by social technologies as well. In fact, this is probably the greatest opportunity and area of growth for organizations of all types and sizes. Through private social networks, intranets and other internal platforms that have incorporated social technology elements, organizations are better able to facilitate employee learning as they perform their job duties and complete work activities. Along with the networks themselves, features like advanced search, identified subject matter experts, digital communities of practice, wikis and more enable employees to access and learn from colleagues who are not just next door or down the hall, but even in another city, state or country!

As organizations move forward with leveraging technology to enhance learning initiatives, it will become increasingly important for them to address issues related to digital literacy and digital competencies. For the past several decades we've generally taken what I refer to as an LIY, or Learn It Yourself, approach to digital knowledge and skills. Although organizations may invest in teaching someone how to use a specific application related to their job, they make virtually no investment in helping individuals learn how to use general digital tools like Microsoft Office and even email. Left to their own devices, most people - and I include myself in this group- are much less efficient and effective at using these tools than they could or should be. As our tools get even more sophisticated, we need the foundational knowledge and skills to be able to use them well - and this foundation should probably be provided via more formal training. In other words, many people need to be "taught how to learn" in the Digital Era. If organizations aren't going to provide the formal training workers need to do that, it's probably in an individual's best interests to pursue those kinds of development opportunities on their own.

● What are social influences on human behavior when talent human number increases?

Social Influences on Human Behavior Because human beings are social and learn from observation rather than depending entirely on instinct, almost all aspects of human psychology and behavior are socially influenced. Languages, modes of dress, gender roles and avoided taboos are all agreed upon at a group level and form the basis of culture. What are the characteristics of social change? Small-scale and short-term changes are characteristic of human societies, because customs and norms change, new techniques and technologies are invented, environmental changes spur new adaptations, and conflicts result in redistributions of power. This universal human potential for social change has a biological basis.

This universal human potential for social change has a biological basis. It is rooted in the flexibility and adaptability of the human species—the near absence of biologically fixed action patterns (instincts) on the one hand and the enormous capacity for learning, symbolizing, and creating on the other hand. Because human beings are social and learn from observation rather than depending entirely on instinct, almost all aspects of human psychology and behavior are socially influenced. Languages, modes of dress, gender roles and avoided taboos are all agreed upon at a group level and form the basis of culture.

On conclusion, when one country can create many talent human, e.g. students, workers. Then they can bring more positive attribution to help or assist themselve country to develop rapidly. Consequently, the country's economic growth speed will be rapid. So, I believe that it has close relationship between economy growth and talent human number to any countries in nowadays societies.

Amazon ecommerce founder successful factors

Nowadays, we are encountering digital age period. Many customers choose to apply websites and mobile apps to buy their products. So,many merchants also choose online e-commerce channel to build online purchase platform to raise its competitive ability in online e-commerce market.

So, customers can apply mobile apps or merchants themselves websites to buy any products in any time and any places conveniently.

However, in electronic (ecommerce) industry, Amazon is the global largest online retail delivery provider. It sells different kinds of products from internet, e.g. books, electronic products, music, movie Cd, DVD, magazine, garden and homw useful tools, children toys, computer,

software, even, cars from online channel to global online shoppers. So, there ate many online buyers choose to buy any products from Amazon web services middle channel. In fact, its products prices can be low, a wide selection, ease website use and convenience to meet all of its customers' needs in one virtual store. So, it can still own the high share market in online retail delivery service industry. I shall indicate that Amazon successful factors as below:

It has a clear aim or mission. It's mission is to be Earth's most customer-centric company , where people can find and discover anything , they want to buy online. So, it will gather data ro analyze whether why and how customers will select to buy the kinds of products from internet. Why do its customers forget to choose to buy any products from shops and they choose Amazon to buy their preferable products from online? I believe that it has these characteristics to attract them such as:

It can provide return after sale services within the reasonable time when the customer feels that he does not need to use the product or feels unsatisfactory to the product, then he can return the product to Amazon and Amazon must refund money to him as well as it can provide free charge of grocery delivery service to every customer home. Instead of these attractive service, it also began to enter publishing market. In July 2002, Amazon started offering services to website developers, marketings its kindle

product, aimed at capturing the publishing market for digital books, then it can sell paper books from online channel. It aims to let readers can choose to either download to read ebooks from its website or borrow ebooks to read from its electronic library or paid visa to print paper books to deliver their paper books to their homes conveniently. So, readers feel that they can enter Amazon publish website to choose any interesting books to buy or borrow to read , they do not need to go to book stores or libraries.It is Amazon's competitive and attractive and unique strengths to build its customers on this online retail market.

On its organization mamagement aspect, it has one effective and efficient management strategy. It has a good CEO manages his e-commerce business. Bezos has been chairman of the board of Amazon , since he founded the compnay in 1994. Amazon has a limitless stock on hand at all time, it enables Amazon to collect high margins when providing low prices, and lets customers to feel consideration every second. So, when the customers feel any enquiries, his customer service team members can apply its intra website email message channel to send email to answer his enquiries when they enter Amazon intra-website email message channel to send email to ask them any enquiries and they can reponse their enquiries immediately in any time or they can phone to Amazon customer service hotline to enquiry them directly. So, its customer service staffs can answer their enquiries either by phone or email communication in short time rapidly. They

won't delay to response their enquiries to avoid they feel worry or unhappy or complain. So, efficient customer service performance can help it to satisy its customer service needs and build good customer service relationship and repeat purchase chance will increase also.

However, global online retail marketplace is expanding rapidly. So, Amazon will have many new or potential online retail competitors, if it neglected to improve its strategy to adapt every online customer individual need or purchase taste, due to customers' purchase need will often change, such as price demand, product delivery time demand, customer service demand etc. spects. So, Amazon needs have different market strategies in different time in order to attract customers' choices in different economic environment, if it hoped to keep online retail leader position.

For example, how to encourage or raise customers' online purchase desires when economy is poor environment. When many people loss jobs, due to many businesses liquidate and loss many clients. So, they need to dismiss many staffs. Then, in society, many families will reduce their consumption desires because their parents loss jobs. So, Amazon needs improve its strategies on above different aspects in order to attract or persuade them to spend much time on internet shopping activities.

Instead of organization management aspect and customer service aspect, the other critical success factors for developing an e-business strategy to Amazon, they may include: How to apply network technology to keep long term close relationship between Amazon its e-commerce organization, online customers, partners, stakeholders and product suppliers. It is very important to influence Amazon's success, because Amazon , such as the e-business delivery service provider will loss the kinds of product sale chance, if the product providers dislike its sale delivery service or feel satisfactory to

its sale strategy or promotion methods or when its online sale delivery service can not let its customers feel its online sale delivery to be satisfactory. Hence, online sale delivery service performance is very important to influence Amazon's success.

Moreover, in its business model, Amazon.com also needs have these key succes factors. They may include: Building strong brand name location, because when online shoppers can remember its brand or loyalty easily when it is famous. Then they won't choose any online retail delivery providers to replace its delivery service easily. So, building one famous and confident online retail delivery service provider loyalty or brand , it can help Amazon to influence many online shoppers have confidence to choose its online retail delivery service in the first time. When they can often remember Amazon and feel it is only one online retail delivery serivce provider, the repeat online purchase chance will also increase, due to they only choose to click on its website to choose any kinds of products to buy more easily.

So, Amazon.com's marketing strategy is needed to design to strengthen the Amazon brand name, increases customer traffic to the Amazon.com web sites, builds customer loyalty, encourages repeat purchases or attracts them to clicks on its websites again to develop incremental products and retail delivery service revenue opportunities. Also, how to design its efficient products delivery value to let product buyers to feel. This factor is important to influence Amazon's products delviery service in success in online

retail delivery service market. Moreover, Amazon publish service also needs to build attractive reading feeling to let readers to satisfy its reading provision needs to replace book stores or libraries.

On conclusion, Amazon ought need to continue to change its marketing strategies in order to adapt to its online retail product delivery service changes as well as lets they believe that it is one online customer care product delviery service provider to comapre other online retail delivery service providers, if it hopes to keep its online retail relviery provider top leader position in this e-commece market.

Skills technological improvement strategy

soft and hard skill to Amazon organization

Skills shortages on developing country market

Nowadays , future global job market competition will be trended serious. Any employers will expert their employees own different skills to know how to do their jobs efficiently and effectively and easily. So, future any organization employees ought considerate how to learn different kinds of skills or knowledges in order to prepare to satisfy their future employers' different new tasks needs. However, if future any new skillful needs or demands will be raised to future employers' demands. It brings these questions: what skills do global any organization employees need own in general? How to improve or raise employees themselves skills more easily and efficiently? What will happen if future employees do not learn new knowledge to improve or raise themselves skills? Why is learning any new skillful knowledge important ? What will be the possible negative and /or positive consequence if future the organizations do not need their employees to learn any new kinds of skillful knowledge?

Future developing countries need to develop their economy, so they need to employ many employees who own technical skills and /or soft skills. What kind of technical skills and/or soft skills , the developing countries' employees who will need to order to raise competiton in local job market ? I shall indicate the developing country

China example. China is one developing country, employers will need different kinds of skillful labors to assist them to develop their businesses. However, China employers will face skillful labour shortage challenge. Although Chinese young age population is high, but many of them do not to be encouraged to learn enough skillful knowledge to fill future new skillful positions. So, the fast speed of training will be important to influence China supply and demand labour market to be more accurately as well as future China's the quality of labour demand number will be influenced to be raised after they have enough training to learn new skills.

How to solve future China skillful shortage of labour? Firstly, nowadays, China employers need to teach their employees to learn how to use and how to operate robotic skills in China's factories. AI robotic has been early developing, so they need to prepare to learn robotic management and operating technical and soft skills in order to satisfy future China factory automation industry development.

China is one world's factory for low-end products to high quality information products, high end technology and services. So, China will need many high skilled workers to assist manufacturers to manufacture many different kinds of products to export or local sale. Moreover, robotic manufacturing skillful workers will also need because robotic will be accepted to assist manual workers to work in China's any factories. This has led to greater demand for labour wirh upgraded skills and competence. So, it seems that China's orkers need to lern any high technological manufacturing knowledge, e.g. learning how to co-operate with robotics to raise productive efficiencies, which will be future many China's manufacturers' skills need intention.

So, when any one of China manufacturer invests robotics to work in its factory . Then, the China manufacturer's labours ought need to know how to co-operate with th robotics to raise productivities and efficiencies. Moreover, these China service industries, e.g. IT, software, accounting, finance, marketing and customer service management, e.g. waiter, property security, shopping center customer service etc. service occupations. In the future, robotics can also used to participate any one of these service industries' part of tasks in order to raise service performance. So, any one of these service industries' employees need to learn how to operate with robotics in order to achieve the most excellent servvice performances to satisfy consumers' needs. So, China service industries labours ought need to learn how to co-operate or manage service natural robotics to work together more efficiently because future China manufacturers will prefer to employ the labours who know how to co-operate and manage and control any service natural robotics more easily and efficiently in order to achieve the most excellent service performance to satisfy customers needs.

Hence, it seems that China manufacturing and service workers need to spend time and effort to learn how to co-operate with manufacturing natural robotics to manufacture any products in factories efficiently or deliver any cargos in warehouses more efficiently or serve customers to let them to feel excellent service performance in restaurants or shopping centers or properties or offices reception counters. Then, when their China employers apply robotics to participate to work in factories, restaurants, shopping centers, cinemas, offices or properties reception etc. different working places . These low skillful labours will be dismissed easily, due to robotics can replace them to manufacture any products or provide services to satisfy clients' needs in order to let them to fell robotics' performances are more excellent to compare human service labours or their productive efficiencies are more effort to compare workers. So, future China workers need to learn how to cooperate or manage or contol with robotics to work more efficiently, if they do not expect to be dismissed easily.

Future global skillful labor
soft knowledge skill need

In the future several occupations have been identified as the most frequent movers between all labour market states. The elementary occupations include: waiters, bar staffs, clearners, catering assistants, construction and security service workers, care workers, sales assistants and general clerks etc. So, the low educational level workers can learn these soft wkills to raise whose professional workering level to prepare to do these above positions in global elementary occupation job market.

The changes of employer were most frequent for IT programmers, doctors, electricians, carpenters, skilled workers in global labour market. These skilled occupations will have manpower shortage supply challenge, due to either people feel the educatonal level is under low. So, there has no many people have interest to know these knowledg to prepare their elementary careers. So, these kinds of low skilled occupations will have not enough human power supply to global labour job market also, the high skilled or educational job support.

Moreover, the high skilled occupations also encounter labour shortage issue. The skills in short supply related to experienced canadidates e.g. five years or more. For example, pharmaceutical , biogharma and food innovation industries. The occupational shortage roles include: Chemists, analytical scientists, product formulation, analytical development for roles in biopharma, quality control analyst includes pharmaco-vigilance, i.e. drug safety roles. The demand for engineering industry aspect which will aos increase the labour shortage includes process and design (research and development, quality control, automation, lean processes) are skillful labours need to help employers to achieve these intentions. They may include raising competitiveness, boosting productivity and skills availability. So, if future these above any one of occupation labours can not achieve these benefits to satisfy their employers' needs. Then, his/her average weekly or hourly wages will be reduced. It means that the unskilled labour under skilled labour wage can not increased more easily, even they own many year working experiences in any one of above these occupations. If the employer feels the labour is unskilled or below skilled level for any one of these occupations in these any one industry aspect, e.g. wholesale and retal , human health, education, accomodaton and food , construction, professional activities, financial service , public administration, and defence, transportation etc. occupations. Then, these industries' unskilled or below skilled level workers' salaries will be lower level to compare the higher skilled workers who work in any one of these industries.

The reason why future employers need to employ skilled labours. One explanation for slow recovery in demand in negative impact on investment is a prolonged period of high unemployment. This is led to job weekers left labour market or became unemployable due. So, future low skillful level will be one important factor to cause unemployment in society as well as nowadays labours ought need consider whether their skills are needed to improve in order to avoid future competition in job market.

2.1 Why do future labours need to learn worldwide readiness skills

Future employers need employees own worldwide readiness skills, such as reading , writing and arithmatic. Why do employees need worldwide readiness skills? In the future, high economic growth countries need high wage positions, high opportunity jobs which need a large number of skills required of job candidates of these positions " job readinss" and not " job training" , which support developments of these importance and widely desired skills won't only support the success to high-opportunity positions, but also be developed for future success in the competitive global economy. Because real-time business intelligence is needed for the talent marketplace to employ talent employees. So, it explains that it will have many future employers hope to employ owning readiness skillful employees to help them to develop their businesse intelligently. Hence, present employees ought need to hard to train readiness skills to prepare whose future employers' job requirements in the future competitive global job market.

2.2 Why these occupations need readiness skills

In the future these occupations will need to raise readiness skills. For example, mathematical science, teachers (post-secondary), management analysts, computer and information systems, managers, first-line supervisors of construction traders, solar photovoltaic installers. All of these occupations , employers need staffs to own good readiness analytic ability to help them to do more accurate real-time business intelligent decisions. The representative occupations include oral and written communication skills, project management, teamwork, marketing and creativity . Moreover, they need to own specific technology skill, deep science and math or even most business skills as well as these skills are "soft" skills more than hard skills. These kinds of occupation employees need own cooperative effort, creativity, problem solving, detail orientation and integrity personal characteristics, which are relevant across all knowledge and domains.

Therefore, in the future, science, technology,engineering and mathematics relevant occupations need to own more readiness and analytic skills more than othe kinds of occupations. Because these organizations need those professionals on knowledge acquisition, literacy analysis, synthesis and critical thinking skills that will impact their organizations to bring more critical thinking beneficial team culture. These occupational top skills will include oral and written communication skills, project management skill, team oriented skill, marketing and creativity skills, problem solving skill, detail oriented skill, self-motivated skills, management and analytical skills, coaching skill, business process modeling skills, work independent skill, strong leadership skills, management experience and business requirements gathering. All of these skills which will be future employers who need to employ these kinds employees who own these skills in preference. Also, all of these skills concentrate on soft skills more than hard skills. It seems that when above occupational applicants who own any one of thes skills, evn more than one skills. Then, he/she will have more chance to be selected to employ. Also occupation specific skills requirements are more needed to compare cross-functional skills for above of any one occupation. Because the high concentraton of cross-functional skills require " job readiness" and not " job training" for success, e.g. communicaton, integraton and presentation skills, entrepreneurialism and related skills, microsoft office software skills.

Of particular interest is communication, integration and presentation skills. These skills include ability to seek, evaluate and examine information and data create a reasoned position, present findings and make a case for or advocate for position. So, these skills are very important and they can help future applicants who expect to win any kinds of these positions easily. However, the hard skills can help these applicants to be more successful to win any kinds of these positions when they own these hard skills, e.g. microsoft offic, powerpoint, excel , word, microsoft project etc. softwares.

In conclusion, the global economy is dynamic and many of the skills required for positons in the future will need good technologies and work practices to be developed. The number of skills required t be successful in the jobs forecast to be most in demand in the future is growing. So, it explains that why future any one of these occupations which will need soft skills more than hard skills, due to organizations like to employ the employees who own managerial and analytical effort more than hard skills productive effort to assist their organizations to develop more easily.

2.3 Data -analysis skill needs

In the future, most organizations will have a number of jobs that include data analysis. Economists and labor market forecasters predict occupations need data analytical skill will need much. In addition, fast technological development means th types of technologies and applications workers in this field will need to be familiar with data analytical skill rapidly. It seems that data analytical jobs will have new job opportunity to employees with in-demand skills in future global labor market.

Why and how do employers demand for data analysis skills? Data analysis skills mean the ability to gather, analyze and draw practical conclusions from data as well as communicate data findings to others. The occupations include: data analyst, data scientist, statistician, market research analyst, financial analyst,research manager. In business career, many employers expect to employ statisticans, operations researh analysts, market research analysts and marketing specialists to assist their organizations to gather useful data from market in order to analyze and draw practical conclusions and finding the best solutions or methods to win their competitors.

Therefore, these data analysis jobs will have much need. Large size organizations with 500 or more employees were more likely than small or medium size organizations with 25 to 499 employees to plan hired data analysis positons in the future. For example, human source department will use big data to help make strategic decisions. How HR uses big data . HR will use big data for sourcing, recruitment, or selection, identifying causes of turnover and/or employee retention strategies or trends, managing talent and performance. Why organizations do not use big data. It is possible that they lack of knowledg expertise, the majority of organizatons will have data analysis positions within accounting and finance department, human resources department, business and administration department, information technology department, marketing, advertising and sales department, supply chain and operations department, research and development department, customer service department and other departments. So, future data analysis skill will need to used in different organizational departments.

However, publicly and privately owned for-profit organizations were more likely than government organizations to have data analysis positions in the marketing, advertising and sales function. Also, data analysis skills are required to different levels in any organizations , such as entry level, non-management / individual contributor level, mid-level management level, seniot management or executive level. The analyst, research analyst, market research analyst, scientist-based titles include: data scientists , research scientist, scientist, other descriptive titles include researcher, statistician, mathematician and other . So, data analysis positions will have many different skills to be selected to any one data analysis professional. For example, the data analysis professional can select either to learn the ability to interpret and communicate data analysis results skill or to learn how gathering or analyzing data skill. So, data analysis skill is not onlyone skill, it is more than one skill to let any one employee to select to learn.

Why do organizations need data analysis professionals? On workforce planning aspect, organizatons expect to let strategic direction and content of workforce needed for future business objectives easier, analyzing workforce: supply analysis, demand analsis and gap analysis more earier, developing action plan : recruiting and training plans to deal with gaps more easier, implementing action plan, monitoring, evaluating and revising plan more easier. So, organizations expect the data analysis professionsla can help them to solve these challenges, such as using of advanced technology solutons to integrate disparate planning sources; data availability and format; accessing to and understanding of the organization's data and analytics, developing business case to gain support from senior management and collaboration among HR staff, managers and executive easier. Future industries need data analysis professionals may include manufacturing health care and social assistance, scientific and technical service, finance and insurance, educational services , government agencies, retail trade, transportation and warehousing, construction, utilities, accomodation, and food services, waste management and remediation services, entetainment, and creation, real estate and rental and leasing , repair and maintenance, agriculture, forestry, fishing and hunting, personal and laundry services etc.

In conclusion, data analysis job need explains why future readiness and data analytical skills will be popular needed in globl labour market , due to these both skills are labour shortage and employers will need employees own big data readiness and data analytical both skills in order to win whose competitors more easier.

2.4 What are regional dynamic skills
of global labour market demand

Businessmen expect to improve better economic environment, they will prefer to recruit the most sought after skills of intelligent employees to bring positive beneficial impact to organizations. However, technology and digisation has had a significant influence on workers. Future globalization will trend digital economic development. Hence, it will influence workers' skills to be changed also. In fact, not all changes are positive because some workers will possible lose jobs, either due to new technology replaces their jobs or they lack enough effort to improve their skills in global digital economic labour market environment.

It brings this question: What are regional dynamic skills need whn digital busines environment is growing. In fact, organizations will continue to deal with skills shortages, labour markets across the global are continually changing. so, more employers and workers will need to adopt innovate working pattern, e.g. on call jobs, freelance jobs will grow popularly. The greater flexibility afforded to employ regardly.

Finally, digitalisation includes artificial intelligence, big data , online platforms. All these new technology will influence future employees how to worker. For example, they can apply online platform to work at home conveniently. So, they do not need to go to offices. They can finish their jobs and send to their employers by email easily. This kinds of job pattern can raise efficiencies and employers do not need go to offices often.

An important implication of innovating working which needs the employees who own digital skills in order to serve organizations more efficiently. So, employers are increasingly able to access demographics that were hitherto less active in labour markets. For example, future more women are joining the labour market because part time and self employment opportunities make it easier. This kinds of job pattern can raise efficiencies and employees do not need go to offices often.

An important implication of innovating working which needs the employees who own digital skills in order to serve organizations more efficiently. So, employers are increasingly able to access demographic that were hitherto less active in labour markets. For example, future more women are joining the labour market because part time and self employment opportunities make it easier to manage family with work life. So, digital skilling needs will cause many women lose jobs in possible. If the women lack digital job skills. Because high digital skill occupations need, like those requiring research, medical treatment and architectural design occupational digital skills are more common in the services sector, more women who own digital skill who can compete to win.

High digital skill occupations more easier than men because employers usually select female to do high skill occupations easier than make. However, if those professional service female employees can not learn how to apply digital skills to do these researchs medical treatmentm architectural design professional service jobs. Then, it is also different for these professional service femal employees to raise competition in global labour professional service market. So, these professional service female employees need to learn how to apply digital to do themselves jobs in future global professional service labour market. Otherwise, if the male professional service employees can attempt to learn how to apply digital skill to do themselves jobs in order to improve efficiencies and service performance to satisfy patients, such as medical service needs, school search service needs, construction firms' building needs. Then, the owning high digital technology skillful female employees will be more easier to find the professional service jobs which need digital skill more easier than the lacking digital skill female service professionals in future global digital service professional labour market.

On the other robotic communication skill need aspect, future employers expect workers to know how to communicate with robots to work efficiently in any working environment if the employers need robotc to serve their organizations. For example, communication between the robots on factory floors, and between people and robots could allow robots to start and stopr processes based on real-time conditions around them and alert people when there is a problem, so robots could increase their own efficiency if the workers could monitor themselves and determine when they needed maintenance; efficiency would also be improved if machines and robots could make production decisions on their own by. For example, ordering new suppliers when existing inputs into a production process run low. The increase in productivity of industrial robots will likely reduce the number of manual jobs on the shop floor.

At the same time, the increased output made possible by such robots will mean that manufacturers need more people in accounting, finance, sales, advertising and other roles. The increase in putput may also drive increased employment on manufacturers' supply chains. Hence, future employers expect to employ the workers who can know how to communicate with robots to work efficiently in order to raise productivity in any working environment. It means that it the worker can know how to control and communicate with the robots to work together in the team. Then, his/her communication and controlling robotic skill will help the organization's team to work efficiently and raise productivity in order to reduce time waste and human waste and resource waste considerately. So, future shortage of communication and controlling robotic skillful workers number will increase. It has much beneficial to workers who choose to attempt to learn how to communicate and control robots to work together in any working environment team efficiently. Because future employers will like to use robots to assist manual workers to attempt to raise productive efficiency in any working environment. So, the need of employees who know how to cooperate or communicate with robots whose talent skills will be useful to any future employers.

Future global business leaders will need human machine cooperation skill. This technological skill includes artificial intelligence (AI and internet of things (IOT), will reshape our working change. These machines will participate to our daily working environment. For instance, many business leaders agree that automated systems will free-up their time as well as they also believe they'll have more job satisfaction by offloading the tasks that they don't want to do to intelligent machines.

Therefore, future leaders will expect humans and machines can work as integrated teams within their organizaton in order to their workforce and machines are already successfully working this way. So, they need to expect future employees can know or learn how to work with automated systems more easily, because many jobs will be participated by automated systems, e..g simple accounting tasks, legal administration tasks etc. clerical tasks. They will be participated with (AI) technology, it learns how to cooperate with (AI) technology to finish simplt clerical tasks efficiently.

Future workers will need have autrmated system operational skills: They include that how to operate automated systems to free -up workers' time. Workers will need to learn how to operate automated system to better with healthcare tracking devices workers will need to learn how to operate automated systems to absord and manage information in completely different ways. Workers will need to learn how to operate automated systems of smart machines to work as admin. in any orking environments. Workers need be needed to learn how to operate (AI) automated machines to mak more accurate clerical tasks or efficiencies. So, the automated system (robotic) operational skillful workers' demand and number will increase.

In the future, employers need automated machine manufacturing and service with workers cooperation reasons include that clear protocols, will need to be established if autonomous machines fail. So, they need their workers to learn how to control and manage and communicate with autonomous machines skillfully. They believe move they depend upon technology, the more they'll have to lose in the event of a cyber attack. So, skillful workers are real required to let them to know how to cooperate with autonomous machines more efficiently and easily. Computers will need to be able to decipher between good and bad commands, so future employers have much chance to need the owning automated machines operating workers to assist any robots to make more accurate good or bad decision when robots and workers have need to make immediate judgement in their any related job responsibilites aspect.

Therefore, future owning automated machines operating workers' skillful level will be high. It bases on automated machine manufacturing environment trend factor. Finally, future technology will connect the right employee to the high task at the right time. It implies that when future global employers began to accept to apply robots to help them to raise any productivities efficiently. It will influence many manufacturing positions which need to employ any proficient skillful workers who own automated machines operational skills to know how to communicate or manage or control , even supervise any robots to work in teams in any organizational manufacturing environmnet efficiently. In the future, employers also expect employees to own sufficient digital vision and strategic skills, manifest among other things. They can know how to apply data to demonstrate any senior support and sponsorship digital technological skill. They expect to reduce a skill gap and avoid a lack of employee buying and a workforce culture to change in their digital technologicl manufacturing organizations. Future employers also believe outdated technology that can't work fast enough, data overload, privary and security concerns. So, it explains why it is possible that future employers also need digital working environment and automated robots machines to attempt to achieve raising productive efficient aim.

Moreover, it also explains why digital transformation need will be raised. The reasons include: They feel digital technology can gain employees' buying in , making customer experience a boardroom concern, achieving fair compensation , training and goals and strategy achievement more easily, tasking senior leaders with digital working environment change putting policies and technology to support a fully remote, flexible workforce , empowering lines of team work more efficient, teaching all employees how to code/understanding how to adopt to work with automatic machines or rots in any team efficiently. So, automate machine can raise efficiency in manufacturing society.

In conclusion, in the future business society, employees need to be stronger human machine partnerships. So , future manufacturing or service industries will have digital technology and automated machine robotic technology to assist workers to work in any working environment efficiently. They expect digital technology and automated machine robotic technology anticipation to workers' daily jobs in order to bring positive impacting to the customer experience from business owners to decision makers in marketing, customer service, research and developmnt and finance etc. They also expect technological productivity can bring positive relationship between technology and workers emerging technologies' impact on business and the way workers and automated machine work together.

Future organizational skillful
needs how to influence workforce
change to what kinds of employees

In the future whether in general organizations need what kinds of employees' skills, they expect employee individual own. It is one interesting question. The common skills that employees need to own in order to any duties to any organizational departments efficiently, e.g. human resource, marketing, administrative, logistic etc. different departments. For hospital, school, business, professional occupations etc. different organizations. Whether future school ought implement one system educational method to teach different common skills to students in order to let them to leave schools to jobs more easier.

Future employers need to create new technologies including automation and algorithms, in order to create new high quality jobs and improve the job quality and productivity of the existing work of human employees in any organizations, e.g. accounting department will need intelligence (AI) to assist account clerks to do simple repeating accounting job tasks in order to share their work load and raise performance efficiency or legal organizations will need (AI) to assist law clerks to do simple repeating legal draft or legal document revising job tasks . All future general clerical jobs will apply (AI) technological tools to assist human to job, it will produce a comprehensive platform for managing workforce change.

Hence, human manual(employees) need to learn how to adopt (AI) job participation to assist them to do different kinds of simple clerical jobs in any organizational administrative departments . They , clerical employees or white color workers need to learn how manage or dominate (AI) tool to improve job performance to be better. However, (AI) administrative workforce change, it is not only one kind of job automation change role in any physical offices. It influences future administrative clerks need change a more flexible manner, utilizing remote staffing beyond physical offices and decentralization of operations organizational workforce change.

Instead of (AI) participation to administrative job aspect, (AI) will also participate to manufacturing industry environment aspect, a new human-machine manufacturing workforce change will exist to any factories, warehouses working environment. Scientists predict that in present an average of 71% of total task hours across the industries are performed by humans, compared a 29% by machines. In this average is expected to have shifted to 58% task hours performed by humans and 42% by machines. In fact, nowadays, in terms of total working hours, no work task was yet estimated to be predominantly performed by a machine or an algorithm (AI). But, this picture is predicted to have somewhat changed with machines and algorithms (AI) on average increasing their contribution to specific tasks by 57% . For example, in the future, 62% of organization's information and data processing and information search and transmission tasks will be performed by machines compared to 46% today.

Therefore, these high technological skillful job change will bring negative influence to some demotive-skillful or low skillful labors to be dismissed, if they can not upgrade or raise or reskillgul their skill level to improve their analytical thinking , technology design and programming skills to cooperate with (AI) tools to work efficiently together in any organizational manufacturing or offie work environment. Because it will have many employers apply (AI) automation tools to participate with blue -color or whiate -color workers' tasks in order to raise efficiencies or improve performance in any working environment. So, it is right time to young or mid age employees need to upskill and/or reskill their rihgt type of skills to prepare future technology risch work environment changeing needs.

Future technological advances will permit an increasing number of tasks traditionally performed by humans to become automated. It seems that , such automation focused primarily on routine tasks, e.g. clerical work, bookkeeping, basic paralegal work and reporting etc. However, with the advent of big data, artificial intelligence (AI), the internet of things and ever-increasing computing power , i.e. the digital revolutions, non-routine tasks are also increasingly likely to become automated. For example, the recent development in robotics and 3D printing allow firms in advanced economies to locate production closer to domestic markets in fully aumomated factories. As a result, the future strongest incentive to automate because of their relatively higher labour costs will be reduced, when production automated will bring the negative influence to dismiss some foolish or low produtive or low skill workers , the owning high automated productive skillful workers will replace the low productive skillful workers in any factories' manufacturing environments. So, technological progress participates to raise quantity of jobs will cause result in significant job losses to low skillful workers. Because future employers will need many high automated productive employees to help them to cooperate with (AI) automated machine to work together efficiently. For example, many proportion of occupations at high risk is greatest in Germany and lowest in Korea, these countries organizations will accept to spend technology investments and education of workers to prepare future automatability manufacturing development successfully.

However, future automatability manufacturing development will bring technological unemployment in possible, due to workers need to adjust to the challenge of automation by switching tasks. Thus, preventing technological unemployment, also technological change does not just destroy jobs, but also generates new roles through its effect on productivity and the demand for new technologies. For example, it has been estimated that, for each high tech-job created in the industries , such as computing equipment or electrical machinery, some 4.9 % additional jobs are created for lawyers, taxi, drivers and waites in the local economy (Moretti, 2011).

Therefore, automated will also influence service industries' job nature change, e.g. taxi drivers need to apply (AI) automated machines to assist them to drive their taxis. When the passenger tells the taxi driver where he/she wants to go. Then, the (AI automated machine will follow the GPS road direction map to be indicated how to drive the taxi to go to the destination automatically . So, future taxi driver is one assistance role to assist the (AI) automated driving tool to dominate the (AI) tool to drive the taxi to catch the passenger to arrive the destination safety in the short time in possible. For another example, future restaurant waiters will need (AI) automated machines's assistance to help them to deliver or dispatch any foods and soft drinks to send to the identified eater's table carefully in accurate and efficient service performance way from the kitchen, in especially in the busy time and many people are sitting in the large size restaurant environment. So, future, waiter roles will be the leader , they need to manage or control or supervise the (AI) robotics how to make decisions to arrange to dispatch which foods or soft drinks to the different tables in preference immediately. Also, future law clerks need to supervise or manage the law robotics how to help them to make decisions to do revision or draft or filing legal tasks in preference in order to avoid any typing words are mistaken to type on computers or revised draft in wrong way to assist manual legal clerks' mistaken words are appearanced on any legal documents. So, the law clerk future role will be the trainer role , he/she eeds to teacher the robots how to check any words, e.g. grammers to correct them to be right grammers, or giving the accurate revision legal documents' instruction to let the legal robots to know how to revise each legal draft to prove whether which part of the legal draft will have wrong to be needed to revise.

In conclusion, future many manual workers' service or manfacturing job natures will become automated assistance to robotics. So, employees need to upgrade their skills in order to adopt new technological work nature change. So future CEO needs to prepare to learn how to apply robotic technological skills to train workers to raise efficiencies and improve performance because there are many future organizations start to apply robotic manufacturing tools to assist workers to work in any departments. Hence, future excellent CEOs must need to own AI knowledge to satisfy their organizational performance improvement need.

Skill training talent human method

Skill is an ability or effort that you need to put time to develop. Talent refers to an inborn and special ability you own it. So, when one person can attempt to learn ths kind of skill. It is possible that he can be trained to be talent person. How to Create Effective Skills Training with Career Pathing ? Your company's ability to address the skills gap is going to be the most significant issue facing HR in the next decade. Relying on the recruitment of new hires will no longer be a viable solution. Digital transformation of the workplace means that AI and automation are continually rendering skills obsolete while creating new jobs in the process. As those new roles emerge, the existing talent pool will be insufficient to meet demand. Employers will no longer be able to fall back on their default strategy of hiring new workers.

● How to improve staff skill to be talent labour ?

As the 'future of work' begins to assume a more defined shape, the majority of employers are placing more emphasis on training of their existing talent, but skills development is not moving fast enough to keep up with demand. Ongoing upskilling and reskilling can help to offset the impact on your workforce from these fundamental changes.

Creating personalized development opportunities

When it comes to developing your talent, there is no 'one size fits all' approach. To succeed in today's workplace the following steps are recommended. Your approach must become more personal, placing development at the center of your overall business strategy.

Personalized development opportunities should be offered to enhance skills acquisition. This approach enables you to provide your employees with the tools they need to acquire new skills.

As well as being targeted to the individual, employees should be able to learn in their own time. Technology can help to support this. A further, critical point to note is that learning and development is not exclusively for the C Suite but should be offered to all of your employees.

● Career pathing strategy improve employee individual skill ?

Career pathing provides a clear route into all of these options, enables you to create individual learning programs for all of your employees and offers the following benefits.

Employees create their own career paths, which are aligned with your organization's business goals. All employees are guided to understand their own strengths and weaknesses and are empowered to identify key areas for development. They are inspired to work towards vertical or lateral moves within your organization, for example, through job rotation (ie, where employees assume new tasks in a different role for a specified period before they 'rotate' back to their original post). Career pathing enables HR and management to understand and analyze employee aspirations through internal mobility programs and aligns well with your succession planning program. So, career pathing strategy is one kind of good skill to raise staff efficiency or improve performance.

Skills shortages on developing country market

Future developing countries need to develop their economy, so they need to employ many employees who own technical skills and /or soft skills. What kind of technical skills and/or soft skills , the developing countries' employees who will need to order to raise competiton in local job market ? I shall indicate the developing country China example. China is one developing country, employers will need different kinds of skillful labors to assist them to develop their businesses. However, China employers will face skillful labour shortage challenge. Although Chinese young age population is high, but many of them do not to be encouraged to learn enough skillful knowledge to fill future new skillful positions. So, the fast speed of training will be important to influence China supply and demand labour market to be more accurately as well as future China's the quality of labour demand number will be influenced to be raised after they have enough training to learn new skills.

How to solve future China skillful shortage of labour? Firstly, nowadays, China employers need to teach their employees to learn how to use and how to operate robotic skills in China's factories. AI robotic has been early developing, so they need to prepare to learn robotic management and operating technical and soft skills in order to satisfy future China factory automation industry development.

China is one world's factory for low-end products to high quality information products, high end technology and services. So, China will need many high skilled workers to assist manufacturers to manufacture many different kinds of products to export or local sale. Moreover, robotic manufacturing skillful workers will also need because robotic will be accepted to assist manual workers to work in China's any factories. This has led to greater demand for labour wirh upgraded skills and competence. So, it seems that China's orkers need to lern any high technological manufacturing knowledge, e.g. learning how to co-operate with robotics to raise productive efficiencies, which will be future many China's manufacturers' skills need intention.

So, when any one of China manufacturer invests robotics to work in its factory . Then, the China manufacturer's labours ought need to know how to co-operate with th robotics to raise productivities and efficiencies. Moreover, these China service industries, e.g. IT, software, accounting, finance, marketing and customer service management, e.g. waiter, property security, shopping center customer service etc. service occupations. In the future, robotics can also used to participate any one of these service industries' part of tasks in order to raise service performance. So, any one of these service industries' employees need to learn how to operate with robotics in order to achieve the most excellent servvice performances to satisfy consumers' needs. So, China service industries labours ought need to learn how to co-operate or manage service natural robotics to work together more efficiently because future China manufacturers will prefer to employ the labours who know how to co-operate and manage and control any service natural robotics more easily and efficiently in order to achieve the most excellent service performance to satisfy customers needs.

Hence, it seems that China manufacturing and service workers need to spend time and effort to learn how to co-operate with manufacturing natural robotics to manufacture any products in factories efficiently or deliver any cargos in warehouses more efficiently or serve customers to let them to feel excellent service performance in restaurants or shopping centers or properties or offices reception counters. Then, when their China employers apply robotics to participate to work in factories, restaurants, shopping centers, cinemas, offices or properties reception etc. different working places . These low skillful labours will be dismissed easily, due to robotics can replace them to manufacture any products or provide services to satisfy clients' needs in order to let them to fell robotics' performances are more excellent to compare human service labours or their productive efficiencies are more effort to compare workers. So, future China workers need to learn how to cooperate or manage or contol with robotics to work more efficiently, if they do not expect to be dismissed easily.

In the future several occupations have been identified as the most frequent movers between all labour market states. The elementary occupations include: waiters, bar staffs, clearners, catering assistants, construction and security service workers, care workers, sales assistants and general clerks etc. So, the low educational level workers can learn these soft wkills to raise whose professional workering level to prepare to do these above positions in global elementary occupation job market.

The changes of employer were most frequent for IT programmers, doctors, electricians, carpenters, skilled workers in global labour market. These skilled occupations will have manpower shortage supply challenge, due to either people feel the educatonal level is under low. So, there has no many people have interest to know these knowledg to prepare their elementary careers. So, these kinds of low skilled occupations will have not enough human power supply to global labour job market also, the high skilled or educational job support.

Moreover, the high skilled occupations also encounter labour shortage issue. The skills in short supply related to experienced canadidates e.g. five years or more. For example, pharmaceutical , biogharma and food innovation industries. The occupational shortage roles include: Chemists, analytical scientists, product formulation, analytical development for roles in biopharma, quality control analyst includes pharmaco-vigilance, i.e. drug safety roles. The demand for engineering industry aspect which will aos increase the labour shortage includes process and design (research and development, quality control, automation, lean processes) are skillful labours need to help employers to achieve these intentions. They may include raising competitiveness, boosting productivity and skills availability. So, if future these above any one of occupation labours can not achieve these benefits to satisfy their employers' needs. Then, his/her average weekly or hourly wages will be reduced. It means that the unskilled labour under skilled labour wage can not increased more easily, even they own many year working experiences in any one of above these occupations. If the employer feels the labour is unskilled or below skilled level for any one of these occupations in these any one industry aspect, e.g. wholesale and retal , human health, education, accomodaton and food , construction, professional activities, financial service , public administration, and defence, transportation etc. occupations. Then, these industries' unskilled or below skilled level workers' salaries will be lower level to compare the higher skilled workers who work in any one of these industries.

The reason why future employers need to employ skilled labours. One explanation for slow recovery in demand in negative impact on investment is a prolonged period of high unemployment. This is led to job weekers left labour market or became unemployable due. So, future low skillful level will be one important factor to cause unemployment in society as well as nowadays labours ought need consider whether their skills are needed to improve in order to avoid future competition in job market.

2.1 Why do future labours need to learn worldwide readiness skills

Future employers need employees own worldwide readiness skills, such as reading , writing and arithmatic. Why do employees need worldwide readiness skills? In the future, high economic growth countries need high wage positions, high opportunity jobs which need a large number of skills required of job candidates of these positions " job readinss" and not " job training" , which support developments of these importance and widely desired skills won't only support the success to high-opportunity positions, but also be developed for future success in the competitive global economy. Because real-time business intelligence is needed for the talent marketplace to employ talent employees. So, it explains that it will have many future employers hope to employ owning readiness skillful employees to help them to develop their businesse intelligently. Hence, present employees ought need to hard to train readiness skills to prepare whose future employers' job requirements in the future competitive global job market.

2.2 Why these occupations need readiness skills

In the future these occupations will need to raise readiness skills. For example, mathematical science, teachers (post-secondary), management analysts, computer and information systems, managers, first-line supervisors of construction traders, solar photovoltaic installers. All of these occupations , employers need staffs to own good readiness analytic ability to help them to do more accurate real-time business intelligent decisions. The representative occupations include oral and written communication skills, project management, teamwork, marketing and creativity . Moreover, they need to own specific technology skill, deep science and math or even most business skills as well as these skills are "soft" skills more than hard skills. These kinds of occupation employees need own cooperative effort, creativity, problem solving, detail orientation and integrity personal characteristics, which are relevant across all knowledge and domains.

Therefore, in the future, science, technology,engineering and mathematics relevant occupations need to own more readniness and analytic skills more than othe kinds of occupations. Because these organizations need those professionals on knowledge acquisition, literacy analysis, synthesis and critical thinking skills that will impact their organizations to bring more critical thinking beneficial team culture. These occupational top skills will include oral and written communication skills, project management skill, team oriented skill, marketing and creativity skills, problem solving skill, detail oriented skill, self-motivated skills, management and analytical skills, coaching skill, business process modeling skills, work independent skill, strong leadership skills, management experience and business requirements gathering. All of these skills which will be future employers who need to employ these kinds employees who own these skills in preference. Also, all of these skills concentrate on soft skills more than hard skills. It seems that when above occupational applicants who own any one of thes skills, evn more than one skills. Then, he/ she will have more chance to be selected to employ. Also occupation specific skills requirements are more needed to compare cross-functional skills for above of any one occupation. Because the high concentraton of cross-functional skills require " job readiness" and not " job training" for success, e.g. communicaton, integraton and presentation skills, entrepreneurialism and related skills, microsoft office software skills.

Of particular interest is communication, integration and presentation skills. These skills include ability to seek, evaluate and examine information and data create a reasoned position, present findings and make a case for or advocate for position. So, these skills are very important and they can help future applicants who expect to win any kinds of these positions easily. However, the hard skills can help these applicants to be more successful to win any kinds of these positions when they own these hard skills, e.g. microsoft offic, powerpoint, excel , word, microsoft project etc. softwares.

In conclusion, the global economy is dynamic and many of the skills required for positons in the future will need good technologies and work practices to be developed. The number of skills required t be successful in the jobs forecast to be most in demand in the future is growing. So, it explains that why future any one of these occupations which will need soft skills more than hard skills, due to organizations like to employ the employees who own managerial and analytical effort more than hard skills productive effort to assist their organizations to develop more easily.

2.3 Data -analysis skill needs

In the future, most organizations will have a number of jobs that include data analysis. Economists and labor market forecasters predict occupations need data analytical skill will need much. In addition, fast technological development means th types of technologies and applications workers in this field will need to be familiar with data analytical skill rapidly. It seems that data analytical jobs will have new job opportunity to employees with in-demand skills in future global labor market.

Why and how do employers demand for data analysis skills? Data analysis skills mean the ability to gather, analyze and draw practical conclusions from data as well as communicate data findings to others. The occupations include: data analyst, data scientist, statistician, market research analyst, financial analyst,research manager. In business career, many employers expect to employ statisticans, operations researh analysts, market research analysts and marketing specialists to assist their organizations to gather useful data from market in order to analyze and draw practical conclusions and finding the best solutions or methods to win their competitors.

Therefore, these data analysis jobs will have much need. Large size organizations with 500 or more employees were more likely than small or medium size organizations with 25 to 499 employees to plan hired data analysis positons in the future. For example, human source department will use big data to help make strategic decisions. How HR uses big data . HR will use big data for sourcing, recruitment, or selection, identifying causes of turnover and/or employee retention strategies or trends, managing talent and performance. Why organizations do not use big data. It is possible that they lack of knowledg expertise, the majority of organizatons will have data analysis positions within accounting and finance department, human resources department, business and administration department, information technology department, marketing, advertising and sales department, supply chain and operations department, research and development department, customer service department and other departments. So, future data analysis skill will need to used in different organizational departments.

However, publicly and privately owned for-profit organizations were more likely than government organizations to have data analysis positions in the marketing, advertising and sales function. Also, data analysis skills are required to different levels in any organizations , such as entry level, non-management / individual contributor level, mid-level management level, seniot management or executive level. The analyst, research analyst, market research analyst, scientist-based titles include: data scientists , research scientist, scientist, other descriptive titles include researcher, statistician, mathematician and other . So, data analysis positions will have many different skills to be selected to any one data analysis professional. For example, the data analysis professional can select either to learn the ability to interpret and communicate data analysis results skill or to learn how gathering or analyzing data skill. So, data analysis skill is not onlyone skill, it is more than one skill to let any one employee to select to learn.

Why do organizations need data analysis professionals? On workforce planning aspect, organizatons expect to let strategic direction and content of workforce needed for future business objectives easier, analyzing workforce: supply analysis, demand analsis and gap analysis more earier, developing action plan : recruiting and training plans to deal with gaps more easier, implementing action plan, monitoring, evaluating and revising plan more easier. So, organizations expect the data analysis professionsla can help them to solve these challenges, such as using of advanced technology solutons to integrate disparate planning sources; data availability and format; accessing to and understanding of the organization's data and analytics, developing business case to gain support from senior management and collaboration among HR staff, managers and executive easier. Future industries need data analysis professionals may include manufacturing health care and social assistance, scientific and technical service, finance and insurance, educational services , government agencies, retail trade, transportation and warehousing, construction, utilities, accomodation, and food services, waste management and remediation services, entetainment, and creation, real estate and rental and leasing , repair and maintenance, agriculture, forestry, fishing and hunting, personal and laundry services etc.

In conclusion, data analysis job need explains why future readiness and data analytical skills will be popular needed in globl labour market , due to these both skills are labour shortage and employers will need employees own big data readiness and data analytical both skills in order to win whose competitors more easier.

2.4 What are regional dynamic skills
of global labour market demand

Businessmen expect to improve better economic environment, they will prefer to recruit the most sought after skills of intelligent employees to bring positive beneficial impact to organizations. However, technology and digisation has had a significant influence on workers. Future globalization will trend digital economic development. Hence, it will influence workers' skills to be changed also. In fact, not all changes are positive because some workers will possible lose jobs, either due to new technology replaces their jobs or they lack enough effort to improve their skills in global digital economic labour market environment.

It brings this question: What are regional dynamic skills need whn digital busines environment is growing. In fact, organizations will continue to deal with skills shortages, labour markets across the global are continually changing.

so, more employers and workers will need to adopt innovate working pattern, e.g. on call jobs, freelance jobs will grow popularly. The greater flexibility afforded to employ regardly.

Finally, digitalisation includes artificial intelligence, big data , online platforms. All these new technology will influence future employees how to worker. For example, they can apply online platform to work at home conveniently. So, they do not need to go to offices. They can finish their jobs and send to their employers by email easily. This kinds of job pattern can raise efficiencies and employers do not need go to offices often.

An important implication of innovating working which needs the employees who own digital skills in order to serve organizations more efficiently. So, employers are increasingly able to access demographics that were hitherto less active in labour markets. For example, future more women are joining the labour market because part time and self employment opportunities make it easier. This kinds of job pattern can raise efficiencies and employees do not need go to offices often.

An important implication of innovating working which needs the employees who own digital skills in order to serve organizations more efficiently. So, employers are increasingly able to access demographic that were hitherto less active in labour markets. For example, future more women are joining the labour market because part time and self employment opportunities make it easier to manage family with work life. So, digital skilling needs will cause many women lose jobs in possible. If the women lack digital job skills. Because high digital skill occupations need, like those requiring research, medical treatment and architectural design occupational digital skills are more common in the services sector, more women who own digital skill who can compete to win.

High digital skill occupations more easier than men because employers usually select female to do high skill occupations easier than make. However, if those professional service female employees can not learn how to apply digital skills to do these researchs medical treatmentm architectural design professional service jobs. Then, it is also different for these professional service femal employees to raise competition in global labour professional service market. So, these professional service female employees need to learn how to apply digital to do themselves jobs in future global professional service labour market. Otherwise, if the male professional service employees can attempt to learn how to apply digital skill to do themselves jobs in order to improve efficiencies and service performance to satisfy patients, such as medical service needs, school search service needs, construction firms' building needs. Then, the owning high digital technology skillful female employees will be more easier to find the professional service jobs which need digital skill more easier than the lacking digital skill female service professionals in future global digital service professional labour market.

On the other robotic communication skill need aspect, future employers expect workers to know how to communicate with robots to work efficiently in any working environment if the employers need robotc to serve their organizations. For example, communication between the robots on factory floors, and between people and robots could allow robots to start and stopr processes based on real-time conditions around them and alert people when there is a problem, so robots could increase their own efficiency if the workers could monitor themselves and determine when they needed maintenance; efficiency would also be improved if machines and robots could make production decisions on their own by. For example, ordering new suppliers when existing inputs into a production process run low. The increase in productivity of industrial robots will likely reduce the number of manual jobs on the shop floor.

At the same time, the increased output made possible by such robots will mean that manufacturers need more people in accounting, finance, sales, advertising and other roles. The increase in putput may also drive increased employment on manufacturers' supply chains. Hence, future employers expect to employ the workers who can know how to communicate with robots to work efficiently in order to raise productivity in any working environment. It means that it the worker can know how to control and communicate with the robots to work together in the team. Then, his/her communication and controlling robotic skill will help the organization's team to work efficiently and raise productivity in order to reduce time waste and human waste and resource waste considerately. So, future shortage of communication and controlling robotic skillful workers number will increase. It has much beneficial to workers who choose to attempt to learn how to communicate and control robots to work together in any working environment team efficiently. Because future employers will like to use robots to assist manual workers to attempt to raise productive efficiency in any working environment. So, the need of employees who know how to cooperate or communicate with robots whose talent skills will be useful to any future employers.

Future global business leaders will need human machine cooperation skill. This technological skill includes artificial intelligence (AI and internet of things (IOT), will reshape our working change. These machines will participate to our daily working environment. For instance, many business leaders agree that automated systems will free-up their time as well as they also believe they'll have more job satisfaction by offloading the tasks that they don't want to do to intelligent machines.

Therefore, future leaders will expect humans and machines can work as integrated teams within their organizaton in order to their workforce and machines are already successfully working this way. So, they need to expect future employees can know or learn how to work with automated systems more easily, because many jobs will be participated by automated systems, e..g simple accounting tasks, legal administration tasks etc. clerical tasks. They will be participated with (AI) technology, it learns how to cooperate with (AI) technology to finish simplt clerical tasks efficiently.

Future workers will need have autrmated system operational skills: They include that how to operate automated systems to free -up workers' time. Workers will need to learn how to operate automated system to better with healthcare tracking devices workers will need to learn how to operate automated systems to absord and manage information in completely different ways. Workers will need to learn how to operate automated systems of smart machines to work as admin. in any orking environments. Workers need be needed to learn how to operate (AI) automated machines to mak more accurate clerical tasks or efficiencies. So, the automated system (robotic) operational skillful workers' demand and number will increase.

In the future, employers need automated machine manufacturing and service with workers cooperation reasons include that clear protocols, will need to be established if autonomous machines fail. So, they need their workers to learn how to control and manage and communicate with autonomous machines skillfully. They believe move they depend upon technology, the more they'll have to lose in the event of a cyber attack. So, skillful workers are real required to let them to know how to cooperate with autonomous machines more efficiently and easily. Computers will need to be able to decipher between good and bad commands, so future employers have much chance to need the owning automated machines operating workers to assist any robots to make more accurate good or bad decision when robots and workers have need to make immediate judgement in their any related job responsibilites aspect.

Therefore, future owning automated machines operating workers' skillful level will be high. It bases on automated machine manufacturing environment trend factor. Finally, future technology will connect the right employee to the high task at the right time. It implies that when future global employers began to accept to apply robots to help them to raise any productivities efficiently. It will influence many manufacturing positions which need to employ any proficient skillful workers who own automated machines operational skills to know how to communicate or manage or control , even supervise any robots to work in teams in any organizational manufacturing environment efficiently.

In the future, employers also expect employees to own sufficient digital vision and strategic skills, manifest among other things. They can know how to apply data to demonstrate any senior support and sponsorship digital technological skill. They expect to reduce a skill gap and avoid a lack of employee buying and a workforce culture to change in their digital technologicl manufacturing organizations. Future employers also believe outdated technology that can't work fast enough, data overload, privary and security concerns. So, it explains why it is possible that future employers also need digital working environment and automated robots machines to attempt to achieve raising productive efficient aim.

Moreover, it also explains why digital transformation need will be raised. The reasons include: They feel digital technology can gain employees' buying in , making customer experience a boardroom concern, achieving fair compensation , training and goals and strategy achievement more easily, tasking senior leaders with digital working environment change putting policies and technology to support a fully remote, flexible workforce , empowering lines of team work more efficient, teaching all employees how to code/understanding how to adopt to work with automatic machines or rots in any team efficiently. So, automate machine can raise efficiency in manufacturing society.

In conclusion, in the future business society, employees need to be stronger human machine partnerships. So , future manufacturing or service industries will have digital technology and automated machine robotic technology to assist workers to work in any working environment efficiently. They expect digital technology and automated machine robotic technology anticipation to workers' daily jobs in order to bring positive impacting to the customer experience from business owners to decision makers in marketing, customer service, research and developmnt and finance etc. They also expect technological productivity can bring positive relationship between technology and workers emerging technologies' impact on business and the way workers and automated machine work together.

In the future whether in general organizations need what kinds of employees' skills, they expect employee individual own. It is one interesting question. The common skills that employees need to own in order to any duties to any organizational departments efficiently, e.g. human resource, marketing, administrative, logistic etc. different departments. For hospital, school, business, professional occupations etc. different organizations. Whether future school ought implement one system educational method to teach different common skills to students in order to let them to leave schools to jobs more easier.

Future employers need to create new technologies including automation and algorithms, in order to create new high quality jobs and improve the job quality and productivity of the existing work of human employees in any organizations, e.g. accounting department will need intelligence (AI) to assist account clerks to do simple repeating accounting job tasks in order to share their work load and raise performance efficiency or legal organizations will need (AI) to assist law clerks to do simple repeating legal draft or legal document revising job tasks . All future general clerical jobs will apply (AI) technological tools to assist human to job, it will produce a comprehensive platform for managing workforce change.

Hence, human manual(employees) need to learn how to adopt (AI) job participation to assist them to do different kinds of simple clerical jobs in any organizational administrative departments . They , clerical employees or white color workers need to learn how manage or dominate (AI) tool to improve job performance to be better. However, (AI) administrative workforce change, it is not only one kind of job automation change role in any physical offices. It influences future administrative clerks need change a more flexible manner, utilizing remote staffing beyond physical offices and decentralization of operations organizational workforce change.

Instead of (AI) participation to administrative job aspect, (AI) will also participate to manufacturing industry environment aspect, a new human-machine manufacturing workforce change will exist to any factories, warehouses working environment. Scientists predict that in present an average of 71% of total task hours across the industries are performed by humans, compared a 29% by machines. In this average is expected to have shifted to 58% task hours performed by humans and 42% by machines. In fact, nowadays, in terms of total working hours, no work task was yet estimated to be predominantly performed by a machine or an algorithm (AI). But, this picture is predicted to have somewhat changed with machines and algorithms (AI) on average increasing their contribution to specific tasks by 57% . For example, in the future, 62% of organization's information and data processing and information search and transmission tasks will be performed by machines compared to 46% today.

Therefore, these high technological skillful job change will bring negative influence to some demotive-skillful or low skillful labors to be dismissed, if they can not upgrade or raise or reskillgul their skill level to improve their analytical thinking , technology design and programming skills to cooperate with (AI) tools to work efficiently together in any organizational manufacturing or offie work environment. Because it will have many employers apply (AI) automation tools to participate with blue -color or whiate -color workers' tasks in order to raise efficiencies or improve performance in any working environment. So, it is right time to young or mid age employees need to upskill and/or reskill their rihgt type of skills to prepare future technology risch work environment changeing needs.

Future technological advances will permit an increasing number of tasks traditionally performed by humans to become automated. It seems that , such automation focused primarily on routine tasks, e.g. clerical work, bookkeeping, basic paralegal work and reporting etc. However, with the advent of big data, artificial intelligence (AI), the internet of things and ever-increasing computing power , i.e. the digital revolutions, non-routine tasks are also increasingly likely to become automated. For example, the recent development in robotics and 3D printing allow firms in advanced economies to locate production closer to domestic markets in fully aumomated factories. As a result, the future strongest incentive to automate because of their relatively higher labour costs will be reduced, when production automated will bring the negative influence to dismiss some foolish or low produtive or low skill workers , the owning high automated productive skillful workers will replace the low productive skillful workers in any factories' manufacturing environments. So, technological progress participates to raise quantity of jobs will cause result in significant job losses to low skillful workers. Because future employers will need many high automated productive employees to help them to cooperate with (AI) automated machine to work together efficiently. For example, many proportion of occupations at high risk is greatest in Germany and lowest in Korea, these countries organizations will accept to spend technology investments and education of workers to prepare future automatability manufacturing development successfully.

However, future automatability manufacturing development will bring technological unemployment in possible, due to workers need to adjust to the challenge of automation by switching tasks. Thus, preventing technological unemployment, also technological change does not just destroy jobs, but also generates new roles through its effect on productivity and the demand for new technologies. For example, it has been estimated that, for each high tech-job created in the industries , such as computing equipment or electrical machinery, some 4.9 % additional jobs are created for lawyers, taxi, drivers and waites in the local economy (Moretti, 2011).

Therefore, automated will also influence service industries' job nature change, e.g. taxi drivers need to apply (AI) automated machines to assist them to drive their taxis. When the passenger tells the taxi driver where he/she wants to go. Then, the (AI automated machine will follow the GPS road direction map to be indicated how to drive the taxi to go to the destination automatically . So, future taxi driver is one assistance role to assist the (AI) automated driving tool to dominate the (AI) tool to drive the taxi to catch the passenger to arrive the destination safety in the short time in possible. For another example, future restaurant waiters will need (AI) automated machines's assistance to help them to deliver or dispatch any foods and soft drinks to send to the identified eater's table carefully in accurate and efficient service performance way from the kitchen, in especially in the busy time and many people are sitting in the large size restaurant environment. So, future, waiter roles will be the leader , they need to manage or control or supervise the (AI) robotics how to make decisions to arrange to dispatch which foods or soft drinks to the different tables in preference immediately. Also, future law clerks need to supervise or manage the law robotics how to help them to make decisions to do revision or draft or filing legal tasks in preference in order to avoid any typing words are mistaken to type on computers or revised draft in wrong way to assist manual legal clerks' mistaken words are appearanced on any legal documents. So, the law clerk future role will be the trainer role , he/she eeds to teacher the robots how to check any words, e.g. grammers to correct them to be right grammers, or giving the accurate revision legal documents' instruction to let the legal robots to know how to revise each legal draft to prove whether which part of the legal draft will have wrong to be needed to revise.

In conclusion, future many manual workers' service or manfacturing job natures will become automated assistance to robotics. So, employees need to upgrade their skills in order to adopt new technological work nature change.Such as Amazon is one super ecommerce organization, it ought need all different departments staffs prepare to ungrade their different kinds of skills, e.g. reading skills for KDP publish review book tasks in order to let authors can have more attractive topics to let readers can buy any Amazon ebooks to read. So, reading skills may be the essential element to Amazon any one book review staff in itself online publish business. Even ebook ecommerce platform design whether Amazon KDP publish online platform can attract to let global readers to feel enjoyment to read its ebooks , it is one essential element to help Amazon to increase e-readers number every day, so Amazon publish platform needs to improve itself ebook reading platform design improve to attract many e-readers like to choose Amazon e-reading platform to read Amazon any authors ebooks. So, E-reading platform design staffs need to upgrade themselves e-reading platform design skills. So, Amazon knolwedge workers number must need to increase in order to continue to improve its e-platform design to attract global e-reading customers or e-shoppers choose to buy Amazon any kinds of products.

Reference

Moretti, E. (2011) local labor market in O, Ashentelter and D. Card (eds.) handbook of labor economics, Elsevier, North Halland.

Amazon organization resource management strategy

Organization tangible and intangible resources function

Any organizations must have tangible and intangible resources. Tangible resources may include: Staffs, lands, equipment, producing machines, factory etc. They may help organizations to produce products or provide services to earn profit, e.g. one shop may be the firm's tangible assets if it can be designed to be the best and provide soft music to let customers to listen and provide clourful light design , they may influence they to bring happy consumption emotion in order to attract many customers to stay long time in the shop and increases shopping chance, the salespeople (staffs) to attract more customers , they may be influenced to feel enjoy to stay long long time by their services. Although, any customers visit any shops , it must not represent that they quarantee to buy any things before they leave the shop. However, I beleive that any business , their products functions and prices is one influential factor to persuade consumers to do shopping activities, their shop design attraction feeling may be also another main factor to persuade them to do shopping decision because when the consumer feels the shop is comfortable , it will cause he/she feels enjoyable to stay long time in the shop. Consequently, shop design attraction may be another influential intangible resource factor to encourage consumers to buy any things easily, if they can be influenced to stay long time in the shop by the ship design attraction. It is one kind of feeling factor to excite consumers to do shopping decision. SO, shop may be one important organization fixed asset resource to influence consumer individual purchase desire in any business environment. It is one good exmaple organizational tangible fixed asset redsource to help any organizations to create income.

The another kind of intangible resources, they are not seen by any customers and they can not be toughed by any customers. BUt they are organizational resources, they also may help any organizations to earn income. Why can intangible resource help organizations to earn income? I shall explain as below:

Customer services and staff skills, they may be organiztional intangible resources and they may help any organizations to create income. For example, when one shop has one kindly and friendly salespeople, when any one customer enters this shop, he will say" Good morning", " Good afternoon", "Good night" and when the customer leaves this shop, he will say " Goodby". Even, when the customer has not bought any thing till to leave this shop, this salesperson also speaks " Goodby". So, all of shop visitors, when the salesperson sees them, he must speaks above words, so any one must feel he is polite person and he can represents this shop's polite image also. Although, some shop visitors do not buy anything when they are staying in this shop, but they must feel that this salesperson's attitude is polite to let them to feel. THis salesperson can bring happy feeling to let all shop visitors feel. So, he must not be complainted easily, because when this salesperson discovers any one person is staying to close to any one producg shelf location in the shop, he will walk to the person to enquire him" DO you need I help you?" politely. Although, it is possible that this person won't need this salesperson to help him, but this salesperson can let this shop visitor to feel that he does not need find any one salesperson to enquire when he feels that he needs purchase help, e.g. whether the shirt has small size stock, or the shoe has organge colour etc. product information enquiries. SO, this salesperson can let this shop visitor feels he can take care to his purchase choice behavior and he can do and purchase help in this shop any time. So, this salesperson , his excellent service performance can let any one shop visitor feels service satisfaction, instead of his essential sale customer service performance. IN fact, this salesperson may let many shop visitors to feel that he does not only considerate whether whom is his real customer in order to enquire any purchase help. The non purchase plan shop visitors may also feel his kindly customer service help during they are staying in shop any time. So, this salesperson's polite and kindly customer service attitude may influence many non purchase planning shop visitors feel happy to see him in this shop. Consequently, it explains why salespeople excellent customer service performance which may help any businesses to increase customers number. It may be one kind of intangible organization resource to any organizations. I mean that when the shop can train many salespeople to raise customer service sale performance improvement.

Overall, these excellent customer service salespeople mus thelp this business to increase customer number easily, because this shop's all salespeople thier positive emotion may influence any one shop visitor feels enjoyment when they can feel they are taking care to their purchase choice need when they are staying in this shop any time. So, the minute, that the shop visitor does not plan to choose to buy any kinds of products, it does not represent that he does not plan to choose to buy any kinds of products next minute. So, any salespeople their excellent customer service performance may influence any one shop visitor to do purchase planning decision any minute. It seems that " salespeople customer service performance feeling" may be one kind of long time intangible resource to help any businesses to earn income in possible. Hence, it explains that any organizations must have tangible and intangible organizational resources to assist them to develop their businesses in long time success. They are essential elelments to influence whether the business's customers number can increase or decrease.

For computer sale business example, its tangible resource may be computer shop and intangible resource may be computer salespeople skills, because if any visitors feel this computer shop's computer desktop or laptop products can be putted in the right and easy seeking locations on any shelves, e.g. the low range price of laptops or desktops are putted on the lowest shelf position as well as the high range price of laptops or desktops are putted on the highest shelf position. So, when the planning purchase of desktop or laptop shop visitors may compare the different design of laptops or desktops their low range price or their high and low shelves locations easily. So, laptops and desktops putting on shelves position, they may influence any one desktop or laptop buyer individual final purchase choice decision. If the laptop planning purchase visitor, he plans to buy one low price of laptop, when he discovers there are all low range price of laptops are putting on the shelf loe position. Then , he may feel convenience to choose any one kind of low price of laptop design products from the lowest range shelf location easily. So, computer shops' computer putting shelves positions may be one kind tangible resource factor to influence any one computer buyer to choose any one kind of design of laptop or desktop priduct convenience. Their computer product choice time whether it is long or short may influence their final computer purchase decision. Hence, the shop's computers ' putting on shelves positions may be one essential tangible resources to influence any one computer visitor to do purchase decision.

The computer shop salespeople computer knowledge may be another intangible factor to influence any one computer buyer decision. For example, when one planning laptop purchaser wants to know whether the laptop's any function, if he enquiries to the computer salesperson, he ften let him to feel that his explanation can not satisfy his any enquiries about the design of laptop product function knowledge, e.g. how to set up password for this computer privacy. If the computer salesperson lets the planning computer buyer to feel that he is difficult to teach him how to set up the passwrod for the computer to use. Then, the computer salesperson's innocence of computer password set up knowledge which may influence the planning computer buyers makes final non purchase decision to this computer, because his innocence can let him to feel this computer is difficult to set up password , if he is one foolish computer user.

Hence, this computer shop's all computer salespeople their computer knowledge, they may influence any one computer buyer final purchase decision. They must need to be trained to learn how to use any one new design of desktop or latop computer products before they are employed to be salespeople in this computer shop。 SO, their computer knowledge may be this computer shop's intangible resource to influence this computer shop's customers number to increase or decrease every day. Hence, decision on any organizational tangible and intangible resources to the organization, they depend on whether what kind of the business needs to sell what kinds of products.

The organization is where resources come together . Organizations use different resources to accompolish goals, e.g. human resources, financial resources, physical resources, and information resources. SO, managers are responsible for managing the resources to accomplish goals. Organizational resources are all assets that are available to a firm for use during the production process. The four basic types of organizational resources are human, monetary, raw material and capital. Managing organizational resources is the ability to understand and effectively manage organizational resources (e.e. people, materials assets , budget). This is demonstrated through measurement, planning and control of resources to maximize resources.

Company resources include tangible assets , such as its plant, equipment, finances, and location, human assets , in terms of the number of empllyees, their skills and motivation and intangible assets (such as technology, patents and copyrights, culture and reputation).

It brings this question: What makes organizational resource unique, in resource based view? Resources are available when they allow a firm to take advantage of opportunities or threats in its external environment. Many resources can either be immitated or substituted over time to any organizations. Hence, effectively managing resources helps companies more consistently deliver projects and services on time. This is because better resource management helps to improve insight into resources availability as well as improves timeline projections. Hence, the types of resources in management they may include: Human resource, natural resource, project resource, financial management, facility management, entertrise asset, public asset management.ON conclusion, I believe that a company's most important resources may be human captial, such as talent employees, their technical knowledge may be intangible resource asset to help the organization to develop its business in longf term success.

Internet will be intangible technology knowledge resource to e-commerce organization
New economy brings new way of resource management. The old loyalty and job security -based organization changes, organizations know that the assets are largely made up employees (HRM), but many new organizations begin to believe technology is important assets, such as Amazon is global ecommerce delivery service organization. It seems internet high technology is its important intangible resource to help it earn global e-buyers number increases . So , many organizations began to believe that technology will be important resource, such as internet can provide online business chance. With all the businesses are taking full advantage of internet, for example, the US department estimates that the value of retail e-commerce in 2000 year was about $25 billion, which represents less than 1% of US retail sales. Despite this, interest in e-business remains high.
● Why internet may be main technology resource to organizations?
E-commere needs strategy in order to win competitors, questions include: What criteria do customers use to choose between our firms and competitors? How do the best employees decision whether to join? What business environment attracts and keeps the best suppliers making with our firms? What characteristics draw the most royal invesdtors to our firms? e.g. Amazon . com's web site and Wal-mart's can apply internet technology resource to create each e-store to let e-buyers to choose any kinds of products to buy athome conveniently. Hence, internet technology, even future other kinds of new technology may be main technology resources to organizations, when they can help organizations to raise sale competitive effort.
I mean that digital economy will be one kind new digital resource to future any organizations. The essential piece is the knowledge, it is what give it life and what makes it an interesting and fulifulling purchase and sale channel for people to spend their time , such as e-commerce virtual organization may be leaded to let purchase and ale transactions carry on easily from online websites. Hence, internet may be main knowledge management (intellectual capital) resource to any e-commerce organizations. It is about the storage, transfer knowledge.
For Amazon publish example, e-books will be knowledge as an object, like a book in library. Amazon can apply internet technology to help it to sell any author's ebooks from its book estores. So, ebooks are Amazon's knowledge resources to help it to create readers incomes. E-books is intangible knowledge resource to Amazon . Any authors' paper and ebooks will be sold cheap price to help Amazon to attract global readers to choose to buy its ebooks from its different countries e-webstores at home conveniently.
Hence, any e-commerce organizations also need HRM (emanagers) to help them to deliver a superior value (world class capabilities) in both te virtual and physical world. E-management will be another main human resources to e-commerce organizations. Why does e-management will be future main HRM resource to e-commerce organization? The reasons may include:
E-management demands in sort of managerial/e-commerce sale strategy effort, skills at positioning the firm within a networm of industries, e-management also demands the ability to see how the firm fits into a value creation-e-management is different because doing it work requires the e-engineering of business eco-systems, e-management demands the ability to be connected to thousands of inputs about specific changes among many industry participants , such as suppliers , customers, employees, competitors, media and shareholders.
Effective e-management requires the ability to monitor developments that can change with unusually high frequency. However, it is also essential that e-managers distinguish between the few meaningful inputs and the many inputs that have limited significance, ability to sustain organizational change, effectie e-managers monitor changes in their markets. So, instead of e-commerce organizations need to employ talent e-managment staffs to help them to manage

overall e-commerce organizations. E-leading staffs (HRM) is another main HRM need. E-leaders need to know how to design online brochures, e.g. online brochures simply involved putting a company's market materials on the web. in order to attract or persuade online buyers visit its websites and choose the most right price of product to buy easily. E-leaders need to lead front-office transactions which involved putting customer facing customers , such as placing on order on the web when leaving back-office activities, such as order fulfillment unchanged.

E-leaders also need to integrate online online purchase transactions in which a firm actually linked its front -office and back -office systems and processes in a fashion, e.g. most companies have developed online brochures , in order to let online advertisement tool to attract e-buyer individual purchase choice from its webstores. Hence, future any e-commerce organizations must need (HRM (e-leaders and e-managers) to help them to bring innovation in order to achieve maximize profit aim. So, internet webstores, e-leaders , e-managers may be future e-commerce organization main resources. So, e-commerce organizations, manages are actors at three levels: In the front line , as entrepreneurs, in the middle , as facilitators, and integrators, at the top as institution builders.

Hence, future new economical society, it creates e-commerce organizations number increases, when consumers began to accept online purchase transaction activities. Hence, it causes e-commerce began to feel internet (e-webstores, e-leaders, e-managers), they will be the most influential resources (intangible knowledge managment and tangible URM both resourcees to influence their success or failure.

● Why does e-commerce organization believe (e-webstore design, e-leaders and e-managers) will be main organizational resources?

The most important question: It asks when e-buyers visit their webstores, wo are their target customers and shich needs of theirs are their trying to satisfy? For exap,e many airlines , e.g. American airlines, China airlines began to feel online e-tickets sale channel is more easily than paper ticket shop sale channel, because many air passengers began to accept e-ticket/online ticket purchase choice more than visiting airline shops . They feel that they do not want to waste time to visit airline shops. They like to pre-book to buy e-ticket to pay from the airline e-websote conveniently. Hence, e-webstore design knowledge management , e-leaders and e-management webstore management skill will be future any one e-commerce organizations their main tangible and intangible resources (assets) to help their e-commerce businesses development.

On conclusion, I believe that the current economy is not a high-tech economy or an internet economy, not an m-commerce economy , but instead customer econoomy. Customers need to gather with information and access, they are demanding, fair, global price, they are demanding that compares deal with them using the distribution channel , they choose manufacturing direct and through dealers and retailers. Base on those factors, they encourage future many e-commerce organizations cause organization change traditional resouce concept, such as land, capital equipment, tangible resource began to change to e-commerce organization's intangibel and tangible resource, such as knowledge management to e-online web store design skills, e-leaders and e-managers e-stores sale management strategy and e-buyer product research and brochure online advertisement design skill. All of these knowledge management skill will be future organizations' main resources to help them to create new economic competition effort.

Organization resources defination

What are organizational resources ? What do organizational resources mean? What kinds of organizational resources are needed? What negative impact may be influenced if organizations lack enough resources to influence organizational development? Does working time belong to organizational time resources to influence employee individual efficiency e.g. how arranging enough employee to do the identified task in the most short time in order to achieve the most efficient performane? I shall attempt to identify examples to explain above questions as below:

In general, organizational resources are all assets, that are available to a firm for use during the production process. The four basic types of organizational resources are human, monetary , raw materials and capital. Organizational resources are combined, used and transofrmed to finished products during the production process. For organizational human resource example, human resource activities full under the following five core functions: staffing, development, compensation, safety and health core functions.

● HR resource

HR conducts a wide variety of activities. However, in any organizations, the major resources used by organizations are often described as follow (1) human resources (2) financial respirces (3) physical resources and (4) information resources. Managers are responsible for acquring and managing the resources to accomplosh goals. Hence, in organizational HR aspect, it may include these function, such as retirement and selection, performance management , learning and development, succession planning, compensation and benefits, human resource information systems. Because considering that for many organizations employees themselves represent a significant cost to the business, if the organization can use its employees in efficiency.

Then, it can avoid human resource in excess or in surplus on wasting challenge. Then , its employee cost or salary can be reduced. I t means that it does not need to employ in excess employees number, but the organization can still achieve itself the most efficient performance. Hence, any organizations must need to learn how to avoid " in excess employees number supply or wasting employee working behaviors" challenge . Because if some tasks do not need many employees to work together, it can still be achieved efficiency . Then , the organization ought not employee too many or excess employees to finish the kind of task. Thus, learning how to use efficient human resources, it can help organizations to avoid wasting working time to any departments employees. For example, when one factory has limited land to be supplied to become warehouse in order to help it to keep sticks. If it has excess logistic or factory workers number. Then, they are wasting working time to do not important tasks in warehouse, it means that if the factory has only one warehouse, but its area is small, it can allow maximum 50 workers to stay in the warehouse , but the warehouse has above 100 workers are staying to deliver goods in the small warehouse . Then, they must not actieve the most efficiency , even their delivery or transport goods performance will be influenced to worse by noise and crowd warehouse working environment. Hence, excess employees number in any working environment, which can not improve organizational performance or riase efficiency any organizations can not neglect " excess employees number" organizatinal HR resource arranging issue.

The solution concerns arranging the most right or the most exact empllyees number in order to supply to any organizational departments. Then, the organization can avoid wasting employee individual talent, reducing employing cost, improvig performance, achieving the most efficiency. Resource capacity means resource pool who are available in the organization to take up to appropriate human resource arrangement to assist any departmental development in long term efficiency. Hence, organizational human rsources may become talent tangible assets or foolish tangible assets. It depends on how the organization's resource capacity tasks arrangement to every employee in different departments. If the organization neglects how to arrange every employee task in the most exact or the most appropriate employees number in the department.

The department's efficiency must be caused worse, because excess employees number, it can not help it to achieve the most efficiency aim, even it may influence the excess employees , themselves feel waste working hours to do the not essential or not important tasks. Then, the organization may cause talent employee to become foolish employee. Otherwise, the organization's efficiency to be worse, because when the department has not enough employees to work. Then , any one employee may feel hard to work, his/her emotion may be influenced to negative, then his/ her workig behavior may b inefficiency or lazy working. On consequence, the organization may bring economic loss, due to employee individual lasy working behavior, negative working emotion, even high working pressure may be caused, when one employee needs to do more , then the employee's task, but his/her salary can not increase. He/she will feel unfair to compare the another department employee, he /she does not need to spend long working hours or overtime to work per day. SO, any organization needs to avoid shortage employee supply or excess employee supply issue to any departments. Appropriare employees number is the best strategy in order to raise overall organizational efficiency.

● Time resource

Instead of human resource, land, raw material, earth natural resource, electricity, gas may be organization resources . Whether time may be organizational resources, organizational time management vires time as a scarce resource that must be invested as effectivity. Time is an infinite resource . If not properly managed on in an organization. It can have a negative impact on both employer's and employee's productivity. So, organizations should ensure that workers are well equipped to manage time in their duties.So, in management view, any organization managers must need to consider how to manage time, eg . how to arrange employees to work in different departments in order to achieve the most efficiency. They need to understand which resources are in short supply and focus on the prioritizing work across shared resources, they need agree on a common approach, they also need to realize resource management is an ongoing process. Thus, time is an often ignored but invaluable resource in any organization. All activities be it procurement.

An organization's time, in contrast, goes largely unmanaged. Although, phone calls, email, instant messages , meetings, they are general daily tasks to any organizations managers, but mangers need to know how to arrange the most urgent tasks in prior. For example, if the manager can not arrange a meeting to the discuss client tomorroe, as well as the manager needs to spend two hours to meeting with overall 200 employees to discuss how to solve improving efficiency challenge tomorroe. So, this manager needs to make choice whether he ought spend two hours meeting to the business client, or two hours meeting to 200 employees. If he chooses to meet the business client tomorrow, he will help his firm to win the important business chance, but he can not discuss how to improve efficiency in order to find the best method to let 200 employees to know tomorrow. Thus, tomorrow time management will be one importat time resource to the manager. The manager needs to arrange tomorrow two hours time how to plan business meting or efficiency imporvement meerting either to his 200 employees or the one business client. Because if the manager decided to meet the client, he must need to spend today time to aplan or organize how to arrange either business proposal content for the business client or organizational operational challenge questions and solutions for his 200 employees . So, today time management is also important time resource to influence tomorrow either the success business meeting or the organizational 200 employees meeting. So, it seems that time management may be one important resource to any managers more than general employees in any organizations. So, Amazon is one big organization, it employees global many staffs, it ought need to manage its different kinds intangible and tangible resources in order to achieve the most efficient departments operational aim.

Organization efficient using resources economic method

In behavioral economic view , any organizations can attempt to apply behavioral economy method to use resources efficiently. Organizational excellence framework performance measurement takes a systematic approach . One of the most effective ways of using resources and minimizing that use of work. Calculating task cost in the most efficient economic method to help organizations to reduce cost and avoid resources waste, e.g. using resource management software, technology, planning and taking a systematic approach , which aims to manage the most efficient steps to follow to finish or implement each task in the most shor time as well as avoiding excess employees number.

Organizational resource efficiency means using the organization's limited resources in a sustainable manner when minimising impacts on the organization performance. It allows the organization to create more with less and to deliver greater value with less money. HR, raw material, technology input to carry on any organizational resources efficiently ? Management is the process of using organizational resources to achieve organizational goals of using organizational resources to achieve organizational goals effectively and efficiently through planning , organizing , leading and controlling. An efficient organization makes the most productive use of its resource in the most short time and the most eficiency and the least cost aspects.

● What is efficient use of resources to any organizations in economics?

Economic efficiency implies an economic state in which every resource is optimally allocated to serve each individual or entity in the best way when minimizing waste and inefficiency. whan an economy is economically efficient, any changes made to assist one entity would harm another . Hence, budget how much spending on resources, e.g. employee saley, office and/or plant technological equipment facilities , before making resource expenditure spending decision. Budget is essnetial to help the organization to deduce resource using and excess purchase waste since budget and resource of organizations have interlock or interconnet relationship. If the organization can make exact udget, then it can avoid excess expenditure or waste resource to use. So, organizations need to acquire a talented resource pool , that can lead projects to success, when any kinds of resources are achieved to be supplied to use inn enough . For example, using an effective enterprise resource management system that delivers capabilities. Regardless of the approach and tools used, organizations must determine how to balance to use any kinds of resources efficiently. Thus, in organizational efficient resource using behavioral economy view, the organizational efficiency factor means that influences the efficiency of the organization's use if its resources can be both internal and external, e.g. how implementing strategic plans, they may include selecting what methods and resources to use, and leadning employees on guideline, working in coalitions with organizations around to deliver those needs in the most resource efficient way.

In organizational studies, resource managemetn is the efficient and one resource management technique of resource leveling, of finding the answers to the question, how to use available resource efficiently, effectively and economically ot organization resource expense. SO , resource management is the process of allocating resources and allocating.

● What is meant by economic using of resource to organizations?

Economic resources are the factors used in producing goods or providing services. Economic resources can be divied into human resources, such as labors and management, and non humann resource, such as land, capital , goods, finished resources and technology , for example, natural resource is a key input in the production process that stimulates economic growth. Natural resources have limited direct economic use in satisfying human need, but transforming them into goods and services enhances their economic value to the socirty. So, if the country has many organizations know how to use their natural resources input in that production processes. Then, they can create themselves economic benefits directly and attribute economic benefit to society indirectly.

Thus, the types of economic organizations can be identified, there are subsistence recipreocal exchange with subsistence, peasant with primary reliance on self-produced food, but containing some exhange elements, market-commercial , redistribution or state socialist. Thus organizations need to learn hoe to use themselves organizational resources efficiently. Organizational resources are all assets that are to a firm for use during the production process. The four basic types of organizational resources are human, monetary, raw material and capital. Organizational resources are combined , used and transformed into finished products during the production process. So, a business that understands how to use resources efficiently. resource management is the process of allocating resources in order for a company to grow easily.

Organizational economic is used to study transactions within individual firms and determine management approach to managing resources. It is broken down into thee major subjects: agency theory, transaction cost economic and property rights theory. Agency theory is a priinciple that is used to explain and resolve issues in the relationship between business principles and their agents. Most commonly, that relationship is the one between shareholders as principles, and company executives as agents. Agency theory is used to understand the relationship between agents and principals. The agent represents the principal in a particular business transaction and is expected to represent the best interests of the principal without regard for seld interest. So, when the relationship between shreholders and company executives is kept the best.

Transaction cost economic is understood as alternative modes of organizing transactions (governance structure, such as markets, firms and bureaus) that mininize transactions costs. This, cost is the primary determinant of such as firm's decision whether it is the most right (the best) or the worst decision. It will influence the firm ho to spend resource behavior. The cost other than the money price that are incurred in trading good and service. SO, if the organization can often make the best decision to carry on any activites. It will avoid to waste resources efficiently. For example, if transaction cost influces the commission, paid to a stockbroker for completing a share deal and booking fee charges when purchase concert tickets. The cost of travel and time to complete an exhange , it means that transaction cost. So if the organization can make the best or the most reasonable decision to carry on any business activities. Then, its transaction cost can be influenced to reduce the most level in order to bring resources economic benefit. e.g. sunk costs are indpeendent of any event and should not resulting from economic trade in a market.

Property right theory means contracted choice, through ownership, property rights theour clarifies the firm's boundary choice. The maon egal property rights are the right of possession, the righ tof excession. So, for the efficiency of property rights al scarce resources are owned by someone. IN the right property rights approsed to the theory of the firm, I assume that in the case of sale ownership by party-property rights define the theoretical and legal ownership of resources and how resources can be used by organizatin. So, above three major organizational theories can assist organizations to know how to spend resources efficiently.

The relationship between organization resources using and social resources

Resources needers may include societies needers ,e.g. government house material householders , electricity , water , natural resources needers, schools, public houses , land number and area needs etc. as well as business organiztions , office building material, office, plant, land area, number need, equipment facilities limited number . So, when global office and plant business users need to buy more land, equipment materials etc. and electricity , water. Social resources number reduces to bring resourcee shortage challenge causes. Have they have shortage relationship (resource demand number is more than supply number) between social resources need and business resource need? I shall attempt to explain this question as below:

I assume global business organization number increases, they will need many natural resources, e.g. water, electricity, gas, land to supply for office, plant building , material and staff office electricity, gas, plant , office daily essential power need. So, when global business organizations number increases, they may need to use much raw material and natural resources for equipment facility, office plant building material, even day office, plant electricity , gas power, staff drinking water etc. basic office operational needs, when global business organizations number increase.

The question concerns whether they will cause natural resources shortage to supply to social need , when global business organizatins number increases. First, I shall explains what social resources needers mean as below:

● Social resource are defined as any concrete or symbolic term that

can be used as an object of exchange among people (Foa & Foa, 1980), money, information, goods and services both tangible items , such as are ususally defined the assessment of social need is of central allocation between organization needers and social citizen needers both stakeholders. So, when global human birth rate and life time increases, population number will increase, then their social resources need are also increasing, if global organizaions and population number are increasing in the same time, due to earth natural resources has limit number to supply in order to satisfy organizations and families daily resources need, e.g. building material resources are used to build either to build offices, plants or private houses , public house, lands resources are used either to build private or public houses or offices , plants , water is supplied to either office staffs drinking or families drinking, electricity , gas resources are limited to supply either offices plants use or families private or public houses use. Hence, due to all of earth, but in the same time, global offices , plants, government organizations and families numbers both stakeholders number is continue increasing. They have possible to encounter natural resources shortage issue when natural resources are using much, but they can nt manufacturers to increase by human easily.

● Can responding to resource scarcity help some kinds business grow?

Foe example, the food and agricultural business organizations, e.g. supermarkets, restaurants, they must send plactic material to manufacture plactic bags to supply to supermarket buyers to carry fruits, breads, mil, etc. foods when consumers need to buy the kinds of foods in any supermarkets, if plactic material supply number is decreasing, then a lot plactic bags can not supply to let buyers to carry their foods, due to plactic bags number is shortage , it will cause any supermarket buyers feel inconvenient when they need plactic bags to carry their foods, they choose to buy the kind of foods from supermarket to themselves homes.

So, if plactic bags manufacture material i shortage, it can not be manufactured to plactic bags to supply to global supermarket organizations. Then, the one supermarket can provide enough plactic bags to let them to carry their foods from supermarkets to themselves homes conveniently. The focus on plactic bag resource scareity is not impossible to occur to supermarket organization case. If families are often using plactic bag to carry rubbish daily at home. Then, plactic bags number can not increase to satisfy global supermarkets food plactic bags and families themselves homes rubbish plactic bags both stakeholders need. Plastic bags can not be manufactured to supply to manufacture lot plactic bags supply to satisfy global families rubbish plactic bags home users and supermarkets food plactic bas users needs. Consequently, plactic bags prices may be influenced to increases, when plactic bags demand increases, but supply decreases. It is one good exaple to explain why plactic bag manufacturered material supply decreases, it may influence plactic bags number decreases and price increases, because families home rubbish plactic bags and supermarket food plastic bags need both increase.

Consequence, supermarket cost may be influenced , due to plastic bags number also increase much, if one day shortage of plactic manufacturing material supply number is shortage. So, it seems that food plastis bags using number, they have close relationship to impact supermarket food plastic bags price, if supermarkets lack enough plastic bag number supplies, then they need to increase food price, even the supermarket may lose customers , if it can not supply plastic bags to let them to use the supermarket itself plastic bags to carry fruits, ,ilk, soft drinks conveniently. Hence, plastic bag material may be one kind of important natureal resource for supermarkets, because any one consumer may be influenced to choose another supermarket when he/she feels the another supermarket can supply plastic bags to let him/her to carry on fruits, milks, soft drinks conveniently.

Another kind of natureal resource , such as steel material for restaurants , steel material can help global restaurants to manufacture kniefs, glass sups for restaurants customers to eat food or drink , if much steels are used to manufactured cars product to satisfy car drivers' driving lesiure need , then it may also influence restaurants s' knieves, glass cups price increases, due to cost increase, restaurants need to increase food price to compensate its knief, glass cups price. even, many families feel need to buy many gloass cups to drink water, then it may also influence global glass cups price increase. If one day steel material is shortage , this kind of natural resource must influence restaurants glass cups , knief cost increases. So, their general food price may be influenced to increase. It is not fair to global restaurants food consumers.

Hence, it explains resource shortage may influence some kinds of business cost increases, as well as consumer foods, products services price increases. It means that " resource shortage may influence some kinds of businesses cost increases".

In fact, in our societies, natural resource shortage may influence any kinds of business cost increases, w.g. car manufacturing industry, if one day stell manufacturing material is shortage. it will cause many car manufacturers can not buy enough steels to manufacture cars. When, global car buyers number increases, but global cars number can not increase rapidly, due to steel material can not supply enough. Then, cars prices may be influenced to raise. SO, it seems that steel resource shortage may bring reasonable chance to let global car manufacturers to raise cars prices. When , global car buyes ' new car purchase needs are increasing, hence, natural resource shortage may influence some kinds of business produce prices increase in possible, when the kind of product , such as many people begin to chose to buy new cars, more than second hand cars. The, when steel material supplies shortage, it may influence new car price increases in global can market.It means that any organizations ought not waste natural resource. Otherwise, it may influence their cost increases.

Environmental resource scarcity would likely have been adaptivve in the human evolitionary parst, resources in the environment and organization resource shortage problem might alsoo effect how satisfied they were. Hence, organizations in virtually every industry face the challenge of new managing resources effectively. The influence would run the other way instability as rival, such as big data platforms for e-commerce organizations, e.g. e-book publishers, online sellers. Big data platforms lift limitations on the size of computing resources that can be applied for data, in other words, data storage and e-commerce organizations can significantly influence computing efficiency.

Hence, organizational resources may also influence computer industry information gathering intangible resources, if the electronic books publish, or online electronic commerce product sellers can gather the most up-date consumer individual purchase behavioral data in short time daily rapidly. Then, they collect the most accurate electronic books readers or the kind of online product buyers past purchase choice in order to judge whther which topics of books are the most popular or which kinds of product to the most popular to let them to implement sale strategy, e.g. whether which topic of e-books prices need to be increased ot decreased, whether which kinds of products prices need to be increases or decreased. So, the big data gathering speed is the technology resource to e-commerce market organizations.

Amazon Organizational Intangible Management Resource Strategy

Management science how applies to Amazon ecommerce organization

Management accounting concept can help organizations to do management budget strategies, e.g. margin analysis, capital budget, inventory valuation and product cost budget, trend analysis and forecast . Management accounting also called managerial accounting or cost accounting, is the process of analysis business costs and operations to prepare internal financial report, records and managers decision making process in achieving business goals.

However, management accountants depend on standard financial statements containing the earning statement, cash flow statement and balance sheet. In addition , it also makes use of additional finds reports in analysizing the information of the organization including budget performance and cost reports. I shall attempt to explain how management account science can help organizations to analyze cost , why and how changes in order to avoid expense increases or excess cost cases or loss increases.

For Amazon e-commerce publish organization example, Amazon publish is a famous publish organization. It applies internet (online) channel to help authors to sell electronic books and paper books to different countries readers. It also cooperate to other publishers to deliver any its anthors books to their webstores, so when one reader chooses its publish partner webstores to buy Amazon any author books, then Amazon publish will share royalty income between them. Hence, Amazon publish may be book distribution partner to its other e-publish partners.

● How resource management can help Amazon publish to manage its cost effectively in order to increase its profit or e-books or paper books sale ability.

Amazon publish is a e-comerce organization. It depends high internet speed to help global authors to register Amazon publish's individual author account , then any global authors may download their book files to produce any ebooks and papers to sell from Amazon publisher webstores as wellas global any readers can apply Amazon publish webstores to buy any author individual paper or ebooks from its web-publish stores rapidly. So, Amazon publish must need have fast speed internet technology to support its books sale ability,

It brings this question: How much does Amazon publish internet expenditure need? Does it need to pay shops rent per month? Because Amazon publish has none any actual book shops to locate in any countries. So, Amazon publish must not pay rent to any countries for its shops. Although Amazon publish does not need to pay rent for any book shops, but Amazon publish needs to pay extra internet expenditure to US internet service provider to support its electronic webstores daily electronic books and paper books every purchase transaction, any countries author individual book electronic files download per day 24 hours . So, Amazon publish must need to pay more expenditure for internet service to support its authors and readers their electronic books and paper books purchase and sale transaction per day 24 hours.

As Amazon publish case, in its financial report indicates , it does not pay any book stores rent expenditure or book stores (shops) building building expediture on its profit and loss account, but Amazon publish must need to pay internet service expenditure to US internet service provider. Moreover, this internet service expenditure must be more amount, due to it needs to provide its webstores online book (electronic books and paper books) to sell and electronic library e-book lending service to global readers, 24 hours. Thus, internet service expenditure must be Amazon publish long-term influential transaction expenditure because, any electronic books and paper books, even e-library books borrow service and readers must need to pay visa card for borrowing book month service fee and purchase books from amazon publish e-publish webstores in any time every day.

Hence, Amazon publish must need have good management account strategy in order to predict whether different countries will have how many readers click to its different countries e-publish webstores to spend time to choose different authors books to buy or borrow to read from intenet channel. So, any countries readers budgeting number, readers reading habit behavior, e.g. US has about one million online readers click Amazon e-publish webstores , but it has only three thousands readers pay visa card to buy its ebooks and paper books from its Amazon electronic publish webstores, in this week , but next week, US has about seven thousands online readers click Amazon e-publish webstores, but it has three thousands readers pay visa card to buy its ebooks and paper books. Hence, it seems tha although this week has one million online readers click to Amazon publish electonic webstores to seek any books, but the book buyer number has only three thousands. Otherwise, although next week, it reduces three thousands e-readers click to visit Amazon e-publish webstores e-readers number , but it still keep same three thousand e-readers to choose to buy Amazon publish's books to read.

I assume that Amazon publish needs to pay a fixed internet service expenditure, e.g. US $500,000, but it design this e-publish webstores can help it to do its different countries e-publish webstores, their daily e-readers visiting number, daily electronic book and paper book sale number and daily e-readers visiting time statistics. It's electronic publish webstores can help it to record any countries' reading habits and reading taste , e.g. how many fiction , story books have sold in the week, how many non fiction books have sold in the week , e.g. business topic books have sold next week.

So, Amazon publish can use its e-publish webstores to gather above data in order to make author book topic sale choice, e.g. whether this week, US market ought sell how many consumer psychological topic book, US market ought sell how many management topic book next week. If this week US market can only sell one thousand consumer psychological topic book to compare its budget is less than one thousand consumer psychological topic books budget sale number reduces, e.g. in the week, there are two thousands readers choose to buy consumer psychological topic books from European market in this week. It implies that there are many European readers who like to read consumer behavior books recently. Hence, Amazon can attempt to concentrate on encouraging authors to write more consumer psychological books to let European readers to read within next several months.

Basic on above effects, Amazon needs to provide rapid internet service to European libraries, schools ,e-book partners to help them to promote Amazon consumer psychology topic books in order to let the European consumer psychological students, consumer psychology lecturers, consumer psychologists to know Amazon publish can provide more different topics concern consumer psychology research in order to increase Amazon 's consumer psychology book European market book buyers bumber.

As above case, I assume Amazon publish needs to pay a fixed internet service expenditure , e.g. US$500,000 per month. Amazon needs webstores to evaluate whether it is value, if it helps European schools, libraries organizations to pay internet fee, in order to let they can let many consumer psychology students and teachers and consumer psychologists to know that Amazon publish may have enough different consumer psychology books to be provided to European publish libraries, schools readers to read. For example, I assume next several month, Amazon publish needs to pay US two million internet service expenditure to global different European countries to help Amazon publish itself to promote its al different authors' consumer psychology topic books as well as it evaluates that it will sell different European countries; students , teachers and consumer psychologists readers, they have about three million readers at least choose to buy its one million consumer psychology topic authors; paper books and electronic books next several months as well as it also needs to evaluate whether it can earn more than US ten million at least royalty income after reducing author royalty from all European countries book markets.

Thus, if Amazon publish makes decision to help European countries schools, public libraries to pay internet expenditure to help it to advertise its one million consumer psychology topic authors electronic and paper books to sell. It must needs to pay fixed US$500,000 internet expenditure for Amazon publish its all e-bpublish webstores and it also needs to pay extra two million internet service expenditure for global all European countries libraries and schools per month. If next month, Amazon publish can earn more than US tem million at least royalty income after reducing author royalty from all European countries book market. Then, Amaozn publish ought attempt to make this internet service expenditure for all European schools, libraries organizations, if it had confidence to earn this royalty amount from European consumer psychology book readers, such as this Amazon publish.

On conclusion, , this Amazon publish organization case, it may attempt to apply management accounting science method to make book sale number budget, royalty income budget, even analysis to reader individual reading habit, book topic choices, book sale price evaluation in order to judge whether the kind or topic book ought concentrates on selling to which countries marekts, such as Amazin publish case, it also may choose different consumer psychology topic books to concentrate on selling to different European countries in next several months, if it can earn all European royalty income more than its internet service expenditure to European schools, libraries, then Amazon may attempt to make this decision. Otherwise, it won't be good decision.

Hence, it implies that management accounting is one kind of business management science, it can apply number to help any organizations to do right or reasonable reason more accurate as well as it is different to traditional financial acounting, it only helps organizations to record and income and expenditure, earn or loss record function. Hence, management accounting may help any organizations to attempt implement useful or effective strategies in order to improve themselves performance.

How resource management helps Amazon makes the most reasonable choice to invest different market ?

Can we apply management hent accounting concept to investment decision aspect? An organization's investment decision may make risk, so they need risk evaluation to decide whether the project can bring ehat benefit before they want any decisions. Risk management is the process of assessing, managing and mitigating losses . This applies to both business and investing risk management exists in many forms throughout the financial world, such as one individual investor decides to buy low risk government securities, instead of high yield corporate bonds in an example of risk managment companies and investors frequently use financial managment method like options, and future and strategies, like portfolio and investment diversification, in order to effectively manage risk.

For investment management strategy example, it is professional asset management of various securities, including shareholdings, bonds and other assets, such as real estate, in order to meet specified investment goals for the benefits of investors. Investors may be insurance companies, pension funds, corporations, charities, educational organizations or private invetors.

The term asset management is often used to refer to the management of investment funds. So managerial accounting is the process of identifications, measurement , analysis and interpretation of accounting information that helps business leaders make financial decisions and efficiently manage their day operation . The main objective of managerial accounting is to maximize profit and minimize losses . It is concerned with the presentation of data to predict inconsistencies in finances that help managers make important decisions, such as investment decision for Amazon publish book sale country market choice for which topic of books which are the most popular, in order to concentrate on selling the topic of books to the country market. So, Amazon publish needs to gather past different kinds for any one country, number data may include each author ebook and paper books sale prices, each author different book topic books sale number , in order t make which topic of book sale to which countries investment decision aims to increase readers number t o the country book sale market. So, Amazon publish may be apply these tools of management accounting to gather datas to concern book sale record. They may include: Financial accounting, financial statement analysis, book cost accounting, fund flow analysis , cash flow analysis, standard costing, marginal cost, budgetary control , management accounting tools.

● How intangible resource management skill helps Amazon publish to make investment decision?

The main aim of management accounting to investment includes planning, controlling and evaluating. Thus, the advatanges to investment may include; better decision making, increase business efficiency, simplify financial statement, raises profitability, motivates employees, cost control, reliability. Hence, management accounting means " mental accouting", it is a concept in the field of behavioral economies. Mental accouting refers to the different values of person places on the same amount of money, based on subjective criteria, often with detrimental results. Mental accouting is a concept in the field of behavioral economies. Developed by economist Richard H, it contends that individuals classify funds differently and therefore are prone to irrational decision making in their spending and investment behavior. It refers to the different values people value on money, based on subjective criteria, that often has detrimental results, mental (managerial)accounting decisions and behave in financially counterproductive or detrimental ways, such as funding a low interest savings account when carrying learge credit card balances, to avoid the mental (managerial) accounting bias, individuals should treat money as perfectly used tools when they allocate among different accounts, be it a budget account (everyday living expenses), a spending account or a wealth account (saving and investment). Also abother author indicates that managerial accounting means mental accounting, which appeared in the Journal of behavioral decision making, the begins with this definition, " mental accounting" is the set of lognitive operations used key individuals and households to organize, evaluate , and keep tracks of financial activities. He considers of how mental accounting leads to irrational spending and investment behavior.

I believe that Amazon publish may apply mental accounting concept to help it to predict whether which topic of books will be the most popular to sell to the country market more accurately. The reason concerns that it can apply all data gathering to analyze whether past has how many readers paid visa to buy the topic of electronic or paper books to prepare to the country , e.g. in this year, Jan. it had 40,000 readers buy fiction electronic books and paper books from Amazon publish US market website to read , it had 100,000 readers buy fiction electronic and paper books to read in European market website and the year Feb. It had 70,000 readers paper books from Amazon publish US market website, it had 200,000 and paper books from Amazon publish European market website. Now, it is Mar. So, Amazon publish may make assumption that fiction (story) topic book is accepted to read by American and European readers, due to US fiction readers had increased 30,000 number in past one month and European fiction readers had increased 100,000 number in past one month.

However, US and European readers number data is not enough to evaluate whether US and European fiction readers number may still keep to increase. It depends on other factors, e.g. fiction e-book and fiction paper book sale price, if one author's ficton's ebooks and paper books rising prices whether it will influence US and European fiction book buyers make book purchas decision to the author's any fictions. So, Amazon publish need s to make the author's past different kinds of fiction books sale prices record in order to judge whether his fiction book's variable price (changing price) will bring negative or positive impact to his readers' fiction book purchase decision. For exmaple, if the author (A)'s one fiction price increased 10% to ebook and paper book sale price between Jan and Feb. His fiction readers number won't be influenced to reduce, even his fiction readers number can still increase 10%. So, it implies that this author's fiction is attract or popular to US and Eurpopean fiction reader market. Amazon publish ought concentrate on helping this author (A) to advertise his fiction to let many US and European readers to know.Hence, it explains that Amazon publish may attempt to gather past every author individual writing book topic book sale proce whether it is increased or decreased how much %, book sale number in order to make book sale investment decision to concentrate on helping whom to advertise to sell to which book sale country market.

So, it seems that mental accounting concept can be applied to Amazon publish to help it to do any author individual book sale country market advertisement investment decision. For example, if Amazon publish can only spend US$10,000 advertieing expenditure to help author (A) to sell fictions to US and European both markets in Mar. , then it can help author (A) to increase 20% more fiction sale number to US and European both markets. This advertisement expenditure is worth to spend for this author (A) in fiction market.

Hence, it implies that mental accounting concept can be applied to publish investment market, such as choosing which country to sell which topic of books, e.g. US sells more which fiction or European sells more fiction or Japan sells more management business topic books or UK sells more consumer psychology business topic books. All of these issues will be any publisher's important book sale market decision . It may influence their royalty income because if the publisher makes wrong decision to sell not popular topic books to the country market, e.g. in the month, US ought have many business topic readers to choose any business topic books to buy from any publishers, if the publisher makes wrong decision to find many fiction authors to help it to increase fiction stock to prepare to sell to US book market. Then, excess fiction stock may cause low fiction price (fiction book supply or publisher's fiction stock number) is more than fiction book demand (readers). Otherwise, it can not increase business topic books royalty inocme to US book market, because it has not enough different topic, such as management, consumer psychology , accounting, economy , marketing topic business books stock to be putted on book shelves to let US readers to choose when they visit US any book shops in the month.

On conclusion, it explains why mental (managerial) accounting has close relationship to influence customer behavior in behavioral economy view. Mental accounting is a management science or behavioral science tool to help any businessmen to make the most effective or the most reasonable busines decision in nowadays society.

Management science accounting concept how to help Amazon to presict market changing

Accounting aims to help any organizations to record whether the year has what kinds of expenditures, how much of every kind of expenditure finds what factors to cause the kind of expenditure needs to be spent too much in order to avoid excess spending, measurement profict or loss level why what factors cause the year had loss or profit growth in order to achieve long term performance improvement or avoiding loss. Hence, accounting system is not only for bookkeeping record financial performance aim. Accoungint may be one kind management science concept to be applied to explain why and how market changes in order to predict whether the company ought implement which strategies to grow up its business groth or increase clients number.

The question concerns why the organization can apply accounting concpet to predict how the market will change in order to avoid profit falls down or loss causes. I shall attempt to explain as below:

For a watch product sale organization example, this watch sale compay own 100 expensive price watch brand products stock to prepare to sell, their sale prices are between US$3,000 to US$5,000 , so the watch brand prices are below than US$3000, they belong to low prices. It has 100 low price watch brand products stock to prepare to sell. Hence, every month, it keeps exact 100 high price of brand watch products stock and exact 100 low price of brand watch products stoc to prepare to sell. I assume this watch company can sell 100 low price watches and 100 high price watches in this month, but next month, it can sell 50 low price watches and 0 high price watches. Hence, it means that next watch , low prices watches sale number falls 50 number and high price watches sale numbe falls 100 number. It ensures that this company's profit may be influenced to fall by the high and low watch price client reducing number factor. However, this company still lacks data to know whether its competitors ; watch price is the main factor to influence its watch buyers number reduces or whether other factors influence its watch buyers number reduces, e.g. whether its high and low watchs are attractive or not attractive to high its watch design buyers number reduces or whether smart phone product invention influences watch users begin feel watchs have not be importnt to help them, because smart phones have time record function, they can replace traditional watch products or this month has higher unemployment rate, so it causes people do not like spend easily , in special, watch is not one kind essential product. Hence, it seems that this watch company can investigate its every month whether its low and high price watch stock sale record in order to attempt tp find whether what are the main factor to cause its watch sale number increases or decreases? I shall follow above every possible points to be investigated by accounting concept in order to explain why its watch low and high price customer number sudden reduces.

I assume that this watch company's last month and this month every high and low price watch brand's sale prices are stable. So, it seems that the influential factor won't be its " increasing sale price" to cause its high and low watch price customers number sudden reduces. If it gathered data concerns its watch competitots similar famous watch brands of general price range. It discovered their general sale prices do not have much difference between itself and their famous brnad of watchs. Also, it discovered that their these famous brand high and low price watch sale number is more than its sale number, e.g. the another similar famous watch brand company can sell 200 high price watchs and 200 low price watchs last month and 400 high price watchs and 400 low prcice watch this month. So, it seems that its high and low price of watch is not main factor to influence its watch sale number, because its high and low price watch's their price level had not changeed within these two months . Mooreve, its watchs manufacture material costs had not increased within these two months. So, it ensures that its profit falls must not be influenced by watch manufacture cost increasing factor. Hence, it may depends on its accounting record to conclude the main factors influence its high and low price watch sale number reduces, they may include; poor watch design feeling to watch buyers factor, smart phones increasing need factor, unemploymenr rate rising factor.

The next step concerns how this watch company can apply accounting concept to find whether the main factor is poor watch design feeling factor, or smart phones are popular accepted to replace watch product feeling factor, or rising unemployment rate factor which one influences it s high and low price range watch sale number decreases can apply accounting cencept to investigate which is the main factor to influences its watch sale number decreased in this two months? I shall attempt to confirm this possibility as below:

Firstly, I assume this watch company's accounting record has marketing promotion expenditure, its expenditure includes advertisement fee, exhibition expense only, however, in its expenditure group accounting record, it has none design expenditure with these two months. Hence, it seems that its high and low price range fanous brands watches had not been improved by its improvement design skill method in order to improve their watch style, picture, shape, colour, function , design to satisfy watch buyers'changing watch fashion need in this competitive market. Hence, it seems that poor watch design feeling factor may be one main factor to influence its watch sale number decreases. It implies that accounting record may help it to find lacking new fashion watch design factor may be one main influential factor to cause watch buyers choose to buy other similar famous brands' watch products.

Next, whether accounting concept can help this firm to judge whether smart phones influences its watch sale number? I assume that smart phone products had been selling more than 10 years in this country in this case indicates US country. So, smart phones mus be its long time similar time seeing function competitors in US. I assume that its past 10 years high and low price range famous brand watches sale number must be more than these two months as well as it had not increases high and low price range of watches prices within this 10 years. Hence, it can depend on its past 10 years accounting record to judge whether smart phones product invention may influence watch buyers number decreases within these two months. basic on its past 10 years , accounting record indicated that its high and lw price range watch sale number had been increasing, and it s watch price had not beedn increased and its markting advertisement promotion expense had been reducing much within 10 years. Thus, its past watching expense and watch price sale amount and profit accounting record may help it to conclude that smart phone product sale to US market is not the main factor to influence its recent high and low price range watchs sale number falls.

Finally, I shall explain whether this watch company may apply accounting concept to explain whether this month's high unmployment rate factor can influence geeral watch buyers' consumption desire as below:

I assume that this watch company employed 20 watch salespeople and their salaries range are between US$2,000 to US $4,000 per month in the first years . It operated till to this month total 20 years . However, its accounting record indicated that its watch salespeople number had been increasing from 20 to 50 number recently and their salaries range had been increading between US$3,000 to US$6,000 permonth. Hence, within these 10 years , this watch company employees number and their salaries range had been continue increasing. . It may depend on its past 10 years accounting record for salespeople salaries and employee number to reflect whether higher unemployment rate is the main factor to influence its watch sale number reduces.

I assume that within these 10 years, its unemployment rare was between 1% to 10%, in US society , although it may had 1% to 10% young people unemployed within 10 years. But, this watch company, I could also increased salespeople employees number and their salaries could also increase more significantly, even their salaries had not decreased in these 10 years. Hence, its accounting record of salsepeople salaries increasing trend , it may reflect this US watch market's local and overseas watch buyer individual buying watch desires ought not be influenced by slight rising unemployment rate factor, it is based on that this watch company will like to increase salespeople employee number, when it discovered there were many potential watch buyers visited its any watch shops every day within past 10 years. Hence, it implies higher unemployment rare won't influence watch potential buyer individual visiting to any one watch shops in US within these 10 years. So, this watch company's past salespeople salaries, employees number, and their salaries rising range record can reflect whether US higher unemployment ratio level can influence its recent high and low price range of watchs sale number decreases in US local watch sale market.

On conclusion, we can depend this watch company past 10 years accounting record to judge whether which one may be the most main fluential factor to influence its recent watch sale number reduces. I make the final conclusion that its poor watch design feeling factor ought be its main factor to influence its recent watch sale number reduces, due to it had not spend any design expenditure to improve its watch style in order to attract many watch buyers' choices within these 10 years. So, I believe that accounting concept can help any companies to revise whether what factos influence their businessess to be better or worse, instead of general booking record function.

Accounting trademark loyalty theory

In accounting theory view, any organizational goodwill or trademark, they are intangible asset because they can not touch, they are the company name. However, when the organization grows up a long time, ususally more than 10 years, if they are famous when consumers choose to buy the kind of product, they will must remember, then the organization's trademark or goodwill, company names will become the company's intangible asset in their balance sheet , financial report, e.g. Cock Coke soft drink, " Coca Coke" may be this soft drink company's trademaek , intangible asset to this soft drink company. Because any country's soft drinkers, they must remember Coca Coke brand soft drink before they make any brands of soft drink purchase choice. The reason may be Coca Coke soft drink . Its brand had been popular to be accept to be the first soft drink choice to any countries people. Hence, Coca Coke soft drink compnay must put is brand name to be intanginle asset in balance sheet, (B/S),

Why does Coca Coke's brand name (intangible asset) value may increase or decrease in B/S. The reason is simple, when general consumers feel Coca Coka drink has better taste to compare other brands soft drinks. Then, they wil choose other brand soft driks to replace Coca Coke soft drink. So, if the year, Coca Coke's any taste of soft drinks sale number decreases, then it will feel its intangible asset of trademark value is devaluation, but if its soft drink sale number increases in this year. Its intangible asset of trademark value will increase in its B/S.

Hence, it explains why Coca Coke 's trade mark value can reflect its soft drink sale number whether it increases or decreases in the year. Thus, any firms mist hope their trademark , goodwill valuation can often increase every year.

The question concerns how they can often keep their trademark valuation to increase? Can the firm increase sale number , it can represent that it has long term goodwill valuation increases? Can other factors influence or impact the firm's goodwill valuation changes? I shall attempt to give examples to explain these questions as below:

In fact, goodwill or trademark represents the company's famility whether how many consumers can remember its brand name , when they choose to buy the kind of product . So, if the firm's products are famous in market, Its products must have many consumers can remember it before they choose to buy the kind of product. So, product's familiar to publish,which ill be one measurement tool to judge whether what may be its goodwill valuation. If there are many consumers remember its brand before they want to buy the kind of products, the firm ought raise its goodwill valuation. It may make market research to enquire whether consumer will choose to buy which brand of product among several similar brands of product. It many people choose to prefer to buy its brand. Then, its brand familiar level to publis will be high grade. It may raise to goodwill valuation inB/S.

So, I think that goodwill fact valuation can not be measured by sale number or sale price or profit or loss amount. It ought be measured by market familiar level. If the product can have many people know its brand exitence in market. Then, its goodwill , intangible asset valuation ought be increased. Otherwise, if there are not may people know or they are familiar its brand existence in market. Then, its probable valuation ought need to decrease . Hence, any firms' goodwill valuation ought reflect their market familiar level for standard.

Do you feel firm goodwill valuation can represent its market value or product sale effort? In accounting principle, goodwill valuation must be measured by money. For example, Coca Coke brand goodwill valuation, in fact, Coca Coke had not pay another in B/S. Its goodwill valuation increases, it is not due to it pays its firm pays cash to buy goodwill. It is due to its capital increase. But, in fact, it does not need to increase cash to capital balance amount in B/S. Because coca Coke has not increase its cash amount, due to goodwill valuation increases. Its goodwill valuation increases, it supposes that is capital amount also be influenced to increase. So, Coca Coke 's goodwill valuation can not represent it has profit growth. Goodwill valuation only represents it has profit growth. Goodwill valuation only represents Coca Coke's present market valuw whether it increases or decreases in soft drink market. It is not actual cash available value. So, why firms need have goodwill valuation. The reason is simple. If one day, the firm hopes to sell its busines to another. When the another potential business buyer feels this firm's goodwill valuation is high. It may persuade b make business purchase decision more easily. because he believes that there are many people are famkliar this product brnad , then they will choose to buy theis product in preference . So, good goodwill valuation can build good business sale image to help the firm can raise business sale price to anyone . Such as Coca Coke soft drink goodwill case, if it can keep high goodwill valuation, then it can persuade any businesses buyers accept to pay high business purchase price. so, B/S goodwill valuation may help any famous business to sell to anyone in the high business sale price more easily.

Can goodwill valuation help the firm to predict market environment changes? For Coca Coke soft drink case example, I assume that it estimated its goodwill valuation is US 3 million , but this year, it estimates its goodwill valuation falls down to US one million. What factors influence Coca Coke feels its goodwill valuation reduces US two million in this year? I believe that is current year goodwill valuatin falls, it has relationship to whole global soft drink taste changes to global soft drinkers. The factors influence global drink makes taste changes , they may include: global soft drinkers begin to dislike to choose to drink any brands of soft drink in preference, if they feel soft drink is one kind of bad health drink. They may choose to buy freash fruits to eat to replace any soft drink. I assume that the other soft drink brand companies' goodwill valuations are decrased. It means that if other soft drink brands' goodwill valuation can increase. Then, Coca Coke may believe that there are many soft drinkers prefer to choose other soft drink brands' soft drinks to drink. So, global soft drink markets still have competitive effort. Coco Coke nees to learn how to change its taste and let soft drinkers believe its soft drink can bring health to them to compare other soft drink brands. So, it seems that goodwill valuation also helps any organizations to eveluate how market changes to influence itself product sale effort. It explains why goodwill valuation is one kind of good market changing predictable tool t any businesses in accpunting concept, instead of sale business valuation measurement tool.

On conclusion, accounting principle or accounintg concept is not only be applied to bookkeeping financial record aspect. If the organization hopes to find what factors to influence its customer number or they hope to predict whether market will ought how to change to be netter or worse. It may attempt to investigate its past every year some kinds of expenditure amount record in order to find how any why the firm itself needed to pay more or less to the kind of expenditure. It aims to research what factors may influence its past and present expenditur changes in order to find whether what the most influential factors are influenced itself buyers number increases or decreases . Hence, accounting is one kind of makret research scientific method to any organizations.

Accounting science how predicts e-commerce consumer behavior

Cash e-commerce organizations apply accounting record to predict consumer behaviors? If it is true, how e-commerce organizations can use past accounting record to predict consumer behaviors? In general, e-commerce sale transactions must need any individual e-buyers to register higher address to their e-store in order to deliver products to any one-buyer homes. For Amazon e-commerce organization, when one China client buys a furniture from US Amazon e-commerce organization, when one China client buys a furniture from US Amazon e-store. The furniture is putted to Amazon US itself warehouse. So, when the China e-buyer pays visa to buy the furniture . He needs to register his address to amazon e-store. When amazon confirms that it can receive cash from the China e-buyer visa card, then amazon will deliver the furniture from US amazon warehouse to the China e-buyer home by plane.

So, amazon must have any e-buyer address record and the product sale price record for any one country e-buyer after it comfirms that the e-buye visa card has enough money to buy the product. Thus, amazon can apply past every online transaction to follow these data to do market research, they may include: which country person buys the product, what the product is, how much to the product price, how many of different product number e-buyer purchase within the year. So, amazon can collect all above data to analyze any one country has the highest e-buyer number,e.g. in the year, there ar one million US e-buyers number, there are two million China e-buyer number,which kind of products are the most popular, e.g. soap , computer, furniture, cloth, shoe, shirt, towel, electronic products etc. what the age range is, e.g. young , old, students , workpeople, they choose to buy the kind of product, how many number , the family buys the kind of product to the e-transaction, how many goods return number to the year total e-transaction, how many goods return number to the year total e-transactions.

Hence, amazon can gather all past every e-transaction data to prepare how to predict whether how every country e-transaction will consumer behavior to predict whether how every country e-transaction will influence consumer behavior will change next year in order to let it to prepare how to implement new market strategy,e.g. how to advertise its product, which countries need to spend more advertise to promote its products, evaluate whether amazon needs to spend how much advertisement expenditure to earn more e-sale transactions number to the targe sale country.

Why does amazon's any one e-transaction's accounting record assists it to predict consumer behavior? For china target e-buyers market example, when one Shanghai city e-buyer pays visa to buy one computer from amazon e-store, if the e-transaction can be accepted . Amazon can gather the e-buyer is living in China Shanghai city, which brand of computer , he chooses to buy, how much sale price to the computer, how many of computers number , he buys, how many e-transaction times to the China, Shanghai city buyer within the year. Hence, when amazon needs know where China target market has how many e-buyers number to every city, how many e-transaction return goods and refind number, which kinds of product are the popular to China e-buyers' purchase needs, which is the highest price and the lowest price sale level to China, Shanghai city target e-commerce market every e-transaction . Thus, when amazon collestc all above China, Shanghai past one year any individual e-transaction data, it can compare whether how its China, Shanghai city.

Nest year, e-buyers behavior change in order to analyze whether which kinds of product price ought need to reduce in order to attract many China e-buyers to click amazn webstores to pay visa to buy its products or which kinds of product price may increase, when the kind of product is popular to sell to China target market, or make out of e-stock shelf decision to the kind of product when Amazon discovers the kind of product is not accepted to buy in popular from its e-store. Thus, it seems that Amazon's past any one e-transaction accountning record can help it to analyze whether how every target market its e-buyer behavior is changing in order to change next year sale changing strategy is more reasonable . Hence, it explains why e-commerce organization's accounting record may help it to analyze how future market changes as well as record how every old e-buyer customer whether he/she will choose to buy the kind of old product again or buy new product, even not buy anything from Amazon e-stores this year.

Hence, any e-commerce organization's e-stores can apply online technology skil and accounting concept to help it to learn how to analyze every year post efficient countries' cities different e-buyer individual product behavioral choice in order to judge/revise whether it ought need to change to buy its products from its e-stores conveniently. So, any e-commerce organization explains why it can attempr to apply its post every accounting e-buyer sale transaction record to make every country consumer behavior marketing analysis to compare transaction visiting shop business model more easily, because visiting shop sale model can let the seller to sell its products in its shop, when it locates in the country. But e-commerce sale model can let the product can be sold to different countries more easily.

So, it seems that if the e-commerce organization can have good accounting record system to keep its past all e-transactions record can gather all data concerns any countries e-buyer individual address , how much sale price for the product, how many sold, and refund to the country e-buyers and the e-buyer age is young or old , male or female e-buyer purchase habit.

Can the e-commerce organizatin predict consumer behavior if it implemented inefficiency accounting record system? Firstly, we need to know good or right accounting record system can help the organization to track or find past any transactions more easily. So, if the organization has none good accounting record system , its accounting record system can not be improved efficiently. Then, its accounting record may bring wrong sale price record, wrong profit (over -profit) or less profit or wrong loss (over loss) number record. Then, this wrong sale transaction record may mislead financial performance to publis to know, e.g. current year, its sale performance is improved, but in fact, its current year sale number is less than last year sale number. Consequently, this organization can not predict its consumer behavior. Whether know to change exactly, due to it often has wrong sale number record, e.g. higher or lesser sale price record, and more or less sale number may influence its gross profit earns high amount, even if its any kinds of expense record is more orless, it will influence its net profit is more or less or less is more or less, for example, if the organization earns US one million dollar prodict this year, but due to it smore sale number transaction to cause over profit. So, its financial performance report indicated its earned US two million dollar. So, it believes its buyers number can increase, if its sale prices do not change. This wrong financial performance report many mislead it has good consumer behavior in this year. Then, it will continue implement its old marketing strategy. Consequently, its next year financial performance may be caused worse to compare present. So, it implies that wrong financial record may cause wrong consumer behavior judgement.

Can robots tangible technological resource helps Amazon to do consumer behavior prediction tasks ?

Our future will experience artificial intelligent development stage. Nowadays, we had had some tasks which can be done by robots, e.g. warehouse delivery, restaurnt kitechen dish cleaning tasks, transport tasks, even non drive manual auto driving tasks, shopping center service etc. cleaning or customer service simple jobs duties. If one day, robots cab be applied to do office tasks, e.g. accounting record tasks, they may replace account clersk, even accountants to deal simple accounting record tasks, even complicate management account analysis tasks in office working environment. If future robots can be developed to help accounts clerks as well as accountants to do simple bookkeeping debit and credit every income ot expense transaction record in order to analyze marketing research tasks, then it brings this question: Can future robots replace accounts clerks and accountants to do their accounting tasks in any organizations. I shall attempt to research the relationship between robots and accounting tasks questions as well as whether robots will bring what social influence if robots can replace future human to do any simple and complex accounting tasks for any organizations.

What is need for development of artificial intelligence to accounting tasks aspect? The first computer language used to create artificial intelligence is USP. This language is quite flexible and extensive . Features such rapid prototyping and macro are very useful in creating AI. LISP is a language that makes complex tasks simple. So it seems that it is possible tobots can learn human to do any kinds of accounting tasks, e.g. financial account record, audit check, management account analysis etc. different kinds of acounting tasks for financial , management account, audit check functions in any organizations.

However, scientists believe that artificial intelligence can help accountants be more productive and efficient. Robotic process automation RPA) allows machines or AI workers to complete repetitive, time-consuming tasks in business processed, such as document analysis, handling that are plentiful in accounting . AI can also significantly reduce financial fraud and maintenance accounting errors. Hence, the stages of AI development to accoutning industry, they may include: internet AI, business AI, perception AI, and autonomous AI ., Internet AI is thr simplest stage of AI, business AI has a limted memory, perception AI. This is the first stage in the future of AI. A key feature of this perceptive form of AI is the ability to compile and draw from past experiences, much like human to accounting tasks. The design phase is essentially in literative process comprising all the steps releveant to building the AI or machine learning model, data acquisition, exploration, management and analsis tasks. So, it seems that future robots may be developed to help human to do simple and complex accounting tasks. Combining AI with other technologies, such as robotic, process automation can follow accountants to redirect the time that they used to spend on multiple tasks, toward performing high-value, high -impact taaks. Adding AI to accounting operation can also increase output quality by miniizing human errors. So, AI and automation won't be replacing finance and accounting professionals in the foreseeable futue.

On the contrary, as AI automates many aspects of business, there is a bug opportunity for accounting and finance professsionals to upskill themselves to meet the requirements of the 21 centurey. For AI audit task aspect, AI enables the analysis of a full populatin of data and can identify outliers or expectations. By making it possible for auditors to work better and smarter. AI will help them to optimize their time, enabling them to use their human judgement to analyze a boarder and deeper set of data and documents.

Can AI be used in auditing and accounting ? In the assurance practice, AI is being used to perform auditing and accounting prcedures, such as review of general ledgers, tax compiance, preparing workpapers, data analytic, expense compliance, fraud accounting skills. So, it seems that future AI can replace market research analysists, compensation and benefits managers , instead of financial accountants, management accountants an auditors in any organizations.For bookkeeping clerks position example, these simple account jobs are expected to decrease, by 8% 2024, and it's non surprise because most bookkeeping is getting automated if it has not been as of now, Quickbook, Peachtrss etc. accounting software that does not need any more, because robots do not need any kinds of accounting software to help them to do any simple or complex accounting tasks.

How has teachnology changed the accounting industry? Computers and accounting softeare has changed the industry complexity, with but when robots develop, it will change global accountancy professional more complex. Can robots replace accountants? Automation had brought significant changes the accounting profession over the last decaed. When some tools have made accountants lives easier. However, since robots invention, it developed these tools have also created a false debate about whether automation will overtake the global accounting industry compexity and make accountants irrelvant . The question should not be whether automation will take over accounting, but where its rreal value lives.

In fact, I believe that no any software can match the critical thinkning and trusted counsel that a human advisor offes, as valued accountants, have become business partners, where software is limited to evaluating concrete inputs, accountants can understand clients business goals and observations voice to make decisions. This allows them to serve as advisors to their clients, whether by adjusting business models in real time, or managing emplyer wellbeing . Sok, future AI development ought not replace human accountant's this kind of skill more easily.

● How robotic process automation impact on accouting industry changes?

Searching for methods to efficiently perform accounting tasks can be dated book to the 1950 s, when process mechanisation involved the use of punched cards to store and retrieve transaction data (Keenoy, 1958). Since then IT ad automation have transtormed the way accountants collect, store, process and share data through a variety of tools (Ellis, 1986); Kaye, Nicholson, 1992; Rom, Rohde, 2007). However, robotis process automation is a technology solution that allows end-users to comfigure a software robot to use existing applications to perform accounting transactions manipulate data and communcation with other systems (introduction to robotis, 2015).

Software robots can be easily programmed or trained to perform repetitive, rules-based , high volume operations by replicating human actions when accessing multiple systems, applications, and documents (Embracing robotic automation 2018). Hence, robotic accounting software can bring cost reduction to counting and finance tasks, e.g. one robotic accounting software can replace two to five full time accounting clerks, increased process speed, software robots perform routime tasks faster than employees would manage mamually (Cacity, Willcocks, 2016) . They do not get distracted or tried and thus avoid delays, cycle times decreases significantly improved process control and performance visibility, e.g the collected analytical information is much more detailed and can be used for audit and compliance checks, higher quality data (accuracy, consistency, compliance), e.g. robots can validate the data before reporting or using them future. Assuming that the appropriate rules have been thoroughly tested beforehand, data inaccuracy and quality risk decrease fill tracking and logging robots' action make internal and external audits easier and reduce compliance risks, continuous operation 24 hours a day, or none working day limits. So, robots are applied on accounting task aspect, it can bring positive impact on employees, repetive tasks taken over by robots release employees' times. They can shift their focus on higher value added tasks, solve employee morale proble,. Any accounting department staffs may feel tired when they need over time works, often but robotic accounting staff won't have tired or bored feeling.

However, robotic process, automatin may be applied on these accounting tasks aspect, they may include: internal control period end clising, general ledger, subledgers, closing , validatin of journal entries, low-risk accounts, reconsiliation, consolidation, reporting-monthly , quarterly close, internal performance and management reportng aggregating and analysing financial and operational data, external statutary report, accounts receivable and payable record-maintaining updating customer/supplier data, creating processing, posting payment, collections, billing, matching invoices, aganist sales and purchase orders, cash management, general accoutning, inter-company transactions, inventory accountancye, travel and expenses reimbursement request, audit and document expense report, payroll, stock keeping, fixed asset accouting record, tax accounting. So, the general simple accounting tasks robots will have effort to finish.

● Can robots perform the same management accounting analytical decision making skills to human management accountants tasks?

Although, robots can perform simple bookkeeping audit accounting tasks, but whether complex management accounting analytical and decision making tasks, robots can do the same level of management accounting analytical, decision making tasks to human management accountants?

I shall attempt to answer this question. How robots impact of mental accounting in valuation? No retailers show this price without considering the " 99" in end. This indicates to our mind that the price is cheaper. Its popularity can be verified gas stations all around the world. The difference between robots mental accounting issue and management accountants.

The Anchoring theory was used to verify its possible impacts on capital venture tech finds decisions, during equity trading for an initial investment starting. Management accountants ususally arrange 68% of the finds use-valuation as a basic, when 21% proposed other methods . But still use valuation and only 11% of the investors said they did not consider valuation at allo. the context considered that the human management accountant will consider that the investment would be made in a startup in early stages. That is with little or any real accounting information can image the amount of uncertainty that exists in the type of analysis?

Moreover, why do even experienced fund managers invest based on an impossible calculation> In simplity, it explains that human management accountant in order to do any investment decision. Although robotis will use alaytic mind more than calculating to estimate any investment risk in order to make investment decsion for any organizations. AI's analytic skill and human management accountant calculation risk skill be their difference on how dealing management accounting investment risk issue aspect. Even, the difference between human management accountant and robotic management accounting automation is their robotic management automation can apply mental accounting theory to judge consumer behavioral choice.

It is a new model of consumer behavior is developed using a hyrod of psychology and microeconomics. The deveopment of the model starts with the mental coding of combinations of risks and losses using the prospect theory value finction. Then, robotic management accounting automatin can attempt to evaluate of consumer purchase for the product is modeled using the new concept of " transaction utility", e.g. one family electronic firm, it is seeling rice cooker, television radio, household electronic products, it can learn how to mental accounting method to help this houseold electronic product firm to predict how any why its different kinds of household electronic products choice may change to its consumer behavior next week, e.g. robots can gather wlectronic product competitors prices data to compare itself company's same kinds of electronic product data e.g. rice cooker prices and its competitors' rice cookers prices, whether its high price , rice cookers price factor or other factors influence its rice cookers sale number decreases in this week. Consequently robotic management accounting software may help this household elecronic product company to analyze whether what are the actual factors to influence its rice cookers prces reduce in this week. It is human management accountants feel difficult to collect past price data in order to make accurate consumer behavior changes, prediction or find whther are the main factors to influence product sale number increases or decreases.

Hence, future robotic management accounting automation can learn the valuation of purchase modeled using the new concept of transactin utulitym such as this houseold electronic product case, robotic management accounting automation many learn the household budget process ,the characterization of mental accounting, in order to find whether household purchase behavior to the company's products whether what the main factors may influence its household producys sale number increases or decreased.

On conclusion, future robots can do simple bookkeeping, audit check , general daily accounting tasks, even robots can also do complex management accounting tasks, they can learn how to apply mental accounting knowledge to gather the company's past all every month different price variable data, sale number, in order to conclude whether what are the main factors to influence the kind of product sale number increases or decreased more accurately to compare human management accountants in any organizations.

Applying HR management accounting learns consumer behavior

Managerial accounting purposes to be used by management in "making by business decision: It includes product caost, budget , forecast and various financial analysis consumer behavior is the series of behaving of patterns that consumers follow before making a purchase through consumer behavior, you can also earn how customers interact with and the year products. So, any organizations may attempt to find any management account past year past per month transaction records to bring consumer behavioral change predictiver knowledge, it can help future decisions about product creation more easily.

Hence , the management accoutning knowledge focuses the process of creating organization goals by identifying, measuring, analyzing, interpreting and communicating informations to managers is call management or manerical accounting. Management accounting focuses on all accounting aimed at informing management about operational business metics. Also, any managers may attempt to gather past product number presentation date to find whether what the main factors can influence consumer buying behavioral change in its any kinds of products, the level of motivation also affects the buying behavior of customers, e.g. whether the products' sale prices sight rise, to influence customer number reduces, or whether the product's traditional old design is not more attractive or popular to accept to compare other linds of competitors' similar product design, or whether the kind of product is not popular to be accpeted to use, the another how invention of similar product ot the market is recession , it need to change another new sale market, if replaces its existence etc. different factors.

Hence, management accounting can help managers to attempt to gather past the product's sale and production past data to carry on analyzing whether what the main factor to influence its customer number reduces or increases in other to improve its sale strategy.

● Computer sale applies management accounting to predict consumer behavior

For computer sale product example, the computer saller may attempt to apply management accounting to analyze why computer buyer behavioral changes, e.g. a study of consumer behavior will reveal what kind of consumers buy computers, could they buy for home and personal use or for office, what features , they look for, what benefit o they seek including post purchase service, huw much they are willing to pay how many they are likely to buy . All of these computer buyer individual purchase behavioral analysis, the computer seller can follow its different models of laptops, desttops, prices, sale number, house or office ise design kind etc. data to research and analyze and predict hether future computer buyer individual need will how changes, in order to prepare and learn how to design new kinds of desktops and laptops to raise competitve effort.

In fact, in computer industry, the factors may influence computer buyer behavioral change, they may include core technical features, past purchase services, price and payment, conditions, physical appearanre, value added features and connectivity and ability are the main seven factors that are influencing consumers' laptop purchases choices.

● How can the laptop computer seller applies management accounting data to analyze whether which is the main factor to influence laptop buyer behavior changes?

for last month, I assume that laptop model (A) laptop computer sale price si per US$1000 and it can sold 1000 number and laptop model (B) laptop computer sale price is per US$1,500 and it can sold 2000 number.SO, it implies that although laptop model (B) computer sale price is more than US$500 to compare laptop model (A) computer, but the model (B) laptop computer can still sell more than 1000 number fo compare model (A) laptop computer last moth. It seems that model (B) laptop's attractive dsign, more fuction, rapid connectivity and mobility and attrative physical appearance main factors may influence laptop (B) model computer products sale number is more than laptop (A) model computer products last month. But, in this month, it has significant change between laptop model (A) and laptop (B). In this month, laptop modle (A) and laptop model (B) prices are not changes, but laptop model (A) can sell 3,000 number and laptop model (B) can sell only 500 number. Consequently, their sale numbers have significantly changes, laptop (A) can increase more 2,000 sale number, but laptop model (B) can decrease 1,500 sale number between these two months. It explains that although it seems that laptop (B) model has possible own attractive physical appearance, and rapid connectivity and mobility, more function to cause it can sell more than laptop (A) model computer produc. But, it ensures that all of anh one these possible factors can not help it to raise sale number in long time. It means that laptop model (B) may have other factors to influence itss sale number, e.g. other brand of laptop computers' physical appearance, more function, connectivity and mobility , features , even they can provide better value added sale service, repair service, product delivery service, feature to compare this brand of laptop seller, or its laptop model (B) buyers had lost confidence to use its laptop model () computer products, because they often need to repair and pay extra repair service fee frequently, e.g. one year has one time to two times at least per year. SO, their past poor frequent repair experience influences they choose to buy other brand of laptops. Otherwise, why laptop model (A) computer products number can sell more 2,000 number , the factor may include non rising price, none frequent past repair experiences to any one model (A) laptop buyer , their individual psychological positive feeling factor . So, it seems that gather these two laptop model (A) and model (B) past sale number, sale price data to conclude whther what main factors may influence its model (A) and model (B) laptop sale number to increase or decrease in long term.

However, this laptop computer seller can not only depend on the gathering these two months short time sale numbers ans sale prices data to model (A) and (B) laptops, in order to make the final conclusion concerns whether what the main factor can influence model (A) and model (B) laptop product sale number changes absolutely. It must need to continue to keep the long time management sale umber and sale prie data record for laptop (A) and (B) in order to conclude whether what the most accurate influential factor is that it can influence laptop model (A) and B() sale number both change in order to implement the improvement strategy for them both.

● Management accounting data can also help this laptop seller to predict future market development or whether which market will have high sale effort, e.g. Japan laptop sale market may have the highest market share ratio, among different Asia countries, or Germany laptop sale market may have highest market share ratio among different European countries next year. For example, in the last year, this laptop computer seller had sold 50,000 laptops to Japan computer market, it has sold 500,000 laptops to China computer market, it has sold 100,000 laptops to US computer market and 50,000 laptops to Germany computer market, in this year. its these laptop markets sale prices are not changed, it has sold 200,000 laptops to japan computer market, it has sold 400,000 laptops to China computer market, it had sold 200,000 laptops to US computer market and 200,000 laptops to Germany computer market . Hence, it ensures that Germany laptop market has increased 4 times sale number from last year and Japan has increased 4 times sale number from last year. Otherwisem China laptop sale number has decreased 100,000 laptops from last year and US laptop sale number has increased 1 time from last year. So, it can imply that Germany and Japan future laptop sale number may grown rapidly to compare US and CHina laptop sale markets. It also indicates this sale trend also may help this laptop computer to attempt to find whether what factors may influence its US and China laptop sale number fells down,,e.g. whether this local laptop choices increasing factor, it laptop physical appearance is not more attraction, or slow connectivity and mobility speed ,even their model (A) and () laptop prices are higher to compare US and China local other similar brands of laptops prices.

In summary, I believe that management accounting technique can be attempted to apply to help any kinds of products to find whether what main factor(S) to influence their product sale number changes, it is one kind of good data gathering and analytical tool to help any businesses to attempt to predict consumer behavioral changes.

Organization management accounting strategy

What is organization management accounting strategy? As its most basic an organization management accounting strategy is a plan that specifies how your business will allocate resources, e.g. money, labour, and inventory to suppoty production, marketing, inventory and other business activities. IN general, the foure organizational straategy and the culture of the organization categorized into four types: Adhocracy, market and hierarchy.

The purpose of an organization management accounting strategy can be defined as the direction an organization takes with the aim of achieving future business success. Strategy sets out how an organization intends to employ its resources, including the skills and knowledge of its people as well as financial and material assets, in order to achieve its mission or overall targets. So, the key element of an organizational strategy may include: define vision, create mission, set objectives, develop strategy, outline approach, get down to tactics. However, an organizatinal strategy plan is an organizational management activity that is used to set priorities, focus energy and resources, strengthen operations, ensure that employees and other stakeholders are working toward common goals established agreement crowd intended outcomes/ results, and access organizational missions.

Adhocracy strategy is a form of business management accounting that emphasizes individual initiative and self organization in order to accomplish tasks. This is in contrast to bureaucracy which relies on a set of defined rules and set hierarchy in accomplishing organizational goals. The term was popularized by Alvin Toffler in the 1970s. Examples of adhocracy include most project or marix organizations. Among private-sector organizations, high technology firms, particularly young firms facing fierce competition are sometimes organized as adhocracies. However, important examples of adhocracy do exist in government. Hence, adhocracy is a flexible, adoptable and informal form of organization that is defined by a lack of formal structure that employs specialized multidisciplinary trams grouped by functions. Adhocracy is characterized by an adoptive , creative and flexible behavior based on non-performance. Adhocray culture in a business context, is a corpoate culture based on the ability to adapt quickly to changing conditions. Adhocracies ar characterized by flexibility, employee empowerment and an emphasis on individual initiative.

The five basic marketing strategies may include: product, price and promotion and people in management accounting strategy aspect. They are key marketing elements used to position a business strategically. A market strategy refers to a business's overall game plan for reaching prospective consumers and turning them into customers of their products and services. For example, the BSC business 2 customed marketing strategies may include : social networks and viral marekting, paid media advertising, internet marketing, email marketing, direct selling, point-of-purchase marketing, co-branding, cause marketing, conversational marketing. Hence, marketing strategy or management accounting strategy is a long term toeard looing approach and an overall game plan of any organization or any business with the foundemental goal of achieving a competitive advantage by understanding the needs and wants of customers.

Hierarchy strategy describes a relations of corporate strategy and sub-strategies hierarchically and logically consistent at the level of vision, mission, goals, and metrics , e.g. HR strategy (human resource strategy), to general, the three levels of strategy are: corporate level strategy, this level answers the foundamental question of what you want to achieve, business unit level strategy focuses on how you've going to grow.

The management accounting strategy planning hierarchy is the organization's mission and vision both of ,which should be long-lasting and motivating. At the base of the hierarchy are the shorter term strategies and tactics that unit members will use to achieve the vision. So, the basic levels of management accounting strategy are: corporate, business, functional and operational level strategy. The strategic hierarchy aims to be concept used to understand the different types of strategy decision made in a organization, e.g. michael porter , three generic strategies (cost leadership, differentation, and focus) that can be implemnted at any organizations. So, hierarchical levels of strategy managment accounting may be concerned with selection of which is the right generic strategy to implement, sale method, such as low product sale price, lot differentiation of product choice, and focus an main product feature market sale methods etc.

● The relationship between organizational management accounting strategy and avoiding resource waste

If an organization can implement good managment accounting strategy whether it can assist it to reduce any organizational internal resource waste, e.g. exceed human resource employment cost, facility used cost, using cost, efficient administration or management cost etc. essential organizational cost. Because any organizations must need to use resources in order to achieve efficient providivities, service activities, if the organization can implement effective strategy in order to measure its performance, whether strategy can assist it to judge how to avoid not essential resources spending. Can efficient strategy help organizations to avoid to waste resources? I shall attempt to explain as below:

Whether formal strategy implement can avoid formal technical measurement of scale and concentrates on the loca resource mobilization using aspect os small, medium and large organization? What does resource mobilization strategy mean? Resource mobilization refers to all activities involved in sesuring new and additional resources for your organization. It also involves making better use of and maximizing , existing resources.What are the stepd in resource mobilization?

Firstly, any organizations need to plan od designing a resource moilization strategy and action plan, secondary , finding key elements of a resource mobilization strategy, thirdly,act of practical step to implementatin, fourth identify, fifth step, engagement, sixth step, negotiate, eventh step, manage and report, final step, communicating results.

What are the source of resource mobilization to any organizations? For example includes spreading flyers, holding community meetings, and recruiting volunteers. Material may include financial and physical capital, like office space, money, equipment, and supplies . Human resources, such as labour experience, skills and expertise in a certain field. How does an entrepreneur mobilize resources? To exploit opportunities, entrepreneurs monilize and recombine a variety of resources, such as financial capital (e.g. cash, ot loan from a bank , human capital e.g. skills from a employees, and social capital e.g. information obtained from social contracts. Hence, the overall objectives of the resource mobilization strategy is to secucre the necessary funds to deliver on the source mobilization strategic outcomes. To achieve this accurate resource used number and expenditure budget and emergency appeals will need sufficient preditable and contrributions. So, the aim of resource mobilization strategy outlines how secretariat will organize the process of prioritising, plannin, selecting projects, monitoring: broadening the resource channels, as well as coordinating with staffs for mobilising and effectively utilizing resources.

So, the genesis of resource mobilization strategy is a good, solid strategic plan, it should articulate activities that are more routine in nature and can be finded through the organizational internal efficient resource mobilization. Resource mobilization refers to all activities involves in securing . These new directions or new business opportunities are pursued using a distinct resource mobilization strategy .

On conclusion , an efficient resource mobilization plan is a term resource mobilization, it refers to all activities undertaken by an organizations to secure new and additional financial, human and material resources to advance its mission. Inherent in efforts to mobilize resources is the drive for organizational sustainability . So, resource mobilization is about an organization getting the resources that are needed to be able to do the work it has planned. Resource mobilization is more that just fundraising, it is about getting a range or resources from a wide range of resource providers for donors, through a number of different mechanisms. How does an entrepreneur mobile resources? To exploit opportunities, entreprensurs mobilize and combine a variety of resources, such as financial captial , e.g. cash or loans from a bank, human capital e.g. skill from an employee and social capital e.g. information obtained from social contract.

Why do organizations need resource mobilization strategy? The reasons may include: The principles of resource mobilization wih examples, it focuses on forging partnerships built on trust and mutual accountability . So, as to attract adequate and more predictable contributions, with the future goal of sustainability, it refers to all undertaken by an organizatin to secure new and additional financial , human and material resource to advance its mission, in efforts to mobilize resources is the drive for organizational sustainability, community mobilization is the process of bring together as many stakeholders as possible to raise people's awareness of and demand for a particular programme to assist in the delivery of resources and services, and to strengthen community participation for sustainability an dself -reliance, resource mobilization is often referrred t as " new business creaating chance" , the organization has a strong, yet flexible structure , such as writing proposal how to spend the least respurce expenditure in order to achieve the most satisfactory effective result to the organization.

Hence, developing a resource mobilization strategy plan , as the source of new business opportunities to the social and behavioral change considerations must be needed the organization as well as resource mobilization target at a minimum level should be needed to raise at transformational change happen on the ground and advocate for the products and may have to develop new business proposal.

● Can resource mobilization change improve organizational performance?

I believe that resource mobilization can help any organizations to change or improve performance to the better, even the best. I shall explain as below:

What are the sources of organizational change? Change originates in either the external or internal environments of the organization. External sources include political, social, technological or economic environment, externally motivated change may involve government action, technology development, competition , social values and economic variables.

How do organizational resources affect change? Results indicate that organizations possessing greater stocks of historically valuable resources were much less likely to engage in adaptive strategic change, but also that this resoure-driven towards change tended to have a even beneficial effect on performance . Wonder of organizational change management is easier spoken about than achieved by resource mobilization strategic in possible? Can create enterprise level value by effective process for resource allocation?

The key to success involves managing organizational change , so it leads to real and lasting improvements, tailoring to resource allocation how mobilization strategy. So, nowadays, organizational capacty for change: Increasing change capacity and avoiding change overload, organization, today risk is overcommitting resources, resulting in an overload condition wih which it how allocates its resources to tbe used efficiently or inefficiently. For example, on new government regulations, ne products development or growth aspect, organizational change efforts often run into some form of human resistance. First, management staffed its human resource departments with spend most of that time in efficiency. So, whether how organizational change is better, it depends on how it changes its old resources, e.g. human resource, facility, equipment resources, even management time resources to change new improvement resources change to be better . It means providing the resources, budget, authority, credibility and commitment for the effort to truly organizational change on improvement.

● Why does organizational resource budget need?

For example, managing a human resource department involves budget planning and execution . The human resources budger refers to the finds that how HR allocates to all HR processes. Unit should include in an HR budget. It may include: number of employees, projected for next year, benefits cost increases or decreases, salary cost increases or decreases, projected turnover rate, calculation, actual cost incured in the current year, new employee welfare benefits. programs planned, other changes in policy, business strategy , it may impact costs on HR cost aspect. So, an organization needs to budget whether it will have how much on what kinds of resources spending aspect, including human resources, facility, equipment and water , electricity etc. natural resource , it budget is a tool used for planning and controlling financial resources. It is a guideline for future plan of action, espressed in financial terms within a set of period time, knowing organization's priorities, objectives and goals helps it prepare organization resource budget. Effectively leveraging people and budget, resource management is critical for organizations to ensure . They are optimizing and allocating resources to the right initiations, e.g. from a human resource perspective, the data needed to create a new budget include the following number of employees, working arrangement tasks time, management time, employee salary cost, due to costs that only impact the human resource department and impacts the entire organization both aspects. So, efficient HR cost budget can help refine goals that reflect realistic resources and how memebers of the organization to use fund because employee retirement can be expensive and it can b increased or decreased expense in any time, when the month needs increase or decrease employees number to any departments. It depends on whether tasks rate is needed to increase or decrease. So, an organization's HR cost budget can help how it makes the most accurate HR resource expenditure.

Organizational facility, equipment, shop, office, warehouse space resource budget why is important. Office space is as an enabling resource, equipment and furniture to enhance the organization's ability to achieve efficient operations and activities of the best organizational performance. In view of this analysis, facility planning personal would be one important factor to influence whether the organizatin can spend the least expenditure to use its resource. During business growth, any facility equipment, office , shop, warehouse space must increase , moreover staff puts increasing number on existing resources, so be sure to budget in order to make another option is to least equipment instead of buying it, whether you need moving insurance for important equipment and machinery, set budget to help prevent overspending.

All of the tasks that are include in maintaining a facility, such as equipment maintenance and building facilities whether are needed to improve, facility oversight, warehouse and special equipment whether is qpproriate space for customer service and uses resource dynamic of an organization's work patterns with work. It depends partly on the resources an organization is willing to invest or not, when it feels this facility resources are very important to influence its performance.

● What does organization office , shop , warehouse space resource management strategy?

Organization and using space must be land resource, if the organization can manage how to use its space in efficiency, then it can improve service performance or productive efficiency. Space management can be defined as a practice where an organization manages its physical space invnetory which includes tracking , control, supervision and utilization, planning of the space available. So, space management is the mangement of an organization's physical space inventory. Ths involves the tracking of how much space an organization has managing occupancy information and creating spatial plans. So, one efficient space resource using organization, it needs to undertake annual property assessment reviews, leverage individual projects to drive portfolio evoluation applya planning methodology on all project rises, utilize planning to define direction and scope focus on mathematics before graphics, define and collect only the required data on warehouse, shops, office, buildind space using aspect. For example, a space management ffice can give the organizatin an accurate picture of how many employees , it needs to have space for an average day, and show it the trends of demand for this space across weeks and months. This can help the organization to determine how many permanent desks could be converted to hot desks in office, warehouse or shop , saving space. For example, space managementin retail aspect, it is the process of managing the floor space adequately to facilitate the customers and to increase the sale.

Shop space management is very crucial in retail as the sales volume and gross profitability depends on the amount of space used to generate those sales. Space management is a multi-step process that requires data gathering, analysis , forecast and strategizing. In prective, it involes creating a space management system that occupants throughout your organization, so whether the organization realizes it or not, every organization needs to know how to manage its space one way or another , if it hopes to improve its service or productive performance. Make use of these strategic space management and planning techniques, efficient and an unplanned, unmanaged office is not likely to magically transofrm into a well organized of productivity. So, space management is the management of an organization's physical space inventoty , employee working environment, shop product putting sheleves locatin, equipment, desk putting location. All of this tangible space physical factor may influence overall organizational service and/or productive performance and /or sale performance. So, space may be an organization's land usng resource because any organization's land using space must be limited size, they must have land space using shortage challenge if their products stock number increases, but warehouse space can not increase or shop products shelves number can not increase, but product sale number increases.

● The relationship netween organization behavior and resource using management accounting

Has organizational behavior and resource spending, they have close cause and effect direct relationship ? When one organization can perform better, whether it represents that it must spend much resource to use or when it perform poor, it represents that it must not spend much resource to use. Organizational behavior is a field of study that investigates the impact that organizational psychology and human resource management, the cause and effect relationship.

How organizational behavior effects an oganization? Organizational behaviors propose that inventives are motivational factors that are crucial for employees to perform well. It changes the way people make decisions, e.g. decision to increase or decrease resources to use, when the organization feels that it has resource shortage or excess. However, businesse that are able to encourage risks in decision making within the company culture can enhance innovation and creativity.

In fact, organizational behavior has four main elements, people, structure, technology and external environment. So , tangible and intangible resources may influence organization behavior when it is needed to change by management, e.g. human behavior in a work environmen and determines its impacts on job structure, performance, communication, motivation, leadership etc. for example, when the manager has less time to prepare how to organize this meeting process to his client. His short managing meeting plan time , intangible time resource, it can influence his business proposal to be either accepted or rejected to this client. So , time resource whether it is enough or not. It can influence this manager's client proposal meeting whether it is accepted or rejected in possible.

Every employee behavior can determine the importance of group departments in business productivity. So, it seems that resources whether they are enough , they can impact on employee's performance. As a result, managers are able to maintain better relation with their employees by effective utilization of human resource. So, cause and effect relationship plays an important rolw in how an individual is likely to behave in a enough tangible and intangible resource provided or not enough organization.

Modern organizational behavior is characterised by the acceptance of a human resource model, e.g. whether the plant can provide enough productive equipment facility and space shelf for product putting location in order to raise or improve logistic transport efficiency in warehouse. So, plant warehouse space management and shelf putting location productive equipment facility these tangible resource factors may influence warehouse productive performance. It seems that tangible resource provision amount and space management or intangible resource time management resource, they have close relationship to influence organizational behavior. Consequently, it can achieve the result either performance improvement or worse performance. So, resource and performance organizations , they ought have cause and effect relationship in resource management mobilization strategy view.

● How applying artificial intelligent management accounting solution accounting challenges

One of the biggest challenges for management accountants nowadays is the preparation to face globalization in local and global market. Globalization competition is changing government regulation and innovation in technology had to change in the market environment which have greater impact to an organization. The role of managemet accounting to AI, it may help managers to make any management strategy decision, e.g. evaluate sale price is the most reasonable, sale market choice, customer age target evaluation etc. within any organizations. Also known of cost accunting, management account of the process of identifying, analyzing and communicating information to managers to help to achieve business goals. However, the most important job of management accountant is t condoct a relevant cost analysis to determine the existing expenses and give suggestion for the future activities and make better management accounting, when management accountants need to learn how to apply these management accounting data: financial planning, financial statement analysis, cost accounting, find flow and cash flow analysis, standard , marginal cost and budgetary control, they can be made by AI.

In general, the job dutures of management accountant may include: generate sale among client accounts, operates as the point of contact for assigned customers, develops and maintains long term relationships with accounts, makes sure clients receives requested produsts ans services in a timely fashion . So, they need to learn these different management accounting technique: margin analys, capital budget, inventory valuation and product cost, tend analysis and forecasting. Future AI may be taught to learn all of these any one management accounting technique to assist organizations to make more reasonable management account strategy implementation.

The basic principles of management accounting include communication presents insight which is crucial , irrelevance information is valuable, the influence one value is estimated, credibility,recognizing the requirement, good accounting manager, they need to learn how conflict, be open to new ideas: In management accounting tehnology apply, there are three elements of management control system to develop to future Artificial intelligent management accounting technology delegated decison authority , performance evaluation and measurement systems and compensation, reward system.

Hence, accounting technology in AI development has always played a past in making the accountant's job just a played a part in making the accountant's job just a easier. Its own knowledge of technology increased to have the accountant's ability to analyze statistical values. Technology advancements have enhanced the accountant's ability to interpret data efficiently and effectively.

● Future AI management accountant may help human to the honest accounting record

However, any one managment accountant needs have good professional personal quality, honestly and integrity play vital roles in accounting because they allow investors to trust the information they receive about companies in which they invest. Honesty in accounting is the primary characteristics of the profession that allows financial decision-makers to make appropriate judgement . So, the main focus of management accounting is to assist the management of a company in efficiency performing its function-planning, organizaing, divesting and controlling . Management accounting helps with these functions in the following ways: provides data, it serves to a vital source of data for planning, for product costing method example, it is used to cost methods available are process costing, job and different production and decision making. for 3 types of controls may include: internal controls are typically procedures or technical safe guards that are implemented to prevent problems and protect organizations' assets. Future AI technology may help an organizations to do above all management accounting decision jobs ,even replace human in offices to avoid losses. The traditional management accounting technique includes" the use of performance measures, three ROI , budget systems for planning and control, divisional profit reports and cost-profit volume relationship, and breakeven analysis for decisions. The management accounting reports may include order information report, project report, competitor analysis. They are either internally aor outsourced. All of these management accounting methods, future AI can replace human accountants to do .

● Can AI be applied to help Amazon organization to implement management account strategies ?

The two widely used types of accounting are: Financial and management accoutning, for the strategic cost management techniques example, it is the cost management techniques that aims at reducing cost , when strengthening the position of the business. It is a process of combining the decision making structure with the cost information in order to do the strategy as a whole . Hence the role of management account in the organization is to support competitive decision making by collecting, processing and communicating information that helps management plan, control and evaluating business processes and company strategy . So, the strategy management accounting can be defined as the process of identifying, collecting , selecting and analyzing accounting data . So, future AI can be applied to assist accounting teams in strategic decision making and organization effectiveness assessment must be defined.

Future AI can be applied to these management accounting aspect: For methods and techniques of costing management , it may include: Job costing, advestment, salepeople,bonus, contract cost, long periods of time job, batch cost, process cost, one operation (unit or output) , cost service or operating costing, farm cost, multiple cooperation unit. The tools of cost analysis, breakeven analysis, budget cost control marginal cost analysis, cost control , minimum price analysis, standard cost development , target cost. All of these management strategies, AI can do .

The various tools and technique of marginal costing may include: contribution, profit volume ratio, contribution : sale value , p/v ratio, features of profit volume , break even point . Hence, the AI tools can control cost monitoring in execution. For that AI can help organizations to make cost control budget, it is defined as a AI tool that is used by the management of an organization in regulating and controlling of a manufacturing organization. AI can also perform cost budget for material to any manufacturing organizations to help them to reduce the manufacturing cost , e.g. making material choice for the cheapest price.

AI can gather the product material price, e.g. standard cost and normal cost. Then , AI can help the manufacturing organization to choose the best quality of the cheapest material in order to compare whether which kinds of material to produce the kind of product can bring the high economic benefit to let consumers get more satisfactory feeling.

Thus, it is future management accounting development direction for AI.

Ecommerce organization resource management strategy

Why does in this e-commerce organization situation, online webstore speed must be the most important factor to influence its sale success. Information technology internet speed, online webstore design, online transation convenience transaction feeling (tangibale and intangible both resource factors) may influence its future clients number ?

In behavioral economic view, any organizations must need to use resources to carry on any business or working activities. Resources may include: management time to managements, working time to employees, information technology etc. office computer to administration, factory equipment to plant workers, plant or warehouse land space to logistic delivery or goods shelves, electricity, gas , water to workplace , even, employees number. HR to any department tasks. So, it seems that before any organization can finish any activities, they must need enough resources supply in order to satisfy any activities need. If the organization overall itself , even overall society. I shall explain as below:

For ecommerce organizatin example, any online trading firms must need to own high speed internet information technology resource to supply to any one technologic staff store to pay visa to buy any product in the most short time rapidly. So, its online store website speeds must need to be very fast in order to avoid to delay any country clients to carry on online transaction. If the ecommerce business organization can not support efficient, high speed internet service to let any countries online buyers to satisfy its online webstore purchase service. Then, any countries' online buyers may choose another online store to replace to buy its similar product easily.

Hence, convenient webstore online purchase service much be very important to influence this online webstore organization. It seems that technologic online internet resource must be the most influential factor to influence this online websore organization clients number. If its online website store can not supply rapid online purchase speed to let any one country to buy its products from its webstores rapidly. Then, its clients number may be influenced to reduce. So, in this e-commerce organization situation, online webstore speed must be the most important factor to influence its sale success. Information technology internet speed, online webstore design, online transation convenience transaction feeling (tangibale and intangible both resource factors) may influence its future clients number . So, judging whether the kind of resource is the most important to influence the organization's success, it depends on whether it needs to use what kind of resource to carry on its daily activities.

In fact, one organizational change has relationship to whether its reponses can have enough supply as well as its behavior can be influenced by the resources variable , the scarcity of any kinds of resources are supplied to be used. So, I believe that whether any kinds of resources are scarcity in the organizational environment, how much they are used, these any kind of resources can bring relationship to influence how organizational perceptions, interpretations and responses.

How an ecommerce organization resource affects society?

Why has online webstore's information technology resource close relationship t influence online buyers number and social job chance?

Organizational impact to the effect on an organization has any reponses to influence how on society chance. However, organizations can also have a positive impact on the economic satisfaction of a town. More oe less jobs supply to the wociety, which can be influenced by whether the organization can have effort to buy how much resources to be used in order to carry on itself any business activities. Hence, it seems that if the organization, such as the above online website sale product organization, if it can have enough money to employ web design professional to help it to design attractive website stores to let attract online buyer purchase choice, as well as paid higher internet service fee to improve its fee to improve its online internet speed in order to let any countries online customers can still click its website rapidly, even in busy online click time. Many people click computer mouse to enter ecommerce website stores in the same time. Then, any one won't choose another websites stores to replace its online sale service easily. Even, if it can buy many advanced computers to let its staffs can use the best quality computers to follow any client's ourchase transaction in short time. When , they confirm that whether the client's visa card payment can accept and what product he has paid to buy from its webstore. Then, the staff can know where the accurate address of the country , the client's product can be delivered rapidly. It will avoid to delay any product delivery. So, if this online store seller can have enough internet information technology source to support its whole computer information department staffs to wrk efficiently. Then, it can increase more online transaction chance in success. Consequently, it can grow up its online sale business, it will create many new potisition, due to its computer information technology department must need to increase employees to help it to deal any countries online buyers online purchase service transactions and online product sale delivery service immediately in order to avoid online product delivery service to global online buyers. So, it can bring more job chance if this online webstore organization can have enough effort to buy high technological computer information products to let its online customer service staffs to use in order to improve online product delivery service store to let global many online buyers' attention . Consequently, it can apply online webstore purchase channel to apply website purchase channel to persuade many global online buyers online purchase choice to its webstore easily. So, it seems that this online webstore's information technology resource has close relationship t influence online buyers number and social job chance.

How do organizational resources affect organizational change?

IN general, resoults indicate that organizations possessing greater stocks of historically valuable resources were much less likely to engage in adaptive strategic change, but also that this resource-driven disinclination towards change tended to have a begin or even beneficial effect on performance . So, in general, if one organization lacks any one of these three important resources. It can influence this organization's performance to worse, they many include: human resource , financial resource, phycial resources and information resource. However, managers are responsible to acquiring and managing the resources to accomplish goals. If the organization can have enough resources to be used. It can bring positive impact to influence its overall organizational performance, even, when it has not any resource scarcity, it can avoid negative impacts on the society, such as increasing jobs chance. Hence, scarcity of capital, human and social resources to be provided to the organization, it will influence the organizational structure changes, even employee individual work attitude is influenced to change worse, when he/she can not have the best resources to be used in order to raise efficiency or improve performance more easily.

How to build organizatonal resource using right psychology

The psychology of management is the branch of psychology studying mental features of the person and its behavior in the course of planning, organization management and the control of joint activity. The human factor is considered as the central point in the psychology of management as its essence and a core. Hence , organizational psychology plays a very important rolw at the time or recruitment very important role at the time of recruitment taking disciplinary action or resolving disputes between employees. HR focus and expertise mainly lies in dealing with people . So , it makes sense that the study of the human mind, how to use organizational resources efficiently.

The organizational side of pschology is more focused on understanding how organizations affect individual behavior, organizational structures , social norms, management styles and role expectations are factors that can influence how people behave within organizations. In general, industrial organizational psychologists use psychological principles and research methods to solve problems in the workplace and improve the quality of life (e.g. avoiding often waste industrial resources in manufacturing process aims). They study workplace workplace productivity and management and employee working styles. They get a feel for the morale and personality of a company or organization, e.g. suggesting to use skills and knowledge relating to psychology how to reduce same productivity level, but the organizational resources can be reduced to use. It is one kind the most efficiency resources using method to any kind of organizations.

On conclusion, industrial and organizational psychologists will often use science to study human behavior organizations and the workplaces. Their aims to help organizations to reduce excess resource using in any manufacturing process in order to reduce cost. Employers who need to attempt to learn how employees use resources to do work activities, it can bring these advanaages : learning how to use neuroscience to attract the right talent, retain high performing employees, because any organizations' resources will be used in order to manufacture any products or work activites by any employees in any time.

Employees are the ones who get the job done. They know how the organization and especially ho w their specigif team works best. So any one employee may be the important factor to influence the amount of resource use, any organizational resource use amount, it has close relationship to any employee work behavior. Moreover, resources, that is , group-level resources associated with shared relationship that foster a quality exchange of information and interaction between individuals within the workplace , helping any one employee to learn more about on the job training, use employee training optios to ensure department leader optimizes the employees' motiviation and potential retention. Aim to give opinions to employees to know how to avoid resource using waste method to achieve cost saving aim to the organization.

Can Amazon resource shortage influence consumer behavior changes?
Can bring either positive or negative or both impact to change consumer behavior when the consumer begins to feel resource shrtage occurrence to choose to buy the kind of product or consume the kind of service?
Consumer researchers have suggedsted that chronic resource scaraity, specially, an inproveished early home environment with fewer resources and high levels of instability and uncertainty can lead to chronic differences in choice behavior (Griskevicius et al. 2011). How are consumers affected by scarcity? Scarcity affects producers because they have to make a choice on how to best ise their limited resources. It also affects consumers because they have to make a choice on what services or goods to chooce. Hence, resource shortage may be situational factor influence, situational influences are external circumstances or conditions existing when a consumer makes a purchase decision. Because the kind of product is facing resource shortage issue to influence the product manufacturer can not have enough resource to manufacture the kind og product. SO, number supply is decreasing, such as cars product, if steel number supply is decreasing, it can influence global car manufacture number decreases. When global new car buyers feel that they can not buy any kinds fo new cars easily. Then, even global new car price rises, they won't influence new car buyers purchase desires. So, in new car sale market, if steel supply number reduces, global new car buyer number will not decrease easily.
How does a consumer make choice with scarce resources?
Like producers, consumers also have to make choices, since consumer resources , such as time, attention, and money are limited. They must choose how to best allocate them by making tradeoff. The concept of trade-offs due to scarcity is formalized by concept of opportunity cost. In fact, research in marketing often begins with two assumptions, by scarcity of products and/or a scarcity of resources, dfferent types of scarcity individually and jointly influence.
Consumer behavior , an integrative analysis of research finding remains that scarcity principle in consumer behavior, it refers that scarcity to the condition of resources shortages, it can affect consumer behavior. So, consumer behavior and resource shortage, they seem have close cause and effect relationship between them. For buying behavior example, when one male consumer with high shopping motivations, when he knows a scarcity arrtibute and thus are a vary limited resources, e.g. he allows to buy the product within 5 minutes , when the shop will close soon and thus a very shop time clising time limited. It can persuade the male customer to make purchase decisin immediately. So, it seems that intangible resource , such as shop closing limited time, scarcity may also be a fundamental phenomenon that influences consumer behavior, when the consumer feels that shop will close, it does not allow himw to continue to stay long time in the shop. The shop closing time nay persuade the customer to buy the product immediately.
It explains that why the influence of quantity scarcity and time restriction on consumer, this implies that when consumers' cognitive resources are not restricted by external environmental factor influence, such as shop soon closing time or web traffic to media, when the online buyer , he dislikes to spend long time to click on any website stores to choose themselves brands of the kind of product choice to make purchase decision. The online buyer may only click one website store to make purchase decision immediately.
So, it explains why online sellers can sell their products firm online stores easily, because their website stores web traffic is not busy at the moment. There are not many online buyers click themselves webiste stores at the moment. So, when there are many online buyers can click themselves webstores to choose any kinds of products in shor ttime rapidly. Then, their online sale chance may be influenced by " not busy website stores web traffic jam to media time factor".
Hence, it seems that when one consumer feels resource shortage, it may persuade the consumer to choose to buy the kind of product immediately. I suggest that people may not only differ in terms of how they choose to consume, this could include encouraging consumers , such as impact pf resource scarcity on price-quality judgement.

It means that the predictable " panic shopping" in response, experiencing resource scarcity can also increase a sense of community by encouraging consumer to share shopping experience. So, product uncertainity , which is able to motivate behaviors, such as urgency to buy.

This, scarcity , also is known as paucity, is an eonomics term used to refer to a gap between the buyer purchase desire and external environmental factor, for exmaple time and money are characteristically scarce resources, to urge consumers to make purchases or else they won't guarantee next day purchase the product.

Howveer, the cost of using a resource is called the opportunity cost, the value of the next scarcity in economics connotes not that something is nearly impossible to finf. In common, consumers must choose between correct consumption and future consumption, for example, the COVID 19 crisisi may bring positive urgent time to save product, e.g. medical mouth cover protection product, when many medical mouth cover protection product buyers believe the brand of covid 19 medical moth cover protection products supply is shortage, they believe they ought buy the brand of medical mouth cover protection product supply is shortage, they believe thay ought buy the brand of medical mouth cover protection products immediately.

Otherwise, they can not find this kind of covid 19 medical mouth cover protection products to buy later. So, the anticipation to the covid 19 crisis will help some brands of medical mouth cover protection proucts, they can be sold rapidly . So, panic buying may be encouraged when the covid19 mouth cover protection product buyers feel a common brand share covid 19 mouth cover protection products shortage resource through a collection action. Hence, even the brand of covid 19 medical mouth cover protection products prices are raised, the covid 19 mouth cover buyers still choose to buy the brand of covid 19 mouth cover protection products, because they believe that they can not buy the brand of covid 19 medical mouth protection cover products later, when this brand of covid 19 medical mouth cover manufacturers won't continue to manufacture this kind of covid 19 medical mouth cover products again.

So, it explains that crisis and product sale time limited intangible resources can influence consumers to make a lot purchase decision suddenly. On conclusion, resource scarcity is essentially about current brand for a resource exceeding available supply. Resource scarcity occurs when demand for a natural resource is greater than the available supply leading to a decline in the stock of available resources.

However, limited time may be one kind of intangible resource shortage to influence consumers to choose to make the purchase decision to avoid that they lose the final purchase chance. So, the intangible limited time psychological factor may help businessmen to sell their products in short time, when the consumers feel that they have no enough time to choose any kinds of product to buy or they believe that they can not buy the kind of product later. So, resource shortage may bring position impact to influence consumer behavior in behavioral economy view.

Do they have relationship between organizational resource economic behavior and social needs?

In organizational behavioral economy view, economic systems that shape behaviors and constrain access to resource necessary to organizations and society both. People are influenced to organizations as employees, consumers. IN behavioral economy view, economics is the social science that examines how individuals, businesses and overall societies manage scarce resources. Because none resource exist in unlimited quantities, even internet technology resource , societies must establish priorities and decide how best to allocate resources in such a way that meets as many needs and wants as possible . So, organizational behavioral and economics to explain why employees sometimes make irrational business decisions , and why and how the organization employee individual behavior does not follow the predictions of economic models . Because any organizational employees are emotional and easily distracted brings , they make decisions that are not in their self interest when they are working in organization. Hence, how whether it is more or less any organizations use themselves resource. It may influence the social whether it has much or less resources to society. It can use which interact within the organization,

Why have they interaction to influence resource supply between orgaizations and societies?

In sociology, a social organization is a pattern of relationship between and among individuals and social groups. Characteristics of social organization can include qualities, such as division of labour, communication system, leadership , structure of a organization. For hospital example, it is one social organization, whether how it uses its resource , it can inluence whether society has how much resources can use. Hospital is one social resource organization (division of labour), e.g. doctors, nurses teams, cleaner teams, patient customer enquire teams, counter service teams. They are a major influence on social behavior and is the link between human nature reaching to the hospital organizational and social environment. Hoe many actual patients number , social need in the year, if the year , there are not many patients need to feel to go to hospital , then it can influence the hospital feels resource excess, or it won't need to use more hospital resource to serve its patients in the year. S, social patients needs and hospital medicine supply needs, they have close relationship every year. It means that the hospital's medicine manufacture material won't need much, it the year has not many patients or patients number is decreasing. So, shopital organzation hoe to need its resource, it has close relationship to patients number in society (nature, demographic, economic, cultural and social behavior patterns and consciousness). So, it explains why the social organization is the best of all organized human society, such as hospital organization example, its patients number will influence medicine resource need.

Another example is bus public transport service social passengers number choice to catching bus transport tool, it can influence whether how buses use oil nature resources needs. If the year , there are less passengers to choose to catch buses, they choose to catch trams, trains, ferries in preference, then due to every bus reduces passengers numer, it does not often driven , following the fixed timetable. If the bus stations often have no many passengers are waiting buses, then many buses are often staying in bus stations. Consequently, bus oil fuel nature resources need must reduce. Thus, social bus passengers number may have indirect relationship to influence buses oil fuel natural resources needs every year. It means that bus oil fuel nature resource use amount is influened by social passengers public transport tool choice needs. It is one good example bus public transport service organization seems to be one social organization.

● How Amazon e-commerce applies resource management principle to bring avoiding resource waste benefit?
For Amazon e-commerce example, it does not apply scientific management principle, due to it is not one product manaufacturing industry, it is online sale service and foreign delivery service organization. It ignores one of the key of scientific management, its creators genuinely believed that you had to pay higher wages to anyone asked to puch themselves to their physical limits. Under scientific management wages are paid to the workers as per the piece-wage system. Minimum wage is not assured, so every work needs to pay incentive wafe when he can manufacture more piece product, but Amazon believes that pay higher wages to any one can bring incentive productivity , such as it only provide online sale and foreign deli ery service to any one online buyer client, e.g. it can pay higher wage to the warehouse workers, because they need to cooperate with robotics to work hard and the human warehouse workers need to learn how to dominate any one warehouse logistic robotics to know hoe to delive and put goods to the right shelves in order to avoid to put wrong goods to the not right shelves position in warehouse.

So, in Amazon scientific management skill to workers view, its warehouse workers are smart workers, they need to know how to dominate any one warehouse robotics to do the right goods delivery to put on right shelves tasks daily. Their wages ought need to pay higher in order to avoid theig goods wrong delivery to wrong sheleves in careless. SO, Amazon feels that it needs to pay higher salary to the warehouse workers because they need have more smart and robotic control skills. When they and robotic to works together in Amazon warehouses.

So, such as Amazon warehouse workers case, Amazon ecommerce organization can apply scientific management principle to reduce resource waste. I shall explain as below:

Amazon 's warehouses have save diffeent kinds of products to prepare to deliver to different countries buyers, after Amazon had confirmed that it has receive visa card payment from online channel by each online buyer successfully. So, it must have smart warehous workers, they know how to control and dominate any one warehouse robotics to cooperate to send every right shelf position message to every one warehouse robotis to know, when the warehouse robotic receives the right product delivery to the right shelf message from the warehouse warehouse, it will delvier the product to the shelf position carefully. So, avoiding none of any wrong goods putting on the wrong shelves positions occurs easily. When, every one, there has none any wrong goods are putted on wrong sheleves positions occurrence, the spending investigation time to any wrong goods putting on wrong shelves position, it does not need to any one warehouse manager to do every day, So, Amazon does not need to waste time to do any goods putting on wrong warehouse workers number, when it applies many warehouse robotics to assist them to work in order to raise goods delivery efficiency in warehouse, e.g. Amazon warehouse can apply three logistic robotics and one human warehouse worker number to do one goods shelf delivery task. Before, it needs to employ ten human warehouse, logistic workers to reponsible to do one goods shelf delivery task. I assume that the goods shelf can put total 300 pieces of different kinds of products per day. So, Amazon can reduce none warehouse logistic workers number when it increases three logistic robotics to help them to do these 300 goods delivery task per day. Hence, its wage expenditure must decrease. Moreover, logistic robotics do not feel tried , bored, overtime work, these three robotics only follow any one of warehouse worker's message to let them to know whether which kind of product is needed to put on which number of the shelf positiion. Then, these three logistic workers can remember where the product is putted on the shelf position and help any one logisitic worker to get the right product to already deliver to the foreign buyer's home from Amazon's warehouses easily, they must raise efficiency more than only workers , they work in Amazon warehouses.

Hence, Amazon believes higher wage can enourage smart logistic workers can have good performance to dominate how every logistic robot , e.g. avoiding to send wrong message to let any one logistic robotic to put wrong product to the wrong shelf number position. SO, Amazon can apply warehouse scientific management method to avoid warehouse worker individual wrong message delviery to any one logistic robotic occurrence, when they can receive higher wage, and the three logistic robotics and one warehouse worker cooperation relationship is the most suitable workers cooperation number.

Amazon 's warehouse does not need more nine workers to often move in the crowd warehouse space environment to avoid worker accident and wrong goods putting on wrong shelves number position occurrences both. Hence, Amazon can apply scientific management method on warehouse avoiding resource waste aspect, when it decides to apply logistic robotics and workers cooperation in order to avoid wasting time to investigate whether which kinds of goods are put on where the wrong shelves number positions per day tasks occurrence in possible and it can bring delay to deliver goods to the online buyer's home. it is one good example of scientific management avoiding time waste method to Amazon warehouse organization.

Can Robotic Help Warehouses To Avoid Resource Waste On Behavioral Economic View
● Behavioral economy view whether robotic can help
warehouse to avoid time and human resource
waste

   IN fact,robts are being used in different types manufacturing to create more efficiency with fewer resource. Robots also reduce errors, to leass waste is produced. Less waste is produced and the robots are able to final and separate the small parts more efficiently than human hands can. For example, on environment recycled aspect, robots can help reduce waste that is incinerated by efficiently sorting materials that can be recycled quickly and more efficiently than humans reducing the input poser and cost control with such processes. So, robots can bring positive affect the environment, because robots use less energy and produce less waste.

As a whole, there are multiple benefits to using robots to fight climate change,e.g. robots can prevent pollution and emissions through careful monitoring optimize the manaufacturing processes to reduce energy consumption. Moreover, robots can help with recycling, the use of robots allows facility operators some new flexibility. Most technologies used in recycling allow to sort materials. The sensing robots (sensoes) allow robots to receive information about a certain measurement of the environment , or internal components. This is essential to robots to perform their tasks, and act upon any changes in the environment to calculate the appropriate response.

● How Amazon warehouse applies logistic robots to help
it to waste resource waste

   Hence, although robots can take our jobs, because they can help organizations to avoid resource waste, and it can bring negative effect to influence we lose jobs. ON behavorioral economic view, robots can help employers to reduce employees number, but it won't influence organizational overall performance to be worse or inefficiency, such as Amazon warehouse applies logistic robots to assist workers to deliver the right kind of goods to put on every correct shelf number position rapidly every day. Hence, one logistic robot can replace at least 10 store workers to do goods delivery tasks every day, e.g. one store worker needs to spend one minute to find the right kind of good to deliver to prepare to arrange to deliver it to fly to overseas client. Logistic robots only need 10 seconds to find the right kind of goods from the near 200 number shelves in Amazon warehouse as well as they are putting 300 different kinds of goods on these 200 shelves in Amazon warehouse every day.

Because each logistic robot has very good memory. Each logistic robot must remember any kinds of goods , their putting number position on which shelf, e.g. when the worker needs to find the model laptop product from 300 different kinds of products,in Amazon warehouse. They are putting on 200 number shelves number following positions. IN general, human worker will need to spend about one minute to find the model of laptop product from these 200 number shelves in warehouse. For example, when one worker needs to find the brand Apple of one laptop product model: PHZ0123, when the warehouse has total 300 diferent kinds of products are putting on total 200 numbers of different shelves positions. Any one Amazon store worker must need to type this Apple brand laptop" Apple" name and its model number" PHZ0123 on the store computer as well as to search its putting on shelf number position from computer. Then, the Amazon store computer will find this laptop product to find its present putting on the correct shelf number position , e.g. 50 number of the shelf positon, or none stock record of all this model PHZ20123 laptop is sold out. So, Amazon store computer must need time to help this store worker to search this laptop product's putting on shelf number position as well as the worker needs time to walk to the right shelf number position to find this laptop product.

However, logistic robotic does not need to spend time to type this laptop product brand name and model number in order to search where it is putted on the shelf number position. The Amazon store worker only needs to speak this laptop product brand name, e.g. Apple and the kind of product, e.g.laptop and model number, e.g. PHZ0123 and its piece number, e.g. one piece number. Then, the Amazon logistic robot can follow the store worker's sound to find its past this kind of product's shelf number position memory to move to this shelf correct number position and finds it to deliver to the worker immediately. So, if the worker speaks 10 kinds f different products one time, then the logistic robotic can help this worker to find these 10 of different kinds products from their correct shelves numbers rapidly. Hence, it seems that logistic robots can help Amazon store workers to reduce each product search time as well as logistic robots can help workers to do goods delviery tasks. So, in logistic robotic behevioral economic vire, logistic robotics can replace many workers to do product position research and delivery tasks, store workers only need to speak the kind of product name, model, brand name and delivery piece number to let the logistic robotic to know. Then, the logistic robotic can follow the store worke's sending message to find the product's past memmory in order to tell the store worker, whether the product has how many stocks on shelf, or none of stock on shelf and where is putted on . Hence, any one store worker does not need to spend much time to search where any kinds of products shelves number position are. They only need logistic robotics to help them to do any kinds of products deliver to , or 20 or more different kinds between products location and the store worker's location. It means that the store worker only needs to stay on the same location to wait the logistic robotic brings his products comes back after he speaks to let the logistic rotic to know whether which kinds of products and piece number he needs . Then, he checks the logistic robotic's all products where they are correct or not. He may put all of these different kinds of gatherng products to the lorry to prepare to send to airport to fly to another country to deliver to the overseas client's home immediately when he confirms that all goods are his correct.

Hence, such as Amazon warehouse case, logistic robotics can help it to reduce many products searching time tasks and avoiding delivering wrong product to any overseas client's home rick occurence. Also, logistic robotics can reduce store workers number, because logistic robotics can replace 10 to 20 human store workers number absolutely. Otherwise, human store workers may have errors in their product search process, e.g. finding the wrong product from shelf or putting the product to the wrong shelf number position, but logistic robotics can reduce to 0 error to put wrong product on the shelf number position or spends long time to search the kind of product from the shelf number position. So, in logistic robotic behavioral economic view, robotics can help businesses to avoid products putting on wrong shelves number position error risk, reduce store workers number, reduce product shelf number position search economic time.

Can Robotic Help Warehouses To Avoid Resource Waste On Behavioral Economic View

● Behavioral economy view whether robotic can help
warehouse to avoid time and human resource
waste

IN fact,robts are being used in different types manufacturing to create more efficiency with fewer resource. Robots also reduce errors, to leass waste is produced. Less waste is produced and the robots are able to final and separate the small parts more efficiently than human hands can. For example, on environment recycled aspect, robots can help reduce waste that is incinerated by efficiently sorting materials that can be recycled quickly and more efficiently than humans reducing the input poser and cost control with such processes. So, robots can bring positive affect the environment, because robots use less energy and produce less waste.

As a whole, there are multiple benefits to using robots to fight climate change,e.g. robots can prevent pollution and emissions through careful monitoring optimize the manaufacturing processes to reduce energy consumption. Moreover, robots can help with recycling, the use of robots allows facility operators some new flexibility. Most technologies used in recycling allow to sort materials. The sensing robots (sensoes) allow robots to receive information about a certain measurement of the environment , or internal components. This is essential to robots to perform their tasks, and act upon any changes in the environment to calculate the appropriate response.

● How Amazon warehouse applies logistic robots to help
it to waste resource waste

Hence, although robots can take our jobs, because they can help organizations to avoid resource waste, and it can bring negative effect to influence we lose jobs. ON behavorioral economic view, robots can help employers to reduce employees number, but it won't influence organizational overall performance to be worse or inefficiency, such as Amazon warehouse applies logistic robots to assist workers to deliver the right kind of goods to put on every correct shelf number position rapidly every day. Hence, one logistic robot can replace at least 10 store workers to do goods delivery tasks every day, e.g. one store worker needs to spend one minute to find the right kind of good to deliver to prepare to arrange to deliver it to fly to overseas client. Logistic robots only need 10 seconds to find the right kind of goods from the near 200 number shelves in Amazon warehouse as well as they are putting 300 different kinds of goods on these 200 shelves in Amazon warehouse every day.

Because each logistic robot has very good memory. Each logistic robot must remember any kinds of goods , their putting number position on which shelf, e.g. when the worker needs to find the model laptop product from 300 different kinds of products,in Amazon warehouse. They are putting on 200 number shelves number following positions. IN general, human worker will need to spend about one minute to find the model of laptop product from these 200 number shelves in warehouse. For example, when one worker needs to find the brand Apple of one laptop product model: PHZ0123, when the warehouse has total 300 diferent kinds of products are putting on total 200 numbers of different shelves positions. Any one Amazon store worker must need to type this Apple brand laptop" Apple" name and its model number" PHZ0123 on the store computer as well as to search its putting on shelf number position from computer. Then, the Amazon store computer will find this laptop product to find its present putting on the correct shelf number position , e.g. 50 number of the shelf positon, or none stock record of all this model PHZ20123 laptop is sold out. So, Amazon store computer must need time to help this store worker to search this laptop product's putting on shelf number position as well as the worker needs time to walk to the right shelf number position to find this laptop product.

However, logistic robotic does not need to spend time to type this laptop product brand name and model number in order to search where it is putted on the shelf number position. The Amazon store worker only needs to speak this laptop product brand name, e.g. Apple and the kind of product, e.g.laptop and model number, e.g. PHZ0123 and its piece number, e.g. one piece number. Then, the Amazon logistic robot can follow the store worker's sound to find its past this kind of product's shelf number position memory to move to this shelf correct number position and finds it to deliver to the worker immediately. So, if the worker speaks 10 kinds f different products one time, then the logistic robotic can help this worker to find these 10 of different kinds products from their correct shelves numbers rapidly. Hence, it seems that logistic robots can help Amazon store workers to reduce each product search time as well as logistic robots can help workers to do goods delviery tasks. So, in logistic robotic behevioral economic vire, logistic robotics can replace many workers to do product position research and delivery tasks, store workers only need to speak the kind of product name, model, brand name and delivery piece number to let the logistic robotic to know. Then, the logistic robotic can follow the store worke's sending message to find the product's past memmory in order to tell the store worker, whether the product has how many stocks on shelf, or none of stock on shelf and where is putted on . Hence, any one store worker does not need to spend much time to search where any kinds of products shelves number position are. They only need logistic robotics to help them to do any kinds of products deliver to , or 20 or more different kinds between products location and the store worker's location. It means that the store worker only needs to stay on the same location to wait the logistic robotic brings his products comes back after he speaks to let the logistic rotic to know whether which kinds of products and piece number he needs . Then, he checks the logistic robotic's all products where they are correct or not. He may put all of these different kinds of gatherng products to the lorry to prepare to send to airport to fly to another country to deliver to the overseas client's home immediately when he confirms that all goods are his correct.

Hence, such as Amazon warehouse case, logistic robotics can help it to reduce many products searching time tasks and avoiding delivering wrong product to any overseas client's home rick occurence. Also, logistic robotics can reduce store workers number, because logistic robotics can replace 10 to 20 human store workers number absolutely. Otherwise, human store workers may have errors in their product search process, e.g. finding the wrong product from shelf or putting the product to the wrong shelf number position, but logistic robotics can reduce to 0 error to put wrong product on the shelf number position or spends long time to search the kind of product from the shelf number position. So, in logistic robotic behavioral economic view, robotics can help businesses to avoid products putting on wrong shelves number position error risk, reduce store workers number, reduce product shelf number position search economic time.

Amazon organizational intangible resource management strategy

● How to implement effective intangible resources management strategy to achieve performance improvement to Amazon e-commerce organization? Why does non intangible resources effective negligence management to Amazon organization, it will cause worse performance to Amazon e-commerce organization any one e-buyer?

One efficient organization must need have efficient and effective resources management strategy in order to provide enough resources for its organization overall different departments cooperation effectively and efficiently. How to implement effective resources management strategy to achieve performance improvement? Why does ersources shortage to organization, it will cause worse performance? I shall explain the reasons as below:

For Amazon e-commerce organization example, it is one global the most large goods transport delivery service moddleman role between global online customers and their product salespeople. Amazon owns its webstores, so global any one country buyer clicks to its different countries webstores , then he/she can choose any kinds of products to buy from Amazon any one country webstore. However, the product is owned the another seller. So, any products are not owned by from Amazon any one country webstores. However, the product is owned by the another seller. SO, any products are not owned by Amazon. It only provides webstores to let global any one e-buyer to buy the product after he/she has paid visa payment. So, Amazon's role is one middleman. It needs to provide goods transport service to help the product's seller to deliver the product to whose e-buyer individual hoime in the most short time, e.g. when one China e-buyer clicks to Amazon China webstore , after he chooses any brands of computers product from Amazon China webstore, he makes purchase of the brand of comouter decision. Then, he needs to pay visa to Amazon 's China webstore . When Amazon confirms that ie can accept payment by the China e-buyer's visa. Then, Amazon will deliver the product to the China e-buyer's home within one week or longer time, the delivery days time depends on how much delivery fee, the China's e-buyer , he can pay. So, Amazon only can receive commision infomr from the computer brand product seller. Because Amazon can build famous loyalty of rapid goods delivery service provider barnad and its different countries websites can provide above one million different kinds of brand products to let global different conuntries e0buyers to choose in order to make the most fair and the most reasonable purchase price decision from its different Amazon different countries webstores per day. So, Amazon can help its different countries sellers to apply Amazon itself unique different countries' websotes design to attract global many different countries e-buyers to click to Amazon's webstores to find any kinds of products to choose to buy conveniently.

So, such as Amazon e-commerce organization case, if it hopes to attract global different countries e-buyers prefer to click to Amazon itself any one webstore more than other firms themselves webstores . Then, it must need have enough resources (tangible and intangible) both in order to provide raoid goods delviery service and many different kinds of goods choice provision service and reasonable price consumption channel to let any one countrye-buyer feels confidence and safe payment transaction and enough product advertisement, photo, price, function information in order to make final purchase decision from Amazon itself different country webstores more easily.

Hence, the tangible and intangible resources are needed to supuply to Amazon e-commerce organization. They may include: Product photos, price information, product advertisement which are shown to Amazon's different countries webstores , enough online customer service enquiry employees number, enough computers number, enough computers number, different countries offices and warehouses number, computers, internnet technology etc. tangible resource as well as customer service enquiries feedbacks, global rapid goods delivery transport service to any one country e-buyer's home, safe e-payment channel, providing to buy global any one country sellers their products in the most reasonable and the most fair purchase transaction. All ot these issues are any one e-buyer individual purchase feeling to Amazon. SO, they are intangibel (non-tangible) resources to Amazon. It means that if Amazon can let global any one e-buyer feels it's e-purchase service provision can let they feel more satisfactory , then they will choose to buy Amazon webstores any kinds of products more than other sellers their webstores products, because Amazon webstores can provide the kind of product of different brands choice, it aims to compare whether which brand's price is unreasonable too high or which brand's product's quality is worse, or design is not very atrraction. So, Amazon's intangibale resource, such as rapid goods delivery service, online or phone customer enquiry service, webstores' products information whether e-buyers can feel satisfactory, e.g. reasonable price, clear product photo many different kinds of brands product choice. All of these intangible resources to Amazon, they may also influence Amazon's future e-buyer number absolutely.

● How can Amazon raise intangible resource number to be effective?

SO, I explain that Amazon hadboth kinds of resources. They may include tangible and intangible resources. Internet speed, whether it is intangible resources. Internet speed, whether it is rapid or slow to satisfy global e-buyers online purchase speed and non online traffic jam accidents feeling. Amazon webstores any brands of products, photos, price information images whether they are clear to let any one global ebuyer to feel when they click to Amazon any one webstores. All of these internet technology resources to Amazon any one webstore will influence Amazon e-commerce organization's e-buyers number will increase or decrease . For example, if Amazon's China webstore can not let Chinese e-buyers to feel that it can not provide different kinds of brand products photos' clear image to let any one Chinese e-buyer to see the product photo clearly. When one Chinese e-buyer clicks to Amazon Chinese webstore to find any brands of laptop products to prepare to choose one to buy. But when he clicks to Amazon China webstore, he can not feel any one brand of laptop's photo is clear to let he feels. Then, theser unclear laptop photos may influence the Chinese e-buyer forgets his laptop purchase decision from Amazon 's China webstore easily. He may clcik to the another brand of laptop seller webstore to buy the brand of laptop from the laptop seller itself webstore. SO, Amazon's webstore design may be the important intangible resource to influence global any one e-buyer's visiting Amazon's any one webstore times or reducing to do to choose to visit Amazon's webstore behavior , due to they do not click to Amazon any one webstore websites again.

I recommend that Amazon ought consider how to design its any countries webstores in order to attract global e-buyers visiting Amazon itself webstores times number increase. So, global e-buyers' visiting Amazon different countries webstores times which will be Amazon's most important intangible resources to cause its future global e-buyers number. This kind of intangible resources may help Amazon e-commerce goods delivery service organization to raise its competitive effort,, because when one country's ebuyer feels Amazon can provide the most attraction and fair purchase channel from its different countries webstores. Then, the country's e-buyer will talk to his friends, families to prefer to choose Amazon if they have online purchase desire. Because Amazon's any one e-buyer , he .she will persduade his/her friends, families to choose Amazon's e-purchase channel., if he feels it can provide excellent e-purchase method to satisfy his online purchase need. Consequently, Amazon's e-buyers number may be influenced to increase.

ON conclusion, such as Amazon case, how to decide its whether which is the most important tangible and/or intangible resources in order to raise competition effort. It depends on whether how the seller sells its product, in order to concentrate on spending to increase the kind of resources number, such as Amazon e-commerce goods sale and delivery service organization case, internet webstores design intangible image dissatisfactory or satisfactory feeling which may be the most influential global e-buyers number increases or decreases. Moreover, Amazon's internet webstores design intangible satisfactory or dissatisfactory feeling resource may also influence e-buyer before or after e-purchase service requiry feedback feeling, safe visa card payment feeling, fair and reasonable brands of products price information and different brands of product photos image seeing satisfactory or dissatisfactory feeling , they are intangible resource asset to Amazon when global any one ebuyer must need to click to its any one webstore to find its any kinds of product to make purchase decision. So, any organizations must need to spend limit money to support its the most influential intangible resource , instead of tangible resources in order to increase clients number. On conclusion, we can increase organizational resources on these several aspects: Organizational resources are all assets that are available to a firm for use during the production process or service process, such as Amazon ecommerce organization case. The four basic types of organization resources are human, monetary, raw materials may be tangible, but internet technology may be another intangible resource to today any organizations. Improving organizational resources aim to improve efficiency, it means as the ability to accomplish something with the least amout of wasted time, money and effort or performance as well as effectiveness, such as improving internet speed, and none online traffic jam accidents occurrence easily. It means as trhe degree to which something is successful in producing a desired result success. However, we can improve resources by these way, they may include : Review who manages resources within the organization, build an-up-to date knowledge raise and company wide resource pool, manage the resource pool in line with the market, focus on education and talent employees growth, keep the customers in mind, work on quality services or products, learn to use technology , such as Amazon needs to learn how to raise high speed internet service for its webstores, and avoid online traffic jam frequent occurrent to its any one country webstore.

To sum up effective resource management strategy can help any organizations to increase resource number. Resource management is acquiring , allocating and managing the reosrces, such as individuals, and their skills, finances, technology , material , machinery, and natural resources required for a project. Hence effective effective resource management strategy ensures that internal and external resources are used effectively on time and budget, resources may be obtained internally from the host organization or procured from external resources. SO, effective resource management can help organizations to save resources being wastes and finances being spend on the wrong things, a significant cost saving factor. Hence, such as Amazon e-commerce organization, it needs to know how to learn how to apply internet technology to improve its different countries webstores design, shorten goods transport delivery time, gathering more different brands of product prices, data and phoducts photos improving safe visa card transaction secret to increase e-buyer individual e-purchase confidence. When Amazon can concentrate on effective allocate limited resource to achiev ethese objectives. Then, its global e-buyer number may increase significantly.

Management accounting science how applies to Amazon ecommerce organization
Management accounting concept can help organizations to do management budget strategies, e.g. margin analysis, capital budget, inventory valuation and product cost budget, trend analysis and forecast . Management accounting also called managerial accounting or cost accounting, is the process of analysis business costs and operations to prepare internal financial report, records and managers decision making process in achieving business goals.
However, management accountants depend on standard financial statements containing the earning statement, cash flow statement and balance sheet. In addition , it also makes use of additional finds reports in analysizing the information of the organization including budget performance and cost reports. I shall attempt to explain how management account science can help organizations to analyze cost , why and how changes in order to avoid expense increases or excess cost cases or loss increases.
For Amazon e-commerce publish organization example, Amazon publish is a famous publish organization. It applies

internet (online) channel to help authors to sell electronic books and paper books to different countries readers. It also cooperate to other publishers to deliver any its anthors books to their webstores, so when one reader chooses its publish partner webstores to buy Amazon any author books, then Amazon publish will share royalty income between them. Hence, Amazon publish may be book distribution partner to its other e-publish partners.

● How management accounting cocept can help Amazon publish to manage its cost effectively in order to increase its profit or e-books or paper books sale ability.

Amazon publish is a e-comerce organization. It depends high internet speed to help global authors to register Amazon publish's individual author account , then any global authors may download their book files to produce any ebooks and papers to sell from Amazon publisher webstores as wellas global any readers can apply Amazon publish webstores to buy any author individual paper or ebooks from its web-publish stores rapidly. So, Amazon publish must need have fast speed internet technology to support its books sale ability,

It brings this question: How much does Amazon publish internet expenditure need? Does it need to pay shops rent per month? Because Amazon publish has none any actual book shops to locate in any countries. So, Amazon publish must not pay rent to any countries for its shops. Although Amazon publish does not need to pay rent for any book shops, but Amazon publish needs to pay extra internet expenditure to US internet service provider to support its electronic webstores daily electronic books and paper books every purchase transaction, any countries author individual book electronic files download per day 24 hours . So, Amazon publish must need to pay more expenditure for internet service to support its authors and readers their electronic books and paper books purchase and sale transaction per day 24 hours.

As Amazon publish case, in its financial report indicates , it does not pay any book stores rent expenditure or book stores (shops) building building expediture on its profit and loss account, but Amazon publish must need to pay internet service expenditure to US internet service provider. Moreover, this internet service expenditure must be more amount, due to it needs to provide its webstores online book (electronic books and paper books) to sell and electronic library e-book lending service to global readers, 24 hours. Thus, internet service expenditure must be Amazon publish long-term influential transaction expenditure because, any electronic books and paper books, even e-library books borrow service and readers must need to pay visa card for borrowing book month service fee and purchase books from amazon publish e-publish webstores in any time every day.

Hence, Amazon publish must need have good management account strategy in order to predict whether different countries will have how many readers click to its different countries e-publish webstores to spend time to choose different authors books to buy or borrow to read from intenet channel. So, any countries readers budgeting number, readers reading habit behavior, e.g. US has about one million online readers click Amazon e-publish webstores , but it has only three thousands readers pay visa card to buy its ebooks and paper books from its Amazon electronic publish webstores, in this week , but next week, US has about seven thousands online readers click Amazon e-publish webstores, but it has three thousands readers pay visa card to buy its ebooks and paper books. Hence, it seems tha although this week has one million online readers click to Amazon publish electonic webstores to seek any books, but the book buyer number has only three thousands. Otherwise, although next week, it reduces three thousands e-readers click to visit Amazon e-publish webstores e-readers number , but it still keep same three thousand e-readers to choose to buy Amazon publish's books to read.

I assume that Amazon publish needs to pay a fixed internet service expenditure, e.g. US $500,000, but it design this e-publish webstores can help it to do its different countries e-publish webstores, their daily e-readers visiting number, daily electronic book and paper book sale number and daily e-readers visiting time statistics. It's electronic publish webstores can help it to record any countries' reading habits and reading taste , e.g. how many fiction , story books have sold in the week, how many non fiction books have sold in the week , e.g. business topic books have sold next week.

So, Amazon publish can use its e-publish webstores to gather above data in order to make author book topic sale choice, e.g. whether this week, US market ought sell how many consumer psychological topic book, US market ought sell how many management topic book next week. If this week US market can only sell one thousand consumer psychological topic book to compare its budget is less than one thousand consumer psychological topic books budget sale number reduces, e.g. in the week, there are two thousands readers choose to buy consumer psychological topic books from European market in this week. It implies that there are many European readers who like to read consumer behavior books recently. Hence, Amazon can attempt to concentrate on encouraging authors to write more consumer psychological books to let European readers to read within next several months.

Basic on above effects, Amazon needs to provide rapid internet service to European libraries, schools ,e-book partners to help them to promote Amazon consumer psychology topic books in order to let the European consumer psychological students, consumer psychology lecturers, consumer psychologists to know Amazon publish can provide more different topics concern consumer psychology research in order to increase Amazon 's consumer psychology book European market book buyers bumber.

As above case, I assume Amazon publish needs to pay a fixed internet service expenditure , e.g. US$500,000 per month. Amazon needs webstores to evaluate whether it is value, if it helps European schools, libraries organizations to pay internet fee, in order to let they can let many consumer psychology students and teachers and consumer psychologists to know that Amazon publish may have enough different consumer psychology books to be provided to European publish libraries, schools readers to read. For example, I assume next several month, Amazon publish needs to pay US two million internet service expenditure to global different European countries to help Amazon publish itself to promote its al different authors' consumer psychology topic books as well as it evaluates that it will sell different European countries; students , teachers and consumer psychologists readers, they have about three million readers at least choose to buy its one million consumer psychology topic authors; paper books and electronic books next several months as well as it also needs to evaluate whether it can earn more than US ten million at least royalty income after reducing author royalty from all European countries book markets.

Thus, if Amazon publish makes decision to help European countries schools, public libraries to pay internet expenditure to help it to advertise its one million consumer psychology topic authors electronic and paper books to sell. It must needs to pay fixed US$500,000 internet expenditure for Amazon publish its all e-bpublish webstores and it also needs to pay extra two million internet service expenditure for global all European countries libraries and schools per month. If next month, Amazon publish can earn more than US tem million at least royalty income after reducing author royalty from all European countries book market. Then, Amaozn publish ought attempt to make this internet service expenditure for all European schools, libraries organizations, if it had confidence to earn this royalty amount from European consumer psychology book readers, such as this Amazon publish.

On conclusion, , this Amazon publish organization case, it may attempt to apply management accounting science method to make book sale number budget, royalty income budget, even analysis to reader individual reading habit, book topic choices, book sale price evaluation in order to judge whether the kind or topic book ought concentrates on selling to which countries marekts, such as Amazin publish case, it also may choose different consumer psychology topic books to concentrate on selling to different European countries in next several months, if it can earn all European royalty income more than its internet service expenditure to European schools, libraries, then Amazon may attempt to make this decision. Otherwise, it won't be good decision.

Hence, it implies that management accounting is one kind of business management science, it can apply number to help any organizations to do right or reasonable reason more accurate as well as it is different to traditional financial acounting, it only helps organizations to record and income and expenditure, earn or loss record function. Hence, management accounting may help any organizations to attempt implement useful or effective strategies in order to improve themselves performance.

How Amazon solves its future marketing challenges

Amazon faces what future marketing competition

Nowadays, any kinds of businessmen may apply internet to do themselves e-commerce sale channel easily and conveniently. So, Amazon needs to find strategies how to persuade any kinds of brands of sellers to choose its e-stores to help themselves to advertise, promote and sell their products to replace themselves online stores from Amazon its e-stores. It will be one long term marketing strategic problem to Amazon needs to consider how to attract global many sellers choose Amazon's e-stores to replace themselves e-stores (online sale channels) easily. How to increase global sellers confidence to choose Amazon e-stores to help them to sell their different kinds of products ? I shall attempt to indicate some useful marketing and management strategies to explain as below:

Firstly, I shall indicate what kinds of challenges Amazon will face in future ecommerce market. Although, Amazon's cloud dominance core online sale marketplace had succeed, but it still faces many challenges.
It needs to implement useful strategies to solve in order to increase its online buyers number and online sellers number both.

` On growth challenge concerning aspect, Amazon needs to learn how to grow investors confidenccs to let Amazon itself can help them to apply its e-stores to help them to advertise their products from Amazon e-stores to replace Google cloud online advertisement service competitor as well as Microsoft cloud online advertisement service competitor both main online advertisement service providers. It seems that global online sellers may also choose Google and Microsoft cloud advertisement to replace Amazon cloud advertisement service.

So, Amazon's marketplace needs to find itself on the defensive for reasons unrelated to the probe improvements in e-commerce technology on the whole could mean that fewer sellers see Amazon as their primary sales channel, instead of Google , Microsoft cloud advertisement sale channel. Hence, Amazon needs to implement strategy how to help any global sellers to change positive shopping experience on traditional web stores improvement, in order to help they to promote their brands more effectively.

ON online shopping confident challenge aspect, Amazon became the dominant e-commerce marketplace in the world by offering hundreds of million of products at competitive prices. However, Amazon will face third-party sellers participation to cloud market online sale agent competitive challenge. Third-party sellers , such as Google, Microsoft have made up an increasing share of products on Amazon in recent years, roughly 58% of sales on Amazon were key third-party sellers, but that comes with its own host of problems, including fakes, counterfeits and unsafe products that Amazon has not been able to successful compete easily in third party cloud e-commerce sale market. Past surveys have shown that Amazon is among the most trusted technology brands out there, but if it gains a reputation as a sketchy products, some consumers could not to do their shopping at first past sites. Hence, Amazon needs to let global many sellers believe that it is the best third party cloud advertisement service provider to compare its another third part cloud advertisement service providers , such as Google. Microsoft in order to persuade many global sellers choose to use its cloud online advertisement service.

What is Amazon marketing strategy? Amazon uses the high runner strategy to market its products. This strategy was data to uncover which products are in the highest demand in every category . Amazon's pricing strategy and bids heavily on advertisement to pull people to those sellers themselves products. In future, Amazon's marketing strategies include: SEOP, cheap price advertisement, user-generated content, video marketing, dedicated website. Hence, Amazon's future marketing strategy or communication strategy aims to increase customer traffic to Amazon websites, create awareness of products or services, promote repeat purchases, develop incremental product and service revenue opportunities.

However, Amazon can improve marketing strategy to help its sellers to boost their products sale by providing free shipping, reviewing [product sale analytics, testing different advertising methods. So, Amazon has three big market sale channels, the retail marketplace, Amazon Prime, and Amazon web services. Moreover, Amazon needs to build effective growth strategy. It's Amazon's secondary intensive growth strategy. It aims to generate more revenue from markets where the company currently operates because Amazon is depended on its customers, which is why when consumerism grows, the business by default grows. It means that whose global e-commerce online e-stores purchase market grows, the global visiting shops market customers number will be influenced to fall down. So, it implies that they have close customer number relationship between e-stores customers number and visiting shops customers number to different kinds of businesses.

Even, future Amazon business may have this competitive strategy, it can be described as cost leadership taken to the extreme strategy. Cost leadership strategy seems as cheap , bulk products sale, such as " discount stores " sale method. All of Amazon's products are sold by the cheapest sale product method. So, Amazon marketing communication mix integrates print and media advertising, sales promotions , events and experiences, public relation and direct marketing. Amazon places a particular focus on print and media advertising and sales promotions elements of the marketing communication channels. So, Amazon was direct marketing. It is so advanced that they see what their customers are searching for, offer products, that are the same of similar and send their emails for when the price changes for an item, the customers have been eyeing up.

However, Amazon's management principles of leadership in organization, it is also important to influence organizational growth. It can drive Amazon to boost sale, they include: customers obsession, leaders start with the customer and work backwards, leaders are owners, invent and simplify, learning and be curious. Hiring and developing the4 best, insisting on the highest standards. So, Amazon company makes include customers are at the top of the company's interests, Amazon wants to make everything as simple as it is possible. Hence, Amazon applies intensive growth strategy. It is a growth strategy that focuses on cultivating new products or new markets and sometimes both. Amazon aims to help its any kinds of product sellers to bring new online advertisement experience feeling to let online buyers to aware their new products existences.

Hence, Amazon needs to help its sellers to change their e-business model from " direct sales" to sales-and-service model, aggregating many sellers under one virtual roof and receiving commission from the other companies sales, because Amazon needs to make income through its online retail e-stores, subscriptions and web services, among other channels. Retail remains Amazon's primary source of revenue, with online and physical stores accounting for the biggest share. Essentially , Amazon is choosing growth over profits. And, Amazon is able to lose money to help its sellers grow their markets shares from e-business model.

In fact, most Amazon sellers market least US$1,000 per month in sales, and some super-sellers make upward US$250,000 each month in sales. However, Amazon also helps someone without cost to create selling, such as Amazon publishers. So, Amazon publishers do not need to spend any cost to sell e-books or paper books when they download their books on Amazon publish. Hence, Amazon can attract many different countries authors choose to cooperate to sell their books from Amazon publish platform. It means that Amazon's business model , which was initially based on ecommerce had changed and now incorporates entertainment, music, cloud computing, meal delivers etc. e-publishing etc. Although, Amazon sells a lot more through its subsidiaries, the core Amazon busi9ness model is based on an e-commerce market platform . Amazon sells products or the platform but, also allows third-party sellers to sell consumers.

How does Amazon future business model? Amazon future business model ought depend on geographically and terms of products and services offered to help its different kinds of product sellers to sell their products, such as continue expanding on selling music, videos, electronics, video games, software, houseware, toys, games, e-books as well as attracted customers were Amazon its personalized recommendation tools and customers reviews, this developing a community of consumers , which is essential free online service to any one Amazon customer.

So, Amazon will obsession rather than competitor focus, passion excellence, and long=term, thinking. Amazon must continue focus on those operations in order to grow income. They may include: Amazon marketplace business model, Amazon asks for a fee from its sellers to promote and advertise their products, Amazon's subscription business model has been vital to the brand growth. In exchange for a monthly fee. Subscribers have access to the platform's video and music streaming catalog, free two days shopping, unlimited photo storage etc.

Amazon was services business model, it is a low cost complete IT structure platform, whose services are contracted by companies, organizations, and institutions around the world. Amazon kindle, business model, it is Amazon's e-reading service, users can buy, browse, and download books, magazines and newspapers , available at kindle store. Amazon patent business model, it has more than 1,000 patents, several of which are licensed by other campaigns. Amazon advertising business model, it is Amazon ad. Platform offers sponsored ads and video. It is a very efficient marketing channel, since the audience there with the intention of buying. Hence, Amazon 's customer segments may include: sellers, buyers and developers. Sellers are all the companies that use Amazon's e-commerce platform to sell their products to all the community involves with Amazon web-services.

Amazon's cloud computing platform, As its own website states, they are customers and partners, e.g. any public sector or private sector organizations. And the buyers are global people, who acquire products and services through Amazon's channels. So, Amazon can track its custo0mer based on some characteristics, such as interest, engagement, and personnel information (e.g. gender, geographical space, language among other), ion order to predict any countries potential consumer behaviors more accurately.

Hence, Amazon's business model is based on three value propositions: low price, fast delivery, and a wide selection of products in order to let consumers feel these benefits, e.g. convenience to connect to Amazon's any web stores to buy any kinds of products, with an reasonable price, safe and reliable delivery service. Also Amazon can build long term good relationship to its global buyers from its web stores, such as product reviews, and comments on the platform, telephone, online chat and email contact. Aside from Amazon's online resource, other key resources to bring Amazon's benefits, they may include physical spaces of the company, such as offices, warehouses, supply chain structure and automation etc.

In fact, human resources are essential for Amazon , which needs to help it to operate daily online purchase and sale activities effectively, such as Amazon's e-stores designers, engineers, developers. Hence, Amazon key partners may include: world wide different brans of product sellers, affiliates, bloggers who earn a commission for any referrals that need to a sale. In addition to helping with sales, they also promote traffic to the Amazon platform. Amazon's platform independent software vendors, who adapt Amazon's online platform technology to work, content creators , they are independent authors, who can publish their works through kindle direct publishing, subsidiaries, include companies that provide storage spaces, stores and systems, in additions to brands and products, developed by Amazon itself, such as Amazon essentials, Amazon elements, kindle , Alexa etc.

Also, Amazon needs to know how to let its future cost structure to reduce in order to achieve saving cost benefit in long time. Its cost structure includes its complete IT structure, customer service center, software development and maintenance, information security, marketing as well as expenses involved in maintaining its physical spaces, such as fulfillment centers, sortation centers, and delivery stations. Hence, future Amazon will need to implement useful methods to help its any departments to reduce operational cost as well as have to persuade partners, sellers, product buyers to help them to raise sales growth, earn more commissions, bringing advertisement effectiveness, subscription income growth, web service growth and patents income.

Amazon's main competitors may include: online stores, Walmart, Alibaba, Otto, Jingdong, ebay, fliplcart, Newegg, ralcuten. So, if Amazon can persuade these any one online competitors to be its future partners, Then, it may reduce its online competitors number significantly. However, Amazon SWOT analysis indicates its strengths may include: Building famous e-commerce brand valuation, customer orientation, such as reasonable prices, personalized suggestions, and reviews make a loyal consumer community, innovation, it always develops new products and services, when improves its regular business, it does not maintain physical stores and has little inventory. It is able to keep a low- cost structure, large selection , it owns an extensive product mix, allowing customers to buy anything on the same platform, more global third-party sale partners, logistics . Also, Amazon's weaknesses may include: limitable business model, kindle e-book publish faces many e-publish competitors, employee workplace conditions may feel worse , focusing dependence on distributors, that exposed Amazon to a wide range to issues, especially considering renegotiation of terms. But, Amazon also has these opportunities, such as expansion. Amazon can expand its operation in developing countries, increasing physical stores number, it can make some big purchases, such as acquisitions and that can increase market share and reduce competition. But, it also has threats, e.g. some government regulations can threaten Amazon distribution inside some countries, exploitations , labor, cybercrime, it can threaten the security of the platform and its users, it faces strong competitors, A video streaming service, such as Disney Add, HBO,. Netflix.

Moreover, it can not estimate when economic recession , online stores are not adapted to alive to economic recession and uncertainty can impact Amazon's sales, fake reviews, customers rely on reviews to make purchase and Amazon needs to have more positive product review more than negative product review from its online customers.

On conclusion, Amazon is one good case to explain future any kinds of e-businesses will face what challenges in order to decide how to implement effectiv3e strategies to help them to solve any possible not predicted challenges in order to raise competitive effort.

CHAPTER THREE

Labors behavior or robot improves organizational performance

The importance of management skills is essential, if any organizations hope to raise efficiency or improve performance. Organizations need to learn how to balance hard and soft skill, how to manage social and human skills whch reflect the ability to get along with other people are increasingly important attributes at all levels of management.

Managers ought need to spend most time operating between the " hard skills" , such as conducting disciplinary matters or how to allocate of budgets, and " soft skills" , such as counselling, or giving support and advice to a member of staff. Managers also needed to be trained to raise technical competence, related to specific tasks, how to supervise and train subordinate staffs, and with day-to-day subordinate staff, and with day-to-day operations concerned in the actual production of goods and services; social and human skills relates to interpesonal relationship in working with and through other people, and how to judge to achieve effective teamwork and direction, and leadership of staff to achieve co-ordinated effort to particular situation and flexibilty in adopting the most appropriate style of management, raising conceptual ability in order to view he complexities of the operations of the organization as a whole, including environmental influences.

Mc Donald soft skill organizational behavior

It also involves decision-making skills, relates to the overall making of the organization and to its stragegic planning in long time, such as McDonald restaurant has good strategic management to manage its global branches of franchise restaurants in organizational behavioral view successfully. So, it can attract many investors buy its franchises to learn how to do McDonald fast food restsurants . It's investors number is increasing, due to it has good significant organizational behavior as well as its managers know how to apply " soft skills" and " hard skills" to manage them effectively.

So, organizational behavior and organizational performance seems have close relationship. If the organization can build the most effective and efficient organizational behavior, managers know how to manage employee individual behavior, then the performance ought will be improved , even customers won't complaint or feel unsatisfactory easily, they will feel satisfactory to their staffs service performance, such as McDonald fast food restaurant case, global McDonald fast food franchise restaurants eating customers complain bumber is low in general, because instead of their front line service staffs performance and attitude can let them to feel satisfactory,

The most influential soft skill to bring its fast food eating customers feel satisfactory or they are persuaded to choose its sale service to replace other similar fast food restaurants sale service. The reason is because that , when they buy its fast food, or soft drink, they must be arranged to give one number ticket. So, they do not need to spend long time to queue in any McDonald fast food restaurants, they can leave McDonald restaurant to go to other places and they wont' worry that McDonald staffs forget to make their fast food or soft drink when they leave. Because they can give the number ticket to indicate their number to the staff to take their fast food or soft drink any time. For example, if the eating customer's ticket number is 30, and the screen indicates next number future cooking is 10, then he will feel that he can leave McDonald to spend about 15 minutes to come back. Even, if his coming back time is exceed 15 minutes, and the screen indicates number is 40. Although, he is late, but he may ask the staff to take his fast food or soft drink immediately. So, he does not need to worry about that he can take his fast food or soft drink even he is late to come back. So they avoid to queue long time in McDonald, they can come back after half hour, even after one hour. When they come back, they only need to give their number ticket to confirm that the had paid money to buy fast food or soft drink. When the front line staff see that number from their ticket. They will go to kitchen to take their prepared fast food or soft drink to give them immediately. it is one effective time management " soft skill" to avoid eating customers feel angry or bad emotion when they need to queue in long time in any one Mc Donald restaurant. They can choose to leave Mcdonald restaurants any long time. It is one efficient and effective 2 soft skill customer service management skill in any one nowadays McDonald front line . So , it's success depends on its front line staff " don't need eating people to queue long time" in any one McDonald restaurant.

Convenient framework of analysis of organizational behavior

Any organizations ought need have a convenient framework of analysis if they hope to manage their organizational behavior efficiently. I shall explain what a convenient framework of organizational behavior analysis means as below: The top level is what nature and purpose of the organization, then next middle level concerns learning how to manage " behavior of people", " process of management", " organizational context" , next is middle level learning how to adapt any environment influences. The final process to any organizations. They hope to achieve improving organizational performance in success as well as organizational processes as well as how to execution of work to the most success.

It is one important service soft skill method to let global McDonald restaurants can continue to attract many eating people to choose to but their fast food or soft drink , instead of reduced price or coupon sale method in global fast food restaurant market. So, its success depends on how to mix of the practical and the soft skill service performance strategy to eating customer long time queue bad emotion theoretical psychological strategy, it must be linked to a single aim, such as Mc Donald has its single aim to front line staffs, is that how to avoid eating people need to stay in McDonald restaurant to queue long time to let them to feel angry and unsatisfactory to its global any McDonald franchise restaurants. So it comfirms that , many its global eating people don't like to queue and to stay in McDonald long time, when the Ms Donald has many people are staying in McDonald in busy time.

Thus, in organizational behavioral view, they will be persuaded to choose to buy MsDonald fast food in perference, because its unique service feature, when other fast food restaurants can not implement this front lines do not need queue method in their fast food restaurants. It implies that effective front line service skill may be one important factor to influence any clients' choices in preference.

How to apply hard skill and soft skill to solve inefficient problem?

The theme of inefficiency will experience to any organizations, if they lack effective organizational behavioral management strategy. It assumed that workers who were not good at one particualr task, would be best at some other tasks in any teams. There is however, no certainty of this in practice. It concerns workers from an engineering view point and as machines , but the one best way of performing a task is not always the best method for every worker. So, the reduction of physical movement to find the one best way is or always beneficial and some " wasteful" movements are essential to the overall rhythm of work.

So, if the organization hopes to achieve effective organizational behavior, the organization needs to concern these soft skill and hard skill issues they may include:

1. High wages from increased output.

2. The removal of physical strain from doing works the wrong way.

3. Development of the workers and the opportunity for them to undertake tasks , they were capable of doing and

4. Elimination of the " boss" and the duty of management to help workers.

For example on factory raising efficient organizational behavior aspect, the factory may implement these soft skill and hard skill both strategies, such as: To assist the stores in better customer service by having the merchandise ready to go on the floor, saving space in the stockroom, and creating customer goodwill, to increase the units per hour produced, to performance the job duties as efficiency and effectively as possible, avoiding bureaucracies organization, it emphasised the importance of administration based on experise (rules of experts) and administration based on discipline (rules of officials). Because one when burea staffs are working in one serious or strict bureaucracies organization, they will feel not happy and unsatisfactory to their manager behavior. So, managers' soft management skill ought often need to revise when need to be changed to be better or improve their performance, such as:

The tasks of the organization are allocated as official duties among the various positions, there is an implied clear -out division of labor and a high level of specialisation, a hierarchical authority applies to the organization of offices and positions, uniformity of decisions and actions is achieved through formally established systems, of rules and regulations. Together work a structure of authority , this enables the coordination of various activities within the organization, an imperaonal orietnation is expected from officials in their dealings with clients and other officials. This is designed to result in rational judgments by officials in the performance of their duties as well as employment by the organization is based on technical qualifications and constitues a lifelong career for the officials, e.g. how to apply specialisation more to the job than to the person undertaking the job.

This makes for continuity because the job usually continues of the present job holder leaves, hierarchy of authority it makes for a sharp distination between administrators and the administered or between management and workers, within the management ranks these are clearly defined levels of authority, system of rules aims to provide for an officials and impersonal operaton, sules are generally stable although some rules may be changed as modified with impersonality means that how allocation and exercise authority should not be complex.

Robotic how helps labours to avoid adnormal working hours

Robotic had direct relationship to influence division of labor in order to avoid labours need work long time in themselves organizations. When the organization applies robotics to assist labours to work togather. It will bring improving efficiency and productive increasing effort advantanges, when their efficiency is improved. Then many labours won't need to work long time, such as adnormal working hours. So, robotic participation is a kind new change by introducing new norms to identify performance inadequately participation, where task forces as set up to develop implementation and identify stakeholders persuasion. when implementation robotic technology and human working together stategies are delegated to technical staff or experts who then sell their ideas back to decision markers and finally, where decision-makers who control and personal power when avoiding any form of only indvidual manual labours participation to any task.

Hence, when the organization can apply robotics to participate to any tasks. Then, its efficiency will raise and productivity will also improve. Consequently, the abnormal working hours challenges will reduce, workers can be happy to work.

● Why can robotic participation assist workers do not need to work overtime or need to work adnormal hours often? I assume that when one organization , e.g. factory will need to increase its productive number in order to achieve sale negotiation with its suppliers , but it has no enough workers to do this sudden increasing productive number task in this time. If it can have robotic to participate its productive task, then its workers will have more chance to avoid overtime hours work. Them worker individual working emotion will be better or enjoy to do their work or more working satisfactory or positive working attitude or improving performance for themselves organization's benefits. They won't feel difficult to produce these sudden increasing products immediately in this time. So, robotic can help workers to solve increasing productive number challenge.

However, robotic;s productive efficiency can be measured and assessment difficulties with technology produce systemic difficulties in managing organizations , (AI, intelligent intelligence or robotic manufacturing technology) and organization's duel natures as increasing productive and process suggest that sociotechnical frameworkers need to change significantly to accommodate longitudinal vires of technology, as well as (AI) or robotic manufacturing technology has increasing become. The manufacturing price is by which tooks and factory workers in the organization change in response to increasing productive demands in this sudden product manfacture number increasing situation.

● Robotic participation will bring these benefits

The " abnormal working hours need" organization will earn advantages from robotic's working participation. When robotics become manager's increasing productive aim of increasing in any projects that in present value terms cost less than the benefits, they bring in , i.e. increasing in positive net present value terms cost less than the benefits, they bring in, i.e. investing in positive value of factory electricity expenditure, reduces overtime working hours increasing wage cost .

So, robotic participation will help the factory reduces long time electricity expenditure cost, the overtime productive hours wage extra cost, when workers do not need to spend long abnormal working hours in factory. Their wage cost and factory electricity cost must reduce. Moreover, productive number will also increase, when the factory can let many robotics' participation to attribute to work for any factory productive prodject tasks with labours together in the factory.

The real asset to the factory may also include: robotic tangibel, instead of machinery to the factory, factories and offices, when robotic's role is productive workers or robotic may be intangible, suchas robotic technical expertise, even the reducing abnormal working hours will be intangible asset because the factory won't often need labours work overtime, then wage cost increases. So, robotic's task participation can increase the factory's real tangible asset benefit as well as intangible technical expertise benefit both, as well as reducing electricity expense, when the robotic can help the factory to manufacture many products, efficiency raises, machine electricity expense will also decreases as well as without none abnormal or overtime working hours need to any workers, then abnormal overtime wage will need to pay , due to robotic productive took assistance to every labour in the factory.

Robotic's productive participation can also help the factory to increase efficient use of assets. I assume the facrory manager owns a relatively small working worker teams that employs them to work to finish the productive project task. In general, the small working worker teams need to spend one hour to manufacture every product in themselves four productive steps. However, if robotic's participation to assist their four teams. Then, they only need half to finish to manufacture every product. So, average their every product productive time can be shortened half hour . Although, the factory may need to spend one time payment expenditure to buy the robotic, buy in long time, the robotic can help them to manufacture double number of product from one piece to two piece product every hour. It is efficient use of robotic asset to help the factory to raise productive number, when the factory does not to spend extra wage to employ extra employees to help it to raise product double productive number from one piece to two pieces product every hour. Hence, robotic's participation to manufacture process can also help the factory to achieve efficient use of assets to raise product productive number.

However, before the factory makes final decision to buy the robotics to assist workers' productive product number raises in order to achieve, these benefits, such as efficient use of resource or asset benefit, avoiding abnormal or overtime working hours need to workers, or extra overtime wage cost, even workers' poor working emotion, productive number increases, electricity expense cost reduces etc. benefits.

It needs to make evaluate properly the results of a risk analysis exercise. They may include: What is the range of possible values for the main product number outputs in the factory? What is the expected rate of return ? What is the downside of this robotic manufacturing investment? How could the factory cope with the downside? Is there any combination of uncertainties that result in robotic's manufacturing participation consequences? Which are that main uncertainty drivers cause the variation in profits or in costs? Can robotic manufacturing participation reduce these uncertainties? How does the risk return profit of this robotic manufacturing participation project companies to other alternatives, e.g. increasing workers number or increasing machines number or increasing workers and machines number both method in order to raise product productive number in long time?

However, risk analysis does not provide simple answers to this factory's manager, such as decision to buy robotics , instead of it provides a means of exploring the trade off between risk and return. It is also an interactive process. Once the factory manager has identified the main uncertainty drivers, he needs to think about ways to reduce these uncertainties by taking advantages of various " increasing product productive opportunities" , market research etc. But risk analysis is certainly a valuable tool for coping with a world in which just about everything is uncertain, such as this manufacturing robotic purchase decision case.

● How robotic reduces restaurant labours working hour

Robotic can apply to a restaurant chain to help it to avoid abnormal working hours to waiters and cookers. I assume that the restaurant has many restaurant chain in any countries. Because it is one famous restaurant and its food taste is good. So, it can attract many eating clients choose to go to its different restaurants to eat in different countries. Hence, every day, its eating clients number is increasing rapidly. Every day , restaurant chain eating clients number is increasing from average 100 to 200 per day. Although, it has many eating clients, but it's waiters and cookers need to often work overtime or work abnormal hours from 8 hours to 12 hours per day, even more hours. Moreover, these challenge will occur to its every restaurant chain in any countries. They may include: level of long waiting time to customers per restaurant. If it hopes to keep its service quality. It can not often need its waiters and cookers work overtime or abnormal work hours. If cookers need often to cook meals in kitchen more than 8 hours. Their meal perceived quality will be worse, when they feel tried to cook. Then, when eating clients feel their meals' perceived quality is worse. Then, they won't like to pay the same price to pay its meals spending on worse quality. Hence, the restaurant chain's revenue will be influenced to fall down. When, its cookers can not keep to cook the same good taste meals to every eating clients to eat every day. Even, their number of restaurant will be influenced to reduce, due to waiters need to spend abnormal working hours to serve eating clients as well as cookers need to spend abnormal working hours to serve eating clients. When clients feel other restaurants can replace any one of this chain restaurants. Then, number of restaurants will be influenced to reduce.

If this restaurant can apply robotic to help cookers to cook simple meals, e.g. vegetable, beef , pock etc. food . They can share their cooking load. Then, these cookers won't feel tried to cook when its eating clients number is increasing. Also, they may not need to work overtime, due to robotic may replace any one cooker to cook simple or complex meals. So, they can still work 8 hours, and meal quality can keep the best perceived to any one eating client when they eat in any one restaurant chain in any one country. Also, when this restaurant chain can apply robotic waiters to help them to deliver any meals to any one eating client's table immediately from kitchen, even robotic can give menu information choice to let any one eating client to make the meal eating decision rapidly, when they need to enquire any one waiter, but there is none any one waiter can serve them immediately. Then, serving robotic can help any one waiter to reduce work pressure and let every eating client feels satisfactory service , when robotic can serve to solve their meal menu choice enquire need.

The most important successful factor is that waiters do not need work overtime to serve many eating clients , when any one restaurant chain needs to increase opening hours to 12 hour or more per day. Serving robotic can help them to do eating client meal menu enquiring choice introducing service task any time , even after 8 hours normal working hours. They can replace any one waiter to do the same restaurant service task after 8 hours. So, waiters do not need spend overtime to work every day. They won't feel tried also, due to any one robotic's service can help than to serve their clients. Hence, it implies that future robotic can help any workers to avoid overtime to do work or need to work abnormal hours in possible.

How robotic changes global future labour market

● Applying management science equation to develop artificial intelligence to do management strategy

How to apply management science equation to develop artificial intelligence to help organizations to solve problem, I shall indicate the management science process may be applied to artificial intelligence mind technology as below:

Any management science techniques may include these steps: First step: From observation, then second step: Defining problem, then third step: model construction, then fourth step: solution finding, then fifth step: implementation management strategy.

From solution stage to implementation stage. Any organization must need to find information in order to achieve the most effective implementation method. Finally, from implementation stage, the organization may give feedback to problem definition step. Model construction step and solution step in order to revise whether this implementation method can be achieved the best aim to satisfy the organization's mission need.

A management scientist is a person skilled in the application of management science techniques. On the observation step, the system must be continuously and closely observed. So that the problems can be identified as soon as they occur or are anticipated. Then, on the definition of the problem stage, the problem must be clearly and defined. Then, on the model construction stage, a management science model is an abstrate representation of an existing problem situation. It can be the form of a graph or chart , e.g. a business from that sells a product. The product costs \$5 to produce and sells for \$20. The model that computes that total profit that will accurate from the items sold is z=

$20-5x$.

In this equation x represent the number of units of the product there are sold, and I represents the total profit that results from the sale of the product. The symbols x and z are variable . The term variable is used because no set number value has been specified for these items. The number of units sold, x and profit, z can be any amount (within limits). They can vary, these two variables can be further distinguished. z is a dependent variable, because its value is dependent on the number of units sold, x is independent variable, because the number of units sold is not dependence on anything else , in this equation.

On the model solution stage, once models have been constructed in management science, they are solved using the management science techniques presented in this text. A management science solution technique usualy applies to a specific type of model. Thus, the model type and solution methods are both part of the management science techniques. We are able to say that a model is solved, because the model represents a problem.

On implementation stage, the final step , the management science process for problem solving is how to implementation the stage. Implementation is the actual use of the model once it has been developed or the solution to the problem. The model was developed to solve. This is a critical , but often overlooked step in the process. It is not always a given that once a model is developed or a solution found is automatically used. Frequently, the person responsible for putting the model or solution to use is not the same person who developed the model and thus, the user may not fully understand how the model works or exactly what it is supposed to do. individuals are also sometimes hesitant to change the normal way, they do things or try new things.

In this situation, the model and solution may get pushed to the side or ignored although if they are not carefully explained and their benefit fully demonstrated. If the management science model and solution are not implemented, then the effort and resources used on its developed have been wasted. Hence, the management science equation models may be applied to artificial intelligent technological tool to learn to help future organizations to solve management challenges, these models may include as below:

Break even analysis, graphical solution, sensitivity analysis, linear math programming analysis, linear math programming technique, probabilistic technique, network technique, forecasting, analytical process, linear programming, multiciteria decision making, nonlinear programming, mathematical equation and function inventory and operational management.

Thus, if artificial intelligence can learn above these management science equation model, then it can help any organizations to solve any management strategic challenges.

● How to apply management skills to let artificial intelligent robotic to learn

The management skills, they can be let robotic to learn. They may include: Management skill is general theory of management . It may include these principles. Division of work, specialization, authority, formal positional authority, discipline, unity of command, unity of direction, subordination of individual interests, remuneration, centralization scalar chain (line of authority), order, equity, stability of personnel, initiative.

Management process period means focuses on the management. Functions of planning, controlling, organizing, staffing and learning. Management theory jungle means to the division of thought that resulted from the multiple approaches to studying the management process. Systems approach to management means that a way of thinking about the job of managing that provides a framework for visualizing internal and external environmental factors as a whole.

Contingency approach to management theory means that different situations and conditions require different management approaches. The Japanese management movement and theory z means their emphasis an individual responsibility with the collected decision making, slow evaluation and promotion for employees.

Robotics can learn communication skill to help organization to let managers and staffs to communicate more easy in order to achieve improving working efficiency and performance in different . So, robotic is a good message sender, he can help managers to deliver any urgent or confident message to let different department staffs to know immediately. Communication is as a management skill reasons may include: Managers must give direction to the people who work for them. Managers must be able to motivate people, managers must be able to convince customers that they should do business with them. Managers must be able to absorb the ideas of others. Managers must be able to persuade other people. An interpersonal communication is an interactive process between individuals that involves sending and receiving verbal and nonverbal messages.

The interpersonal communication process: from sender (event or condition generates information). This creates a message. The sender , such as message communication sender , robotic is such as a manager assistant, needs to initial message communicated both verbally and nonverbally. To the receiver (perceives the message, dervies meaning and reacts to the message). Then, the receiver needs to reply message communicated both verbally and nonverbally , sometimes referred to as feedback to the sender, perceives messages dervies meaning and reacts to the message from robotic message assistance between any organizational departments.

Hence, if the manager can let robotic remember any important and urgent messages to help him to send any verbal or nonverbal message to communicate between individuals, especially between the manager and subordinates , it is critical to achieving organizational objectives, and as a result, to managing people effectively. Estimates vary,but it is generally agreed that since managers spend must of their time with their dubordinates, effective communication is criticial to the wise and effective use of then time.

- ● Why does robotic need to learn customer satisfaction skill

Developing good listening skills to robotic is also important in management skill. Active listening means absorbing what another is saying and responding to the person's concerns. Listening , know how to listen is an important part of dealing with customers . Using active listening skills can help robotics understand why customers are dissatisfied. Responding : The way robotics, respond to complaints can be just as important as the way, they solve the customer's problem. Businesspeople should always be courteous and friendly when dealing with customers. Managers need to determine what went wrong and figuring out what they can do to solve the problem as well as making sure the customers are satisfied.

Hence, teaching robotics can learn how to determine to know whether customers have satisfied their services or their needs and giving feedback they receive from the customers. Written and overall communication is the most communication method for any robotic needs to learn communication skills. Writing communication may include: email, letters, draft report, memo, oral communication is formal and takes place at meetings or interviews or phone.These communication skills are robotics need to learn in any organization.

Moreover, robotic also needs to learn rational skills how to make the most reasonable decision making. The learning steps may include: recognize the need for a decision, establish, rank and weigh the decision criteria, gather, available information and data, identify possible alternatives, evaluate each alternative with respect to all criteria and select the best alternative.

Moreover, robotic also needs to learn satisficing skill. What is satisficing approach? The satisficing approach is a believing the assumptions of generally unrealistic. The capacity of the human mind for formulating and solving complex problems is very small compared with the size of the problems whose solution is required for objectively rational behavior , or even for a reasonable approximation to such objective rationality.

The steps of satisfied skill that robotic needs to learn. The first step: satisfied with best alternative found ? " yes", then making decision, if " no" search for additional alternative, then value of new alternative found either achieving value of best previous alternative or achieving current level of aspiration.

So, satisficing approach assumes: If person's knowledge of alternatives and criteria is limited. People act on the basis of a simplified, ill-structured, mental abstraction of the real world. People do not attempt to optimize , but will take the first alternative that satisfied their current level of aspiration , it is called satisficing.

An individual's level of aspiration concerning a decision fluctuates upward and download, depending on the values of the most recently identified alternatives. If the decision marker, such as robotic's knowledge of alternatives is incomplete, the individual commit optimize , but can only satisfice. Optimizing means selecting the best possible alternative, satisficing means selecting the first alternative, that meets the decision maker's such as robotic's minimum standard of satisfaction .

Assumption , it is based on the belief that the criteria for a satisfactory alternative are determined by the person's current level of aspiration. Level of aspiration refers to the level of performance a person expects to attain, and it is impacted by the person's prior successes and failures.

These environment factors will influence any robotic decision maker's decision . They may include: the patterns of the organizational manager his authority by the formal organization structure, for example, when robotic is one management strategic tool in a military organization , it requires to learn a different style of decison making than a volunteer organization does, whether the organization's formal and informal group structures. The decision maker, such as robotic's superiors and subordinates, personalities, backgrounds and expectations of these people influence the decision markers. So, robotic's decision making may be revised by his mangers , the labor market, the political climate and competition. These factors will influence the robotic's final decision making can be accepted or not by the organization.

● Worker lazy behavior applies to robotic

Why can robotic help workers to avoid lazy. Taylor's studies find that enterprisers can not satisfactorily benefit from workers and believed that forming and programming of doing works should be regulated by a scientific analysis and more output would be gained if they were standardized . He found about human factor may include: Lazy and least work, unproductive can be avoided when robotic can assist workers together in any organizations.

Robotic also is observed that this unproductive work order and environment existing in enterprise may give big damages at a degree tat can reach to losses at an extent effecting national economy. Some radical decisions must be taken from robotic to turn factors causing inefficiency ad effecting production negatively into neutural or to minimize them. Robotic can assist worker to avoid lazy working behavioral worker management principle may include: workers and managers must work according to scientific principles rather than working haphazardly , when carrying out organizational activities, organizational activities must be performed in a coordinated and consistent way, not in an inconsistent way, organizations and their methods, rather than submitting low unpredictiveness , must reject this and must try to provide the highest productivity, each labor must be parted to sub-factors forming it, when defining activities which workers and robotic must carry out, not only intuition and experience, but also scientific methods must be chosen, that say, the most suitable staff member and robotic must be chosen to work together in order to achieve raising efficiency and improve performance aims.

Why can robotic's participation assist workers to improve performance? Because people whose mental and physical skills are sufficient for works being standardized must be chosen, that say, the most suitable staff member must be chosen, specialization in every part of a defined labor and robotic must be provided. When robotic and workers work together, standards and specialization of workers, functions, such as organization, planning, controlling and coordination in management.

On the contrary to the representatives of scientific management's aiming to increase productivity of by dealing with the form of works' and robotic's being done and work design more at factory level. So, robotic and workers work together, they can raise productivity, economical efficiency and rationalism. Views as them both about the human and machine cooperative factor in enterprises from the workers and robotics, instead of the ability to manage, have desired to be managed and generally avoid taking responsibility.

What is robotic participation to working environment advantages ? In every step of hierarchy, authority and duties are determined formally by pre-determined law, method and administrative regulations, labor's being distingushed to parts is carried out in according with determined rules and standards by specialized staff member, processes and communication are done in written form, workers obey to directives, as they are based an legal authority. So, robotic participation can bring benefits to staff to know how to follow company's regulation to do their task together in order to achieve the reasonable performance. It means inefficiency or low production will be reduced when robotic and workers can work together.

● How robotic and workers coordination in factory condition

The scientific management conditions in factories were unplanned, there was absence of standardization of methods of work, these was no rational method of assigning workers to their jobs and they were often placed in jobs that they preferred. The work to be done and the methods to be adopted and selection of tools were also determined by workers and robotics. When robotic and workers coordination , it can help organization to reduce a lot of waste of materials, loss or production and inefficiency, there was no coordination between departments and managers did not posses decision making skills, they had no clear idea of the responsibilities. Decisions and standards of work performance were made on the basis provision to the workers and robotics with an opportunity for a " systematic " as well as the purposed restriction of output.

Hence, the reason why robotic and workers cooperation can raise productivity or improve performance, it is based on management science on these observations, a scientific theory of management aimed at discovering the one best way of performing any task as well as increasing productivity, revolutionized the idea of optimizing productivity. So, robotic and workers cooperation focused on the most efficient way of managing and making the workers more productive.

However, robotic and workers efficient principle may include: To find the best way of doing a job, so that the best method for performing each task could be determined . The most efficient ways of completing tasks and standard work procedures were delivered to enhance productivity. It involved the scientific selection and progressive development of the workers, when robotic can participate to task with workers together. So, when robotic can participate to workers' team tasks, each worker and each robotic would be assigned responsibility for the task for which expected that management can better identify strengths and weaknesses of each worker. Robotic aims to help workers to maximize his/her capacity. The successful factors include to raise productivity, equal division of work and responsibility between managers and robotics and workers, promoting friendly cooperation between managers and workers and robotics would help management for better supervision of its workers as well as reduction of disputes between robotics and workers, raising productivity and efficiency were the primary ends of scientific management aim when robotic participation is implemented to any workers' tasks and they do not need to spend long time training, due to robotic can do the complex tasks.

In conclusion, robotic participation can bring these advantages to any organizations. They may include: reducing time and expenditure for staff training, determination of standards of performance, the real problem concerns that no one exactly knew how much work a worker was expected to do in a specific / given time, rather than following any scientific basis, e.g. time and emoton how determines the standard of work performance, avoiding functional supervision and recommended functional foremanship in the organization in which robotics can do complex tasks , when workers can do simple tasks together, managers do not need to spend long time to supervise workers , when robotics can do more complex tasks, every worker is responsible for some specific aspect of the worker's simple task, the division of work between managers and workers and robotics favoring a compute separation of the planning function from the doing function. For example, the linear system or military type of organization in which each worker is subordinate to only one boss; piecework system of wage payment means that workers did as little as possible because under prevalent system of wage hard. Avoiding piece productive number reducing problem, when robotic participation to piecework for motivate then to achieve the highest level of efficiency. Finally, robotic participation can help workers to reduce mental pressure to work, in its essence, it involves a complete mental revolution in the attitudes of workers toward their work and in the attitudes of management toward their duties and ways in which they handle their daily piece productive number problems. According to robotic participation to determining standards of work benefits, they may include that eliminating wasteful operation and piecework system of wage payment would benefit both the workers and the employer/management, which will result into a mental revolution among the workers and the management, since they would develop a cooperative attitude toward workers and managers and robotics together.

● How and why robotic participation can bring personnel selection benefit

To answer this question. we need insight in terms of human resource management . Indeed, " piece rate " , payment method is popular to be used to evaluate workers performance, but when robotic participation can help organizations to evaluate every worker wage/salary easily. For example, in factory manufacture environment, when robotic participation to workers team cooperative tasks, this wage system can motivate workers to work hard. It emphasizes the necessity of high wage and low cost per unit, and therefore the manager and workman and robotic collaboration in the selection and reducing time to train staffs when robotics can participate to every worker's tasks. It assumes that reducing training time to ever worker was taken into consideration more than systematic managerial work when robotics can participate to do complex tasks, workers can do simple tasks when they cooperate to work together.

However, robotic participation can help workers to reduce working pressure as a mental revolution rather than an means of productivity which came into fashion at that time. Thus , the cooperation with managers and workers and robotics is as an essential principle. Although, scientific method seems to adopt the increase in production, it can also solve the problems between the managers and workmen and robotics. It seems that robotic participation can help workers to raise interest to work when they only concentrate on doing the simple task part and robotic can help them to do complex task part. It assumes that every worker work performance and wage decision is based on their simple task process part to piece productive number finishing every hour, due to robotics can help them to finish the complex task process part to piece productive number finishing every hour. So, if one worker can finish 100 piece productive number simple task part every hour, but another worker can finish 200 piece productive number simple task part every hour, when robotics can participate to complex process task part to finish every product piece productive number process, it can ensure that the 200 piece productive number simple task part worker can have higher efficiency and better work performance to compare the only finishing 100 piece productive number simple task process worker. So, robotic participation can bring benefit to help organization to evaluate every worker salary level more reasonable.

● Why can robotic bring talent working place benefit and reduces long time training and development cost

The quality of a working place is determined by the quality of its employees to a great extent. The success of many establishments depends on the labour and robotic force which has the talent to carry out the task required for the job and the ability to perform the strategic aims to the establishment. So, the success of personnel recruitment, when robotic can participate to do complex task part, So, robotic participation can help organization to choose right employee to do any simple task part, when they can finish the more piece productive number to simple task part. So, when robotic participation do not need workers to do complex task part, they only needs to concentrate on finishing the simple task part. They do not need to be trained. If the worker is one talent worker, they must not need more training time to learn how to finish the simple task part. So, robotic participation to manufacture complex task part which can help organization to know whether who is the talent worker to continue to be selected to employ , when he can finish to produce to manufacture many pieces when they only manufacture simple task part in factory. Hence, robotic participation can also help organizations to reduce long time training and development cost.

Hence, robotic participation can help organizations to measure whether whom workers can have productive efficiency or improve performance, when they only concentrate on manufacturing the simple task part to finish every product. Capitalists can not accurately know the worker's labor efficiency, when they need to manufacture every product in both simple and complex task parts. A worker is under normal working conditions and work flow can do how much work, but all too workers work less, get more salary and then by extending the worker's labor time, when robotic can not participate to assist them to manufacture complex task part. But, when robotic can not participate to their product productive process. Sone workers feel they are doing more, but they are paid less. When they need to learn to manufacture the more complex task part to every product. So, it explains that why robotic can encourage workers feel less working pressure or more lazy to finish the only simple task part to finish every product. If they only concentrate on manufacturing simple part to every product. Then , the workers who can manufacture many products when they only concentrate on manufacturing the simple task part. Their salary may be reasonable increased and they can feel more fair. Then, they won't perform poor. Also, the under manufacturing workers will be encouraged to raise productive number, if they hope that their wage can also be increased. When robotic can participate to help them to manufacture the complex task part to finish every product in the whole finishing process in the talent factory working environment. During the poor performance workers do not feel unreasonable days work often, then prevailing daily wage and general piece work wage system . It is not short coming and it can motivate their productivity to be increased in the factory talent working environment, when robotic can participate to help them to do any complex task part to every product. So, it explains why factory piece production wage system can raise productivities or efficiency when robotic can participate to help workers to do the complex task part to every product in whole manufacturing process. For example, one skilled labour wage calculation only depends on how much piece , he can produce. This skilled worker's wage rates calculation methods can not excite his piece manufacturing number in factory. The low skilled workers may apply piece wage system to excite their productivities when robotic can participate to simple task part manufacturing process. Robotic participation to complex task part, it aims to upgrade their low skills to high skilss in order to manufacture the kind of product in proficient. But for computer hardware equipment manufacturing workers example, their skills need to apply robotic scientific standardization to meet the raising efficiency and productivities needs of the production of each simple and complex task both parts. So, if the management hope the whole computer hardware manufacturing process can be improved the efficiency of the team work with the process and development of robotic technology, the proportion of brain labor is needed to increase when robotic can help the skilled workers to manufacture the complex task part of every hardware product. So, it explains why the piece wage system is suitable to skillful workers, such as computer hardware manufacturing tasks. The computer hardware organization needs to change its compensation management, pay a high wage rate in order to encourage these high skilled employees to do their work on the simple task part to computer hardware products on time. They can make corresponding incentives. Hence, robotic participation to hardware product complex task part, it can help computer manufacturing company to evaluate whether whom can be talent to learn the simple task part more easily, when they can manufacture the simple task part to finish every hardware in short time.

- How to implement the mind of strategy skills to robotic?

I shall indicate how robotic's strategic thinking process as below:

Robotics need to be learnt to own managers' judgement abilities, if organizations hope robotics can make the best strategic skills . The strategic skills need robotic to learn , the skills may include: Deciding whether the consumers likely to favor a quality product, if " yes" robotic needs to learn hoe to reflect quality in marketing strategy . Otherwise, if " no", robotic needs to learn hoe to design analysis, or deciding whether the company can make uneconomic purchases, if " yes", learning how to improve purchase methods, replace suppliers, " no" learning how to improve production process control or deciding whether the work in pace too slow, if " yes", learning how to improve employee education and training: install incentive system, if " no", deciding there are many rework, if " no" there is too much down time. Are of these analysis strategy process which be any robotics need to learn in order to achieve the most effective strategy management skills to recommend themselves organizations how to solve any management challenges.

For this profit analysis price flexibility case to robotic to learn example, the whole learning process to make decision may include this strategic thinking to let robotic to learn: the question may be " can the ex-factory price to raised?" It has two questions possibilities:

One is " can the market price be raised? "

Then it may has two possibilities:

The first possibility is simple increase in the list price possible. Then robotic can make these solutions: price elastic, possibility of price rises differentiate by geographical areas, models or by distribution channels, results achieved by competitors (possibility of " follow-the-leader" price increase.

The another possibility is that it is possible to raise the price by changing the product model to more than cover the increased cost? Then it may make solutions: Basic consumer needs in each market segment, price elasticity, cost -benefit analysis.

The another question may be: Can distribution margins be reduced? Then, it may have three possibilities: The first possibility may be " would integration of retail outlets enable margins to be reduced?" The solutions may include: Basic economic analysis of distribution system, analysis on economic of scale, correction between number sales outlets and market coverage. The second possibility may be " could volume be maintained if only low-margin channels were used?"

Then, the solutions may include: flexibility in physical flow of goods by distribution channels, degree of motivation and sales effort exerted by different channels.

The final possibility may be " could a switch to direct sales reduce distribution margin?" Then solutions may include: analysis of long -term strategic effect, analysis of short-term,, cost-benefit and possibility of maintenance of sale skills.

All of above strategic analysis process, robotic must need to learn in order to achieve human's mind process to make the most reasonable decision making to help managers to solve challenges.

Hence robotic ought need to be trained , such as one management consultant helps the organization's manager to recommend any useful strategic in order to make the most reasonable solution. However, robotic needs to learn how to determine the critical issue. The first stage in strategic thinking is needed to know what the critical issue in the situation for its organization. Robotic needs to learn how to make strategic thinking. In problem solving, it is at the start to formulate the question in a way that will facilitate the discovery of a solution. Hence, robotic needs to learn how to find the critical question that its organization needs to solve to avoid low efficiency or poor performance causes. Discovering the most influential problem will be robotic duty.

Suppose , robotic discovers the overtime work has become serious hurt to a company to cause low profit . It needs to find solution how to reduce overtime. Recommendation may include: work harder during the regular working hours, shorten the lunch period and coffee breaks, forbid long private telephone conversation, product quality, involves the participation of all employees. So, robotic's role participation task may include: How to gather ideas, screened and later incorporated in the improvement program. Returning to this overtime problem. Suppose the question in a more solution-oriented way: Is this company's work force large enough to do all the work required? Hence, robotic's strategic thinking needs to be better than manager. Otherwise, the firm manager can attempt to solve this problem.

To this question: There can be only one of answers, " yes or no". To arrive at answer " yes", a great deal of analysis would be needed, probably including a comparison with other companies in the same industries. The historical trend of workload per employee, and the degree of automation and computerization and their economic effectiveness. On the other hand, if after careful check sales record, profit per employee, ration between direct and indirect labor, compensation with other companies, the answer should be no (i.e. the company is currently understaffed. So robotic ought to be trained to learn to make the most reasonable solution for this problem.Such as " understaffed" causes " overtime" to cause low profit reasonable recommendation to this company manager. If robotic can make this "understaffed" reason causes low profit result to let manager to solve. Then, this company manager may find this solution, the probability increases that desired adopts this robotic 's follow.

However, a shortage of suitable personnel should be sought either in staff training or in recruiting capable staff. In the other hand , if the owner is " yes" this indicates that the problem of overtime lies in the nature of the work, but in the amount of the workload. Thus, not training but adding to the work force would be the critical factor in the solution. Hence future robotic needs to how to find the critical question to cause any organization's low profit as well as making the judgement how to recommend the most reasonable solutions in order to give the most reasonable recommendation to its organization manager. All of these are future robotic needs to be learn in order to make human's strategic thinking mind.

Finally, the observed phenome to any organization's problems, in general, they may include these problems aspects that future robotics need to learn organization's strategic thinking process.

On personnel problems aspect, they may include these aspects: Increase in average age, seniority system of promotion, low mobility of personal among divisions. Then, robotic ought make the " inflexibility in organization" decision to determine of " reorganization strategy" , e.g. how to reorganization itself organization to solve its organization overall personnel problems.

On cost problems aspect, they may include these factors: Increase in number of managers, decline in morale among younger employees, increase in personnel costs, delays in new product development. If robotic can ensure those factors may cause its organization's cost problems. Then, robotic ought may make judgement because costs high with competitors to cause its cost problem.

Finally, robotic needs to learn how to plan for improving profitability determination. On strategic problem aspect, they may fall in profitability, increase in unprofitable products factors to cause strategic problems. If the organizational robotic can find these phenomena to cause strategic problems. Then , it ought make judgement to know hoe to determine to implement its revised strategic in order to solve its organization's inflexibility in corporate strategy problem.

Thus, this organization's robotic is needed to learn how to analyze its organization's current different problem aspects whether are existed to influence its organization's high cost, inflexible corporate strategy or inflexible in organization influences. Then, this robotic needs to learn how to help its manager to find the most suitable pan to reorganization or how plan for improving profitability or how revised strategies in ordr to assist its ,anger to solve present existed actual problem effectively.

In conclusion, future robotics ought need to learn strategic thinking skill in order to give the most effective recommendation to assist their managers to solve any problems if the organization hopes it can keep long time competitive effort. Thus, future management ought need robotic participation to their strategic thinking discussion in order to achieve the most excellent strategic plan implementation to win their competitors.

● How robotic can manufacturing and service job market?

In the future, when robotic participate to any organizations' tasks. It will bring significant positive and negative impact to influence global labour market change. I shall indicate as below:

when robotic participation can improve efficiency, then it will cause the low skilled workers lose job ,e.g. factory workers, restaurant waiters, cookers etc. low skilled and low educational level occupations. , if they expect employers can pay same or higher wage for these low skilled and poor performance workers in this low skilled workers group in any organizations. They will loss their jobs more easily, due to robotic may replace these low skilled and poor performance workers in any one working places.

Robotics can work in service industry, instead of factory manufacturing industry in the future, e.g. cinema front line ticket sale service staff, public bus or train or tram driver, (non manual auto AI driver), shopping center security or customer service staff etc. occupations. So , in these service market, they can not perform to satisfy customer service need, then employers will feel their services are " price out of market", due to robotic can be popular to be accepted to serve clients in any service working environment in possible. Then, these poor service performance staff's salary may be influenced to reduce, even robotic can replace them to perform better service. So, many poor performance service and manufacturing workers will lose jobs , if their service or manufacturing performance can not perform better or improve better to compare general performance level staffs.

So, robotics tasks participation may impact many poor performance workers to influence they lose their jobs , due to employers will seek better performance staffs and/or robotics can replace them. So, the unemployment ratio will have possible increase, when global employers begin apply robotics to assist workers to manufacture products or serve clients.

Robotic participation helps companies to maximize profit. The fundamental assumption of labor theory is that firms, the employers of labour seek to maximize profit. So, firms are assumed to continue ask " Can we make changes that will improve profit, when robotic is participated to either manufacturing task or service task?"

First , a firm can make changes only in variable that are within its control, because the price , a firm can change for its product and prices, it may pay for its inputs are largely determined by other (" the market"). However, robotic role can only help it to raise efficiency or improve performance. So, robotic participation can not guarantee to raise profit or profit maximization, but it can help organizaions to raise efficiency or improve performance, when robotic can assist manufacturing or service workers to work together in any manufacturing or service workplaces.

● How artificial intelligence influence e-business workers market?

E-business is popular to be applied to sell any products from website. However, when artificial intelligence is participated to e-operation management environment. It can influence some e-business labor to lose jobs , due to artificial intelligence can provide better e-service task performance to compare these e-service labor, the e-service may include, such as online customer service support or e-inventory management, e-distribution and logistics, technical infrastructure.

When any e-commerce management tasks can be applied to robotic to replace any human e-service provision workers. Then, many e-service provision workers will lose jobs. Any website e-business management tasks will apply artificial intelligent e-service provision tool to replace human e-service provision workers , when they can perform better e-service provision to manage their websites, as well as satisfy e-clients' needs.

How to operate their websites to achieve the most attracting and efficient online sale performance? For example, applying (AI) development to define the customer online purchase experience in the e-operation planning process. It may include these three stcps" The first step is that developing high level customer view process, flows of the online seller's production processes. The second step is that identifying quality metics, (AI) helps the online seller to decide whether what need to be measured to indicate the quality level of the online customer's shopping experience and the quality of the production process. The final step is that identifying types of requirements. There are two types: By resource (technical, organizational and informational) as well as by operational management function. When (AI) tool can help the online organization to design e-operation planning process to improve the best online shopping experience to any one client to feel. Then, many e-service provision workers can be replaced in e-business related any e-operation management task aspect.

● How robotic becomes one kind of factor of production to the owning robotic task participation organizations?

However, robotic will be one kind of factors or production to the owning robotic task participation organizations. Instead of land, labor, capital and entrepreneurship factor of production. Robotic will be tangible talent technique manufacturing tool or service worker machine to factor of production to these owning robotic task participation organizations, as well as intangible skilled technique to upgrade works to improve individual performance or raise efficiency factor or production to these businesses.

Hence, in economics the factors of production view, robotic can be the basic inputs of any productive goods or service-producing system to businesses. When robotic participation to the shopping center, factory, restaurant, cinema , e-commerce etc. different organization tasks. It can be one kind of skilled technique worker. It has different to general labour, general labour is the mental and physical effort available to produce goods and service, the human resource. Unskilled, semi-skilled and skilled are terms that describe different types of labour. Management skill is also a type of labour.

How much a firm produces and the quality of what it produces are affected by the motivation, skills, and efforts of its labour. Japan's development from a devastated economy to an economic superpower in four decades is due in part to its highly productive human resource. However, when the organization applies robots to participate its daily task, like this one at a Joh Deere plant are capital goods that helps to mechanize and automate the production process. Hence, robotic can be one tangible machine capital to this plant, but when it can improve worker skills to be upgrade or raise efficiency, it can be also intangible skilled asset to this plant. Hence robotic may have effort to help this plant's low skilled labours to upgrade. Their low skills can be upgraded to be higher skills. Their skills can be trained to upgrade or improved from robotic's task participation in this plant. Then, this plant will have not many low skilled workers, if most of them can be upgraded skills or improve skills. It means that robotic helps this plant's low skilled workers to be trained to raise high skills when they can cooperate to work together. Then, manufacturing industry will have more high skilled workers if many plants apply robotics to participate and cooperate low skilled workers to manufacturing process. It will influence the country's factory labour market will have none high skilled workers shortage challenge, due to if many plants apply robotic participation to any workers' tasks cooperation to work together in order to improve their efficiency and raise any product productive number. Then, , due to many robotic participation , it can influence many high skilled workers number increase to the country. In consequent, the high skilled workers supply number is more than the labour demand in plant manufacturing industry. Then, the high skilled workers' salaries will be influenced to reduce. So, robotic's participation to plant manufacturing process, it may influence the high or proficient skilled workers' wages level to be gone down or reduce in the country's plant manufacturing labour market.

● Why can robotic avoid productivity challenge and the firm does not need to employ extra worker ?

Robotic's participation can help the manufacturers to avoid not enough productive number challenge and they do not need to employ extra workers . The reason is that when the plant workers can learn how to cooperate with the robotic to work together effectively. Then, their productivities ought be influenced to increase, because robotic can assist them to reduce their work pressure, when they only need to do the simple task, robotics need to help them to do complex task. In this robotic and worker long time cooperative working behavior, these factors may help them to raise productivity, they may include that: The plant do not need often to replace outdated plants and equipment, due to robotic's participation to this plant's complex task part. This plant does not need to invest in research and development to find new ways to design, produce, and market products, due to this plant had found new application for robots, this plant does not need to develop new ways to manage employees by raising their layers of management and getting workers more involved in decision making. Because robotic has assist these workers to finish complex task part in whole manufacturing process, these workers only need to concentrate on doing simple tasks part every day. For example, more robotic complex task participation firms are using self-managed teams to rejuvenate the work ethic. So, when the firm can let robotict o participate complex task part and its staffs only need to do simple tasks part as well as they do not need to spend time to participate and learn how to making decision with managers or spend time to learn in training., due to robotic's complex task part participation. So, in long time, their productivities may be influenced to raise, when they only concentrate on doing simple task part, due to robotics can help them to do complex task part daily.

However, this owning robotic complex task part participation to plants won't need to employ extra workers, but their productivities may be raised. Then, it will influence labour demand will reduce, even employers will dismiss some low skilled workers, when managers feel they can not raise productivities as well as when robotic helps them to do complex task part. It may influence the unemployed low skilled and poor performance workers number increases or/and their wage may be influenced to reduce in the country's plant manufacture industry labor market.

In conclusion, robotic's participation to complex task part, it may influence labour market to change to raise low skilled workers unemployed number, and reduces their wage level, but productivity may be influenced to increase, low skilled workers may be ungraded their skills by robotic's complex task part participation, can bring positive influence to employers, e.g. raising productivities number, increasing profit, reducing machine purchase and employee number salary expense, upgrade low skilled worker skill, or creates talent workers, reducing training time and expense. But it can bring negative influence to employeeees, e.g. it canuses low skilled worker unemployment, their wages reduce in themselves countries labor market.

How robotic brings positive and negative social change
● Why does robotic seem to McDonaldization franchise sale method

Robotic's invention can influence global society has large change. I shall explain what it seems to be similar to McDonaldization global fast food restaurant sale method in possible. How it can be franchise to commodification , ration and globalization to sell any kinds of robotic products to bring global franchise income for robotic inventors. Robot's invention can let robotic inventors to own franchise to sell their different kinds of robotic in factories, manufacturing places, factories warehouse delivering goods places, hospital room food delivery places, restaurant food delivery places, restaurant kitchen cooking places or restaurant waiter serving clients places, shopping center securities or customer service counter places or office computer documents delivery or clerical working places etc. different kinds of service or manufacture tasks.So, robotic's influence to future service or manufacture model can be changed to machines. Many people will lose jobs if they are replaced by robotic in factories or restaurants or offices or hospitals or shopping center etc. different working environments.

If robotics inventors own franchise , it seems that it can be similar to McDonaldization global fast food restaurant to sell its robotics to different business buyers or householders to satisfy their needs. When every robotic sellers need to buy franchise from the robotic inventors. So, robotic inventors seem to be similar to McDonaldization founder to own franchise to sell its fast foods. The different view, is that robotic inventors sell robotic price must be more expensive to compare McDonaldization's fast food. So, it will influence future any business buyers or householders need to pay high price to buy any one robobit's founder's inventing robotic products when they owns franchise to sell their different robotic in society.

This phenomenon will bring social much change, such as restaurants won't need many waiters or cookers if they have robotic cookers to help them to cook food or robotic waiters help them to serve eating clients, cinemas do not need many bringing seat position serving staffs or from counter ticket sell service staffs ,because robotics can replace them to do simple servicing tasks in cinemas, factory warehouses also do not need many workers to help them to deliver goods because robotics can deliver goods to any right places very rapidly, such as Amazon is applying robotics to help their goods to deliver to any places in warehouses nowadays, they can perform more better to compare warehouse workers.Also robotic can help them to manufacture products to replace manufacture workers, so manufacturing workers number will be influenced to reduce.

● Why robotic seems to McDonaldization's operation?

They have these similar points to raising service aspects: Computerization, product-predictability, managerial control, efficiency, raising production value, quantity manufacturing value, providing excellent convenience and rapid delivery service. So, robotic franchise can be similar to McDonaldization to let robotic inventors to continue to own franchise to invent different kinds or function robotics to satisfy our different services or manufacture needs aspects.

Nowadays, education organizations had begun to attempt to apply robotics to replace teachers to teach students in classrooms, or householders had begun to apply robotics to help them to do cleaning tasks, e.g. cleaning kitchen, toilets or security job etc., even robotic can help parents to take care parent's children at home when they leave homes. So, future robotic won't only influence business jobs change aspect, it may also influence householder's life aspect. When robotic is popular to be accepted to be used for anyone. Then, the robotic inventors can be seem to McDonaldization founder have themselves own franchise to sell their unique robotics to global different countries markets. Then, our societies will feel robotics are our living part. We need to apply them to help us to do any simple . even complex tasks in order to satisfy our living needs. So, robotic's invention will be possible serious to influence our future society to become " machine man " society. Anyway, working environment, service environment or home environment will own at least one robotic to serve our organizations or homes.

Hence, robotic seems to be one kind of new resource to motivate own society to change to be more better. Our part traditional living model or living attitude is need to be change. We need to learn how to adapt the live or to work with robotic in anywhere together. Robotics seem to be our future social capital. It is rooted in social networks and social relations and is conceived as resources embedded in a high technique social structure that are accessed and/or mobilized in purposive actions. So, robotic's invention seems to one big artificial intelligent organization. The different kinds of robotic inventions will organize how to design different kinds of robotics to satisfy human's unlimited needs to be applies to different aspects in our society. For example, future public transport tool drivers, e.g. bus , tram, ferry, train, mass transit rail drivers will be replaced by robotics. Non-manual drivers will be popular to be replaced to different countries by robotic's automatic drivers. many drivers will also lose driving jobs. They will be assistant role to the robotic drivers. So, if robotic invention can be invented in success to make more accurate to drive any kinds of transport tools in order to avoid road accidents occurrence chance to be the least minimum level to compare manual drivers. Then, our societies will be non-manual driving transport tools. We need to adapt to accept or believe their driving skills must be better than manual drivers. Otherwise, we only may choose to buy cars to drive.

So, robotic will be our future important resources. They will help to do complex tasks, instead of simple tasks, e.g. seeking the suitable land or ocean to attempt to discover any new milling or oil or gas resource and help human to do the difficult exploration oil or gas tasks. We ought believe that they have much accurate judgement to compare human's talent. So, they will be talent machine to replace human to do much complex mind judgement tasks. Even, they may be space scientists to help us to find many undiscovered natural resources from outside earth or planet. When robotic can be invented to own high mind judgement effort or talent effort to compare humans. So, in science research aspect, future human scientists may be needed to accept themseleves to be robotic's assistant to assist them to do any science research tasks in laboratory, when robotic can be invented to own human talent effort.

Hence, robotic's invention will influence our societies to be changed more advanced or more fun or most technological development. Human can not predict how robotic's change to influence our future society in which aspects accurately. But, many robotic scientists are continue attempting to research robotics how to invent on which aspects to satisfy our different living needs. I believe that robotics will help us to serve our societies much better.

It is simple , that our post industrial society, and such social change is needed traditional computer will be replaced by (AI) artificial intelligence or called robotics. So, our industrial society will change to encounter technological society. It continues to fascinate those commentators seeking to understand transitions from a modern to a post-modern world also preoccupies those who prefer to think about the " transformation" society or technological society.

The invention is which global tendencies are taking hold are arguably more about countinue than they are about change. The extent to which new technologies, such as robotic invention fundamentally alter our lives is debatable.

How important is the internet, for instance? Who is to say that ultimately it might prove more controlling than it is enabling? Indeed, our part most industrial society, notably as regards the spread of scientific rationality , such as robotic invention.

Our post-industrial society has none limited staying power, such as robotic's invention. The extent to which such ideas really illuminate our understanding of contemporary social life beyond the general insights provided by its technological dimension is questionable.

● Why does robotic seems to be common social commodity?

Thus robotic will be seemed to common commodity first and foremost as something to be sold and exchanged on the marketplace. It therefore had a role in determining our social position. From Marx's point of view, determined by how you actively engaged with consumer goods. When, robotic is popular to be accepted to use and robotic's manufacturing number will increase. Then, it's price will reduce,when supply is increased. The robotic's commodity therefore plays a fundamental role in relating the individual (householder user) to the capitalist system (business organization user) . It promotes a sense of false consciousness that camouflages the realities of alienation.

Robotic's commodification seems to be McDonaldization commodification, by process , by which everything is valued according to its value in the system of exchange, creates a world in which a person's (householder's or business organization's priorities become subject to the requirements of the job making or our living need.

Marx therefore believes that robotic becomes a situation in which the worker is aliented by the fact he or she no longer has ownership of the artificial commodity he or she helps to work together in any organization. The worker is a assistant who no longer is needed to do his/her tasks in his/her organization when the organization applies robotic to be own labour.

Marx (2000) therefore decides the fetishism of the commodity, such as artificial intelligence or robotic. By this, Marx means that the commodity such as robotic was a mystical quality: To the extent that objects become to the self, and are therefore ascribed a significance beyond their use-value. The robotic commodity is treated with an awe and reverence previously reserved for religion. But even, in this analysis, for Marc, the fetishism of the robotic commodity is only a by-product of independent labour to our future society.

The fetishism of the world of commodities arises from social character of the labour which produced them, such as robotic objects of utility become commodities, such as robotic only because they are products work independently of each other . The special social characteristics of employers' private labours such as robotics appear only which this exchange. Hence, Marx was certainly accurate , there can be no doubt that the process of commodification, such as robotic has reached new extremes to enter our society to bring benefit to influence our daily lives.

● How can robotic bring global social stratification positive and negative change?

Why does robotic have relationship to social stratification? Firstly, we need to know that social stratification mean? Some of the world's nations are wealthy, other poor and some in between. This division of nations as well as the layering of groups of people within a nation, is called " social stratification".

Social stratification is one of the most significant topics to discuss . It will affects one life chances, such as robotic's invention from our access to material possession to the age at which we die.

Social stratification also affects the way we think about life. If you had been born into the rich family, you can be illiterate and would assume that your children would be as well. You also would expect hunger to be a part of life and would not expect all of your children to survive. To be born into the family, however, would give you quite a different picture of the world. You would expect your children not only to survive, but to go to college as well. You can see that social stratification brings with it ideas of what we can expect out of life. So, it has different between rich countries and poor countries people, business organization AI users or householder AI users their thinking to need robotics' attitude in social stratification view.

Social stratification is a system in which groups of people are divided into layers according to their relative property, power. It is important to emphasize that social stratification does refer to individuals. It is a way of ranking large groups of people into a hierarchy according to their relative families. It is also important to note that every society stratifies its members. Some societies have greater inequality than others, bur social stratification is universal. In addition, in every society of world, gender is a basic for stratifying people. On the basic of their gender, people are either allowed or denied access to the good things offers by their society.

Hence, due to social stratification or unequal born occurs in our nowadays society, it will influence different countries people will have different needs to AI. For example, the people born in US, UK etc. developed countries, they will have high quality of living need in order to improve their daily needs , e.g. more living comfortable feeling. So, non-manual driving cars or robotic driven cars can help them to drive themseleves cars on the roads. These developed countries householders will have much needs to buy non-manual driving cars to replace themselves manual driving cars. They do not like or do not enjoy to drive themselves cars on the roads. Otherwise, the developing countries people, because they are common poor, they need to work to earn to satisfy their daily essential needs, e.g. buying food, paying rent. So, it is common these developing countries poor people , they do not like to buy non-manual driving cars to replace themselves to drive cars on the roads. So, on comfortable living aspect,developed countries rich people , they are common to accept robotics to help them to do any simple or complex tasks . Otherwise, developing countries poor people they are not common to accept robotics to help them to do any simple or complex tasks in society. The reason is that " money spending" problem developing countries poor robotic consumers. But, it does not mean developing countries poor people do not pursue to enjoy to apply robotic to help them to do simple or complex tasks. They are common lazy, they also hope robotic can help them to do any simple or complex tasks in their organizations or houses. If these developing poor countries people can save enough money to buy robotics, or robotic price is cheap, then they will like to spend some money to buy robotic to satisfy their material lives needs.

So,, in the future, it seems that robotics ought influence developed countries people pursue much material lives to satisfy their living needs more than developing countries people in short time. But, when robotic is popular to be accepted to use for anyone. Robotic;s manufacturing number will also increase, then supply number is also influenced to increase. It is possible to influence common every robotic price goes down, then its demand number is global maker. So, when robotic 's price goes down . In general, when developing countries people can save enough money to buy cheaper robotic to use for their living needs. The, many developing countries' people will need robotics to help them to do any simple or complex tasks to householder AI users or organizations AI users . Then, global society will be influenced to change among technology's amazing technological advance, such as robotic makes many people more valuable to their daily lives.

Our society will encounter " pulseless electronic social activity" . it means that our daily activities will need to include robotic's activities to assist our simple or complex active needs. When technology changes, robotic's invention electronic activities satisfy our simple or complex living activities needs, such as non-manual driving activity, hospital non-manual food delivery activity, home non-manual cleaning activity, restaurant non-manual food deliver activity, restaurant non-manual cooking activity, factory non-manual manufacturing or warehouse non-manual goods delivery activity etc.

Hence, robotic will be participated to our daily simple or complex activity to satisfy our lazy needs . I assume that human is lazy animal, human needs some technological thing, such as robotics to help us to do any simple or complex tasks.So, it may say that robotic encourages human's lazy behavior is caused on occurrence in our future society, when robotic is invented to be used to satisfy to different living need aspects. It also means that future robotic may replace computers to help human to do any simple or complex computer tasks. Then, robotics may be applied to replace office workers to do clerical tasks in possible. Our office working environment will be influenced to change robotic clerical workers. Consequently, any working environments will have robotics to be participate to satisfy raising efficiency or improving client service performance or raising productivities needs. Robotics will be needed to any working environments in our society. Talent office or talent restaurant or talent factory or talent warehouse or talent transport tool etc. will be changed to robotic task participation.

In conclusion, our robotic invention may be human's society final change point, our society had experienced from hunting and gathering society to change to pastoral and horticultural society, then from agricultural society changes to industrial societies, till to changes to nowadays postindustrial (information) society. It is unlike the industrial society, this new type of society is not material and manufacture . Rather its basic component is information. Teachers pass on knowledge to students, when lawyers , physicians, bankers , pilots and interior decorators sell their specialized knowledge of law, the body , money to clients. Unlike the factory workers of an industrial society. These individuals don't produce anything. Rather they transmit or use information to provide.

Service that others are willing to pay for such as internet can help any e-commerce to develop online business. Till to biotech society, e.g. in this new biotech. society, the economy will counter on applying and altering genetic structures, both plant and animal to produce food, medicine and material. If there is a ne society, when did it begin ? So, such as robotic invention will bring another new change to our society. Will cloning humans become a reality? Many people object that cloning is immoral, but some will arge the opposite. They will explain why we should leave human reproduction to people who have inferior traits, generic diseases, low IQ, perhaps even the propensity for crime and violence. They will suggest that we select people will finer characteristics, high creative ability, high intelligence, compassion and propensity of peace. Hence, it seems that if future robotics can invented to achieve high IQ, become talent to compare human, such as us. Do you think that it should be our moral obligation to populate society with people like this ? To try to build a society that is better for all, one without terrorism , war, violence. Could this perhaps even be our evolutionary destiny from robotic talent technology. Hence, robotic may help our society to avoid more crime fight, violence, stealing occurrence , they can be such policemen to protect our societies to be more safe to live. It ought mean that robotic can satisfy our living safe need, instead of householders' daily living useful needs and organizations' raising efficiency and improving service performance or raising productivities needs.

Robotic how influences global economic change
Whether robotic invention can bring global economic change to be either improved or better or worse or recession. It depends on many different factoors to influence. I shall indicate some factors as below:
● Encouraging new economic development competitive factor
On new trend in economic development aspect, its invention ought may bring these benefits to our society. Raising social additive utility, technological innovation can bring new economic to competition to our societies or encourage social competition. Then, economics may grow in the social science development view, because robotic;s manufacturing technique can help factories to raise productivities . Then, it encourages manufacturers need to participate competition. For example, when one vehicle manufacture factory decides to apply robotics to assist it to manufacture any cars in the whole manufacturing process. Then, when their cars in the whole manufacture process, when their its worker individual efficiency can raise, performance can be improved. Moreover, its car quality can satisfy to different countries' car buyers. The most importance is that its car productivities number can increase. Thus, it can supply be enough to be sullied to satisfy different countries' car buyers' needs. If its other manufacture competitors do not follow its robotic's participation , so that car manufacture process. Then, they will have much chance to lose their car buyers. So, robotic's manufacture technique to car industry can encourage the global whole car manufacture industries to develop robotic manufacture skills. It encourages whole car manufacture industry will choose robotics to help them to manufacture efficiency and productivities and improve worker's manufacture performance aim. Then, car industry will may increase sale number to increase GDP growth rapidly. So, robotic is intellectural development was perhaps the most significant of this century. It was the explicit negotiation of property rights and transaction costs as contraints on behaviors.

● How much robotic productivity can raise competition to cause effects of limited competition disadvantage to our society.
Economists had begun to observe the effects in markets of monopolies and of fierce competition. So, when robotic investors own monopolies to manufacture any kinds of robotics or adrtificial intelligence. Then, they will rise robotic's sale price to any business organizational roboticsbuyers or householder buyers, They found that robotics monopolies manufacturers will tend to restrict robotic's limited supplying number to keep high sale prices and profit high in robotic selling market, where there was plenty of competition robotic prices were driven down to the level of costs, profit were low and artificial intelligent robotic output was high.
French economist Anotoine Cournot wanted to find out what happened when there was only few firms had as robotic manufacturers sale is similar to robotic products . In future , robotic manufacturer market, Cournot created

his model based on a duopoly of two firms selling indentical spring water to consumers. The two firms are not allowed to turn a cartel by working together, no other firms can enter the industry, because there are no other natural springs and each firm has to decide, how many bottles of water to supply. At this point, each firm is selling the most profitable amount given what the other firm is doing.

Hence, each firm must choose the output that maximizes its profit based on what it thinks that other firms output will be. If firm (A) thinks that firm (B) will produce nothing. Firm (A) will select the low output of a monopolist to maximize the profits. On the other hand, if firm (A) thinks that firm (B) will produce a high output. Firm (A) may choose to produce nothing. Because prices would be too far to make production worthwhile. Due to each firm knows that the other firms' output will affect their own profits. Each firm reacts by selecting its best output given the level of output the other firm chooses (plotted on a reaction curve). The market will be in a Cournot equilibrium where the two reaction curves meet. Consequently, this is low much the firm showed produce, given the competition. Such as robotic manufacturing cases, if two robotic manufacturing firms are not allowed to other firms to enter manufacturing robotic products easily, because they lack robotic's technology to manufacture and each firm has to decide how many robotic products to supply to different countries' robotic organizational buyers and householder buyers both.

The total robotic output of the robotic manufacture industry is the sum of the two robotic manufacture firms' output decisions . Each robotic manufacturer firm must choose the output that maximizes its profit based on what it thinks the other robotic manufactuing firm's output will be. Consequently, they may be unfair to any countries robotic organizational buyers and house holder buyers both. They may give the unreasonable high selling price to by any one robotic product, due to they both control global robotic products number supply and selling price. Consequently, their robotic manufacturing monopolies tended to restrict robotic output to keep high sale prices and profit high to global robotic organizations and householders buyers both. It is very unfair to global robotic consumers. So, however, future when economic is recession, global robotic's sale price will not be influenced to go down easily, due to these two robotic manufacturing monopolies companies control global robotic product manufacturer market. Future robotic consumers will need to pay unreasonable high price to buy any kinds of robotic products, if these are only two robotic manufacturers own monopolies to control global robotic supply output number ans sale price leve. It is one case to explain unfair robotic manufacturers' competition to bring global future unreasonable robotic high sale price as well as limited supply number disadvantages to any countries' robotic to consumers.

So, in game theory, future robotic manufacturers number must need to above at least two firms, even more than ten firms when global has many robotic buyers number will increase. Consequently, when economic recession occurs, robotic's price will climb up. It will influence many robotic buyers can not buy any kinds of robotic product to help them to raise efficiency or productivities if many factories have need, but they can not buy any robotic to assist them to workers to raise productivities or efficiency. Then, their productivities number can not satisfy consumers' needs. Consequently, GDP will also influenced to go down. Because robotic will be future manufactur industry's important asset, they may help any manufacturers to raise productivities in long time. If many manufacturers have enough money to buy robotic to assist workers to manufacture any products. Then, global product export number will redice. So, robotic manufacturer market can not be monopolies to control by at least two firms. They will influence global manufacturing industry export can not increse to satisfy consumers needs easily. Then, economic recession will be more serious indeed.

In conclusion, future robotic manufacture market will influence economic recession or not. It depends on a system of free robotic manufacturing market is needed to stable. Because when shortages of robotic supply in own area of the economy create surplues of supply. Either where there are robotic supply shortages, so prices rise or when these are robotic supply surpluses prices fall. When price riase, global robotic demand falls and robotic supply rises, aims to eliminating shortageto robotic or robotic prices fall, global robotic demand rises, and robotic supply falls aims to eliminating surplus to robotic. Consequently, they will cause that economics is as a whole tend towards equilibrium as long as they are free to do so. Also , a system of free robotic manufacture market is needed to stable, global robotic sale price is to be more reasonable and fair and output supply number to robotic organization and housholder consumers in order to satisfy raising efficiency or improving productivity or performance aim to factories organizations. Hence, robotic supply output number and sale price will have direct relationship to influence future GDP growth or recession.

● How and why robotic brings long time intellectural development to global factories ?

Rarely, in any science, has a new development turned so rapidly influence global different industries aspects, such as robotic technological development can influence different industries aspect to bring more intelligent and creature attributies. The economic of property and rights of robotic has major change in the direction of economic thinking has to do with the purpose or intent or research to encourage global robotic scientists can compete to cooperate to achieve the more advanced or intellectural of any kinds or functions to different robotic's industries uses.

Whereas, earlier economists began to believe that cooperative competition work bring more creative ability more than non-cooperative competition. So, whan different professional robotic scientists can cooperate to work together, they will raise " brain storm" creative ability to continue to create non-discovered or non-reserch future robotic products. So, nowadays, our robotic products do not only to limit to reash the final invention number. In the future, economists had predicted our future society ought have many new kinds or new functions of robotics new products are invented to satisfy robotic consumers different needs, e.g. applying to space or earth or ocean non manual exploration science tasks aspects, non pilot driving flying aspect, hospital medical non manual surgeon or non manual patient food delivery aspects. Then, due to future our society's different industries aspects can be participated by robotics to help to cooperate to achieve any mission in oder to achieve any reasearchs more successful. Thus, future robotics' role are not only to do complex or simple tasks for manufacturers or householders. They may be used for any scientists to participate to achieve any important research missions more successful. Thus, future robotics will be applied for scientists in order to assist them to achieve any important research missions more successful. For example, robotic is applied to garment and toy industries. It can bring more advantages to factory works and manufacturers. Pieceworkers may work either in a factory where space and tools are provided or at home using their own equipment, before none any robotic's participation to pieceworkers' tasks . But when robotic invention, home factory robotic's coordination of activities is improved when all workers perform under one tool supplementing with work sent out to home craftsman only at times of people loads. So, robotics help factory workers to reduce workload. Moreover, pieceworkers in factories are often assigned specific machines to avoid careless use random rotation, and fast workers are often assigned the better equipment. But when robotic's participation to their tasks. However, foolish and clever workers must give advantages , robotics can assist foolish workers to raise efficiency as well as clever workers can be improved their productivities number predictably. Piece rate work which do not require the use of heavy machinery, it tends to apply robotic to be produced in a factory. So, home workers do not need. They do not need machinery in a home, dangerous to children and requires repair, it may not also be so costly that few home workers woud willingly invest without assurance of long term use. When robotic can be replaced to any home or factory machine.

So, robotic can assist foolish and clever workers to raise management productivities more than traditional simple machine. Thus, future management ought make clear judgement whether whom is clever or foolish workers when they need to cooperate to robotics to work together. Also, they may give more reasonable wage to the worker, if the worker can cooperate to robotic to raise more productivites number. Then, he ought need to give bonus , instead of basic piece number wage calculation method. Otherwise, if the worker can nor improve his productive performane after ne needs to cooperate with robotic. Then, he must need time to learn how to cooperate to robotic in order to adapt together factory working environment. So, new robotic's participation to any factory, every worker will need time to adapt how to cooperation with its change. The bonus paid system will depend on whom can adapt to cooperate with robotic in order to achieve the most rapid raising efficiency or improving productivities perform objective. Thus, in economic view , robotic's factory participative tasks, which can assist worker's cooperation more effectively. Consequently, when one factory all workers can adapt to cooperate with robotic to work together . The factory's productivities number must be raised in long time. Consequently, the factory's worker efficiency and productivity number must be improved , due to robotic can improve its manufacturing skills to be upgrade absolutely. Also, factory management can decide advantages result to determining piece wage rates , then would be possible if contributes were only be measured by machine . When, robotic's participation to every clever or foolish worker tasks, it can influence their performance to be accepted or rejected more easily . So, in general, foolish workers need long time to learn how to cooperate with robotic to work together, tey must not earn bonus or increase piece wage easily in short time. Otherwise, clever worker can adapt how to cooperate with robotic to work. So, their piece productivities number must increase in short time. So, bonus or increasing piece wage paid method may be evaluated to compensate to every workers more fair in the factory . It is robotic's factory participation to worker individual tasks economic benefit to any future factories manuacturing environment.

● How can robotic help manufacturers to raise productivitied or improve efficiency?

In modern economic view, robotic's participation to worker tasks, it ought achieve better productivites number. We need to make choice because productive resources are scare. Hence, in factory environment, manufacturing resources ought only include workers, traditional old machines and advance robotic. If the factory expects to achieve the most effective productivites. When they have robotic choice to be productive resources. Therefore, they make robotic productive resources, they may ask these questions: Can robotic assist economy growing or stagnant?

Growth means greater output and potentially higher levels of living for a society; stagnation removes that possibility for improvement. IS a society using its productive resources fully and efficiently? Anything less will mean unemployment of people, machine and other productive agents? For whom to produce? It concerns that distribution of the output, who in a particular society will get the goods and services that are produced? How to produce? such as factory choice to productive resources case, factory may still choose machine and worker together production or workers only productin or robotic only production or robotic and workers together productive method. It concerns the methods that a society can use to undertake its production. Usually, an item can be produced, with various different techniques , a lot of labor and only a few machines as a lot of labor and only a few robotics , or few labours and a lot of robotics , or a lot of machinery and very few workers. What to produce? Which goods among the endless possibilities will a society decide upon, an in what quantity? What decision-making process will be used to arrive at the answer?

So, in microeconomics, manufacturers consider how to make industrial productive decision in order. It concerns how resources are allocated, such as workers and/or machine and robotic's factory managers. However, microeconomic takes how that it is divided by product, how to minimize the resources, such as workers number nnd without machine, when robotics can replace machine to assist workers to raise productivities and improve efficiencies in any factory environment, but on the same time, in macroeconomic view, when robotic participation to few workers tasks. It will also increase high unemployment or stagnating growth , due to many factory workers lose their tasks, due to robotics may help them to raise productivities.So, workers ' roles will be assistants, but robotics will be the main important actor to produce and products in the factories.

● Why does production possibilities curve may explain why robotic participation may assist few workers to raise productivities in factories ?

One simple model, known as the production possibilities curve, is very helpful to explain traditional machine and workers cooperation can not produce more products more than robotics and workers cooperation, how choices must be made among scarce economic alternatives. Supposing a vehicle manufacturing factory , factory area/floor size is fixed, the factory supply of tools can only choose either machine or robotic altered. So, the factory can not choose both productive resources to assist workers to produce any vehicels, and th number of working hours can not increase, but many decrease. There is not extra money supply to consider . Hence, if the factory sells all with resource scarce limited tools, either robotic or machine choice, worker working time can be increased, but may decrease and managerial worker ability can not improve, because managers number can not increase, may only decrease.

If the factory expects to raise vehicle productive number, it only may choose to apply robotic to replace machine. Robotic can bring cost reducing advantage in long term, when the foolish workers can not be trained to apply robotic to cooperate to raise vehicle productivities number. the talent workers can be trained to raise vehicle productivites number. Even, when some talent managers can be trained to supervise many robotic and workers to work together efficiently. Then, the factory may reduce the foolish managers and foolish workers. It 's whole vehicle productivities number may still be raised, when trained talent workers and managers can adapt to work with robotics to raise their productivities number in long time.

It is based to explain why robotic can help workers to raise productivities in this productive possibilities curve. When the factory needs to manufacture two kinds of unique vehicles. f this factory still choose machine and workers to manufacture the (A)kind of vehicles and the (B) kind of vehicles . It can manufacture the maximum (A) knid of number vehicles is 20 pieces as well as the maximum (B) kind of number vehicles is 20 pieces every hours. Otherwise, if this factory changes productive resource to apply robotics to replaced machine and foolish workers to manufacture the kind (A) of vehicles, the kind of (A) vehicles maximum number is 40 pieces as well as the kind of (B) vehicles maximum number is 40 vehicles also every hour.

The kind of maximum (A) and (B) vehicles number manufacturing effect per hour, shows production level higher than actually be attained and more efficiency, when the factory applies effectively the rpbotics and trained talent workers and trained talent managers resources to replace the traditional old machines and the foolish workers resources to manufacture the both kinds of (A) and (B) unique vehicles in this factory.

Although, this factory's factory floor size can not increase and money is limited . So, it has only twenty productive resource machine number can not increase to buy more twenty robotic to replace them,even robotic's number may be reduced, as well as it has fifty workers and five factory manager number, it can not increase more than these number. But due to when managers and workers can be trained to proficient to know how to control any one of these ten only robotics to manufacture the kind (A) and kind (B) unique vehicles. Then, this factory's robotic purchase expenditure must be decreased to only ten number, even when some trained workers can be traned to be talent to proficient how to shorten time manufcture every kind (A) an kind (B) unuqie vehicels from the maximum number 20 pieces to (A) and 20 pieces to (B) vehicles per hour to the maximum number 40 pieces to (A) and 40 piece to (B) vehicles per hour.

Thenm this factory can attempt to reduce the foolish workers and foolish managers umber and ot only employ the talent workers and managers to cooperate with ten only robotics number, when these talent workers and managers can ensure to know hoew to control these ten robotic together in order to achieve the maximum productivites kind (A) 40 piece and kind (B) 40 piece every hour effort in possibility.

In this both (A) and (B) unique vehicle manufacture case, this simple robotic production possible productive curve represents an important modern economics. The prdocutive cost is property defined as opportunity cost . This factory only may choose two methods ot productive resources. Either is lot clever and foolish workers and managers number and lot machine number or few worker number (only trained) clever workers and few robotics number. This factory have no money costs of production , when it sells all machines to buy few robotic number, even it can save money if robot purchase cost is less than all machine selling cost. Moreover, the factory will only dismiss the low skilled ot inefficient workers and the low managerial abilities managers to reduce salary expenditure when they can not be trained to proficient to control any one robotic to raise the both kinds (A) and (B) vehicles productivites number for a period. For example, after three months training time, their productivities number to kind (A) and (B) vehicles can not be increased absolutely.

Thus, production possibilities curve can explain why this factory ought choose to decide to sell its all machines and buy robotics to replace them in order to participate to the only trained talent workers and manager teams to cooperate to concentrate on onlymanufacturing the both (A) and (B) vehicle number per hour and in order to achieve improving performance, raising both kinds unique (A) and (B) vehicles productivities and efficiency aim.

Must Developed And Developing Countries Need Artificial Intelligent To Replace Human Job

Must developed and developing countries need artificial intelligent development? If one developed country, e.g. US, UK , Japan , Singapore it does not continue to develop artificial intelligence, robotic, then what disadvantges or weaknesses , it will encounter to compare when it chooses to continue to develop this artificial intelligent technology in society. If one developing country, e.g. China, Korea, Taiwan, it does not continue to develop artificial intelligence, robotic, then what disadantages or weaknesses, it will also encounter to compare when it chooses to continue to develop this artificial intelligent technology in in society. I shall explan the reasons why the results may cause to either the developed country, or the developing country as below:

● How AI help developing countries to communication and agriculture and learning and medical delivery development

Why can AI help developing countries ? Drones that pick inaccessible crops and mobile phones that give medical advice are two of the ways AI can transform life in the developing world. Artificial intelligence (AI) may improve the lives of the world's poor, the technology needed to revolutionise inefficient, ineffective food and healthcare systems in developing countries is well. For example, in low-income areas, agriculture and healthcare are two critical ecosystems that we can apply AI to immediately; this is not the far future, or even in five years.

Artificial intelligence (AI) has seeped into the daily lives of people in the developed world. From virtual assistants to recommendation engines, AI is in the news, our homes and offices. There is a lot of potential in terms of AI usage, especially in humanitarian areas. The impact could have a multiplier effect in developing countries, where resources are limited.

Emergency Response to developing countries' earthquake natural damage suddence occurrence predicting

AI and machine learning are still finding importance in emerging markets, but certain applications have emerged and are now widely used. For instance, predictive models for disaster relief enable first responders to automatically analyze large-scale behavior and movement through multiple sources of data including social media platforms, web forums, news sources, etc. Based on collected data, responders can scale reconstruction efforts and distribute supplies in a timely manner.

Why and how AI can assist farmers to predict when the earthquake occurs suddenly in order to avoid or reduce the natural damage to their agriculture productive number loss. For example, In 2015, when a major earthquake hit Nepal, more than 8 million people were affected. During the aftermath, drones were used to map and assess the destruction and speed up the rescue mission. The town of Sankhu, situated about 20 kilometers northeast of Kathmandu, was among the highly affected locations. In May 2018, my company Fusemachines and GeoSpatial Systems partnered with Sankhu's city officials to use drones and artificial intelligence in an effort to automatically estimate the reconstruction need. After processing data accumulated from a drone-powered aerial mapping of the region, the team fed this data to advanced machine learning algorithms. Combining drone imagery, digital mapping and machine learning, the team configured region modeling and infrastructure development with higher accuracy. Another organization known as One Concern, a California-based startup, has created a predictive AI program called Seismic Concern to accurately predict seism and is also working on solutions for wildfires, floods and hurricanes.

Smart AI Agriculture

Another application of AI in developing countries is smart agriculture. Farmers monitor crops more effectively and make better predictions on planting, weeding and harvesting using AI tools. It can also be used to analyze one plant at a time and add pesticides only to infected plants and trees instead of spraying pesticides across large swaths of crops. One California-based tech company is an example of this use of AI. So, the developing countries farmers in rural parts of India are also using AI to increase yields through better access to information about the farming season than they would normally have. Technology-enabled process automation offers the agribusiness industry the chance for remarkable growth -- not only in developed countries but around the world. There's a unique opportunity to increase yields, cut down labor costs and improve people's health.

Medicine Delivery to developing countries' patients urgent need

Companies are also leveraging AI to improve access to health care in some of the most remote areas of the world. In Rwanda, for example, Zipline is using drones to deliver medical supplies and blood to hospitals and clinics that are difficult to access by car. This has dramatically impacted people living in remote parts of the country because they are able to get medical help when needed. The drone system in Rwanda has also helped reduce waste of blood by 95%, as noted by Zipline. One Concern has created an AI program called Seismic Concern that accurately predicts seismic events and is also working on solutions for floods, wildfires and hurricanes. The medical field may actually benefit the most from emerging technologies in developing countries.

Assistance to reduce teaching work workload or psychological pressure to teachers in developing countries' schools

Another vital area benefiting from innovative technologies like AI is education. Advanced technologies can enhance how we learn, teach and perform tasks. In most developing countries, schools lack experienced teachers and resources to enhance students' knowledge. As a result, many students still have to walk long distances to get to the nearest school, which has created education gaps, especially in rural areas. AI tools such as personalized learning assistants can simplify learning by making tutoring services and learning materials accessible to all students, wherever they are. Machines can be automated to help students learn basic concepts without a tutor, which companies like Carnegie Learning are working on. This would allow students to learn at any time from anywhere. With AI, education is made easy and accessible to more people.

The initial usage of AI in developing countries has been at a micro level -- solving small, specific problems in a defined industry. As machine learning advances and there is a higher utilization of AI, we will see more complex issues being targeted and resolved. When duly adopted, AI can positively impact future developing countries people everyday lives not just in disaster intervention, education, health care and agriculture but can also help in mitigating poverty, malnutrition and pollution. Especially, in developing nations, to leverage AI's true potential and create a snowball effect. Startups are defining a holistic and humanitarian approach to building more sophisticated, AI-ready societies. Stakeholders in the AI landscape should understand the strengths and nuances of the developing world as well as the limitations of AI and create localized solutions and applications.

Why does smart phone help developing countries communication ?

Internet Seen as Positive Influence on Education but Negative on Morality in Emerging and Developing Nations. Internet access differs substantially across the 32 emerging and developing countries polled, with the lowest rates of internet use in South Asian and sub-Saharan African nations. Within countries, computer owners, young people, the well-educated, the wealthy and those with English language ability are much more likely to access the internet than their counterparts. To access the internet, people increasingly use smartphones rather than more cumbersome fixed landline connections and computers. Around the world, both smartphones and basic-feature phones alike are used for sending messages and taking pictures.

In fact, many developing countries young people, students are popular to use smart phones for internet usage aim, instead of communication. Moreover, many developing countries working people are also popular to use smart phones for any working usage in their working time , even non working time any time. So, smart phones (AI) phones will be important communication or leisure tools to developing countries people in the future. Unless, it is one day, scientists can develop another new communication tool to replace smart phones. So, artificial intelligence will be important to influence developing countries people , how to improve or bring positive learning attitudes to students in their daily learnnng lifes. as well as how to raise developing countries people, how to raise working people efficiency or improve performace in their daily working lifes. So, AI may bring positive learning or working attitudes to developing countries working people and students both.

The Positive Impact of Mass Media in Developing Countries

Radio, newspapers, television, Internet, social media, etc., all of these are forms of mass media. Each of these outlets has the capability of bringing information to thousands of people with one device. While in some communities it is easy to take advantage of these communication outlets such as television and Internet access, not everyone has access to such outlets. Radio is one of the most common forms of mass media in developing countries because it's affordable and uses less electricity than many other forms of mass media, but only approximately 75 percent of people in developing countries have access to a radio, and roughly 77 percent of people in rural areas have access to electricity.

For developing countries that have implemented forms of mass media in their communities, there have been numerous positive outcomes are influenced to impact developing countries mass media by artificial intelligence as below:

When AI is participated to developing countries mass media, it can influence any radio, television audiences raise more attention to each other through social media platforms such as Facebook and Twitter and create, organize and initiate street protests and campaigns. Furthermore, having access to social media in developing countries, people are able to connect to those that they usually wouldn't have the chance to talk to. Moreover, AI Provides educational opportunities- In many countries, the division between local and national languages as well as issues of literacy can make communication difficult. With the use of mass media, a bridge can be built between these two gaps. In India, there is a radio station that provides information in local languages and respects local culture and traditions. One of the main ways is to create public awareness of what is going on with businesses and government officials. The media plays an important role in giving people the opportunity to act against injustice, oppression and misdeeds that they otherwise wouldn't know about. Information on available healthcare, a mass radio broadcast was sent out encouraging parents to seek treatment at local healthcare facilities for their sick children. With this mass outreach on healthcare, the encouragement of people to take their children to healthcare facilities saved thousands of lives. This easy way of encouraging others and bringing awareness about certain diseases was made possible through a simple radio broadcast. Finally, when AI is particiapted to media, it may bring many social issues to life that otherwise would remain unknown to many people. In developing countries and communities like Burkina Faso, when the radio broadcast was released about malaria, diarrhea and pneumonia, people were educated and moved to action and knew to take their children to healthcare facilities for preventative care. As it is seen, having access to different media outlets is vital for those in developing countries. Here are three ways that those in developing countries can implement mass media to help their people and communities.

When AI is participated to any internet radio or internet newspaper mass online listening or reading channel. It can provide online radios or newspapers in public places- By providing online radios and newspapers in public areas it gives community members to access news, information and emergency warnings. Even though radios can be on the cheaper side, there are still many people that can't afford to have a radio in their home. By providing one in a local place, not only would it better educate the community members but also it will bring the community together. So, it can make media outlets a two-way platform- Creating a two-way platform between the community and those who are behind the radio stations, newspapers or broadcasts makes the community feel involved and that their voices are being heard. An organization called Soul City in sub-Saharan Africa is showing how well two-way platforms work by engaging their listeners and having them contribute thoughts and ideas about complex issues. Because developing countries radio listening audiences or newspaper readers are popular to accept computer online radio listening channel or online newspaper reading channel to replace traditional paper newspapers or radio machines. So, AI may raise their listening news or reading news leisure feeling from online mass media channel in the future.

● Why do developed countries need to develop AI
Artificial intelligence, or AI, is driving massive shifts across the globe, and every day more questions arise. What impact will AI have on the workforce and how can we prepare for it? How can we encourage economy-boosting and job-creating technologies? How can we ensure that AI will be implemented ethically and with minimal bias? How will society benefit? For developed country, such as US example. None of the US, Israel and Russia have a formal national AI policy yet. Private sector companies such as Google, Amazon and Apple and the US department of defence are driving the bulk of AI investment in the United States. Though Israel does not have a specific policy, it is keenly focused on AI and has seen the number of AI start-ups triple since 2014.

Developed country may learn whether what weakness it is lacking when it does not continue to develop AI from one another developed country. Which countries are approaching AI most effectively, and to what degree is there opportunity for greater international collaboration? It may be too early to tell; however, when analyzing the best practices of existing national AI policies, there is much that can be learned. These are the specific areas to consider. When one developed country continue to develop or research AI, it may bring these benefits as below:

On gathering Data aspect, from self-driving vehicles to smart cities, data is the driver behind AI. Innovation in the United States is limited without a national strategy that answers questions about protocol and ownership. France and Denmark, on the other hand, are opening government data. France is hosting troves of centrally collected public and private data that it plans to make available as part of its strategy. Conversely, by taking a restrictive position on issues of data collection (as indicated by the implementation of General Data Protection Regulation), the EU is putting manufacturers and software designers at a disadvantage while balancing the demand for privacy. On raising technologica talent aspect, the demand for AI talent far outweighs the available supply. As a result, almost every nation's strategy addresses talent development. Canada's AI strategy is distinct in that it primarily focuses on research and talent strategy. The country boasts AI degree programmes and is building a $127 million research facility in Toronto. Companies like Facebook and my own company, Uptake, are investing in Canada to access this talent pool. On AI legal technological innovation aspect, a whole host of legal questions swirl around AI. The country is developing a bill for AI liability that will be ready in March 2019. The government hopes the legal framework will attract investors by providing a simple, comprehensive guideline to enable the broad use of AI systems. So, when the developed country applied AI technology to assist any lawyers to work, then AI can help them to reduce the workload to draft any legal documents more easier. So, any developed countries lawyers' draft legal documents time must reduce if the developed countries lawyers accept to apply AI to assist their legal works. One of the great promises of AI is its potential for improving quality of life. But without the right planning and oversight, we risk exacerbating problems of inequality or marginalizing groups of people. As an example, India's AI strategy is focused on leveraging the technology not only for economic growth, but also for social inclusion.

AI may bring what benefits to developed countries

From SIRI to self-driving cars, artificial intelligence (AI) is progressing rapidly. While science fiction often portrays AI as robots with human-like characteristics, AI can encompass anything from Google's search algorithms to IBM's Watson to autonomous weapons. Artificial intelligence today is properly known as narrow AI (or weak AI), in that it is designed to perform a narrow task (e.g. only facial recognition or only internet searches or only driving a car). However, the long-term goal of many researchers is to create general AI (AGI or strong AI). While narrow AI may outperform humans at whatever its specific task is, like playing chess or solving equations, AGI would outperform humans at nearly every cognitive task.

Why research AI safety? Would AI bring war when AI is continued to develop by developed countries? In the near term, the goal of keeping AI's impact on society beneficial motivates research in many areas, from economics and law to technical topics such as verification, validity, security and control. Whereas it may be little more than a minor nuisance if your laptop crashes or gets hacked, it becomes all the more important that an AI system does what you want it to do if it controls your car, your airplane, your pacemaker, your automated trading system or your power grid. Another short-term challenge is preventing a devastating arms race in lethal autonomous weapons.

In the long term, an important question is what will happen if the quest for strong AI succeeds and an AI system becomes better than humans at all cognitive tasks. As pointed out by I.J. Good in 1965, designing smarter AI systems is itself a cognitive task. Such a system could potentially undergo recursive self-improvement, triggering an intelligence explosion leaving human intellect far behind. By inventing revolutionary new technologies, such a superintelligence might help us eradicate war, disease, and poverty, and so the creation of strong AI might be the biggest event in human history. Some experts have expressed concern, though, that it might also be the last, unless we learn to align the goals of the AI with ours before it becomes superintelligent.

There are some who question whether strong AI will ever be achieved, and others who insist that the creation of superintelligent AI is guaranteed to be beneficial. At FLI we recognize both of these possibilities, but also recognize the potential for an artificial intelligence system to intentionally or unintentionally cause great harm. We believe research today will help us better prepare for and prevent such potentially negative consequences in the future, thus enjoying the benefits of AI while avoiding pitfalls.

How can AI be dangerous when developed countries continue to develop AI to become weapon to replace soldiers?

Most researchers agree that a superintelligent AI is unlikely to exhibit human emotions like love or hate, and that there is no reason to expect AI to become intentionally benevolent or malevolent. Instead, when considering how AI might become a risk, experts think two scenarios most likely:

The AI is programmed to do something devastating: Autonomous weapons are artificial intelligence systems that are programmed to kill. In the hands of the wrong person, these weapons could easily cause mass casualties. Moreover, an AI arms race could inadvertently lead to an AI war that also results in mass casualties. To avoid being thwarted by the enemy, these weapons would be designed to be extremely difficult to simply "turn off," so humans could plausibly lose control of such a situation. This risk is one that's present even with narrow AI, but grows as levels of

AI intelligence and autonomy increase.

The AI is programmed to do something beneficial, but it develops a destructive method for achieving its goal: This can happen whenever we fail to fully align the AI's goals with ours, which is strikingly difficult. If you ask an obedient intelligent car to take you to the airport as fast as possible, it might get you there chased by helicopters and covered in vomit, doing not what you wanted but literally what you asked for. If a superintelligent system is tasked with a ambitious geoengineering project, it might wreak havoc with our ecosystem as a side effect, and view human attempts to stop it as a threat to be met. So, a super-intelligent AI will be extremely good at accomplishing its goals, and if those goals aren't aligned with ours, we have a problem. You're probably not an evil ant-hater who steps on ants out of malice, but if you're in charge of a hydroelectric green energy project and there's an anthill in the region to be flooded, too bad for the ants. A key goal of AI safety research is to never place humanity in the position of those ants.

Why the recent interest in AI safety ?

Stephen Hawking, Elon Musk, Steve Wozniak, Bill Gates, and many other big names in science and technology have recently expressed concern in the media and via open letters about the risks posed by AI, joined by many leading AI researchers. The idea that the quest for strong AI would ultimately succeed was long thought of as science fiction, centuries or more away. However, thanks to recent breakthroughs, many AI milestones, which experts viewed as decades away merely five years ago, have now been reached, making many experts take seriously the possibility of superintelligence in our lifetime. While some experts still guess that human-level AI is centuries away, most AI researches at the 2015 Puerto Rico Conference guessed that it would happen before 2060. Since it may take decades to complete the required safety research, it is prudent to start it now.

Because AI has the potential to become more intelligent than any human, we have no surprise way of predicting how it will behave. We can't use past technological developments as much of a basis because we've never created anything that has the ability to, wittingly or unwittingly, outsmart us. The best example of what we could face may be our own evolution. People now control the planet, not because we're the strongest, fastest or biggest, but because we're the smartest. If we're no longer the smartest, are we assured to remain in control?

A captivating conversation is taking place about the future of artificial intelligence and what it will/should mean for humanity. There are fascinating controversies where the world's leading experts disagree, such as: AI's future impact on the job market; if/when human-level AI will be developed; whether this will lead to an intelligence explosion; and whether this is something we should welcome or fear. But there are also many examples of of boring pseudo-controversies caused by people misunderstanding and talking past each other. When one developed country continue to develop AI, can itself country's all factories workers will lose jobs, due to AI can replace them to do simple works in factories, or any public transport drivers, e.g. bus drivers, ferry , tram, train drivers, they will lose jobs, when AI (non manual driving drivers) can replace all public transport drivers. So, some occupations will lose if developed countries continue to develop or research AI to replace human to do some simple jobs, such as some cooking jobs can be done by AI. So, it is possible that future cookers won't be needed, because AI cooking skills may be better than them to cook any good taste chinese or western food in restaurants. If you drive down the road, you have a subjective experience of colors, sounds, etc. But does a self-driving car have a subjective experience? Does it feel like anything at all to be a self-driving car? Although this mystery of consciousness is interesting in its own right, it's irrelevant to AI risk. If you get struck by a driverless car, it makes no difference to you whether it subjectively feels conscious. In the same way, what will affect us humans is what superintelligent AI does, not how it subjectively feels.

In fact, AI may be make any brokers jobs in financial market. the main concern of the beneficial-AI movement isn't with robots but with intelligence itself: specifically, intelligence whose goals are misaligned with ours. To cause us trouble, such misaligned superhuman intelligence needs no robotic body, merely an internet connection – this may enable outsmarting financial markets, out-inventing human researchers, out-manipulating human leaders, and developing weapons we cannot even understand. Even if building robots were physically impossible, a super-intelligent and super-wealthy AI could easily pay or manipulate many humans to unwittingly do its bidding. So, future brokers will be replaced by AI, when AI can be made to own financial brokers' analytical mind to make more accurate whether the share price will rise up or fall down to compare human financial brokers' analytical mind. The robot misconception is related to the myth that machines can't control humans. Intelligence enables control: humans control tigers not because we are stronger, but because we are smarter. This means that if we cede our position as smartest on our planet, it's possible that we might also cede control.

Not wasting time on the above-mentioned misconceptions lets us focus on true and interesting controversies where even the experts disagree. What sort of future do you want? Should we develop lethal autonomous weapons? What would you like to happen with job automation? What career advice would you give today's kids? Do you prefer new jobs replacing the old ones, or a jobless society where everyone enjoys a life of leisure and machine-produced wealth? Further down the road, would you like us to create superintelligent life and spread it through our cosmos? Will we control intelligent machines or will they control us? Will intelligent machines replace us, coexist with us, or merge with us? What will it mean to be human in the age of artificial intelligence?

Why do developed countries people need AI ?

Why do we assume that AI will require more and more physical space and more power when human intelligence continuously manages to miniaturize and reduce power consumption of its devices. How low the power needs and how small will the machines be by the time quantum computing becomes reality? Why do we assume that AI will exist as independent machines? If so, and the AI is able to improve its Intelligence by reprogramming itself, will machines driven by slower processors feel threatened, not by mere stupid humans, but by machines with faster processors? What would drive machines to reproduce themselves when there is no biological incentive, pressure or need to do so?

Who says superior AI will need or want to have a physical existence when an immaterial AI could evolve and preserve itself better from external dangers. What will happen if AI developed by competing ideologies, liberalism vs communism, reach maturity at the same time, will they fight for hegemony by trying to destroy each other physically and/or virtually. If AI is programmed to believe in God, and competing AI emerges programmed by muslims, christians or jews, how are the different AI's going to make sense of the different religious beliefs, are we going to have AI religious wars? What if the "powers that be" greatest fear is the emergence of a super AI that police's and rationalizes the distribution of wealth and food. A friendly super AI that is programmed to help humanity by, enforcing the declaration of Human Rights (the US is the only industrialized country that to this day has not signed this declaration) ending corruption and racism and protecting the environment.Most benefits of civilization stem from intelligence, so how can we enhance these benefits with artificial intelligence without being replaced on the job market and perhaps altogether?

Key to the process of machine learning are neural networks. These are brain-inspired networks of interconnected layers of algorithms, called neurons, that feed data into each other, and which can be trained to carry out specific tasks by modifying the importance attributed to input data as it passes between the layers. During training of these neural networks, the weights attached to different inputs will continue to be varied until the output from the neural network is very close to what is desired, at which point the network will have 'learned' how to carry out a particular task. A subset of machine learning is deep learning, where neural networks are expanded into sprawling networks with a huge number of layers that are trained using massive amounts of data. It is these deep neural networks that have fuelled the current leap forward in the ability of computers to carry out task like speech recognition and computer vision.

In conclusion, when developed countries continue to develop AI, it may bring positive advantages to bring raising productivies, or efficiencies, but it may also raise unemployment ratio to any low skill or low knowledge jobs in ther societies. However, human future society will need to change to be better to raise our living standard. But AI is one kind the best choice tool to achieve this aim in our future, so I agree developed countries continue to develop or research AI to be the super -human machine.

Reference

A. Castano et. al. " Automatic detection of dust devils and clouds at Mars" Machine vision and applications, Oct. 2008, vol. 19, no 5-6, pp. 467-482.

Accenture, " Why artificial intelligence is the future of growth"(2017) <http://www.accenture.com/us-en/insight-a rtificial-intelligence-future-growth>.

D. Schedidt , Unmanned Air Vehicle Command And Control, Handbook Of Unmanned Air Vehicles, Springer-Verlag, 2014. Facebook (AI) Research Available at https://research.facebook.com/ai, research at google, machine intelligence available at

http://research.google.com/pubs/machineintellige nce.html; micro soft research-machine learning and artificial intelligence available at <http://research.microsoft.com/en-us/research- areas/machine-learning-ai.aspx>.

International Federation Of Robotics, 2016. IFR press release world robotics report. IFR, org . 29 Sept. Accessed Feb. 01, 2017. http://www.ifr.org/news/ifr-press-release/world-robitics report -2016-8321.

K, Fedra , "GIS and environmental modelling" in environmental modelling with GIS, edited by M.F. Goodchild.B.O. Parks and L.T. Steyaert, Oxford University press, pp. 35-50, 1994.

Keynes, J.M. (1933). Economic possibilities for our grandchildren (1930). Essays in persuasion, pp.358-73.

Mckinsey & Company (2013, May). Disruptive technologies: Advices that will transform life, business and the global economy , USA.

Ministry of economy, trade and industry, Japan, 2015, Japan's robot strategy. Ministry of economy, trade and industry.

Ray Kurzweil , The age of spiritual machines (1999) is cited numerously through this chapter: Kurzweilai.net http://www.kurzweilai.net

Rich, Elaine & Knight, Kevin, Artificial Intelligence Second Edition, 1991, New York; Mc-Graw-Hill.

Artificial intelligence bank service working environment

Focus on outcomes not technology.Artificial Intelligence: Waiting to be unleashed? The Insider Column - When Digital Transformation misses. Are you meeting the demands of the new digital consumer? Will your legacy mindset compromise your digital competitiveness? Can artificial intelligence create online remote office new business service market in global ?

The Future of Artificial Intelligence In The Workplace:

Is AI going to displace workers or come as a benefit to them?

Is AI going to displace workers or come as a benefit to them? Getty

Smart technologies aren't just changing our homes; they're edging their way into their numerous industries and are disrupting the workplace. Artificial Intelligence (AI) has the potential to improve productivity, efficiency and accuracy across an organization – but is this entirely beneficial? Many fear that the rise of AI will lead to machines and robots replacing human workers and view this progression in technology as threat rather than a tool to better ourselves.

With AI continuing to be a prominent online office service business to replace human actual office working environment, businesses need to realize that self-learning and black-box capabilities are not the panacea. Many organisations are already beginning to see the incredible capabilities of AI, using these advantages to enhance human intelligence and gain real value from their data. As there is increasing evidence demonstrating the benefits of intelligent systems, more decision-makers in the boardroom are gaining a better understanding of what AI can really offer. Research conducted by EY explains "organizations enabling AI at the enterprise level are increasing operational efficiency, making faster, more informed decisions and innovating new products and services." Can articial intelligent technology create remote office working environment to replace our traditional actual office work environment ? Can we do not need to go to office to work , when any office staffs ,e.g. managers, clerk, etc. they can apply artificial intelligent technology and online technology to work at home, such as remote office working environment ?

The first companies employing AI systems across the board will gain competitive advantage, reduce cost of operations and remove head counts. Whilst this may be a positive from a business perspective, it is obvious why this a worry for those working in roles at risk of displacement. The introduction of these technologies will likely trigger an issue with unions and job security due to the substantial operational changes. Although AI will affect every sector in some way, not every job is at equal risk. PwC predicts a relatively low displacement of jobs (around 3%) in the first wave of automation, but this could dramatically increase up to 30% by the mid-2030's. Occupations within the transport industry could potentially be at much greater risk, whereas jobs requiring social, emotional and literary abilities are at the lowest risk of displacement.

A positive future with artificial intelligence to bring remote online office working environment chance:

Many businesses and individuals are optimistic that this AI-driven shift in the workplace will result in more jobs being created than lost. As we develop innovative technologies, AI will have a positive impact on our economy by creating jobs that require the skill set to implement new systems. 80% of respondents in the EY survey said it was the lack of these skills that was the biggest challenge when employing AI programs.

It is likely that artificial intelligence will soon replace jobs involving repetitive or basic problem-solving tasks, and even go beyond current human capability. AI systems will be making decisions instead of humans in industrial settings, customer service roles and within financial institutions. Automated decisioning will be responsible for tasks such as approving loans, deciding whether a customer should be onboarded or identifying corruption and financial crime.

Organisations will benefit from an increase in productivity as a result of greater automation, meaning more revenue will generated. This thus provides additional money to spend on supporting jobs in the services sector.Due to the vast array of jobs that could be impacted by AI, it is fundamental to address the potential pitfalls of these technologies. Business need to overcome the trust and bias issues surrounding AI by achieving an effective and successful implementation that makes it possible for everyone to benefit.

Governments must ensure that gains from AI are shared widely across society to prevent social inequality between those affected and unaffected by these developments. For example, this could be through increased investment into training. With the additional cost-savings from implementing AI systems, employers should also focus on upskilling their current employees.

To properly leverage the power of AI, we need to address the issue at an educational level, as well as in business. Education systems needs to focus on training students in roles directly associated to working with AI, including programmers and data analysts. This requires more emphasis to be put on STEM subjects (science, technology, engineering and mathematics). Also, subjects centered around building creative, social and emotional skills should be encouraged. Whilst artificial intelligence will be more productive than human workers for repetitive tasks, humans will always outperform machines in jobs requiring relationship-building and imagination. Hence, artificial intelligence will change our world both inside and outside the workplace. Instead of focusing on the fear surrounding automation, businesses need to embrace these new technologies to ensure they implement the most effective AI systems to enhance and compliment human intelligence.

Artificial Intelligence (AI) in Banking working environment

Artificial Intelligence (AI) is a fast-evolving technology, gaining popularity all around the world. Several industries have already adopted AI for various applications, getting better and smarter day by day. In the past few years, the banking sector has also become one of the leading adopters of Artificial Intelligence. Most banks and financial institutions are implementing AI to add more efficiency to their back-office and lessen security risks.

As per Statista, the AI market in the United States is forecasted to reach 7.35 billion U.S. dollars in 2018. Some major applications of AI include classification, image recognition, object identification, and automated geophysical feature detection. Speaking of banking and financial institutions, JPMorgan Chase, Wells Fargo, Bank of America, CitiBank, and other leading U.S. banks have already implemented AI in their systems, helping consumers manage their daily banking needs more efficiently.

AI technology can bring better Customer Support in bank service environment

Several pieces of evidence advocate that the customers willingly prefer self-service options which allow them to chat with a virtual assistant as if it were a live customer representative. Most leading banks have already added virtual assistants to their instant website chatbots, voice response systems, and mobile applications. Artificial Intelligence considers each interaction as a teachable moment, so the chatbots (virtual assistants) keeps getting better while understanding customers. With AI, virtual assistants can deliver better customer support. It also allows sentiment analysis, so the virtual assistant can determine when individuals are getting frustrated and instantly transfer them to a live agent.

Enhanced Banking Services

AI streamlines the banking process while giving customer service a new level of comfortability. It allows banks to meet customers' expectations with comprehensive digital support. With Artificial Intelligence, you can achieve greater precision and accuracy. From cash transfer to bills payment, cards management, and other support, AI can significantly enrich the satisfaction level of your customers. All of these operations can be easily managed through desktops, smartphones, and other mobile devices.

Scam Recognition

With an immense growth of banking fraud, scam recognition and reduction has become challenging for the banking sector. Several banks tried to identify the factors and powerful solutions but couldn't succeed. However, AI makes it easier to detect the factors involved in frauds and support investigators. It improves financial security with advanced fraud prevention tactics. Artificial Intelligence works as a real-time scam solution for the banking sector while handling complex situations and tactics. Based on advanced data crunching, AI can detect fraud by flagging unusual transactions. It also feeds back into the consumer's profile which subsequently builds a secure environment.

Advanced Data Analytics

One of the main advantages of AI is its ability to complete tedious tasks through intricate automation, resulting in better productivity. Based on a machine learning algorithm, AI can quickly consume and process a massive amount of data at an expedited level. The enormous speed brings efficiency to financial services, providing scope for personalized offerings to consumers. What's even more, AI makes faster decisions while carrying out actions quickly. With such advantages, it is nearly obvious that the majority of banks and financial institutions will adopt AI to stay competitive and deliver better customer support. However, several cons are also associated with a machine learning algorithm. As it continues to learn and grow, the decision-making capabilities may create problems in the near future.

Disadvanages of AI in Banking Sector

Artificial intelligence is also expected to massively disrupt banks and traditional financial services. Some of its disadvantages are listed below.

Highly Expensive

Production and maintenance of artificial intelligence demand huge costs since they are very complex machines. AI also consists of advanced software programs which require regular updates to meet the needs of the changing environment. In the case of critical failures, the procedure to reinstate the system and recover lost codes may require enormous time and cost.

Bad Calls

Though Artificial Intelligence can learn and improve, it still can't make judgment calls. Humans can take individual circumstances and judgment calls into account when making decisions, something that AI might never be able to do. Replacing adaptive human behavior with AI may cause irrational behavior within ecosystems of humans and things.

Distribution of Power

There is a constant fear of AI superseding or taking over the humans. Artificial intelligence can give a lot of power to the few individuals who are controlling it. Hence, AI carries the risk and takes control away from humans while dehumanizing actions in several ways.

Unemployment

Replacement of the workforce with machines can lead to wide-reaching unemployment. Moreover, if the use of AI becomes rampant, people will be highly dependent on the machines and lose their creative power. Unemployment is a socially undesirable issue. Individuals with nothing to do can lead to the devastating use of their minds. Be it banking or any other sector; Artificial intelligence can effectively increase the unemployment rate.

Artificial Intelligence delivered to wrong hands can turn out to be a serious threat to humankind. If individuals start thinking destructively, they can generate havoc with these advanced machines. The challenges introduced by the emergence of artificial intelligence revolve around several things. However, AI is a right balance of skill and emotions which is continually growing. Artificial intelligence provides banks, financial institutions, and tech companies with significant competitive advantages. Nevertheless, it can completely transform the financial sector and make it faster, but this will only be possible if the financial industry can manage the security risk of systems based on AI.

What does artificial intelligence mean for the bank service office workers?

With all these new artificial intelligence use cases comes the question of whether machines will force humans into obsolescence. The jury is still out: Some experts vehemently deny that artificial intelligence will automate so many jobs that millions of people find themselves unemployed, while other experts see it as a pressing problem.

"The structure of the workforce is changing, but I don't think artificial intelligence is essentially replacing jobs in bank service working environment. It allows us to really create a knowledge-based economy and leverage that to create better automation for a better form of life. It might be a little bit theoretical, but I think if you have to worry about artificial intelligence and robots replacing some bank service jobs, e.g. bank security, bank enquiry service,. But, AI can not replace bank counter service staffs to do saving or withdrawing money transfer tasks when any customers prepare to save money or withdraw money in bank counters. As this technology develops, the AI bank service will see new startups, numerous saving or withdraw transactions from consumer won't be raise more easily.

AI to Banking and Finance industry

The banking and finance industry plays a major role in our lives. I mean the world runs on money and banks are essentially the gatekeepers that regulate that flow. Did you know that the banking and finance industry heavily relies on artificial intelligence for things like customer service, fraud protection, investment, and more? A simple example is the automated emails that you receive from banks whenever you do an out of the ordinary transaction. Well, that's AI watching over your account and trying to warn you of any fraud.

AI is also being trained to look at large samples of fraud data and find a pattern so that you can be warned before it happens to you. Also, when you hitch a little snag and chat with bank's customer service, chances are that you are chatting with an AI bot. Even the big players in the finance industry use AI to analyze data to find the best avenues to invest money so they can get the most returns with the least risk. That's not all, AI is poised to play an even bigger role in the industry as major banks across the world are investing billions of dollars in the AI technology and we all will observe its effects sooner than later.

The Future of Artificial Intelligence In The Workplace

Smart technologies aren't just changing our homes; they're edging their way into their numerous industries and are disrupting the workplace. Artificial Intelligence (AI) has the potential to improve productivity, efficiency and accuracy across an organization – but is this entirely beneficial? Many fear that the rise of AI will lead to machines and robots replacing human workers and view this progression in technology as threat rather than a tool to better ourselves.

With AI continuing to be a prominent buzzword in 2019, businesses need to realize that self-learning and black-box capabilities are not the panacea. Many organisations are already beginning to see the incredible capabilities of AI, using these advantages to enhance human intelligence and gain real value from their data. As there is increasing evidence demonstrating the benefits of intelligent systems, more decision-makers in the boardroom are gaining a better understanding of what AI can really offer. Research conducted by EY explains "organizations enabling AI at the enterprise level are increasing operational efficiency, making faster, more informed decisions and innovating new products and services."

Today In: Cybersecurity

The first companies employing AI systems across the board will gain competitive advantage, reduce cost of operations and remove head counts. Whilst this may be a positive from a business perspective, it is obvious why this a worry for those working in roles at risk of displacement. The introduction of these technologies will likely trigger an issue with unions and job security due to the substantial operational changes. Although AI will affect every sector in some way, not every job is at equal risk. PwC predicts a relatively low displacement of jobs (around 3%) in the first wave of automation, but this could dramatically increase up to 30% by the mid-2030's. Occupations within the transport industry could potentially be at much greater risk, whereas jobs requiring social, emotional and literary abilities are at the lowest risk of displacement.

A positive future with artificial intelligence

Many businesses and individuals are optimistic that this AI-driven shift in the workplace will result in more jobs being created than lost. As we develop innovative technologies, AI will have a positive impact on our economy by creating jobs that require the skill set to implement new systems. 80% of respondents in the EY survey said it was the lack of these skills that was the biggest challenge when employing AI programs. It is likely that artificial intelligence will soon replace jobs involving repetitive or basic problem-solving tasks, and even go beyond current human capability. AI systems will be making decisions instead of humans in industrial settings, customer service roles and within financial institutions. Automated decisioning will be responsible for tasks such as approving loans, deciding whether a customer should be onboarded or identifying corruption and financial crime. Organisations will benefit from an increase in productivity as a result of greater automation, meaning more revenue will generated. This thus provides additional money to spend on supporting jobs in the services sector.

How to take advantage of AI to any offices

Due to the vast array of jobs that could be impacted by AI, it is fundamental to address the potential pitfalls of these technologies. Business need to overcome the trust and bias issues surrounding AI by achieving an effective and successful implementation that makes it possible for everyone to benefit. Governments must ensure that gains from AI are shared widely across society to prevent social inequality between those affected and unaffected by these developments. For example, this could be through increased investment into training.With the additional cost-savings from implementing AI systems, employers should also focus on upskilling their current employees.

To properly leverage the power of AI, we need to address the issue at an educational level, as well as in business. Education systems needs to focus on training students in roles directly associated to working with AI, including programmers and data analysts. This requires more emphasis to be put on STEM subjects (science, technology, engineering and mathematics). Also, subjects centered around building creative, social and emotional skills should be encouraged. Whilst artificial intelligence will be more productive than human workers for repetitive tasks, humans will always outperform machines in jobs requiring relationship-building and imagination. Artificial intelligence will change our world both inside and outside the workplace. Instead of focusing on the fear surrounding automation, businesses need to embrace these new technologies to ensure they implement the most effective AI systems to enhance and compliment human intelligence

How AI can help office workers to do tasks more easily

Companies are currently spending big on artificial intelligence and machine learning initiatives to the tune of $12 billion, but estimates put that figure as high as $57.6 billion by 2021, according to the International Data Corporation (IDC). With such massive shifts, the focus is usually on what we might lose, but it shouldn't be. A recent report on the future of work from the McKinsey Global Institute suggests that while only about 5% of jobs can be completely eliminated by automation, the rise of AI requires workers to beef up both technical and soft skills in order to stay competitive.

What's seldom discussed is how AI can revolutionize our jobs. It's now possible to pinpoint peak productivity for a single day, improve communication in meetings (even before people ever work together face to face), or even teach you to be a better leader, all thanks to AI platforms. I shall indicate these advantages to bring any office benefits from AI assistance as below:

1. AI can help any companies to get better to hire the best applicants

AI has the greatest potential to change the way companies find candidates, according to Alexander Rinke, cofounder and CEO of Celonis. The company's process-mining technology helps businesses to understand the areas where automation can help humans, he says. In HR departments, Celonis can help identify how fast workers come and go, the cost per hire, and which positions take the longest to fill. AI helped enable one customer's ability to identify bottlenecks in recruitment and reduced process costs internally by 30% as well as get them hired more quickly, he says.

Crafting a resume has never been easier, nor has landing an interview. Another example is how recruitment software provider iCIMS, in partnership with Google, is helping job seekers find jobs directly through the search engine, thanks to Google's AI and machine learning capabilities. Susan Vitale, iCIMS's chief marketing officer says that in addition to reducing the number of expired job postings, machine learning is underlying a private beta program of Google's Cloud Jobs Discovery model. "For a candidate searching for, say, a CTO role, Cloud Job Discovery will serve up CTO positions as well as jobs with titles that are similar, but not verbatim, such as chief technology officer or chief technical officer," says Vitale. This model also allows for conceptual search results, such as serving up job listings for cashiers, sales associates, and store associates when someone searches for one versus just only showing jobs that exactly match the keyword search criteria, she adds.

2. AI can help any office workers to raise much more productive efficiencies

John Furneaux, CEO and cofounder of Hive, says predictive analytics will help us better understand how we work. "It can tell us just about everything we want to know about teams and collaboration, for example, if men or women get more done in the afternoon, and if summer Fridays are a myth," he says. (Everyone thinks summer Fridays aren't productive, but in reality there's no difference between those and other Fridays during the year–productivity is equally low.)

Using a data set of over 30,000 completed actions across Hive workspaces, Furneaux says they were able to identify some notable trends in productivity. For example, men were far more productive early in the day, with a sharp decline in the afternoon, while women had a slower start to the day but were far more productive in later hours than their male counterparts. And analyzing chat messages revealed that women appear to complete more tasks when chatting, suggesting they use communication as a key tool to completing work. Similarly, Nintex Hawkeye analyzes data on business processes by types, users, roles, and departments to see who's doing the work and how long it takes them to do it. Management can monitor and analyze those metrics in real time.

3. AI can help any managers to make the most fair compensation and eliminate wage gaps to every staffs

Tanya Jansen, cofounder of the compensation management platform beqom, says that AI and predictive analytics can eliminate unconscious bias from compensation. Jansen says that AI based on a variety of rules including education, experience, certifications, and more can make compensation more fair and help businesses move closer to closing pay gaps. "Specifically, AI can help solve gender pay gaps and the CEO-to-worker pay gap, in which pay ratios of Fortune 500 companies range from 2:1 at the low end to nearly 5000:1 at the high end," she says. Additionally, the use of AI-driven compensation technology to make pay more fair can mitigate the risk of employee turnover, which costs businesses as much as 33% of a worker's annual salary to replace them.

4. AI can help any office staffs to arrange better meetings

Augmented Reality (AR) is still in its infancy, but AI and machine learning are the core components that make it work. As such, Christa Manning, the vice president and solution provider research leader at Bersin, Deloitte Consulting LLP, says that AR can help workers find the right information, in the right place, at the right time to make the best decisions wherever they may be working. For example, as more companies adopt video meetings and collaborative workspaces, it's likely we'll begin to see HR-curated information like talent profiles and work styles layered over interactions through AR."Imagine being in a video conference with a colleague and having direct insight into their communication style, seeing tips on how to best interact with them or reminders of what needs to be discussed. SO, AI can help any organizations to conclude or find the best methods to solve any problems after their every discussion in any meetings.

How AI is improving onboarding and training. AI coaching tools first learn by observing how different employees conduct specific tasks. Then these tools can walk new employees through how to complete those tasks—or even coach existing employees on how to do things more effectively or efficiently. Chorus is a great example of this technology. It analyzes sales calls while they happen, offering tips to help sales reps manage the cadence of meetings and use the most effective messaging. It also records all sales calls and compiles statistics for each sales rep, providing everyone with the tools they need to help them close more deals and conduct more effective calls. Another example is Cogito, a tool that combines AI with behavioral science to help customer service employees provide better phone support. It monitors calls for voice signals, providing real-time suggestions to representatives on how to improve the conversation.

5. AI can help any managers to be better leaders

Indiggo, a platform powered by a proprietary AI tool called "indi," functions as a brain that has consumed all the knowledge the company has gathered in its 15 years of operation. It also uses an algorithm to provide an estimate of how much time is wasted by a company by analyzing the size of its management team. Then it taps their calendars to see how they spend their time, and walks individual managers through a type of Q&A to make sure they are clear on what their top three priorities are, and how that relates to the organization's priorities, which will indicate if that strategy is moving forward or not. "The counterintuitive impact of these advances is that they actually make human work truly irreplaceable," Alexander Rinke, the cofounder and CEO of Celonis says. As such, he reminds us, "Humans are much better at processes that involve reasoning, judgment, and interaction with people." So, AI can recommend more accurate and useful opinions to help any managers to solve their managing challenges in office any time.

How AI is eliminating repetitive administrative tasks

There are a lot of tasks that knowledge workers spend time on that provide little—if any—value.For example, say you need to schedule a meeting to get consensus on a decision before moving forward, but you need five people to join the meeting. It's easy to spend a ton of time sending email back-and-forth or finding an open slot on everyone's calendar.That's not the most rewarding use of your time for you or your company.Tools like X.ai give employees AI-powered personal assistants that perform administrative tasks like scheduling, rescheduling, and cancelling meetings.

How AI is transforming internal communications and support

Personnel on the teams that provide employee support have their hands full with other responsibilities, too. HR teams work on building the kind of company people love working for. IT maintains the company's network and keeps data secure. Office managers frequently run big events like holiday parties.These tasks are crucial, but they're often hard for teams to focus on because they're busy answering routine questions. AI service desks like askSpoke allow employee support teams to balance their service commitments with other important responsibilities by reducing interruptions from rote, repetitive requests.Employees can askSpoke for whatever they need over Slack, email, SMS, and the web. askSpoke's friendly AI will automatically provide a prompt response.

How AI is transforming marketing, sales, and customer service

AI-powered chatbots help with external support as well. Just like with internal support tools like askSpoke, these chatbots learn from real marketers, salespeople, and customer service reps and are eventually able to answer questions as accurately as a knowledgeable person.For example, chatbot for Messenger helps customers plan their vacations. It books flights, hotels, and cars, highlights destination attractions, and even provides answers to questions like "Where can I go for $100 expense budget only?"

How AI is transforming business data and analytics

It's hard to run a competitive business today without data. But even massive amounts of data are useless without a way to transform that data into valuable insights. That's typically why you'd want to hire a data scientist—which just happens to be one of the most difficult roles to fill. How AI is fighting fraud and transforming security. Have you ever taken a call from your bank to find that someone used your debit card fraudulently? Most likely, your bank used some form of AI to detect the fraudulent transaction and decline it. Applying the same basic technology to the workplace helps identify security risks and keeps customer, employee, and company data safe. AI-powered software can automatically detect and address threats among thousands or millions of signals that humans would never be able to parse (especially not in real-time).

How AI is transforming productivity

While AI is transforming the workplace in many different ways across every industry, it's impacting productivity most of all. When your office staffs don't have to scroll through calendars to look for open meeting times, build reports in spreadsheets to look for insights, or spend your day answering the same questions over and over again, you're more productive. Workers are freed from redundant and mindless tasks, giving them more time to do work that matters, solve problems, and exercise their creativity. Some tools use AI to specifically monitor and boost productivity. For example, Deloitte's LaborWise provides company leaders and managers with productivity analytics that help them identify areas where labor costs are too high, impediments that slow people down, and departments that need additional staff.

In conclusion, what AI means for the workplace of the future. While some will dramatize the negative impacts of AI, cognitive computing, and robotics, these powerful tools will also help create new jobs, boost productivity, and allow workers to focus on the human aspects of work. Essentially, automation frees companies and their employees up to be more empathetic, to focus on things like the customer experience, employee engagement, and workplace culture.

What are traditional office tools to be replaced by AI ?

Artificial intelligence (AI) is predicted to eliminate over a million jobs in the next few years, potentially replacing lower level positions like administrative assistants with humanoid robots or voice assistants. But in the nearer future, fresh AI-driven software and products are also moving to eliminate non-human elements of the workplace by replacing traditional office tools, including both physical products and everyday electronic processes. Why should businesses switch from the tried-and-true to emerging technology? Many of the experts TechRepublic talked to said the AI options streamline business practices, making their adopters work smarter instead of harder. I shall indicate these office tools ,they can be applied to help any office staffs to finish their these tasks in office, they may include as below:

1. Scheduling

Workloud's end-to-end, cloud-based workforce management software takes scheduling from paper or Excel and moves it to the cloud. Everything from clocking in and out to monitoring employee absences is fully digitalized.Schedules and timesheets are accurate, created easily, and accessible through the service's web, tablet, and mobile apps. The software can also be used for absence management.

2. Employee talent selection

Using AI and organizational behavior science, can be used to replace internal spreadsheets and databases designed to monitor human capital. By mining employee attributes and experiences, the software can recommend who would be best for a project. The software also collects reviews after projects to better predict successful employee-project matches.The traditional hiring process is slow, biased and inaccurate, By removing humans from the beginning stages of the process, it can become faster and more fair, and result in better hires.

AI software automates the hiring process, using online simulations instead of manual screenings and interviews. Using the software, employers can include tasks in a job application, allowing job candidates to show technical skills that may be necessary for a job. Employers can't rule out candidates until they see how the candidate performs, eliminating bias that occurs in the resume reading stage. Both sides also automatically receive updates about each other's steps, reducing the amount of time it takes to .

3.Timesheets: Allocate

Using AI and machine learning, the software registers an employee's computer activity throughout the day. The data, which can also pull information from email and calendars, is used to suggest timesheet entries to reflect a more accurate amount of time an employee spent working. The employee can review and revise as necessary. However, the software doesn't spy on or monitor employees. The data is only available to each employee, while others in the company can only see the timesheet's output, which Allocate said would be the same information available if a manual sheet was used. So,replacing manual timesheets with Allocate has three advantages: More accurate time entry, project analytics, and "'unsucking' the work experience."

4. Document storage

By using AI to read and analyze business and legal documents, AI can store all of the important document-based information in the cloud. The severe reduction in print-outs means less paper and ink, fewer products like binder clips and boxes to store and organize all of the paper, and more employee time freed up from not needing to manually sort through every document.

For example, in any lawyer offices, legal professionals' morale in the industry can suffer when they are pushed into performing such dull, repetitive tasks like sorting through and coding documents by hand, With AI tools to automate those duties, lawyers can focus on more meaningful projects and boost the business's and clients' success as a result. While focused on law firms, businesses that have a lot of unstructured data in documents may also be able to use the service to free up employee time and save on printing costs.

5. Scanners: Adobe Scan

While documents are moving to the cloud more and more, sometimes a physical copy of a document still needs to be scanned using a bulky office scanner. Adobe Scan, an app that condenses a scanner to the size of a smartphone, can rid offices of the need for an in-house scanner. Users can download and open the app, then hold their device over whatever they need to scan. Adobe Sensei then turns the scan into a PDF, and sends it to the Adobe Document Cloud. The app can transform any image into digital text that can then be searched and used electronically. The app streamlines the scanning process, making scans cleaner and more immediate. For businesses already using Adobe services, the app makes documents easily accessible.

6. Landline phones

While landlines in homes are increasingly less common, the same cannot be said for offices. But using chatbots and AI integrations, RingCentral is trying to replace traditional office landline phone systems. The platform offers over 100 integrations, including that AI landline phones can let employees check their voicemail, and a Gong.io option that listens to call recordings to find traits of successful employees than can be used in training. An add-on for Gmail lets users switch from emailing back and forth to a voice session without needing to look up contact information. AI landline phone is easy to adopt and use in the workplace, and is more customizable than standard phone systems, said David Lee, vice president of platform products. Compared to the traditional option, the cloud-based option is "future-proof.

How artificial intelligence can raise office efficiency

Artificial Intelligence is already impacting every industry through automation and machine learning, bringing concerns that AI is on the fast track to replacing many jobs. But these fears aren't new, says Dan Jackson, director of Enterprise Technology at Crestron, a company that designs workplace technology. "I'd argue this is no different than when we moved from an agricultural to an industrial economy at the turn of the last century. The percentage of people working in agriculture significantly decreased, and it was a big shift, but we still have plenty of jobs 100 years later," he says. Anytime society experiences a major technological advancement, we need to be prepared for it to change the way we live and work. It's hard to imagine what the future of jobs will look like with AI, but that future exists. And optimists suggest that, like the sewing machine to the textile industry, AI will make us better, more efficient and faster workers.

In fact, many experts agree that AI has the potential to eliminate mundane, administrative work, while we will always rely on human workers to be empathetic, collaborative, creative and strategic. But it's impact on any industry lies in the hands of the business leaders who are responsible for adopting AI strategies.

● Training presents challenges

A recent study of 1,000 global companies by Accenture found that AI is already creating three new categories of jobs: trainers, explainers and sustainers. Trainers are the people who teach AI systems how to act -- whether it's language, human behavior or the intricacies of human interaction. Explainers are the liaison between technology and business leaders, providing more insight and clarity into machine learning for the non-tech workers. Sustainers are the workers required to maintain AI systems and troubleshoot any potential issues. Some jobs were highly technical and required advanced degrees, but other roles demanded innately human things such as empathy and interaction. Downstream jobs, such as those in sales, marketing, or service will change to take advantage of the insights from AI, but many of the core skills will remain. However, it might sound like any job related to AI will require years of technical knowledge, but that isn't the case. We've already seen a shift in tech hiring -- companies often need highly specific skill sets that are hard to find in potential candidates. As a result, more businesses are hiring employees with the right soft skills, and then training them in technical skills.

An office effort measured approach to AI

The real takeaway is that any approach to AI will need to consider the human aspect of every business. AI has great potential to increase efficiency and accuracy and it's already been proven in certain industries. For example, the use of AI In banking to identify and money laundering schemes. It's also improved healthcare by "increasing the speed and accuracy" of cancer diagnosistics. AI can also help reduce the cost and length of human trafficking investigations, a situation where time is precious. In these examples, AI hasn't replaced jobs, but has positively impacted efficiency. Thus, we need to ensure our education system responds to equip young people with the appropriate skills and adaptability, while businesses and public organizations must invest in training. Perhaps most of all, we need to encourage imagination and willingness to experiment. The organizations that can innovate with AI will reap the benefits. Their growth will make them the primary source of future jobs. Companies have a choice when implementing AI. They can choose to effectively implement systems that make employee's lives easier and find creative ways to leverage the technology. It's up to employers to ease fears for workers around AI and build strategies that benefit everyone. Hence, some AI experts believe AI can only raise efficiency to some office tasks, however, AI can not still raise efficiency to all office tasks for any office deparments. The reasons are because some office tasks which can only dominate to finish by human office workers. These office tasks are as below:

How can leaders and managers improve employee productivity while still saving time? These below tasks, AI experts ensure that AI can not help any office workers to raise their efficiencies as below:

1. Office managers can not delegate to AI to help them to do. While this tip might seem the most obvious, it is often the most difficult to put into practice. We get it—your company is your baby, so you want to have a direct hand in everything that goes on with it. While there is nothing wrong with prioritizing quality (it is what makes a business successful, after all), checking over every small detail yourself rather than delegating can waste everyone's valuable time. Instead, give responsibilities to qualified employees, and trust that they will perform the tasks well. This gives your employees the opportunity to gain skills and leadership experience that will ultimately benefit your company. You hired them for a reason, now give them a chance to prove you right.

2. Office managers can not match Tasks to Skills to AI. Knowing your employees' skills and behavioral styles is essential for maximizing efficiency. For example, an extroverted, creative, out-of-the-box thinker is probably a great person to pitch ideas to clients. However, they might struggle if they are given a more rule-intensive, detail-oriented task. Asking your employees to be great at everything just isn't efficient—instead, before giving an employee an assignment, ask yourself: is this the person best suited to perform this task? If not, find someone else whose skills and styles match your needs.

3. Office managers can not teach AI to replace them how to communicate and teach their low level staffs how to work effectively. Every manager knows that communication is the key to a productive workforce. Technology has allowed us to contact each other with the mere click of a button (or should we say, tap of a touch screen)—this naturally means that current communication methods are as efficient as possible, right? Not necessarily. A McKinsey study found that emails can take up nearly 28% of an employee's time. In fact, email was revealed to be the second most time-consuming activity for workers (after their job-specific tasks). Instead of relying solely on email, try social networking tools (such as Slack) designed for even quicker team communication. You can also encourage your employees to occasionally adopt a more antiquated form of contact...voice-to-voice communication. Having a quick meeting or phone call can settle a matter that might have taken hours of back-and-forth emails. All of above communication tasks, I believe that AI can not do better than managers in offices.

4. AI can not keep Goals Clear and focused to be better than managers. You can't expect employees to be efficient if they don't have a focused goal to aim for. If a goal is not clearly defined and actually achievable, employees will be less productive. So, try to make sure employees' assignments are as clear and narrow as possible. Let them know exactly what you expect of them, and tell them specifically what impact this assignment will have. One way to do this is to make sure your goals are "SMART" – specific, measurable, attainable, realistic, and timely. Before assigning an employee a task, ask yourself if it fits each of these requirements. If not, ask yourself how the task can be tweaked to help your workers stay focused and efficient.

5. AI can not know how to incentivize Employees to work more efficiently. One of the best ways to encourage employees to be more efficient is to actually give them a reason to do so. Recognizing your workers for a job well done will make them feel appreciated and encourage them to continue increasing their productivity. When deciding how to reward efficient employees, make sure you take into account their individual needs or preferences. For example, one employee might appreciate public recognition, while another would prefer a private "thank you." In

addition to simple words of gratitude, here are a few incentives managers can know how to incentivize their staffs to work efficiently, but AI is only one machine, it can not perform very good.

6. AI does not know how to assist managers to train and Develop employees. Reducing training, or cutting it all together, might seem like a good way to save company time and money (learning on the job is said to be an effective way to train, after all). However, this could ultimately backfire. Forcing employees to learn their jobs on the fly can be extremely inefficient.

So, instead of having workers haphazardly trying to accomplish a task with zero guidance, take the extra day to teach them the necessary skills to do their job. This way, they can set about accomplishing their tasks on their own, and your time won't be wasted down the road answering simple questions or correcting errors. Past their original training, encourage continued employee development. Helping them expand their skillsets will build a much more advanced workforce, which will benefit your company in the long run. There are a number of ways you can support employee development: individual coaching, workshops, courses, seminars, shadowing or mentoring, or even just increasing their responsibilities. Offering these opportunities will give employees additional skills that allow them to improve their efficiency and productivity. But, AI do not know how to improve any office workers' performance more easily than managers.

● How can AI be dangerous to office working environment?

Most researchers agree that a superintelligent AI is unlikely to exhibit human emotions like love or hate, and that there is no reason to expect AI to become intentionally benevolent or malevolent. Instead, when considering how AI might become a risk to any office working environments, experts think two scenarios most likely:

The AI is programmed to do something devastating: Autonomous weapons are artificial intelligence systems that are programmed to kill. In the hands of the wrong person, these weapons could easily cause mass casualties. Moreover, an AI arms race could inadvertently lead to an AI war that also results in mass casualties. To avoid being thwarted by the enemy, these weapons would be designed to be extremely difficult to simply "turn off," so humans could plausibly lose control of such a situation. This risk is one that's present even with narrow AI, but grows as levels of AI intelligence and autonomy increase. So, if some businessmen apply AI to be business weapon to attack or steal their business competitors' business secret, e.g. contract document, employee performance report, profit report, even business secret document. Then, AI will be one business competitor weapon more than business assistant role in any business market. So, whether AI is office assistant or business competitor weapon, it depends on how the businessmen apply them to assist their business development.

The AI is programmed to do something beneficial, but it develops a destructive method for achieving its goal: This can happen whenever we fail to fully align the AI's goals with ours, which is strikingly difficult. If you ask an obedient intelligent car to take you to the airport as fast as possible, it might get you there chased by helicopters and covered in vomit, doing not what you wanted but literally what you asked for. If a superintelligent system is tasked with a ambitious geoengineering project, it might wreak havoc with our ecosystem as a side effect, and view human attempts to stop it as a threat to be met.

As these examples illustrate, the concern about advanced AI isn't malevolence but competence. A super-intelligent AI will be extremely good at accomplishing its goals, and if those goals aren't aligned with ours, we have a problem. You're probably not an evil ant-hater who steps on ants out of malice, but if you're in charge of a hydroelectric green energy project and there's an anthill in the region to be flooded, too bad for the ants. A key goal of AI safety research is to never place humanity in the position of those ants. Because AI has the potential to become more intelligent than any human, we have no surefire way of predicting how it will behave. We can't use past technological developments as much of a basis because we've never created anything that has the ability to, wittingly or unwittingly, outsmart us. The best example of what we could face may be our own evolution. People now control the planet, not because we're the strongest, fastest or biggest, but because we're the smartest. If we're no longer the smartest, are we assured to remain in control?

A captivating conversation is taking place about the future of artificial intelligence and what it will/should mean for humanity. There are fascinating controversies where the world's leading experts disagree, such as: AI's future impact on the job market; if/when human-level AI will be developed; whether this will lead to an intelligence explosion; and whether this is something we should welcome or fear. But there are also many examples of of boring pseudo-controversies caused by people misunderstanding and talking past each other. To help ourselves focus on the interesting controversies and open questions — and not on the misunderstandings — let's clear up some of the most common myths.

There have been a number of surveys asking AI researchers how many years from now they think we'll have human-level AI with at least 50% probability. All these surveys have the same conclusion: the world's leading experts disagree, so we simply don't know. For example, in such a poll of the AI researchers at the 2015 Puerto Rico AI conference, the average (median) answer was by year 2045, but some researchers guessed hundreds of years or more. There's also a related myth that people who worry about AI think it's only a few years away. In fact, most people on record worrying about superhuman AI guess it's still at least decades away. But they argue that as long as we're not 100% sure that it won't happen this century, it's smart to start safety research now to prepare for the eventuality. Many of the safety problems associated with human-level AI are so hard that they may take decades to solve. So, any businessmen ought have business moralty to know whether they ought how to apply their AI to assist their business development in our future office environment to be more moral.

● Five ways to use AI to improve business efficiency to these office tasks

Regardless of a company's size or type, its executives typically look for ways to help it operate as efficiently as possible. They understand the link between efficiency and profitability. If employees waste too much time with drawn-out processes or complicated tasks, it'll be hard for the enterprise to remain profitable and adapt to challenges. Fortunately, artificial intelligence (AI) supports the need for effective business operations. Here are five ways enterprises can use AI for help: 5 ways to use AI to improve business efficiency image.Getting the best results from AI means looking at where bottlenecks exist, then figuring out if and how it might remove or minimise them. AI can help any offices to improve or raise efficiency to these tasks aspects as below:

1. Use AI to answer queries and support customer engagement

Chatbots are an increasingly popular option for businesses to try, and they use AI to work. Companies often build chatbots that can answer any questions from customers that come through outside of business hours. Some identify the nature of a person's problem, then either attempt to tackle it with preprogrammed answers or pass the communications to a human support worker. The retail industry, in particular, saw success by deploying chatbots. Global data collected by Juniper Research shows an estimated 2.6 billion retail-based chatbot interactions in 2019, and the company forecasts the number to rise to 22 billion in 2023.

Chatbots are excellent for answering simple questions like "How late are you open today?" or "Do you have gluten-free menu options?" Getting quick answers to queries like those increases the chances customers will choose to do business with one company over another. Equally importantly, when chatbots can give responses in a matter of seconds, there's no need for humans to stop what they're doing and address the questions.

2. To enhance reporting speed and accuracy

Company reports reveal things such as which products are selling the fastest and where they're most popular. They can also confirm the impacts of marketing campaigns on product sales, break down the costs of a new packaging choice or shipping method, and much more. However, as anyone that files reports knows, creating them is a painstaking task, and trying to rush through the process could cause mistakes. Some forward-thinking companies are combining AI with big data analytics. Doing this brings better forecasts and takes some of the burdens off the people who prepare the reports. AI also helps conquer the inevitability of mistakes. Even the most careful people make blunders, often because of mental fatigue.

AI learns to spot patterns in data and gets smarter with time. This means reports get finished faster and contain more-reliable information. The reliability aspect is crucial, especially since recently published research indicated two-thirds of the senior executives polled had no confidence or trust in big data. Using AI does not mean companies can do without data scientists. However, depending on the technology allows them to reduce the uncertainty that may otherwise exist. It also prevents employees who work with a company's data from being asked to recheck the findings, even if they initially took appropriate precautions to ensure accuracy.

3. To improve data transfer speeds

Fast data transfers help AI technology work. Concerning some information-intensive applications like virtual reality (VR), any slow transmissions greatly interfere with the realism, and content immersion people should enjoy after strapping on a VR headset. As it turns out, AI can improve data transfer speeds, too. For example, services exist that boost speeds across any wide-area network (WAN). Users enjoy consistently accelerated rates regardless of the kind of information transferred. Some companies have solutions that can reduce WAN job times by up to 98%. These AI-driven options work particularly well when companies need to move information between data centres or cloud environments.

4. To assist the IT team with identifying genuine cyberthreats and anomalies

One of the ongoing challenges faced by IT teams of all sizes is to separate the true cyber threats from false alarms. The difficulties associated with categorising the two types may mean cybersecurity professionals waste time getting to the bottom of things that are ultimately nonissues. They might miss the actual threats that could derail a company's operations. Besides detecting possible intrusions associated with a network, AI can screen for software abnormalities that may make it easier for cybercriminals to orchestrate their attacks successfully. It can also find malicious software hackers installed. Due to this kind of information and the advantages of receiving it through real-time updates, IT security teams can work more productively. They can use the majority of their resources on the threats that matter most to the company's stability.

Some organisations have even used AI to help them conquer the substantial skills shortage in the cybersecurity industry. At Texas A&M University, the Security Operations Center deals with about a million attempted hacks each month. The facility has some full-time workers, but students comprise most of the staff. They work alongside AI that aids in threat monitoring, detection and remediation. Before students see possible threats, the smart technology finds and groups them. This approach saves time and lets the team get to work investigating the problems and deciding how to handle them.

Can AI replace office workers

Can AI replace all office workers to do their different tasks in office different department ? If AI can only replace some department office workers to do their simple tasks, how it can raise more efficiency to compare them in some business office environments. I shall indicate some office tasks to explain how AI can help these businesses to raise their efficiency in officesas below:

● AI insurance workers

Nowadays, some country offices begin apply robotics to replace human office workers in their companies. For example, Japanese company replaces office workers with artificial intelligence in insurance industry. A future in which human workers are replaced by machines is about to become a reality at an insurance firm in Japan, where more than 30 employees are being laid off and replaced with an artificial intelligence system that can calculate payouts to policyholders.

Fukoku Mutual Life Insurance believes it will increase productivity by 30% and see a return on its investment in less than two years. The firm said it would save about 140m yen (£1m) a year after the 200m yen (£1.4m) AI system is installed this month. Maintaining it will cost about 15m yen (£100k) a year. The move is unlikely to be welcomed, however, by 34 employees who will be made redundant by the end of March.

The system is based on IBM's Watson Explorer, which, according to the tech firm, possesses "cognitive technology that can think like a human", enabling it to "analyse and interpret all of your data, including unstructured text, images, audio and video".The technology will be able to read tens of thousands of medical certificates and factor in the length of hospital stays, medical histories and any surgical procedures before calculating payouts, according to the Mainichi Shimbun.

While the use of AI will drastically reduce the time needed to calculate Fukoku Mutual's payouts – which reportedly totalled 132,000 during the current financial year – the sums will not be paid until they have been approved by a member of staff, the newspaper said.

Japan's shrinking, ageing population, coupled with its prowess in robot technology, makes it a prime testing ground for AI. According to a 2015 report by the Nomura Research Institute, nearly half of all jobs in Japan could be performed by robots by 2035. For example, one Japan insurance company, Dai-Ichi Life Insurance has already introduced a Watson-based system to assess payments - although it has not cut staff numbers - and Japan Post Insurance is interested in introducing a similar setup, the Mainichi said. AI could soon be playing a role in the country's politics. Next month, the economy, trade and industry ministry will introduce AI on a trial basis to help civil servants draft answers for ministers during cabinet meetings and parliamentary sessions. The ministry hopes AI will help reduce the punishingly long hours bureaucrats spend preparing written answers for ministers.

● AI public service workers

The automated city: do we still need humans to run public services? If the experiment is a success, it could be adopted by other government agencies, according the Jiji news agency. If, for example a question is asked about energy-saving policies, the AI system will provide civil servants with the relevant data and a list of pertinent debating points based on past answers to similar questions.

The march of Japan's AI robots hasn't been entirely glitch-free, however. At the end of last year a team of researchers abandoned an attempt to develop a robot intelligent enough to pass the entrance exam for the prestigious Tokyo University. "AI is not good at answering the type of questions that require an ability to grasp meanings across a broad spectrum," Noriko Arai, a professor at the National Institute of Informatics, told Kyodo news agency. Hence, AI will have possible to replace some public service workers' tasks.

● AI replace warehouse workers

Denso's use of Drishti shows how some jobs will be transformed by artificial intelligence even when they're unlikely to be eliminated by AI anytime soon. Many jobs in manufacturing require dexterity and resourcefulness, for example, in ways that robots and software still can't match. But advances in AI and sensors are providing new ways to digitize manual labor. That gives managers new insights—and potentially leverage—on workers. For example,some workers say the results are unpleasant. Last year, Amazon warehouse employees in Minnesota staged a walkout to protest how the company uses inventory and worker-tracking technology. They allege that Amazon uses it to enforce a punishing working pace that causes injuries. The company has disputed those claims, saying it coaches employees on how to safely meet quotas.

Workers at Denso were initially wary of the prospect of being video-recorded all day to feed machine-learning algorithms, but Huffman says they have since come to appreciate Drishti's technology. After something goes wrong, workers can now look at the data and video with their managers, instead of having to hope bosses take their account of what happened seriously. Huffman says having a constant readout on productivity also helps managers be more responsive to nascent problems. "If somebody's struggling, not every associate is going to call for help," he says. "If we see their cycle time is jumping through the roof, we can go over and say 'Are you having any issues?'"Workers on Denso lines equipped with Drishti's technology now get a personal feed of their own data. Monitors on each workstation display how a worker is doing, says Raja Shembekar, a Denso vice president. If the worker completes their assembly step on time, they see a smiley face—if not, a frowny one. Hence, Amazon had begun to apply AI robotic to replace some warehouse workers' tasks.

For another factory manufacture working environment example, AI can replace many manufacture workers to do their tasks in factories. Route 9 skims by Boston and cuts clear across Massachusetts to Pittsfield, a city of roughly 50,000, the largest in Berkshire County. Well east of Pittsfield, Route 9 becomes Worcester Road, named for a city that in earlier times was the nation's largest manufacturer of wire—barbed wire, electrical wire, telephone wire and the wire used in the making of undergarments by the Royal Worcester Corset Co., once the largest employer of women in the United States. Older Worcester residents can still recall the factory bells pealing to signal the start and end of the workday. Now, the bells are silent, and the wire and corset factories have been replaced with three of the nation's largest employers: Walmart, Target and Home Depot. If this sounds familiar, it should. It has been nearly two decades since retail overtook manufacturing as the nation's most important job creator, employing roughly one of every 10 American workers—more people than in health care and construction combined. That's a lot of jobs.

Of course, not all retail jobs qualify as what most of us consider good jobs. Today, the average hourly wage for a nonsupervisory retail worker is $11.24, and less than half of retail workers receive benefits of any kind. Still, as a nation, we've come to a sort of uneasy peace with this trend. We know that manufacturing employs far fewer

Americans today than it once did—that iPads and Macs aren't made in America and neither are many televisions, appliances, tools, toys or clothes. We also know that shopping for these appliances, tools, toys and clothes is an all-American pastime: On average, we spend nearly 45 minutes a day (more than 270 hours per year) purchasing goods and services. Retail has become the world as we know it, and many of us expect to make our living working in that world.Thanks to automation and a killer business model, Amazon is so efficient that it reaps nearly twice the revenue per employee of Walmart, despite the fact that Walmart, too, has a substantial online presence. Worldwide, Amazon has installed over 100,000 robots to labor in "perfect symbiosis" with humans in its warehouses and has plans to install many thousands more. While it's not clear what constitutes perfect symbiosis, the robots are said to save the company $22 million annually, per warehouse. The company's master plan of an autonomous future also includes goods delivered by drones and self-driving vehicles.

For while Amazon continues to open warehouses around the globe and staff them with many thousands of human beings, estimates are that every human on the Amazon payroll—whether full- or part-time—displaces two humans at traditional brick-and-mortar operations. And that's a feature, not a bug: As Tim Lindner, a veteran IT analyst, confided in a note to industry insiders, eradicating jobs is the explicit goal of any online retailer. As he once wrote: "Labor is the highest-cost factor in warehouse operations. It is no secret that Amazon is moving to highly automated operations within its distribution centers, and...it has additional technology that can further reduce the number of humans it needs to process customer orders.... You have heard the old programmer's phrase, 'Garbage in, garbage out.'... [With] the diminishing reading abilities of humans on the Receiving dock, finding an automated solution to eliminate the 'garbage in' problem is the holy grail. Amazon may have just patented it."

By garbage, Lindner meant human error, the alternative to which is apparently robotic precision. And robots can be very precise, especially when it comes to routine tasks. Sawyer, an industrial robot created by the former Boston-based Rethink Robotics, offers an impressive illustration of how all-embracing a robot arm can be. Sawyer is the brainchild of Rodney Brooks, the inventor of both Roomba, the robotic vacuum, and PackBot, the robot used to clear bunkers in Iraq and Afghanistan and at the World Trade Center after 9/11. Unlike Roomba and PackBot, Sawyer looks almost human—it has an animated flat-screen face and wheels where its legs should be. Simply grabbing and adjusting its monkey-like arm and guiding it through a series of motions "teaches" Sawyer whatever repeatable procedure one needs it to get done. The robot can sense and manipulate objects almost as quickly and as fluidly as a human and demands very little in return: While traditional industrial robots require costly engineers and programmers to write and debug their code, a high school dropout can learn to program Sawyer in less than five minutes. Brooks once estimated that, all told, Sawyer (and his older brother, the two-armed Baxter robot) would work for a "wage" equivalent of less than $4 an hour.

Robots loom large in discussions of work and its future, a conversation that can get mired in false assumptions. Until recently, many economists were skeptical that automation could permanently displace human workers on a large scale. People have always shifted away from work better done by machines, but the economic principle of "comparative advantage" predicts that humans will maintain an edge in many fields. Under this logic, technology will not displace us but set us free to do less dangerous, more challenging things, essentially the very things that make humans human. Of course, human workers are complicated. We get tired, hungry, distracted, angry, confused. We make mistakes, sometimes egregious ones. Machines lack our frailties and biases and are better equipped to weigh evidence fairly, without prejudice or false assumptions. Perhaps most critically, machines can retain and process data far more accurately than we can, and that data is growing exponentially.

Every minute of every day, Google services 3.6 million searches in the United States alone. Spammers send 100 million emails. Snapchatters send 527,000 photos, and the Weather Channel broadcasts 18 million forecasts. This and more data—properly collected, codified and analyzed—can be applied to automate almost any high-order task. Data can also serve as a surrogate for human experience and intuition. Online shopping and social media sites "learn" our preferences and use that information to make values-based assessments to influence our decisions and behavior. And, increasingly, machines excel in the tasks once thought uniquely human."Computers are able to see and hear, and have face-recognition capabilities that are significantly better than humans," says Vardi. "Machines understand the human world far better than they did just a few years ago. And we haven't discovered anything in the human brain that can't be modeled."

● AI can replace counter cashier service staffs

And robots need not be perfect, only equal to—or a tad better than—complicated and expensive humans. And technologists are working hard to make sure they are a tad better. For example, in the case of retail, it's become clear that many of us avoid the self-service checkout line—we prefer the cashier to punch in our purchases rather than do so ourselves. So it seems that the job of cashier—among the largest retail employment categories—is not directly at risk. But Zeynep Ton, an MIT management expert who focuses on the retail sector, says self-service checkout is only a first step and not a terribly smart one. "Customers recognized that self-service checkout is not an innovation, but merely a way of outsourcing the job to them, so they didn't like it," she says. "But new technology is coming that will make self-service checkout so much easier and faster, and that will have a real impact on retail employment."

Experts caution that the so-called apocalypse in retail predicted a few years ago has not yet come to pass. In fact, for every company closing existing stores, two more are opening new stores. Retail is a highly competitive industry, and technology is transforming not only the way we shop but the way we connect with brands—for example, just a few years ago, who would have imagined that Amazon would open actual retail stores? And while e-commerce has grown to 10 percent of retail, that still leaves 90 percent for brick-and-mortar stores. But those brick-and-mortar stores, too, are undergoing radical change that has serious implications for America's workforce.

As example, Lobaugh cites food trucks, which he says increasingly pose a threat to many fast-food outlets. Unlike restaurants pinned down by a pair of Golden Arches, food trucks are nimble—they can home in on areas where customers are most likely to gather at any particular time. They can also tailor their offerings to a particular region or even a neighborhood, as well as use Facebook or other media to get out the word on their menu items and locations. Small, specialty stores also have far more flexibility than large department stores. "Technology has reduced the cost of entry into new markets, so in retail there are fewer big, monolithic companies, but more small competitors," he says. "Companies are diversifying to meet the specific needs and desires of consumers—everyone's piece is getting smaller, but there are many more pieces."

But despite what it predicts will be a banner holiday season, this year Amazon took on far fewer seasonal employees than usual—100,000 employees versus 120,000 the previous two years. And while an Amazon spokeswoman insisted that automation is not a factor in this reduced workforce, others seem to not agree. In a recent report, Morgan Stanley analyst Brian Nowak soothed the fears of Amazon shareholders concerned with the wage increase by pointing out that automation had already and would continue to reduce the call for labor, and therefore reduce overall costs. When asked about this, Lobaugh again tactfully declined to comment—other than to say that while the retail sector had lost less ground than most people assume, retail employees were another matter. "There are winners," he says, "and then there are losers."

● AI can replace accountants in accountancy service industry

Not that long ago artificial intelligence (AI), robots and machine learning (ML) were thought to be things only found in science fiction films. Today, this type of technology is taking center stage in workplaces across the globe. Industries, including manufacturing, retail, agriculture, and customer service have already had AI replace some job positions that left workers scrambling to find new career options. This AI revolution is not expected to slow down anytime soon. In fact, experts anticipate that as many as 800 million jobs could be replaced with AI technology by the year 2030. Initially, AI technology and automation in the workplace seemed to only affect pink and blue-collar workers. As this technology advances and becomes more powerful, professional, white-collar workers, including accountants, are starting to worry about what the future holds for their career and if AI will be developed to own their professional skills in accounting service industry.

In basic terms, AI technology is intelligent machines that are able to complete repetitive, mundane tasks at a fraction of the time it takes humans and with greater accuracy. The emergence of Machine Learning now allows AI platforms to observe, analyze and self-learn data and processes to improve its performance and accuracy over time. AI technology is already able to handle many accounting functions, such as tax preparation, payroll, and audits. Many of the leading accounting software providers, including Xero, Intuit and Sage have incorporated AI technology into their software to handle basic accounting tasks, such as bank reconciliations, invoice categorization, risk assessment, and audit processes, like expense submissions and invoice payments. Many of these standard tasks are extremely time-consuming, which has many accountants across the country worried about how the emerging AI technology will affect their billable hours. An even bigger concern is that AI technologies will replace the need for companies to work with accountants at all.

● AI Will Transform not Replace Accountants

While there is no doubt that AI technology is capable of handling many standard accounting tasks faster and more efficiently or that these capabilities will only increase over time, it doesn't mean the end for accountants. There always will be a need for that human element - human intelligence - at the other end of AI technology. In fact, according to leading research firm, Gartner, AI is set to create more jobs than it will replace, leaving workers, including accountants with options. Accountants don't have to worry about their job being replaced by AI any time in the near future. Companies will always need accountants that can analyze and interpret AI data, as well as provide consulting services. Rather than replacing the role of an accountant, AI technology will transform the duties an accountant performs.

With AI technology and machine learning handling many of the mundane, repetitive tasks, accountants will have more time to focus on other aspects of the job, such as consulting and data analysis. This is good news for many accountants. Rather than spending hours completing menial tasks, accountants of the future will be able to use and analyze AI data to provide their clients with sound business solutions.

In many ways, AI will help accountants improve their services. AI technology will improve data entry accuracy and lower the liability risk for accountants. In addition, emerging technology is more efficient at fraud detection, adding an extra layer of protection for accountants and their clients. It also provides real-time data, which allows accountants to provide real-time solutions. Even more impressive is the ability of machine learning to analyze large amounts of data instantly, evaluate past successes and failures in an effort to accurately predict future outcomes.

There is no way to escape the use of AI technology, at least not if you hope to remain competitive in the upcoming years. The speed, efficiency and accuracy of AI technology just cannot be beat. The only thing accountants can do is to embrace this new technology and learn how to maximize its use. The better equipped you are to help your clients integrate and utilize AI technology in their accounting processes the more valuable you will be. For example, many universities today are already incorporating IT and database management courses into their accounting program. This means that graduating students are coming into the workforce with the skills they need for future accounting work. Accountants already in the workforce must find ways to acquire these skills in order to remain relevant to their employers and/or their clients. Accountants can obtain the IT skills they need by attending seminars, using self-learning online programs or attending college-level courses. It is equally important for accountants to stay up-to-date on the latest accounting trends, emerging technologies and industry news. This will allows accountants to not only keep their jobs but to also provide more efficient services to their clients. Rather than worry about AI taking over their jobs, accountants should embrace this technology as a powerful solution to enhance customer services. Finally, accountants will be able to use all their training and experience to provide customer will real and effective business solutions, whether it's in reference to tax consulting, real estate deals, mergers, growth options, or any other business practice.

On conclusion, technology is advancing at record rates so now is the time to obtain the IT and database management skills you need to advance into the future. With the right skills and training, accountants are guaranteed a lucrative career that will last well into the future.

Why Developed And Developing Countries Need Artificial Intelligent Development To Assist Office Tasks

Must developed and developing countries need artificial intelligent development to assist office tasks ? Ought AI is needed to prefer to develop technique to assist office staffs to reduce workload to compare other kinds of occupation environment tasks aspects ? If one developed country, e.g. US, UK , Japan , Singapore it does not continue to develop artificial intelligence, robotic, then what disadvantges or weaknesses , it will encounter to compare when it chooses to continue to develop this artificial intelligent technology in society. If one developing country, e.g. China, Korea, Taiwan, it does not continue to develop artificial intelligence, robotic, then what disadantages or weaknesses, it will also encounter to compare when it chooses to continue to develop this artificial intelligent technology in in society.

I shall explan the reasons why the results may cause to either the developed country, or the developing country as below:

● How AI help developing countries to communication and agriculture and learning and medical delivery development

Why can AI help developing countries ? Drones that pick inaccessible crops and mobile phones that give medical advice are two of the ways AI can transform life in the developing world. Artificial intelligence (AI) may improve the lives of the world's poor, the technology needed to revolutionise inefficient, ineffective food and healthcare systems in developing countries is well. For example, in low-income areas, agriculture and healthcare are two critical ecosystems that we can apply AI to immediately; this is not the far future, or even in five years.

Artificial intelligence (AI) has seeped into the daily lives of people in the developed world. From virtual assistants to recommendation engines, AI is in the news, our homes and offices. There is a lot of potential in terms of AI usage, especially in humanitarian areas. The impact could have a multiplier effect in developing countries, where resources are limited.

Emergency Response to developing countries' earthquake natural damage suddence occurrence predicting

AI and machine learning are still finding importance in emerging markets, but certain applications have emerged and are now widely used. For instance, predictive models for disaster relief enable first responders to automatically analyze large-scale behavior and movement through multiple sources of data including social media platforms, web forums, news sources, etc. Based on collected data, responders can scale reconstruction efforts and distribute supplies in a timely manner.

Why and how AI can assist farmers to predict when the earthquake occurs suddenly in order to avoid or reduce the natural damage to their agriculture productive number loss. For example, In 2015, when a major earthquake hit Nepal, more than 8 million people were affected. During the aftermath, drones were used to map and assess the destruction and speed up the rescue mission. The town of Sankhu, situated about 20 kilometers northeast of Kathmandu, was among the highly affected locations. In May 2018, my company Fusemachines and GeoSpatial Systems partnered with Sankhu's city officials to use drones and artificial intelligence in an effort to automatically estimate the reconstruction need. After processing data accumulated from a drone-powered aerial mapping of the region, the team fed this data to advanced machine learning algorithms. Combining drone imagery, digital mapping and machine learning, the team configured region modeling and infrastructure development with higher accuracy. Another organization known as One Concern, a California-based startup, has created a predictive AI program called Seismic Concern to accurately predict seism and is also working on solutions for wildfires, floods and hurricanes.

Smart AI Agriculture

Another application of AI in developing countries is smart agriculture. Farmers monitor crops more effectively and make better predictions on planting, weeding and harvesting using AI tools. It can also be used to analyze one plant at a time and add pesticides only to infected plants and trees instead of spraying pesticides across large swaths of crops. One California-based tech company is an example of this use of AI. So, the developing countries farmers in rural parts of India are also using AI to increase yields through better access to information about the farming season than they would normally have. Technology-enabled process automation offers the agribusiness industry the chance for remarkable growth -- not only in developed countries but around the world. There's a unique opportunity to increase yields, cut down labor costs and improve people's health.

Medicine Delivery to developing countries' patients urgent need

Companies are also leveraging AI to improve access to health care in some of the most remote areas of the world. In Rwanda, for example, Zipline is using drones to deliver medical supplies and blood to hospitals and clinics that are difficult to access by car. This has dramatically impacted people living in remote parts of the country because they are able to get medical help when needed. The drone system in Rwanda has also helped reduce waste of blood by 95%, as noted by Zipline. One Concern has created an AI program called Seismic Concern that accurately predicts seismic events and is also working on solutions for floods, wildfires and hurricanes. The medical field may actually benefit the most from emerging technologies in developing countries.

Assistance to reduce teaching work workload or psychological pressure to teachers in developing countries' schools

Another vital area benefiting from innovative technologies like AI is education. Advanced technologies can enhance how we learn, teach and perform tasks. In most developing countries, schools lack experienced teachers and resources to enhance students' knowledge. As a result, many students still have to walk long distances to get to the nearest school, which has created education gaps, especially in rural areas. AI tools such as personalized learning assistants can simplify learning by making tutoring services and learning materials accessible to all students, wherever they are. Machines can be automated to help students learn basic concepts without a tutor, which companies like Carnegie Learning are working on. This would allow students to learn at any time from anywhere. With AI, education is made easy and accessible to more people.

The initial usage of AI in developing countries has been at a micro level -- solving small, specific problems in a defined industry. As machine learning advances and there is a higher utilization of AI, we will see more complex issues being targeted and resolved. When duly adopted, AI can positively impact future developing countries people everyday lives not just in disaster intervention, education, health care and agriculture but can also help in mitigating poverty, malnutrition and pollution. Especially, in developing nations, to leverage AI's true potential and create a snowball effect. Startups are defining a holistic and humanitarian approach to building more sophisticated, AI-ready societies. Stakeholders in the AI landscape should understand the strengths and nuances of the developing world as well as the limitations of AI and create localized solutions and applications.

Why does smart phone help developing countries communication ?

Internet Seen as Positive Influence on Education but Negative on Morality in Emerging and Developing Nations. Internet access differs substantially across the 32 emerging and developing countries polled, with the lowest rates of internet use in South Asian and sub-Saharan African nations. Within countries, computer owners, young people, the well-educated, the wealthy and those with English language ability are much more likely to access the internet than their counterparts. To access the internet, people increasingly use smartphones rather than more cumbersome fixed landline connections and computers. Around the world, both smartphones and basic-feature phones alike are used for sending messages and taking pictures.

In fact, many developing countries young people, students are popular to use smart phones for internet usage aim, instead of communication. Moreover, many developing countries working people are also popular to use smart phones for any working usage in their working time , even non working time any time. So, smart phones (AI) phones will be important communication or leisure tools to developing countries people in the future. Unless, it is one day, scientists can develop another new communication tool to replace smart phones. So, artificial intelligence will be important to influence developing countries people , how to improve or bring positive learning attitudes to students in their daily learnnng lifes. as well as how to raise developing countries people, how to raise working people efficiency or improve performace in their daily working lifes. So, AI may bring positive learning or working attitudes to developing countries working people and students both.

The Positive Impact of Mass Media in Developing Countries

Radio, newspapers, television, Internet, social media, etc., all of these are forms of mass media. Each of these outlets has the capability of bringing information to thousands of people with one device. While in some communities it is easy to take advantage of these communication outlets such as television and Internet access, not everyone has access to such outlets. Radio is one of the most common forms of mass media in developing countries because it's affordable and uses less electricity than many other forms of mass media, but only approximately 75 percent of people in developing countries have access to a radio, and roughly 77 percent of people in rural areas have access to electricity.

For developing countries that have implemented forms of mass media in their communities, there have been numerous positive outcomes are influenced to impact developing countries mass media by artificial intelligence as below:

When AI is participated to developing countries mass media, it can influence any radio, television audiences raise more attention to each other through social media platforms such as Facebook and Twitter and create, organize and initiate street protests and campaigns. Furthermore, having access to social media in developing countries, people are able to connect to those that they usually wouldn't have the chance to talk to. Moreover, AI Provides educational opportunities- In many countries, the division between local and national languages as well as issues of literacy can make communication difficult. With the use of mass media, a bridge can be built between these two gaps. In India, there is a radio station that provides information in local languages and respects local culture and traditions. One of the main ways is to create public awareness of what is going on with businesses and government officials. The media plays an important role in giving people the opportunity to act against injustice, oppression and misdeeds that they otherwise wouldn't know about. Information on available healthcare, a mass radio broadcast was sent out encouraging parents to seek treatment at local healthcare facilities for their sick children. With this mass outreach on healthcare, the encouragement of people to take their children to healthcare facilities saved thousands of lives. This easy way of encouraging others and bringing awareness about certain diseases was made possible through a simple radio broadcast. Finally, when AI is particiapted to media, it may bring many social issues to life that otherwise would remain unknown to many people. In developing countries and communities like Burkina Faso, when the radio broadcast was released about malaria, diarrhea and pneumonia, people were educated and moved to action and knew to take their children to healthcare facilities for preventative care. As it is seen, having access to different media outlets is vital for those in developing countries. Here are three ways that those in developing countries can implement mass media to help their people and communities.

When AI is participated to any internet radio or internet newspaper mass online listening or reading channel. It can provide online radios or newspapers in public places- By providing online radios and newspapers in public areas it gives community members to access news, information and emergency warnings. Even though radios can be on the cheaper side, there are still many people that can't afford to have a radio in their home. By providing one in a local place, not only would it better educate the community members but also it will bring the community together. So, it can make media outlets a two-way platform- Creating a two-way platform between the community and those who are behind the radio stations, newspapers or broadcasts makes the community feel involved and that their voices are being heard. An organization called Soul City in sub-Saharan Africa is showing how well two-way platforms work by engaging their listeners and having them contribute thoughts and ideas about complex issues. Because developing countries radio listening audiences or newspaper readers are popular to accept computer online radio listening channel or online newspaper reading channel to replace traditional paper newspapers or radio machines. So, AI may raise their listening news or reading news leisure feeling from online mass media channel in the future.

● Why do developed countries need to develop AI

Artificial intelligence, or AI, is driving massive shifts across the globe, and every day more questions arise. What impact will AI have on the workforce and how can we prepare for it? How can we encourage economy-boosting and job-creating technologies? How can we ensure that AI will be implemented ethically and with minimal bias? How will society benefit? For developed country, such as US example. None of the US, Israel and Russia have a formal national AI policy yet. Private sector companies such as Google, Amazon and Apple and the US department of defence are driving the bulk of AI investment in the United States. Though Israel does not have a specific policy, it is keenly focused on AI and has seen the number of AI start-ups triple since 2014.

Developed country may learn whether what weakness it is lacking when it does not continue to develop AI from one another developed country. Which countries are approaching AI most effectively, and to what degree is there opportunity for greater international collaboration? It may be too early to tell; however, when analyzing the best practices of existing national AI policies, there is much that can be learned. These are the specific areas to consider. When one developed country continue to develop or research AI, it may bring these benefits as below:

On gathering Data aspect, from self-driving vehicles to smart cities, data is the driver behind AI. Innovation in the United States is limited without a national strategy that answers questions about protocol and ownership. France and Denmark, on the other hand, are opening government data. France is hosting troves of centrally collected public and private data that it plans to make available as part of its strategy. Conversely, by taking a restrictive position on issues of data collection (as indicated by the implementation of General Data Protection Regulation), the EU is putting manufacturers and software designers at a disadvantage while balancing the demand for privacy. On raising technologica talent aspect, the demand for AI talent far outweighs the available supply. As a result, almost every nation's strategy addresses talent development. Canada's AI strategy is distinct in that it primarily focuses on research and talent strategy. The country boasts AI degree programmes and is building a $127 million research facility in Toronto. Companies like Facebook and my own company, Uptake, are investing in Canada to access this talent pool. On AI legal technological innovation aspect, a whole host of legal questions swirl around AI. The country is developing a bill for AI liability that will be ready in March 2019. The government hopes the legal framework will attract investors by providing a simple, comprehensive guideline to enable the broad use of AI systems. So, when the developed country applied AI technology to assist any lawyers to work, then AI can help them to reduce the workload to draft any legal documents more easier. So, any developed countries lawyers' draft legal documents time must reduce if the developed countries lawyers accept to apply AI to assist their legal works. One of the great promises of AI is its potential for improving quality of life. But without the right planning and oversight, we risk exacerbating problems of inequality or marginalizing groups of people. As an example, India's AI strategy is focused on leveraging the technology not only for economic growth, but also for social inclusion.

AI may bring what benefits to developed countries

From SIRI to self-driving cars, artificial intelligence (AI) is progressing rapidly. While science fiction often portrays AI as robots with human-like characteristics, AI can encompass anything from Google's search algorithms to IBM's Watson to autonomous weapons. Artificial intelligence today is properly known as narrow AI (or weak AI), in that it is designed to perform a narrow task (e.g. only facial recognition or only internet searches or only driving a car). However, the long-term goal of many researchers is to create general AI (AGI or strong AI). While narrow AI may outperform humans at whatever its specific task is, like playing chess or solving equations, AGI would outperform humans at nearly every cognitive task.

Why research AI safety? Would AI bring war when AI is continued to develop by developed countries? In the near term, the goal of keeping AI's impact on society beneficial motivates research in many areas, from economics and law to technical topics such as verification, validity, security and control. Whereas it may be little more than a minor nuisance if your laptop crashes or gets hacked, it becomes all the more important that an AI system does what you want it to do if it controls your car, your airplane, your pacemaker, your automated trading system or your power grid. Another short-term challenge is preventing a devastating arms race in lethal autonomous weapons.

In the long term, an important question is what will happen if the quest for strong AI succeeds and an AI system becomes better than humans at all cognitive tasks. As pointed out by I.J. Good in 1965, designing smarter AI systems is itself a cognitive task. Such a system could potentially undergo recursive self-improvement, triggering an intelligence explosion leaving human intellect far behind. By inventing revolutionary new technologies, such a superintelligence might help us eradicate war, disease, and poverty, and so the creation of strong AI might be the biggest event in human history. Some experts have expressed concern, though, that it might also be the last, unless we learn to align the goals of the AI with ours before it becomes superintelligent.

There are some who question whether strong AI will ever be achieved, and others who insist that the creation of superintelligent AI is guaranteed to be beneficial. At FLI we recognize both of these possibilities, but also recognize the potential for an artificial intelligence system to intentionally or unintentionally cause great harm. We believe research today will help us better prepare for and prevent such potentially negative consequences in the future, thus enjoying the benefits of AI while avoiding pitfalls.

How can AI be dangerous when developed countries continue to develop AI to become weapon to replace soldiers?

Most researchers agree that a superintelligent AI is unlikely to exhibit human emotions like love or hate, and that there is no reason to expect AI to become intentionally benevolent or malevolent. Instead, when considering how AI might become a risk, experts think two scenarios most likely:

The AI is programmed to do something devastating: Autonomous weapons are artificial intelligence systems that are programmed to kill. In the hands of the wrong person, these weapons could easily cause mass casualties. Moreover, an AI arms race could inadvertently lead to an AI war that also results in mass casualties. To avoid being thwarted by the enemy, these weapons would be designed to be extremely difficult to simply "turn off," so humans could plausibly lose control of such a situation. This risk is one that's present even with narrow AI, but grows as levels of AI intelligence and autonomy increase.

The AI is programmed to do something beneficial, but it develops a destructive method for achieving its goal: This can happen whenever we fail to fully align the AI's goals with ours, which is strikingly difficult. If you ask an obedient intelligent car to take you to the airport as fast as possible, it might get you there chased by helicopters and covered in vomit, doing not what you wanted but literally what you asked for. If a superintelligent system is tasked with a ambitious geoengineering project, it might wreak havoc with our ecosystem as a side effect, and view human attempts to stop it as a threat to be met. So, a super-intelligent AI will be extremely good at accomplishing its goals, and if those goals aren't aligned with ours, we have a problem. You're probably not an evil ant-hater who steps on ants out of malice, but if you're in charge of a hydroelectric green energy project and there's an anthill in the region to be flooded, too bad for the ants. A key goal of AI safety research is to never place humanity in the position of those ants.

Why the recent interest in AI safety ?

Stephen Hawking, Elon Musk, Steve Wozniak, Bill Gates, and many other big names in science and technology have recently expressed concern in the media and via open letters about the risks posed by AI, joined by many leading AI researchers. The idea that the quest for strong AI would ultimately succeed was long thought of as science fiction, centuries or more away. However, thanks to recent breakthroughs, many AI milestones, which experts viewed as decades away merely five years ago, have now been reached, making many experts take seriously the possibility of superintelligence in our lifetime. While some experts still guess that human-level AI is centuries away, most AI researches at the 2015 Puerto Rico Conference guessed that it would happen before 2060. Since it may take decades to complete the required safety research, it is prudent to start it now.

Because AI has the potential to become more intelligent than any human, we have no surprise way of predicting how it will behave. We can't use past technological developments as much of a basis because we've never created anything that has the ability to, wittingly or unwittingly, outsmart us. The best example of what we could face may be our own evolution. People now control the planet, not because we're the strongest, fastest or biggest, but because we're the smartest. If we're no longer the smartest, are we assured to remain in control?

A captivating conversation is taking place about the future of artificial intelligence and what it will/should mean for humanity. There are fascinating controversies where the world's leading experts disagree, such as: AI's future impact on the job market; if/when human-level AI will be developed; whether this will lead to an intelligence explosion; and whether this is something we should welcome or fear. But there are also many examples of of boring pseudo-controversies caused by people misunderstanding and talking past each other. When one developed country continue to develop AI, can itself country's all factories workers will lose jobs, due to AI can replace them to do simple works in factories, or any public transport drivers, e.g. bus drivers, ferry , tram, train drivers, they will lose jobs, when AI (non manual driving drivers) can replace all public transport drivers. So, some occupations will lose if developed countries continue to develop or research AI to replace human to do some simple jobs, such as some cooking jobs can be done by AI. So, it is possible that future cookers won't be needed, because AI cooking skills may be better than them to cook any good taste chinese or western food in restaurants. If you drive down the road, you have a subjective experience of colors, sounds, etc. But does a self-driving car have a subjective experience? Does it feel like anything at all to be a self-driving car? Although this mystery of consciousness is interesting in its own right, it's irrelevant to AI risk. If you get struck by a driverless car, it makes no difference to you whether it subjectively feels conscious. In the same way, what will affect us humans is what superintelligent AI does, not how it subjectively feels.

In fact, AI may be make any brokers jobs in financial market. the main concern of the beneficial-AI movement isn't with robots but with intelligence itself: specifically, intelligence whose goals are misaligned with ours. To cause us trouble, such misaligned superhuman intelligence needs no robotic body, merely an internet connection – this may enable outsmarting financial markets, out-inventing human researchers, out-manipulating human leaders, and developing weapons we cannot even understand. Even if building robots were physically impossible, a superintelligent and super-wealthy AI could easily pay or manipulate many humans to unwittingly do its bidding. So, future brokers will be replaced by AI, when AI can be made to own financial brokers' analytical mind to make more accurate whether the share price will rise up or fall down to compare human financial brokers' analytical mind. The robot misconception is related to the myth that machines can't control humans. Intelligence enables control: humans control tigers not because we are stronger, but because we are smarter. This means that if we cede our position as smartest on our planet, it's possible that we might also cede control.

Not wasting time on the above-mentioned misconceptions lets us focus on true and interesting controversies where even the experts disagree. What sort of future do you want? Should we develop lethal autonomous weapons? What would you like to happen with job automation? What career advice would you give today's kids? Do you prefer new jobs replacing the old ones, or a jobless society where everyone enjoys a life of leisure and machine-produced wealth? Further down the road, would you like us to create superintelligent life and spread it through our cosmos? Will we control intelligent machines or will they control us? Will intelligent machines replace us, coexist with us, or merge with us? What will it mean to be human in the age of artificial intelligence?

Why do developed countries people need AI ?

Why do we assume that AI will require more and more physical space and more power when human intelligence continuously manages to miniaturize and reduce power consumption of its devices. How low the power needs and how small will the machines be by the time quantum computing becomes reality? Why do we assume that AI will exist as independent machines? If so, and the AI is able to improve its Intelligence by reprogramming itself, will machines driven by slower processors feel threatened, not by mere stupid humans, but by machines with faster processors? What would drive machines to reproduce themselves when there is no biological incentive, pressure or need to do so?

Who says superior AI will need or want to have a physical existence when an immaterial AI could evolve and preserve itself better from external dangers. What will happen if AI developed by competing ideologies, liberalism vs communism, reach maturity at the same time, will they fight for hegemony by trying to destroy each other physically and/or virtually. If AI is programmed to believe in God, and competing AI emerges programmed by muslims, christians or jews, how are the different AI's going to make sense of the different religious beliefs, are we going to have AI religious wars? What if the "powers that be" greatest fear is the emergence of a super AI that police's and rationalizes the distribution of wealth and food. A friendly super AI that is programmed to help humanity by, enforcing the declaration of Human Rights (the US is the only industrialized country that to this day has not signed this declaration) ending corruption and racism and protecting the environment.Most benefits of civilization stem from intelligence, so how can we enhance these benefits with artificial intelligence without being replaced on the job market and perhaps altogether?

Key to the process of machine learning are neural networks. These are brain-inspired networks of interconnected layers of algorithms, called neurons, that feed data into each other, and which can be trained to carry out specific tasks by modifying the importance attributed to input data as it passes between the layers. During training of these neural networks, the weights attached to different inputs will continue to be varied until the output from the neural network is very close to what is desired, at which point the network will have 'learned' how to carry out a particular task. A subset of machine learning is deep learning, where neural networks are expanded into sprawling networks with a huge number of layers that are trained using massive amounts of data. It is these deep neural networks that have fuelled the current leap forward in the ability of computers to carry out task like speech recognition and computer vision.

In conclusion, when developed countries continue to develop AI, it may bring positive advantages to bring raising productivies, or efficiencies, but it may also raise unemployment ratio to any low skill or low knowledge jobs in ther societies. However, human future society will need to change to be better to raise our living standard. But AI is one kind the best choice tool to achieve this aim in our future, so I agree developed countries continue to develop or research AI to be the super -human machine.

Artificial Intelligence Worker Brings

Working Environment Influences

Robots were once known only for the manufacturing business but today they are very much part of many workplaces. The future is even more promising for this wonder of artificial intelligence.Imagine a robot doing some of the major tasks of managers like using data to evaluate problems, making better decisions, monitoring team performance, and even setting goals.

Technology is playing a pivotal role in helping humans work more effectively. Since automation has become an integral part of business operations, we can predict that robots are soon going to replace many jobs that are today performed by humans. Now that the corporate world is also on the cusp of entering the robotic age, let's see what pros and cons this technology offers business world. If one day, our global working environments have any kinds of robotic participates to our service and warehouse and office etc. different working environment in order to assist office workers, service workers, warehouse workers, professional lawyers, doctors accountants job duties, what positive or negative influences, it will bring to what negative or positive effects to any office , warehouse, shopping center, hospital, transport , restaurant etc, different working environments. Can robotic help office , warehouse to raise efficiency ? Can robotic help hospital, restaurant, cinema, shopping center to improve service performance? Can robotic influence working environment to be worse? Can robotic help office or any working places to reduce expenditure or reduce long time machine and salary cost when they do not need more employees or machines , due to robotic workers assistance.

I shall attempt to explain whether robotic workers will bring what positive or negative influence to our future working environment as below:

Advantages to robotic bring to working environment

What advantages that robotic will bring to working environment? They may include: Many people fear that robots or full automation may someday take their jobs, but this is simply not the case. Robots bring more advantages than disadvantages to the workplace. They enrich a company's ability to succeed while improving the lives of real, human employees who are still needed to keep operations running smoothly. If you're thinking about investing in some robots, share the advantages with your employees. You might be surprised at how many of them are quick to support the idea.

1. Safety

Safety is the most obvious advantage of utilizing robotics. Heavy machinery, machinery that runs at hot temperature, and sharp objects can easily injure a human being. By delegating dangerous tasks to a robot, you're more likely to look at a repair bill than a serious medical bill or a lawsuit. Employees who work dangerous jobs will be thankful that robots can remove some of the risks.

2. Speed

Robots don't get distracted or need to take breaks. They don't request vacation time or ask to leave an hour early. A robot will never feel stressed out and start running slower. They also don't need to be invited to employee meetings or training session. Robots can work all the time, and this speeds up production. They keep your employees from having to overwork themselves to meet high pressure deadlines or seemingly impossible standards.

3. Consistency

Robots never need to divide their attention between a multitude of things. Their work is never contingent on the work of other people. They won't have unexpected emergencies, and they won't need to be relocated to complete a different time sensitive task. They're always there, and they're doing what they're supposed to do. Automation is typically far more reliable than human labor.

4. Perfection

Robots will always deliver quality. Since they're programmed for precise, repetitive motion, they're less likely to make mistakes. In some ways, robots are simultaneously an employee and a quality control system. A lack of quirks and preferences, combined with the eliminated possibility of human error, will create a predictably perfect product every time.

5. Happier Employees

Since robots are often assigned to perform tasks that people don't particularly enjoy, like menial work, repetitive motion, or dangerous jobs, your employees are more likely to be happy. They'll be focusing on more engaging work that's less likely to grind down their nerves. They might want to take advantage of additional educational opportunities, utilize your employee wellness program, or participate in an innovative workplace project. They'll be happy to let the robots do the work that leaves them feeling burned out.

6. Job Creation

Robots don't take jobs away. They merely change the jobs that exist. Robots need people for monitoring and supervision. The more robots we need, the more people we'll need to build those robots. By training your employees to work with robots, you're giving them a reason to stay motivated in their position with your company. They'll be there for the advancements and they'll have the unique opportunity to develop a new set of tech or engineering related skills.

7. Productivity

Robots can't do everything. Some jobs absolutely need to be completed by a human. If your human employees aren't caught up doing the things that could have easily be left for robots, they'll be available and productive. They can talk to customers, answer emails and social media comments, help with branding and marketing, and sell products. You'll be amazed at how much they can accomplish when the grunt work isn't weighing them down.

8. Cost reduce

The first and the foremost advantage of having robots in workplaces is their cost. Robots are much cheaper than humans and their cost is now decreasing. It's a fact that we cannot compare human abilities with robots but robotic capabilities are now growing quickly. For example, if you run an essay writing service, you can use robots to perform every kind of research related to any subject. Because robots are more active and don't get tired like humans, the collaboration between humans and robots is reducing absenteeism. The pace of human cannot increase hence robots are helping humans.

However,robots are more precise than humans; they don't tremble or shake as human hands. Robots have smaller and versatile moving parts which help them in performing tasks with more accuracy than humans. There is no doubt that robots are significantly stronger and faster than humans. Robots come in any shape and size, depending upon the need of the task. Robots can work anywhere in any environmental condition whether it is space, underwater, in extreme heat or wind etc. Robots can be used everywhere where human safety is a huge concern. Robots are programmed by a human; they cannot say no to anything and can be used for any dangerous and unwanted work where humans may deny to offer their services. For example, many robotic probes have been sent into space but have never returned. Robots in warfare are saving more lives and have now proven to be very successful. For example, in chemical factory environment, robots are now being used in the chemical industry and can, for example deal with chemical spills in a nuclear plant, which would otherwise pose a major health concern. Cost-effectiveness is one of the most sound arguments to be made for the case of industrial robots. Robots will reduce production costs by eliminating internal costs to compensate human salaries. Businesses are forecasting that their profitability will increase once they implement robots into production, or that they will have more financial mobility to invest in new products or technologies.

9. productive efficiency

Quality assurance is expected with the use of machinery in production. Industrial robots will be able to ensure consistency with mass production of manufactured products. The possible human error that assembly line workers pose the threat of will be removed. Optimized production efficiency means that a general manager will be able to have set quantity and quality standards that will be met by robots. Production quotas will not be jeopardized by low concentration, break time and employee injuries, among other things. The efficiency of production forecasts and supply levels will be increased with robots, able to be programmed to work at the optimal speed for a given plant. Limiting human work in hazardous environments, because manufacturing jobs often place workers at more physical risk compared to a lot of other industries. Lowering the level of a hazard presented to employees on the job is attractive to executives to preserve company reputation and minimize potential legal liabilities.

10. Reducing longer working hours

Typically people have to have breaks, get distracted and after time attention drops and pace slows. With a robot it can work 24/7, and keeps running at 100%. Typically if you replace one person on a key process in a production line with a robot the output increases by 40% in the same working hours just because a robot has more stamina and never stops. Robots also don't take holidays or have unexpected days off sick.

11. Increased profitability

By increasing the efficiency of your production process, reducing the resource and time needed to complete it, and also achieving higher quality products, industrial robots can thus be used to achieve higher profitability levels overall, with lower cost per product.

12. Improved working environment

Industrial robots are often used for performing tasks which are deemed as dangerous for humans, as well as being able to perform highly laborious and repetitive tasks. Overall, by using industrial robots you can improve the working conditions and safety in your factory or production process. Robots don't get tired and make dangerous mistakes, neither do they suffer from repetitive strain injury.Due to their high accuracy levels, robots can also be used to produce higher quality products which adhere to certain standards of quality, whilst also reducing the time needed for quality control.Industrial robots are able to complete certain tasks faster and better than people, as they are designed to perform these tasks with a higher accuracy level. This and the fact that they are used to automate processes which previously might have taken significantly more time and resources, means that you can often use industrial robots to increase the efficiency of your production line.

13. Improved Quality Assurance

Few workers enjoy doing repetitive tasks and after a certain period of time concentration levels will naturally decline. This lapse in concentration is known as vigilance decrement and can often lead to costly errors for the business and sometimes serious injury to the member of staff.Robotic automation eliminates these risks by accurately producing and checking items meet the required standard without fail. With more product going out the door manufactured to a higher standard, this creates a number of new business possibilities for companies to expand upon.

14. Increased Productivity

Using robotic automation to tackle repetitive tasks makes complete sense. Robots are designed to make repetitive movements. Humans, also by design, are not. The introduction of automation into your manufacturing process has many different productivity benefits, some of which are shown here.Giving staff members the opportunity to expand on their skills and work in other areas will create a better environment which the business as a whole will benefit from. With higher energy levels and more focus put into their work, the product can only improve, which will also lead to extremely satisfied clients.

15. Avoiding workers need to work In Hazardous Environments

Aside from potential injuries in the workplace, staff members in particular industries can be asked to work in unstable or dangerous environments. For example, if a high level of chemicals are present, robotic automation offers the ideal solution, as it will continue to work without harm. Production areas that require extremely high or low temperatures typically have a high turnover of staff due to the nature of the work. Automated robots can minimise material waste and remove the need for humans to put themselves at unnecessary risk.

Disadvantages to robotic bring to working environment

1. Increase unemployment rate and job loss

On working environment cost increasing aspect, where robots are increasing the efficiency in many businesses, they are also increasing the unemployment rate. Because of robots, human labour is no longer required in many factories and manufacturing plants. They can certainly handle their prescribed tasks, but they typically cannot handle unexpected situations.The ROI of your business may suffer if your operation relies on too many robots. They have higher expenses than humans, so at the end of the day you may not always achieve the desired ROI.

However, robots may have AI but they are certainly not as intelligent as humans. They can never improve their jobs outside the pre-defined programming because they simply cannot think for themselves. Robots installed in workplaces still require manual labour attached to them. Training those employees on how to work with the robots definitely has a cost attached to it.Moreover, robots have no sense of emotions or conscience. They lack empathy and this is one major disadvantage of having an emotionless workplace.Also, robots operate on the basis of information fed to them through a chip. If one thing goes wrong the entire company bears the loss. Where a robot saves times, on the other hand it can also result in a lag. It is, after all, a machine so you cannot expect too much from them. If a robot malfunctions, you need extra time to fix it, which would require reprogramming.If ultimately robots would do all the work, and the humans will just sit and monitor them, health hazards will increase rapidly. Obesity will be on top of the list. So there are advantages, but there are disadvantages as well. It is the twenty first century and we cannot work without machines.Humans are still considered far more efficient than robots when it comes to decision making powers, handling difficult situations, brainstorming, and generally bringing a sense of emotion and empathy into a workplace. Besides, you cannot rule out the significant role of humans in a business. After all, no machine can replace the human factor 'real employees' bring into a workplace. So, AI can raise unemployment and increase factory or shopping center or office working environment cost when their working environment are applied robotic to replace many workers, then machine electricity expense will also increase. Otherwise, human workers can not spend too much electricity expense in cost aspect.

Whilst industrial robots can prove highly effective and bring you a positive ROI, implementing them might require a fairly high capital cost. That's why, before making a decision we recommend considering both the investment needed and also the ROI you expect to achieve. Often the easiest way to get round this issue is to take out asset finance and the ROI of the robot more than pays for the interest on the asset finance.

This is typically the biggest obstacle that will decide whether or not a company will invest in robotic automation, or wait until a later stage. A comprehensive business case must be built when considering the implementation of this technology. The returns can be substantial and quite often occur within a short space of time. However, the cash flow must be sustainable in the meantime and the stability of the company is by no means worth the risk if the returns are only marginal. Yet, in most instances there will be a repayment schedule available, which makes it a lot easier to afford and control finances. Our downloadable automation payback calculator also has a finance scheme option so you can see how this would work for you.

On job loss increasing aspect, Job loss is by far the most significant opposition frequently brought against the use of robots in the manufacturing industry. Industry workers of all levels, from entry-level to veterans, worry about the security of their employment status, and the ability of their job to be replaced by a robot. This panic is more widespread in this industry compared to others because of the closer immanence of a robot takeover in manufacturing.

Macro effects are another topic that usually comes up with job loss. More "big picture" thinkers wonder how the national, and eventually global economy will be affected when manufacturing workers' jobs are displaced. How can this mass unemployment possibly be compensated for, and how can the robots' presumed success be limited from seeping into other industries. However, increased investment costs are a financial counterpoint to industrial robots, with the idea that manufacturing companies will rack up their debt investing in robotic technology. Firms that do not have the funding might even go bankrupt in an effort to keep up with industry trends rather than continue on with normalized operations.Hence, elimination of a whole labor class would presumably occur a bit of a ways down the road, but the implications of this point are too large not to consider. Bringing in robots to take unskilled labor jobs will place more pressure on the economy, education system, and financial market, just to name a few. The United States has always been associated with the grit and work ethic of its blue-collar workers, and robots are threatening to eliminate this aspect of the human population, with a take over of production jobs.

One of the biggest concerns surrounding the introduction of robotic automation is the impact of jobs for workers. If a robot can perform at a faster, more consistent rate, then the fear is that humans may not be needed at all. While these worries are understandable, they are not really accurate.The same was said during the early years of the industrial revolution, and as history has showed us, humans continued to play an essential role. Amazon are a great example of this. The employment rate has grown rapidly during a period where they have gone from using around 1,000 robots to over 45,000

   2. Robotic can not perform better to compare human workers, when they need to work long time in any working environment

Robots need a supply of power, The people can lose jobs in factories, They need maintenance to keep them running, It costs a lot of money to make or buy robots, The software and the equipment that you need to use with the robot cost much money. Robots cost much money in maintenance & repair, The programs need to be updated to suit the changing requirements, the machines need to be made smarter, In case of breakdown, the cost of repair may be very high, The procedures to restore lost code or data may be time-consuming & costly.

Robots can store large amounts of data but the storage, access, retrieval is not as effective as the human brain, They can perform repetitive tasks for a long time but they do not get better with experience such as the humans do. Robots are not able to act any different from what they are programmed to do, With the heavy application of robots, the humans may become overly dependent on the machines, losing their mental capacities, If the control of robots goes in the wrong hands, Robots may cause the destruction. Robots are not intelligent or sentient, They can never improve the results of their jobs outside of their predefined programming, They do not think, They do not have emotions or conscience, This limits how the robots can help & interact with people. Robots can take the place of many humans in factories, So, the people have to find new jobs or be retrained, They can take the place of the humans in several situations, If the robots begin to replace the humans in every field, They will lead to unemployment.

Humans fear robots, Robots inspire two types of fear: firstly, that they might take over our jobs, and secondly, that they could take over the world, Robots will steal our jobs, Robots have the effect of increasing productivity rather than eliminating jobs.Robotics become increasingly present in our everyday life, with household robots, medical, industrial, on production lines, not to mention airports, banks, and hotels, So, Robots may dominate the human species. Robots can operate on the basis of information fed to them through a chip, when one thing goes wrong the entire company bears a loss.The robot can save times, but it can also result in a lag, It is a machine so you can't expect too much from them, If the robot has malfunctioned, you need extra time to fix it, which would require reprogramming, If robots would do all the work, and the humans will just sit and monitor them, health hazards will increase rapidly, Obesity will be on top of the list and less labour at workplaces.

3. Increasing training expense

Whilst industrial robots are excellent for performing many tasks, as with any other type of technology, they require more training and expertise to initially set up. The expertise of a good automation company with a support package will be very important. To minimise your reliance on automation companies you can train some of your engineers on how to program robots, but you will still need the assistance of experienced automation companies for the original integration of the robot.

In recent years the number of industrial robots and the applications they can be used for has increased significantly. However, there still are some limitations in terms of the type of tasks they can perform, which is why we suggest that an automation company looks at your requirement to assess the options first. Sometimes a bespoke automated system may give a better or faster result than a robot. Also, a robot does not have everything built into it, often the success or failure of an industrial robotic system depends on how well the surrounding systems are integrated e.g. grippers, vision systems, conveyor systems etc. Only use good trusted robot integrators to be sure of the optimum results if you do choose to use industrial robots.

Artificial intelligent working participation how brings economic growth

● How AI impacts economy

What is AI non-manual shops? Why and how it can assist economic growth? I shall explain as below:

Artificial Intelligence, as we see it, is a collection of multiple technologies that enable machines to sense, comprehend and act—and learn, either on their own or to augment human activities. Compelling data reveal a discouraging truth about growth today. There has been a marked decline in the ability of traditional levers of production—capital investment and labor—to propel economic growth. Artificial intelligence (AI) is a new factor of production and has the potential to introduce new sources of growth, changing how work is done and reinforcing the role of people to drive growth in business. Accenture research on the impact of AI in 12 developed economies reveals that AI could double annual economic growth rates in 2035 by changing the nature of work and creating a new relationship between man and machine. The impact of AI technologies on business is projected to increase labor productivity by up to 40 percent and enable people to make more efficient use of their time.

To fulfill the promise of AI as a new factor of production that can reignite growth, Accenture recommends the following steps be taken to help navigate the complexity of issues:
· Prepare the next generation – integrate human intelligence with machine intelligence so they can successfully co-exist in a two-way learning relationship and reevaluate the type of knowledge and skills required for the future.
· Encourage AI-powered regulation – update and create adaptive, self-improving laws to close the gap between the pace of technological change and the pace of regulatory response.
· Advocate a code of ethics for AI – ethical debates should be supplemented by tangible standards and best practices in the development and use of intelligent machines.
· Address the redistribution effects – policymakers should highlight how AI can result in tangible benefits and preemptively address any perceived downsides of AI, helping groups disproportionately affected by changes of employment and incomes.
Our research strongly shows that AI can unleash remarkable benefits across countries, countering slow economic growth and lagging productivity. To fulfill the promise of AI, relevant stakeholders must be thoroughly prepared – intellectually, technologically, politically, ethically and socially - to address the benefits and challenges that can arise as artificial intelligence becomes more integrated in our daily lives."
How AI impacts economy? AI has the potential to markedly increase industry growth. Information and Communication, Manufacturing and Financial Services are the three sectors that will benefit most from the application of AI. AI offers unprecedented profitability opportunities. For example, manufacturing has a forecast share-of-profit increase of 39 percent due to AI-powered systems whose ability to learn, adapt and evolve over time can eliminate faulty machines and idle equipment.

● How AI will reverse falling profit growth IN 2035

AI can reverse the cycle of low profitability across industries through three channels: It includes these three aspects:
INTELLIGENT AUTOMATION
Image
Whether enhancing the production chain with improvements to supply chain management or streamlining the sales process, AI offers huge advantages over traditional automation.

LABOR & CAPITAL AUGMENTATION
Image
Workers can delegate low value-added tasks to AI and be more productive in their main tasks. AI can also help businesses maximize their asset utilization rates.

INNOVATION DIFFUSION
Image
By accelerating the development of new products, AI helps to increase innovation, eliminate redundant costs and generate new revenue streams to increase profitability.

Annual growth rates in 2035 of gross value added (a close approximation of GDP), comparing baseline growth in 2035 to an artificial intelligence scenario where AI has been absorbed into the economy. AI offers unprecedented profitability opportunities. For example, manufacturing has a forecast share-of-profit increase of 39 percent due to AI-powered systems whose ability to learn, adapt and evolve over time can eliminate faulty machines and idle equipment (Accenture and Frontier Economics).

Source: Accenture and Frontier Economics https://www.accenture.com/us-en/insight-ai-industry-growth
Louis Columbus (2017) also gave opinions to show that AI will increase economic growth an average of 1.7% across 16 industries by 2035. Information and Communication, Manufacturing and Financial Services will be the top three industries that gain economic growth in 2035 from AI's benefits.
AI will have the most positive effect on Education, Accommodation and Food Services and Construction industry profitability in 2035.
The research compares the economic growth rates of 16 industries, projecting the impact of Artifical Intelligence (AI) on global economic growth through 2035. Using Gross Value Added (GVA) as a close approximation of Gross Domestic Product (GDP), the study found that the more integrated AI is into economic processes, the

greater potential for economic growth. One of the reports' noteworthy findings is that AI has the potential to increase economic growth rates by a weighted average of 1.7% across all industries through 2035. Information and Communication (4.8%), Manufacturing (4.4%) and Financial Services (4.3%) are the three sectors that will see the highest annual GVA growth rates driven by AI in 2035. The bottom line is that AI has the potential to boost profitability an average of 38% by 2035 and lead to an economic boost of $14T across 16 industries in 12 economies by 2035.

· AI will increase economic growth by an average of 1.7% across 16 industries by 2035 with Information and Communication, manufacturing and financial services leading all industries. Accenture Research found that the Information and Communication industry has the greatest potential for economic growth from AI. Integrating AI into legacy information and communications systems will deliver significant cost, time and process-related savings quickly. Accenture predicts the time, cost and labor savings will generate up to $4.7T in GVA value in 2035. High growth areas within this industry are cloud, network, and systems security including defining enterprise-wide cloud security strategies.

· AI will most increase profitability in Education, Accommodation and Food Services and Construction industries in 2035. Personalized learning programs and automating mundane, routine tasks to free up colleges, universities, and trade school instructors to teach new learning frameworks will accelerate profitability in the education through 2035. Accommodation & Food Services and Construction are industries with manually-intensive, often isolated processes that will benefit from the increased insights and contextual intelligence from AI throughout the forecast period.

· Manufacturing's adoption of Industrial Internet of Things (IIoT), smart factories and comparable initiatives are powerful catalysts driving AI adoption. Based on the proliferation of Industrial Internet of Things (IIoT) devices and the networks and terabytes of data they generate, Accenture predicts AI will contribute an additional $3.76T GVA to manufacturing by 2035. Supply chain management, forecasting, inventory optimization and production scheduling are all areas AI can make immediate contributions to this industry's profits and long-term economic

· Financial Services' greatest gains from AI will come automating and reducing the errors in mundane, manually-intensive tasks including credit scoring and first-level customer inquiries. Accenture forecasts financial services will benefit $1.2T in additional GVA in 2035 from AI. Follow-on areas of automation in Financial Services include automating market research queries through intelligent bots, and scoring and reviewing mortgages.

· By 2035 AI technologies could increase labor productivity 40% or more, doubling economic growth in 12 developed nations. Accenture finds that AI's immediate impact on profitability is improving individual efficiency and productivity. The economies of the U.S. and Finland are projected to see the greatest economic gains from AI through 2035, with each attaining 2% higher GVA growth.The following graphic compares the 12 nations included in the first phase of the research.

Source:

Louis Columbus Senior Contributor Artificial Intelligence Will Enable 38% Profit Gains By 2035 June. 22 . 2017 https://www.forbes.com/sites/louiscolumbus/2017/06/22/artificial-intelligence-will-enable-38-profit-gains-by-2035/#5121455a1969

Human Behavioral network job brings social economic benefits

What does human network job mean ? Why may human network job be popular? Why human network job behavior may influence economy ?

Nowadays internet is popular to use. We can apply internet to find data , search any new things, even earn money. Why does internet

may become huma network job source. For example, e-publish may be one kind of new human network job. Any authors may apply internet

channel to help them to sell electronic or paper books from e-publisher web store. They may apply facebook, you tub etc. any online

channel to promote themselves new books to let new readers to know whether when they may buy themselves favourable new topic books to read from electronic publisher web store.

Thus, future electronic publisher industry may help any authors to build internet network platform to help them to sell and promote

ot advertise their any one new electronic or paper book topic to let global any one reader to choose to buy their any new topic books from electronic publisher web store easily and conveniently. However, it implies that electronic network platform author may be one kind of future new human network job in our societies.

How electronic network platform author job may bring economy benefit in macro economy view? A person can have few friends, contacts and still be very influential if these few

friends and contacts are themselves highly influential, e.g. one author must not need to know any one reader in global society. When they like to choose any electronic books from electronic internet network platform. They may become the author's any one topic book buyer, when they feel the author's any one topic book is fun and attract they make decision to buth the strange author whose the topic book from electronic book publisher's platform web store conventiently in short time. Although, they are strangers, they do not know themselves , but the reader can understand what it way that made Google from writing platofrm to create new creative mind and typing network job method to replace traditional hand writing book method for global authors. It will be one kind of new human network writing job.

Hence, global any one reader can apply an innovative search engine , such as google.com to find whether whom author personal new topic books are value to read from internet.

Then, the electroniuc publisher's web store may be new book store platform sale network to help the author to sell many electronic or paper books from electronic network platform

in short time. So, internet may be future new network plaform to help global any one author to create network writing job absolutely. Furthermore, internet may be popular social media

to help any one author to build goold relationship between his/her readers. It is one kind of new network, human network job. New authors do not need to buy many paper books to prepare to put in any one book shop warehouse. Their every book can print on demand to reduce out of book stock in any one book shop. They may choose to sell either electronic books or paper books both from any one book publisher web store. So, electronic network platform may be one kind of good writing channel to help human authors to create income and it can also help authors to bring new creative mind and new topic fun content books to let readers to know and buy to read from electronic publisher network platform.

Why does human behavior may be one kind of new human network job to bring global economic advantages. ALthough, it may be free income or without inocme, but the person does the network behavior, his/her behavior may be bring advantages to influence many other people's health. For this case, when a worker in a coffee shop in an airport gets a vaccination aganinst the flu, it does not only helps him or her stay healthy, but also helps the many travellers who might otherwise have been inflected if that workers caught the flu. So, the externality , the result implies the vaccination of even a part of a community conveys benefits to the whole community. For example, governments pay special attention to the vaccinations of school children, teachers, health mothers, and the elderly, categories of people particularly susceptible not only to catching, but also to transmitting a disease.

It is not accidental that governments are heavily involved with vaccination . When there are externalities, free market, fail to persuade individual incentives with society's

their the worker's decision of whether to get a vaccine ends up attracting whether other people get sick. The workers might not fully take all these other people's potential suffering into account when making her or his vaccination decision.

As Stanford University does many suggestions, understand this and tries to help them make the right decisions and so providers free flu vaccines for its staff and students.

Small pockets of unvaccinated individuals can allow a disease to gain a spread more widely well-being. For example, parent weighing the costs and benefits of a vaccine for their child is not always thinking of the consequences of that vaccination to other people. THese are markets in which subsidizing or regulating behavior can make everyone better off. Because the reason for requiring that a child be vaccinated before enrolling in school is not just to protect that child, because each child's vaccination affects others via potential contagions.

Robots take our jobs behavioral and economy influences

Robot job behavior brings economy influences

If one day robots can replace human to do simple, even complex jobs. They will bring what influences to our global societial economy.The popular economic refrain declares that the

global middle class is dying and robots will soon take our jobs, e.g. shopping center customer service jobs, library service jobs, cinema ticket sale jobs, restaurant kitchen cooker jobs,

even, bus drivers, taxi drivers etc. public transport driving jobs, accountant, doctors etc. professional jobs. Whether it is beautiful or petty matter if our future societies have many human jobs can be replaced to do from robots. Businessman must may reduce to employ employees and reduce to pay salary or wage, when robots can be replaced to do their employees tasks. But, societies must bring unemployement rate rises , due to societies will have many people loss jobs when their employers choose to buy robots to serve their clients or do any office tasks or customer service or cleaning etc. tasks.

In micro economy view, employers may save money in long term, but in macro economy view, it will cause unemployment ratio rises , even crime rate rises when there are many people lose

jobs in societies. These models of doom, though, fail to account for the hundreds of businesses riding the waves of change in their industries when robots may be invented to replace human to do many simple , even complex tasks in our future societies.

WE may image that one small factory needs to manufacture fishes canes to sell to supermarket, the small , cheaper stuff and higher margin parts of the fishes manufacture industry. Before, this factory needs to employe many human factory workers need to help every fresh customer makeing the perfect fishing gear, designed for performance, durability, and cost in order to achieve to manufacture every fish cane in whole fished processing manufacturing stages. Every worker needs to spend about 15 to twenty minutes to finish every fish cane , till to delivery to any supermarket to sell. If this fish canes manufacturing factory can apply manufacturing robots to help them to finish any one working tasks , every robot can only spend five minutes to finish whole fresh fish cane manufacturing process. Thus, every robot can

help this factory save 10 to 15 minutes time to finsh every fish cane manufacturing process. IN fact, time is money, because when every robot can help this factory to reduce 10 to 15 minutes time to compare human worker. Then, this factory can finish about 20 fish canes in one hour if it can use robot to help it to manufacture fish canes. Otherwise, if this factory still use human workers to help it to manufacture fish canes, then it can finsh about 3 to 4 fish canes in one hour. SO, the manufacturing efficiency ensures that robots must help this fish manufacturing factory to raise fish canes number more than human workers. So, in robotic behavioral economy view, manufacturing robots must help this fish canes manufacturing factory to raise fish canes manufacturing number and deliver increasing number to supermarkets to prepare to sell every day. Robots can help this fish canes manufacturing factory bring manufacturing time saving, rising manufacturing efficiency, improving performance and reducing wages expenditure long time advantages in micro economy view. However, manufacturing robots can also bring disadvanages to society, e.g. increasing unemployment ratio, increasing crime rate,

this factory workers will lose jobs and income, they need earn social welfare from government and increasing government finance pressure in short time, even long time in macro economic view.

Stanford University graduate program in economics, Scott lecturer explained that "in demand and supply economic theory for robots supply and demand case, robots supply number increasing may influence human workers demand number decrease. It sometimes calls " the efficient frontier".

No specific human beings were mentioned in any of economics classes. As robots supply and demand in market case, They (robots) may be purely theoretical " agents" who reached to the most reasonable sale prices in order to persuade any one businessman buyer to make manufacturing robot buying decision whether robots can help him / her to bring how much saving time , saving money, saving cost, improving performance, efficiency economic benefit before he/she plans to reduce workers number when he/she decides to apply robots to replace human workers in his/her factory or office or any service department, e.g. cinema ticket sale service, shopping center customer service, shopping center cleaning , supermarket customer service etc. service or sale tasks. When robots can replace human to do any one of these tasks in any organizations. So, robots may be human worker agents who reached to prices the way robots would react to a software

command. There was nothing that explained why some people thrived and others did n't or why truly brilliant, hardworking people could fail when much lazier folks succeeded." Having been admitted to the Stanford University graduate program in economics, Scott lecturer hoped to get his answers there.

How robots influence our future social changing? Using the right technology can be a boon to your business in this economy. For internet example, it is easier than ever to find well-matched customers all around the world, to stay in contact with them, and to more quickly design the products they want. If you focus solely on being cutting -edge, though you risk letting the technology

take over what should be very robust relationships with your customers , employees, and colleagues. IN nowaddays society, technoligical advances and cutomation, personal

relationships in business are more crucial than ever. I mean that robots can not replace human to serve clients to let them to feel more comfortable and passion more easily. For shoe shop case example, if the shoe shop apply one robot to serve its clients to replace human shoe salesperson to serve its shoe customers. Robots ensure that they can not persuade every shoe potential buyer to make shoe buying decision more easily when robots need to contact every shoe potential buyer. The reason is simple, because robots can not touch any one shoe buyer individual emotion very easier.

If the shoe buyer needs the robots to help him/her to choose any right shoe styles when he/she can not feel himself / herself can make the most right shoe style choice decision. The robots can not replace human shoe salesperson to make shoe style choice judgement more easily. They must need longer time to analyze whether which shoe style may be the most suitable to the shoe buyer. Otherwise, human shoe salesperson may attempt to make the most right shoe style choice decision to help any one shoe buyer to chooce the most right style shoe because he/she owns shoe style sale experience, shoe style knowledge, the most important reason is that they can feel every shoe customer individual emotion to touch whether he/she will feel comfortable or happy when they attempt to help every shoe customer to seek the most right shoe style in every shoe customer whole shoe searching processing. Othwerwise, serving robots are only one machine, they can not touch or feel every shoe customer individual emotion whether he/she feel comfortable or unhappy or happy when they need to contact them in whole shoe searching processing. Hence, I believe that some tasks robots can

not repalce human staff to do very easily. Otherwise, robots may bring disadvanatges to let any one businessman to loss his/her customers, due to robots can not touch every customer

emotion to compare human staff in service tasks more easily. Robots serving customer behaviors may cause money lose and customers number lose to the shop in micro economic view.

Intellectual human economic behaviors

What does intellectual human economic behaviors mean ? I believe that when we choose or decide to do intellectual behaviors, then our societies will be influenced to bring economic growth in consequence.I shall attempt to indicate pollution case to explain how and why eithet our intellectual or foolish behaviors may bring economic growth or recession in consequence as below:

On one hand, for air pollution social case aspect example, if we only consider to buy cars to drive for working aimr or holiday leisure aim. Then, our societies air will be polluted. Our health will be influenced to bad. Our car driving behaviors may cause global environment air pollution serously. In long tiem, global air pollution will bring our bodies health to be bad. Although, ourselves car driving behaviors may bring our driving travelling leisure enjoyment and comfortable feeling in short time, also we so not need to pay public transport fare often, but we need to compensate ourselves health economic intangible loss due to air pollution , when cars number increases, dirty air will cause ouselves health to become bad.

In the result, we will need to pay more medical expenditure when we are old age, due to ourselves bodies will become bad, due to we breathe global dirty air every day, due to ourselves cars pollute air in long time, e.g. 10 to 20 years, even 30 more without limited air pollution environment. So, driving cars behavior may be one kind of human foolish behavior and our foolish behavior may bring ourselves future long time medical expenditure absolutely.

One the other hand, water pollution social aspect, if we often keep much rubblish to pollute sea, oil exploration porcessing pollute ocean , ships gas pollute ocaen, then fishes will eat polluted food and drive dirty water, due to global ocean is polluted.

In fact, because human only to conside how to buy boats to carry on leisure enjoyment activities, or catch cruises to travel on the sea. Also, oil manufacturers only consider researching anywhere to find new oil exploration places to manufacture oil product, when their oil exploration processes pollute ocarn . Consequently, global fishes drink polluted warer or eat polluted food. They will have poison. SO, human will have high chance to eat poison polluted fishes, due to fishes are poison or are polluted.

So, human is doing foolish activities, we only hope to find oil exploration places to pollute ocean or we only spend money to buy ticket to catch ships to travel anywhere in global ocean. All of these human foolish behaviors will bring pollution to global ocean. On consequently, we will need to compensate to eat polluted or dirty or poision fishes, ourselves bodies health will be bad. In long time, we need have high chance to pay medical expenditure when we are old. So, pollution case may be one good example to explain how and why human foolish behavior may influence ourselves future need to compensate serious medical loss.

All of these human foolish behavior will bring pollution to global ocean. On consequently, we will need to compensate to eat polluted or dirty or poison fished , ourselves bodies health will be bad. In long time, we will have high chance to pay medical expenditure, when we are old. So, pollution case may be one good example to explain how and why human ourselves intellectual or foolish behaviors may influence future long time economic loss or economic growth or recession in micro and micro economic view.

On another water pollution aspect hand, if we often keep rubbish to sea, oil exploration processing pollutes ocean and ships' gas pollute ocean, then fishes will eat polluted food and drink dirty water, due to fishes will eat polluted food and drink dirty sea water because the global ocean is polluted seriously.

In fact, because human only consider how to buy boats to carry on any leisure water activities, or catches cruises to travel on the sea. Also, oil manufacturers only consider any where to find oil exploratin places to manufacture oil products from ocean, when their pol exploration processes can plooute ocean. Consequently, global fishes drink polluted water or eat direty food. They will have poison. So, human will have high chance to eat poison fishes.

Otherwise, such as pollutin case, it can infuence inflation or deflation. Consequently, the reason indicates supply and demand theory. If air pollution is serious, then we will consider health issue, global cars demand number may be influenced to reduce, when global cars number demand will reduce, global car prices and supply number will need to change to fall down in order to attract or persuade global car consumers choose to make car purchase decision.

Hence, global car manufacture number and car price will be influenced to reduce, due to global air pollution issue. Consequently, deflation will occur because when the country citizen usually does not spend much extra saving money to buy car expensive goods. Money value will be low. Otherwise, if global cair pollution is not serious, human considers to buy cars to enjoy driving leisure lives. So, global car demand is influenced to increase , also global car price will also influenced to increase.

Consequently, gobal human will choose to buy cars to drive. Due to we accept to spend extra saving to buy expensive car goods. Car sale price and supply may be influenced to rise up. Money value is influenced to reduce. Inflation may be influenced, due to global car consumers number increases, we would not have extra money to spend easily. Car expensive goods expenditure influences our spending habit to avoid to make car purchase decision more easily. So, human intellectual or foolish activities may bring inflation or deflation consequency in possible indirectly in macro economic view.

On conclusion, above pollution case explain that how and why human intellectual or foolish economic behaviors may bring inflation or deflation consequency as wll as economic growth or recession consequency as well as any goods demand and supply increasing or decreasing consequency. It implies that human behavior may have indirect relationship to influence any goods demand and supply number to either increase or decrease result as well as any goods price will be influenced to increase or decrease in micro and macro economic view.

The relationship between social change and human behavior

Why does economic changes may influence human individual behavioral change? I shall attempt to indicate shopping behavior and staying at home behavior to explain their case and effect relationsip as below:

Human behavior can be influenced by economic change or economic change can be influenced by human behavior? Why does recession may influence consumers reduce shopping desire? In social recession suitation, it is possible that many people lose jobs suddenly, due to businessmen lose many customers. They need to make decision to reduce employees number in order to continue to keep businesses. Consequently, many firms (organizations) their employees may lose jobs. When they have much time, due to lose jobs, they will feel to avoid to spend too much time and money to go to shopping often. Many losing jobs people, they will often stay at homes.

So, they will reduce time to go to shopping, then non essential products won't their preferable choice purchase products. Hence, recession will change many losing jobs people their shopping or consumption desires to avoid to buy non essential products often . Usually when economic boom, many people have jobs to do because consumers number must increase when many people have jobs to do. Then, many people can accept to spend money to buy non essential products often. Many people feel spend time to go to shopping can satisfy their purchase of any kinds of new products useful psychology or desire. So, recession is one good example to explain it can influence many people do not like often to leave homes to go to shopping easily. Many people like to stay at homes, becaue they feel worry about spending too much shopping time when they leave homes. Their staying home time is one good negative shopping behavior example. So, economic change may influence human individual behavior changes , they have direct cause and efect relationship in behavioral economic view.

May human behavior influence economic change? Is it possible that human behavior may bring the country social economic change in macro economic or micro behavioral economic view ? I shall indicate publishing industry example. Do you feel that if there are many students feel learning is very important when they read many books or many of students feel interesting to read or they have reading new books in habit, then it is possible that the country will have many students like to spend time to go to any book shops to choose the books, they feel that they can help they learn new knowledge. Then the country will increase students number, they often spend time to visit any one book shop every week. Their visiting book shops behavior which may become their habits. So, the country will increase students number, they often spend time to visit book shops. Also, it implies that visiting book shops behaviors may be their behavioral habits.

So, when the country has many students often spend time to visit book shops , their visiting book shops behaviors may help any one book shop to raise books sale chance. So, the country's student individual often visiting book shop behaviors, their habitual visiting book shops behaviors must may assist help any one book shop to increase books sale number absolutely.

Consequently, any one book shop , its books sale bumber must be influenced to increase to increase because the country will have many students like or feel need visit book shops habit in order to choose any suitable books to buy to read at home in order to raise themselves learning effort. When the country has many bok shops often have many students visit their book shops, then their books sale number may be influenced to increase. It explain why student individual visiting book shop behavior may help any one book shop sale number increases also.

How human productive behavior may influence economic development

May any country which citizen behavior assist themselves country development? It is one cause and effect economic question. I mean that if the country itself citicen can not concentrate mind or energy to choose to do one kind of industry in order to let themselves country can bring the most benefit, then whether the counry itself economy can bring the most serious economic benefit. I shall attempt to indicate these countries themselves indistry choice to explain whether these countries themselves citizen productive behavior may help themselves countries to achieve the largest economic benefits. I shall indicate as below:

New Zealand farmer individual wine productive behavior

For New Zealand country example, this country concerns itself effort is foucs on farming agricultural aspect. So, this country has many farmers concentrate on farming agricultural aspect. May New Zealanders choose to spend time to produce different kinds of wines, e.g. wine or red grape wine is for the people are eating meat, or they are eating dinner.

When these New Zealanders their behaviors choose to do farming or agriculture to grow and produce different kinds of taste of white or red grape wine drinking products job. Themselves grape agriculture behavior will influence these New Zealanders themselves, they can learn how to improve different kinds of grape wine drinking products in order to achieve every kinds of white or read grape wines taste improving aim during their white or red grape producing process.

Why can New Zealander every individual white or read grape wine producers improve their white or read grape wine taste more easily? In behavioral economic view, it can explain that why any one New Zealander white or read grape wine producer can be encouraged or excited or persuaded to concentrate nervous and energy and effort to learn how to improve their white or red grape wine products easily.

In fact, New Zealand is one agricultural food export country. It has good natural environment resource , e.g. land, seed to provide any one farmer to produce themselves any kinds of agricultrual food products, e.g. fruit, or wine food products. Because New Zealanders know themselves country has enough natural resource . So, in common, many New Zealanders choose to attempt to do farming agricultural jobs in order to export themselves any kinds of fruit or meat or wine products to overseas or sell to domestic in order to earn profit.

So, when these New Zealand farmers number has been increasing every year. This country farmers will feel themsleves competition between this New Zealand farmers themselves are serious due to they may feel New Zealanders choose to do agriculture businesses in order to export themselves different kinds of farming food to overseas or sell to local to earn profit.

Hence, when many New Zealand farmers feel that farmers number has been increasing every year. They will feel themselves competition is serious. They must need to spend much time and nervous and effort to research what method is the best how to produce the best taste of white or red grape wine products in order to let local or overseas wine buyers to choose to buy his/her producing white or read grpae products to drink.

Hence, in competition psychological view, may influence many New Zealand white or reaad wine producers had been beginning to change their learning behavior on researching what method is the best in order to produce the best quality of taste red or white wine products to sell in order to attract overseas or local white or read grape wine drinkers to choose to buy his/her wine products. Their behavior will focus on learning how to raising or improving white or read grape wine taste method more than only focus on producing a large number white or red grape wine products. They believe wine quality is more important to compare wine producing number. So, New Zealand wine producers themselves wine producers behaviors have been changing on concentrating on researching wine quality method aspect more then wine producing number aspect in behavioral economic view.

America high technological productive behavior

For America example, US is one high technological country, it owns many high technological knowledge talent inventors, e.g. computer science inventors. Hence, US must attract many diferent countries owning high technological computer inventors choose to go to US to develop their computer science profession career. Also, it seems that when many computer science inventors or professions choose to go to US to develop themselves computer science new career. In behavioral economic view, due to their leaving themselves countries choice, which may bring influence themselve country job behaviors need to be changed. They must need to adapt US new live. Because they will forgive their past computer science job. These computer science professionals need to spend time to adapt US new lives. They " past computer science job behaviors" will need to be changed to their new US any computer employer's new computer science job model.

Because their traditional computer science jobs needed to be forgot in their themselves countries. They will feel their old computer science job knowledge and behavior needed to change in order to let their US any one new of computer company employer feels satisfactory to accept their new working behavior in any one US computer organization.

So, on the other hand, many US computer company employer will feel that they must need time to accept any one new overseas computer science professions their working behaviors, their working attitude daily, because these foreign comouter science professional, their past computer working behaviors and working attitude must be different to US domestic computer science professions.

In behavioral economic view, these overseas computer science professions, their working behaviors and attitude must be needed to change in order to adapt any one US new computer company itself domestic or local computer science professional stafs themselves daily working behaviors and attitude because these overseas and local computer science professionals must need to team work together.

In behavioral economic view, it is only one way that foreign computer science professionals must need to change themselves past country traditiona daily working behaviors and attitude in order to cooperate with these US local computer science professionals in teams more easily.

Consequently, if these foreign compute science professionals can change their past working behaviors and attitude to let any one US local computer science professional feels to cooperate with them easily in short time. Then, the US computer company itself whole computer professional teams themselves efficiencies will be influenced to raised or improved by the changing past working attitude and working behaviors of these foreign computer science professionals. So, in behavioral economic view, only if US any one computer company hopes itself computer teams themselves efficiency can be raised or improved when it decides to employ foreign computer science professionals and US domestic computer science professionals. They need to work in teams together. They must need to let these foreign computer science professionals to know how to change their working behaviors and attitude to let their domestic computer science professionals feel easy to work together. Then, the US computer company itself whole team efficiency must be rasied or improved easily in short time.

● China share market investing behavior

For China share market example, economic development depends on financial market. Because if many Chinese have interest to invest to carry on shares buying and selling activities in orde to learn how to earn shares interest and share profit when the China shareholder can make decision to sell himself/herself shares in the the high price, then he/she can earn money when he/she can sell the China company's shares in the high sale share price position.

If China has many Chinese like to spend time to carry on investing shares activities. Themselves shares buying and selling behaviors will influence China has many companies can increase fund from many Chinese shareholders in order to have enough money to expand or develop themselves businesses in China in long term.

Consequently, when China can have many Chinese like to attempt to carry on buying and selling shares investing behaviors in China share market. Themselves buying and selling shares behaviors can help many Chinese companies have effort to increase enough money or capital in order to continue to do their businesses in long term absolutely. So, it explains why when many Chinese become shareholders , they can assist China will have many companies continue to develop their businesses if many Chinese like to carry on shares buying and selling investing behaviors in long time in China financial investment market nowadays in behavioral economic view.

Why has any individual country have many people invest share behavior which can influence the country's macro consumption desire?

I shall apply shares market buying and selling investment behavior to explaiin why shares investment behavior which may impact the country's overal consumption desire as below:

In behavioral economic view, I assume that when the coutry has many people have interest to attempt to carry on shares buying and selling investment behavior, then their frequent shares buying and selling behaviors which may bring negactive consumption desire or shopping desire of these shares investors their consumer behavior.

The reason is simple, when the country has many share buyers number suddenly been increasing rapidly. Consequently, these large group share investors must need to spend much time to research any kinds of company shares variations, whether when their share prices will rise up of fall down in order to achieve buying the company's shares in the lowest price and selling the company's shares in the highest price level in order to earn profit.

Basic on this reason, they must need to spend much extra time to research share prices changing behavior every day, e.g. one working person will wait to leave his/her job, after he/she can spend time to gather data to research the day's share price changing behavior after dinner. So, the working person's right time may be his/her share price market research behavior. Before he/she may spend his/her night time to go to shopping after dinner, but nowadays, he/she will fogive to do his/her shopping behavior before dinner or after dinner at hight sometime. He/she will make decision to spend much night time to turn on computer to click on share market website to research his/her share purchase choice to investigate whether his/her share price whether it rises up or falls down at the moment in order to make his/her share buying or selling decision at ever night time.

I mean the when the country has many people are share investors, their shares investment behavioral spenging time which will influence many shops lose customers at might often because the country will have many people feel need to spend night time to turn on computer or watch television to investigate share price variation. So, the country will have many people / share investors choose to stay at home in order to carry on share price variation investigation behavior, they need to listen share market update news from radios or watch the share market update news from computer or TV at home every night. Consequenly, they must reduce times to leave themselves homes at night. So, their shopping behavior also will be reduced. Because these share investors feel need to spend time to investigate share price variation news at homes which can bring economic benefits (high opportunity benefits) when they choose to forgive to leave homes to go to shopping times (opportunity cost) every night.

On conclusion, it seems that when the country has many people are share investors, then their share price investigating behavior may bring negative shopping emotion at night. Consequently, the country's any one shop may lose many customers from this share investor consumer group in behavioral economic view. Hence, when the country's share investors number had been increasing rapidly, it will influence any shops lose many customers from this share investing customer group at night frequently in short time, even long time in behavioral economic view, because their shopping desires or shopping emotion will be brought negative feeling when they make decisions to spend much time to listen radios or watch TV or computers share price update nes at night. Hence, share market will bring negative impact to influence consumer shopping desire or negative shopping emotion in behavioral economic view.

Can technology influence human shopping behavioral change?

Nowadays, technological development has reached mature stage, whether technological mature stage may bring positive or negative shopping emotion influence to global consumers. I shall aplly internet inventin or ecommerce shopping channel tool to explain whether internet technology can bring postive or negative influence to global consumer behavior in behavioral economic view.

Internet is a good technological tool, it brings e-commerce business chance. In fact, commonly, global has have many businessmen choose to use internet channel to carry on their products transactions between global online-buyers and their electronic websites. So, global many shoppers had begun to feel online shopping is more convenient to compare visiting shops shopping. Their shopping behaviors have been changed from internet technological tool. Global has many shoppers choose to buy any products from any overseas or local businessmen their web stores. They only need to spend time to find any businessmen their webstores to choose the most suitable products to pay visa to buy from their webstores. at homes. So, in general, global had have may shoppers had changed their shopping behaviors from visiting shops to visiting webstores at homes often.

So, it seems that internet technological tool had influenced global many shops disappear, but internet webstores will be replaced their actual shops on streets. Some of businessmen either they choose webstores to replace shops or choose websotes and shops both or still keep shops only. Hence, internet tool influences global businessmen have three kinds of products sale channels to let globa local and overseas consumers to choose how to buy their products. However, in fact, many of global shoppers, youngers and olders had begun to accept to buy any products from webstores. They feel to spend time to leave homes to visit shops , their shopping behaviors will be wasted time to not essential part to their daily lives. Hence, since internet technological invention, it had changed many consumers their traditional visiting shops shopping habit to change to buying products from webstores channel.

However, on the one hand, internet creates webstores ecommerce shopping channel to let global many consumers do not need to leave homes to go to shopping. It brings negative visiting shops shopping emotion to global general consumers nowadays. But on the other hand, it also brings positive visiting internet webstores shopping emotion to global general consumer nowadays. So, it seems that global many consumers feel that they often do not need to spend much time to go out shopping. Many global consumers feel convenient and enjoy to choose any products to buy from different internet webstores, when the online buyer chooses the most suitable product, he she only needs to pay visa card to buy the product from the online seller's webstore conveniently at home.

Hence, online shopping can bring economic benefit to online buyers, e.g. avoiding walking time or spending transport fare to visit the shop to go to shopping, shortening or reducing shopping time to do another important matter.

On conclusion, global many consumers began feel online shopping can bring more economic benefits on shortening shopping time, avoiding transport fare spending aspect. So, online shopping will be popular shopping behavior for future long time. It may encourage global many shoppers can make rapid shopping decision in short time in order to carry on any products buying transaction to global any one online shopper in short time easily in behavioral economic view. So, global many businessmen had begun to build themselves one attraction webstore in order to persuade different countries consumers to choose to click themselves webstores from internet channel to buy any kinds of products in short time easily.

So, internet technology had changed consumers traditional shopping behaviors to build positive online shopping emotion as well as raise online sellers' any products sale chance easily in behavioral economic view.

Why and how human behavior may influence the country's economic growth or recession?

When one country has many people choose to do the same matter for one period, whether their behavior may influence the country's pvera; economic growth or recession . I shall attempt to indicate cases toexplain their relationship as below:

For flowing rubblish behavioral case example, do you feel that when the country has many people often flow rubblish on the streets, instead of their flowing rubblish behavior may bring streets dirty? But, their flowing rubblish behavior may explain that this country has people may have enough money to buy food to ear, or enough cloths to wear, enough bottles of water to drink, even they may have enough money to buy new television, radio, refrigeraters , washing machines, desktops or laptops electronic home products from old to new to use in order to satisfy their living needs. So, when they flow old electronic home products, their flowing old home electronic products behaviors may seem that they have enough money to buy other new home electronic products to replace old home electronic products to use at homes.

However, it seems thaat this country ought have many people have jobs to do. So, many of them, they can easy to make purchase decison to flow any old home electronic products and buy any new home electronic products to use . Because this country has many people have jobs to do. So, they can often not use old home electonic products to become rubblishs to flow on streets after they had bought any kinds of new home electronic homes.

In fact, it also implies that this country's economy grows rapidly. So, many businesses can glow up rapdly. When they expanded their businesses, they must need to increase employees number in order to let they help themselves to raise productivity or serve their clients absolutely. So, when the country has many businesses can grow up, it seems that its economy must be better or it is improved to compare past. Due to many different kinds of home electronic products had been often bought to use by this country people in this period. So, this country's any streets can be observed that expensive electronic home products were flowed on streets anywhere. then, this country will have many electronic home products sellers can sell their home electronic products very easily. When this country has many people can find any kinds of jobs to do easily. So, due to unemploymen rate had been decreasing.

In behavioral economic view, as this many electronic home products rubblish country case, we can observe this country may have many people have jobs to do. So, consumption number has been increased long time. So, cheap food, or expensive home electronic products may be rubblish on any streets. This country's people , their flowing rubblish behaviors may be explained that many of people have enough jobs to do, so they have ability to buy any good taste food to eat or buy any kinds of expensive electronic home products to use. So, this country's economy may be improved for this long period. So, in behavioral economic view, when this country can have many electronic home products rubblishs are flowed on anywherer in streets frequently. It seems that this country will have many people have jobs to do, so it causes they often change old home electronic products or replaced them easily, when they have enough income to spend to buy any kinds of new home electronic products to use at homes easily. Moreover, their flowing old electronic home products behaviors also indicate that this country has many people their salaries may be increased in possible from their emplyers. When this country can have many different kinds of home electornic products are sold. It means that this country's electronic home products needs or demand had been increasing, due to many people have jobs to do and income increases to excite their living of needs also improve. Consequently, this country may seem have better economic improvement. We can observe from this country's electronic home products rubblish increasing income in theis period.

On conclusion, this country ought experience economic growth at this period. So, " flowing expensive electronic home rubblish increasing number " may seem that this country's economic growth is rapidly in this period, due to many people have jobs to do as well as salaries increase in this period.

Technology how impacts human behavior changing?

Technology how influences human behavior to bring changing? For example, online share purchase and sale transaction from smart phone brings share investor can do share buying or selling transation in any where and any time conveniently, non manual driving auto vehicle, bring car owner feels comfortable and spends free time to do other matter, e.g. reading, listening mucis in himself or herself car freely. electrical energy vehicle can help car owner to reduce air polluton and it can brings the drivers do not feel drive long time in any journeys in order to avoid air pollution for environmental protection responsible car drivers in our societies. Thus, they will drive long time in any journeys when they can drive electronic energy cars to replace oil energy cars.

However, online technology can also bring consumers can choose to stay at homes to buy any things from seller individual online webstore conveniently. Such as online technology can bring shoppers do not need to spend much time to visit shops to buy any things. They can choose any kinds of products from any online sellers individual online webstores conveniently at homes. Online technology excite busy consumers can make purchase decision easily as well as it can help online sellers sell any kinds of products from internet easily.

In behavioral economic view, technology can change human behavior to be improved, it can let human feels comfortable, more free time ro use, rapid making any decisions, such as apply smart phones to make share purchase or sale transaction decision, online shopping decision, even travelling any where decision in short time, when the traveller finds the most cheap hotel accommodation room price and air ticket price frm any travel agent online tourism webstore, then the potential travel customer can follow the online hotel accommodation price and air ticket price data to make decision when to buy the air ticket from the airline travel agent or make decision when to prebook which hotel accommodation room to go to the country to travel from online travel agent tourism webstores. So, technology can encourage global any country travelers to make anywhere to trvel rapidly. If the traveler can find the country's general hotel rooms and airline tickets prices had been decreasing more sightly. The traveler may make travel decision to choose the country to travel in short time, then he/she can prebook the country;s any hotel room and airline ticket to pay by visa fraom the country's any hotel and airline travel agent webstores., before one week, even one month or more easily. Hence, online technology can also encourage traveler individual frequent travel times to be increased, due to global travelers can find any hotel rooms and airline tickets prices from internet conveniently at homes. They do not need to spend time to visit any airline travel agent to enquire travel choice country's hotel rooms prices and airline ticket prices. They can compare global travel of countries choices ' all hotels rooms and airline agents air tickets prices to make prebook airline seat and hotel room decision before one week, one month even six months early.

On conclusion, online technology can encourage global travelers can make travelling any where and when traveling time desicions easily. It can excite tourism industry develops in long time. Also, such as electricity cars invention can encourage environment protection car owners do car purchase decision easily, because they can choose to drive electronic energy cars to replace oil energy cars in order to avoid air pollution occurs easily. So, electronic cars can increase electronic car purchasrs number, due to many of environmental protection attitude of car owners can choose to drive electricity cars to bring air cleans, even non -manual driving cars can encourage lazy driving and free time driving car owners to choose to buy non-manual (artificial intelligent) cars to drive , because they can spend much free time to read, listen music or do any matters in themselves cars, they do not need to drive cars, robotic (AI) auto driving machine is such one non-manual driver to help them to drive themselves cars confidently. So, non-manual driving cars can attract lazy and enjoying free time driving car owners to choose to buy to replace traditional manual cars to drive easily. Moreover, online share transaction can help any share investors to make share buying and selling decision in short time easily. When they can apply smart phones technological tool to carry on share buying and selling activities easily. They can observe any share rising or falling price suitation from smart phones in any where any any time easily. So, smart phone technology can help global any shareholders to make share purchase and sale transaction easily. So, technology can encourage human makes decision in short time rapidly.

How and why employees behaviors may influence economy development?

In behavioral economy view,I believe the country's any organizational employees behavior may bring indirect relationship to influence the country's long term economic development. I shall indicate past manufacture industry social development period to explain their relationship. For many countries' past business activities had belonged to manufacturing industry, such as US, UK past before 1980 year, it focused on steel manufacturing and steel manufacturing related machine products. So, US, Uk developed countries manufacturing industries may be past main country's economic income sources. I assume US , UK past had one million number different kinds of industries. They ought had about seven houndred thousand number organizational businesses were belonged to manufactured industry. They may include:

Steel manufacturing and steel related machine manufacturing, e.g. vehicle manufacturing, home appliances, e.g. washing machine, television, radio, refrigerate cooler, heater, air condition etc. different kinds of different kinds of steel -related manufacturing machine, they were manufactured from US, UK steel machine manufacturers. So, US, Uk the other three hundred thousand number industry may be general service industry, e.g. hotel service, restaurent, cinema, public transport service, tourism lesiure , wine bar, supermarket etc. different kinds of non-manufacturing industries business organizations were operated in UK, US past before 1980 year.

So, in UK, US developed countries industry development history, they ought have high percentage of businesses belonged to steel related manufacturing machine and steel products. Also, in the past before 1980 year, US, Uk business employers , they employed many workers are manufacturing workers. They needed to spend long time to work in factories. They were skillful workers, and they are trained to manufacturing cars, washing machine, television, heater, etc. even steel itself different kinds of steel related products to prepare to deliver to their shops to sell to US, Uk local or overseas clients.

So, I believe that past UK, US ought employ many employees, they belonged to skillful manufacturing workers, manufacture increasing steel machine or steel related machine number of products rapidly daily. So, if UK, US had had many of these manufacturing factories owned high skillful workers, then their manufacturing steel-related machine or steel both kinds of products number must be influenced to raise rapidly. Consequently, their steel machine manufacturing products would been exported to overseas or would been sold to local both markets , they may be influenced to raise sale number. They (these manufacturing workers) needed to be trained to know how to manufactur these different kinds of machine products in the efficient teams and they ought to be trained to raise their efficiencies in order to shorten time to manufacturing many kinds of steel related manufacturing machine or steel itself products rapidly. So , if their efficiencies and manufacturing performance was improved, these US, UK any one manufacturing worker and their teams ought achieve raising productivities significantly.

Hence, when past UK, US manufacturing industry development period, if these two countries' any manufacturing factories could have many manufacturing workers could be trained to be skillful and proficient manufacturing workers. Then, in past every day to these factories workers, they ought help their steel or steel related manufacturing employers to raise any kinds of machine or steel products number in every team. So, when past in the manufacturing industry development, US, UK could have many factories' manufacturing workers themselves steel or steel related machine products manufacturing skill could be trained to to improve to any kinds of these machine or steel manufacuring products quality as well as their products number could be influenced to raise by themselves skillful improvement significantly every day.

Then, what would be influenced to occur to past UK, US manufacturing industry period? In behavioral economic view, when these two manufacturing industry developed countries, such as UK, US , if they had many factories workers can be trained to improve their skill in order to achieve any kinds of steel or steel-related machine products quality could be improved as well as products manufacturing number could be also increased absolutely.

In consequence, past UK and US both countries ought increase themselves any kinds of steel and steel related machine products number to be supplied to themselves local shops to let local clients to choose any one kind of machine manufacturing products to buy easily as well as they could also export to supply overseas any countries to buy their different kinds of steel or steel related machine products to let overseas steel or steel related manufacturing machine product buyers, they can have many of these different kinds of these steel or steel-related different kinds of manufacturing machine from UK and UK these both countries easily to compare other countries.

On conclusion, I believe that past US, and UK macro manufacturing industry income GDP would increase significantly. So, they would have good economic growth performance because when many of these manufacturing workers themselves manufacturing effort could be improved. So, it explained when employees manufacturing abilities can influence economic growth indirectly.

Robots invention whether they can help organizations to raise efficiencies or inefficiencies?

In behavioral economic view, in any organizations, when the organization hopes its worker teams can raise efficiencies , the organization may choose to increase more workers number and/or it can provide training to improve these workets themselves skills in order to raise their efficiencies. For one warehouse example, when the warehouse increases many goods , they are needed to delivered these goods from the shelves to the delivering destination locations. If this warehouse supervisors feel these workers themselves goods delivery speeds are slow, which is possible due to this warehouse's workers number is not enough. So, this warehouse supervisor ought increase workers number in order to increase their goods delivery speed in order to deliver goods from the shelves to every indicated goods delivery destination in order to let any one lorry driver can transport the right kinds of goods and ensure the accurate goods number to transport to any one client home rapidly.

However, if this warehouse supervisor planed to buy several warehouse goods delivery robots to assist these warehouse workers to find the right kinds of goods from shelves and then deliver to the right destination location in the warehouse. So, these warehouse orkers can concentrate on counting the accurate goods number and ensuring the right kinds of goods in order to prepare to let lorry drivers to transport these goods to these goods of buyers themselvers homes rapidly. Consequently, in the first step, robots can concentrate on finding th right goods from shelves and delivers them to the right goods transportation of location destination. Then, in the second step, these warehouse workers can concentrate on counting the accurate goods number and ensuring the right kinds of goods in order to prepare to put them to the lorry. Consequently, when warehouse robots and warehouse workers can cooperate to work together, the most important, robots, can deal on finding the right kinds of goods and deal on delivering the accurate number of goods of job duty as well as these warehouse workers can only concentrte on counting the right kinds of goods number in order to avoid it has none any mistake of wrong kinds of goods and inaccurate goods of delivery number to be transported to the lorry and to deliver to any one buyer's home.

So, it seems that warehouse robots ought help any one warehouse worker to raise himself efficiency and avoid goods delivery of mistake occurrence easily as well as their help to warehouse workers that can let any one goods buyer feels their goods can be delivered to their homes rapidly. Moreover, warehouse robots can also help these warehouse workers to raise efficiencies because warehouse robots can help them to shorten goods delivery time between any one shelf and any one goods delivery destination of location in the warehuse because robots may help them to find the right kinds of goods from the right shelf in the short time. So, any one worker does not need to spend long time to seek anywhere is the right shelf location for the kind of goods when the kind of goods are needed to deliver to the buyer's home from lorry. Warehouse robots can help them to do this aspect of " finding the goods from the right shelf in short time job duty". So, any one warehouse worker only needed tospend less time to do the counting of any right kind of goods number and ensuring the right kind of goods job duty. Consequently, this warehouse 's any one worker, his any one kind of goods delivery time may be reduced, because robots' assistance and they may have more confidence to avoid mistake to deliver the wrong number of goods and/or the wrong kind of goods to any one goods buyer's home.

On conclusion, it seems that warehouse robots ought may help any one warehouse worker to raise efficiency for any one team in the warehouse as well as the warehouse any one supervisor does not need to spend much time to observe any one worker individual performance for " goods delivery job duty aspect" because their goods delivery job duty that had been replaced to do by these several warehouse robots. Robots can achieve the more accurate of right kinds of goods and the right number of goods delviery job performance to compare any one of human warehouse worker themselves right kinds of goods of delivery and right number of goods of delivery job performance. So, when robots can participate to cooperate with this warehouse's any one worker to do their goods of delivery job duty in this warehouse every day. Then, robots can raies any one of supervisor individual confidence in order to let they do not need to spend time to observe any one of worker individual whose goods of delivery job performane. They can concentrate on supervising any one worker whose goods transport to lorry in the final step in order to avoid to deliver wrong goods number and / or wrong kind of goods to any one goods buyer's home every day. Consequently, this warehouse's overall teams of their delviery of goods performance many be improved by robotss' participatin to goods of delivery task as well as this warehouse's oveall teams themselves efficiencies may be influenced to raise by robots' goods of delivery task participation.

Why social behavior may influence organizational strategy needs to be changed ?
Why any organizations need to know whether nowadays social behaivor how has been changing in order to implement the kind of the most right strategy to achieve the profit aim pursue in possible. I shall indicate nowadays ecommerce or online, customer shopping behavior to explain above question concerns they ought have close relationship between social behavior and organizational strategic choice or organizational behavioral changing need. On nowadays ecommerce business, or online shopping model, this kind of shopping model in global many young and old age consumers like to apply internet tool to choose any country sellers website stores in order to stay at home to buy any kinds of products from themselves webstores in global societies.
In fact, online shopping model had been popular for long time above to twenty years. Most of global sellers will make decision to design themselves webstores in order to attract global many online buyers to choose to buy their products from themselves webstores. So, it seems that social consumers purchase behaviors had been changed to online shopping from internet invention.
Hence, social consumers purchase behavioral changes may influence any organizations' strategies need to be changed from visiting shops purchase strategy model to online purchase strategy model, if the seller still concentrate on concentrate on considerate how to design itelf , but neglects to considerate how to design itself webstore, e.g. how to design attract product photos to put on itself webstore, how to arrange sale price information location to be putted on webstore and visa card payment location on itself webstore in order to let any one online buyer can feel very easier to buy itself any kinds of products from itself webstore. Then, its potential online buyers will be influenced to increase number when they can find this online seller itself any kinds of products photes and every kinds of product sale price information and visa card payment channel locations easily from itself webstore.
So, it implies that nowadays any one seller ought need to design one webstore to let any one online overseas and domestic consumers can have chance to click itself webstore to choose any one kind of product to buy conveniently when he/she does not hope to leave him/her home to go to shop, because nowadays social shopping behaviors had been influenced to change when internet invention, them it gives another online purchase method to replace visiting shops purchase method to global any one buyer in nowadays societies.
So, if nowadays any one seller still concentrate on how to design itself shop display in order to put any kinds of product on shelf in order to let any one visiting shop customer to find the kind of product to buy, but it neglects to change to choose to pursue another new technological shopping method, such as webstore purchase method in order to implement effective strategy to design the most right webstore as well as in order to attract global overseas and local consumers to find itself webstore easily from website and find its any one kind of product phots and sale price and visa card payment button in order to choose to buy itself any kinds of products in the short time. Consequently I believe that the seller will lose many customers from overseas and local when its other same or similar product sellers choose to design themselves webstores in order to let global any one product buyer can buy themselves any one kind of product when they can pay visa card to buy their products from them webstores conveniently when they stay at home habitly. Then, the seller will lose many global potential customers in long time.
On conclusion, in behavioral economic view, any consumer behavioral social changing, which will influence any in

order to avoid customers number loses significantly . In future time, organizations need to make rapid decision in order to implement the most reasonable and the most useful strategy in order to avoid global potential customers number reduces or lose them in long time. So, social behavioral changing environment ought influence any global organizations need to decide how to change themselves strategies in order to avoid customers loses significantly in future time.

How and why human behavior may influence economic growth or recession?
May ourselves daily behaviors influence our global societial continue economic growth or recession? Do they have cause and effect close relationship between human behaviors and global economic growth or recession? I shall apply behavioral economic theory to analyze and explain whether ourselves daily behaviors and our global societial economic growth or recession which have close cause and effect relationship as below:
Every country itself economic development must depend on any business activities, otherwise, any kinds of business activities must need ourselves business activities or behaviors in order to achieve any business activities as well as achieve the country's overall economic development in macro view.
However, any country's overall business activites or behaviors which must depend on any kinds of individual businessmen, themselves employees daily working behavior or activity or performance in order to help them to attract or increase many clients number to acieve " earning profit" aim. So, it seems that any individual business, itself overall every department individual working behavior is one main factor to influence the company's overall business performance.
For agricultural fruit and meat food farming industry example, such as New Zealand is a farming main target industry country. It had had many New Zealanders were daily themselves own farming businesses for many years. Their farming businesses include growing fruit, sheep, cow, pig pork, meat etc. food sale business. If the New Zealand farmer owned a large size farming land, then he will choose either growing fruit or feeding sheeps, pigs, cows to be meat to to transport to New Zealand supermarkets to help them to sell to their farmers meet to New Zealanders in order to earn profit. Thus, if the New Zealand farmer owned large size of farming lands, then he needs to employ many farming employees (farming workers) to help him to carry on farming business daily tasks, e.g. picking up friuts, feeding pigs, cows, sheeps to eat food daily. These daily farming jobs are very important to influence this New Zealand farmer's meats or fruits sale number whether they can be easy or diffcult to sell in New Zealand supermarkets , if these farming workers can own encough farming knowledge or skill to know how to pick up fruits method and make judgement to know whether it is right time to pick up the kind of fruits from the trees , as well as know how feed this pigs, sheeps, cows to eat food in order to let they are better health. Consequently, their farming behaviors which can let these animals can provide the best taste and enough meat from these animals to let New Zealander to buy to eat from New Zealand any one supermarket. Even these New Zealand farming workers can know whether the kinds of fruits, e.g. oranges, apples, gapes etc. fruits whether they ought be picked up from the trees at the right time. Consequently, they can make judgement to decide to pick up any kinds of the best taste fruits to let any one New Zealander to buy to eat from any one supermarket in New Zealand. Otherwise, if they do not make judegement to know whether the kind of fruit ought not be picked up because they still need longer time to continue grow up to increase fruit size and better taste from the trees in order to let any one fruit buyer can feel better taste when they eat this kind of fruit later. If they can buy this kind of fruit to eat later, then this New Zealand farmer's his fruit buyers can buy the best taste of this kind of fruit to eat from an yone supermarket in New Zealand. Consequently, many New Zealand supermarkets will choose to buy any kinds of fruits from this farmer fruit supplier when they feel this farmer's fruits can provide more better taste fruits to compare other farmers' fruits.
Thus, due to New Zealand is one farming main income source country. It's any kinds of fruits and meats need to be export to overseas to sell , instead of local sale. It's GDP percent is very high to whole country 's overall income source. So, any one New Zealand farmer individual and any one farming worker individual working behavior will influence its economy whether it is influenced to grow or recession possible. Moreover, it also seems that farming workers' farming knowledge and skill will influence themselves farming daily activities to achieve the aim of the number of increase or decrease to any kinds of fruits whether they are better taste or the number of increase of

decrease to any kinds of meats whether they are better taste to supply to any one New Zealand fruit or meat buyers to eat from any one New Zealand supermarket. So, it implies that any one New Zealand farming worker individual farming behavior may influence any kinds of fruits or any kinds of meat taste because they are transported to any one supermarket to sell in New Zealand.

Consequently, if New Zealans had many farmers can teach god farming knowledge and skill to let their any one farming workers know how to decide judgement to decide when it is right time to pick up any kinds of fruits from trees , or how to grow them on soil in order to let they can grow rapidly. Then, many different kinds of fruits can be provided to let any one New Zealanders can eat the best taste of fruits when their fruits are supplied to any one New Zealand supermarkets. Even, if they knew how to feed foods to pigs, cows, sheeps to eat daily. Then they can be more health and they can provide the best taste of meats to let any one New Zealanders can buy their meats from any one New Zealand supermarkets. Moreover, their fruits and meats can be transported to overseas to let any one country fruits or meats buyers can choose any kinds of New Zealand meats and fruits to buy to eat from themselves countries supermarkets. Then, many overseas fruit and meat buyers will perfer to choose New Zealand any kinds of fruits or meats to buy to compare other countries fruits or meats to buy when they go to any one local supermarkets. On conclusion, it seems that New Zealand farming workers themselves farming behavior may influence their farming employers any kinds of fruits or meats sale number and income because their farming task behaviors must influence whether their fruits or meats taste are the better taste or worse taste to compare their other local farmers (the farmer competitors) whose fruits or meats taste. If tthe farmer's any one farming worker can be trained to learn how to know to feed animals skill and when is the most right time to pick up any kinds of fruits from trees or how to grow them on the soil methods. Due to these farming worker individual farming behavior may influence his different finds of fruits and meats sale number to be increase or decrease, so these any one New Zealand farmer must need to depend on any one farming worker whose farming working methods, if their farming working behaviors can be the best to influence any kinds of fruits to grow rapid or any kinds of pigs, cows, sheeps animals grow up rapidly , then their sale number may be increase significantly and their taste can be improved to let any New Zealand or overseas meat or fruit buyer to buy to eat to feel from any one New Zealand or overseas supermarkets, then New Zealand's agriculture industry must be influenced to increase. In the world, any one fruit or meat buyer must choose to buy New Zealand's fruit and meat to eat in prefer to compare other countries' fruits and meats. So, New Zealand's GDP may be influenced to raise from any one New Zealand farming worker individual farming working behaviors.

www.ingramcontent.com/pod-product-compliance
Lightning Source LLC
Chambersburg PA
CBHW081912120726
47996CB00010B/3294